HÖLDERLIN · POEMS AND FRAGMENTS

FRIEDRICH HÖLDERLIN

Poems and Fragments

TRANSLATED BY MICHAEL HAMBURGER

FOURTH BILINGUAL EDITION
WITH A PREFACE, INTRODUCTION AND NOTES

ANVIL PRESS POETRY

Fourth edition published in 2004
by Anvil Press Poetry Ltd
Neptune House   70 Royal Hill   London SE10 8RF
www.anvilpresspoetry.com
Reprinted in 2005

First edition published by Routledge & Kegan Paul Ltd 1966
Second edition published by Cambridge University Press 1980
Third edition published by Anvil Press Poetry Ltd 1994

Designed and set in Monotype Fournier by Anvil
Printed at Alden Press Limited
Oxford and Northampton

ISBN 0 85646 360 4

This book is published with financial assistance from
The Arts Council of England

A catalogue record for this book
is available from the British Library

Contents

THE DEATH OF EMPEDOCLES

THE HYMNS (1799–1805)

FRAGMENTS OF OTHER HYMNS (1800–1805)

PINDAR FRAGMENTS AND COMMENTARY (1805)

LAST POEMS (1807–1843)

Preface, 2003

BECAUSE THIS WILL BE the last of a succession of Hölderlin editions on which I have worked since my adolescence, and the first of which appeared sixty years ago, a few afterthoughts seem to me to be called for. Though I translated many other poets, not only German, over that period, none of them held my attention quite so continuously. One reason for that could be the state of his later manuscripts and drafts, so far from ever being finalized that they are still in the process of being repeatedly re-edited, rearranged and reinterpreted, so that every return to them for translation could be a rediscovery and a new challenge.

The very earliest poem of my own I was able to include in my *Collected Poems 1941–1994* was a Hölderlin persona poem, a self-identification with his person I had to outgrow even as a translator, let alone as a poet; but this juvenile self-identification forbade anything like free 'imitations' or naturalizations of his poems, which would have ironed out their singularity, an oddity of which he himself was quite aware, apologizing for it in his tiny preface to the poem 'Friedensfeier'. This little apology was intended for the poem's publication, but was never printed before 1954, more than a century and a half later, when his fair copy suddenly appeared – in London, of all places, where I had the luck to be asked to identify it as the long-lost definitive version it was.

Since I have never shared Hölderlin's religious allegiance to an idealized ancient Greece, or his grappling with its poetic forms, epic, lyrical and dramatic, inseparable as these were for him from a neo-Hellenism always in a state of tension with the culture of his time and place, what drew me to Hölderlin's work must have been something other than his themes and forms, something no more palpable, it may be, than his way of breathing in verse; and although I never know what has 'influenced' me, or how, I suspect that it was this, if anything, in Hölderlin, that entered into the writing of my longer poems and sequences. Once I had decided that I must retain his adaptation of classical forms in my versions, much more refractory though these forms have proved in English over the centuries than in German, my assimilation of his metres and rhythms also helped me to overcome the iambic compulsion dominant in most English verse later than the Anglo-Saxon, other than in verse measured by stress rather than sylla-ble or 'foot' count or as free as some of Hölderlin's later poems became when 'free verse' was not a term in currency. This may be how dactyl and spondee came to mix freely in some of my later verse with the iambic beat.

Looking back now, I recall an altercation with W. H. Auden who – in a text I can't now trace, any more than I can trace my letters to him, of which I kept no copies – had written that Hölderlin was easier to trans-late or more translatable than other poets because he was mad – or 'dotty', I'm sure was the word in the original text to which I objected. Well, Hölderlin is not easy to translate, nor to put across – far from it, not only because of the dubious and open state of his later texts, whose 'meaning' could be suspended in a polysemy by no means accidental down to unprecedented syntactical and grammatical twists. Nor was he mad, or dottier than poets have been expected to be if not since Plato's time, certainly since Shakespeare's, until he ceased to be Hölderlin, to the point of disowning both his name and his work. In his answer to me of January 15th, 1967, Auden explained that he had meant not easy to translate, but to put across: 'I do not of course mean that, because he was mentally peculiar, this detracts from the greatness of his poetry, any more than it does from Blake's. I was trying to account for what I'm sure you'll agree with me is a fact, namely that Hölderlin is easier to get across in translation than, say, Goethe. Perhaps, though, if you try your hand at the 'Marienbad Elegie' (*sic*), you can prove me wrong. I tried, but could do nothing with it.'

Though I never came to attempt the 'Marienbader Elegie', I found Goethe's other late poems – those that appealed to me – easier to trans-late or get across than most of Hölderlin's, even where his technical virtuosity was hard to match, as in that elegy. When he came to substan-tiate his claim in his commonplace book *A Certain World*, published in

1970, Auden did so with a poem not by Hölderlin but Scardanelli; and in a prose version of it at one time required of me by Penguin Books for purposes that must have been mainly educational, but already superseded by my verse translation in the first edition of *Poems and Fragments*, available both in Britain and the USA. (Auden's quotation of part of an earlier Hölderlin ode in the Introduction to Vol. IV of the anthology *Poems of the English Language* had been not only less questionable, but illuminating in its context. So I minded less that this, too, was drawn from a superseded version in my juvenile first Hölderlin book.) In another letter, of August 20th, 1969, written after a conversation with me in London, Auden clarified the matter again for the editor of his commonplace book: 'I never said that Hölderlin was easy to translate, only that the aspects of his poetry which reflect his insanity come across in translation because they do not depend on language.' But all poetry depends on language, being made of it, even where its language aspires to a condition beyond the reach of prose; and Hölderlin's poems – middle period, late or too late – are no exception to that. If a flat prose version of such poetry retains some of its power – as Dante's *Commedia*, for instance, did for me and many others in the Temple Classics crib – this may say something about its quality and nature; and the Scardanelli text chosen by Auden for his book was one of his few in the ode forms salvaged by Scardanelli from the work of Hölderlin, carried over, briefly, from the wreckage. The analogy with Blake was not far-fetched; but even in his time Blake was not locked up as a madman, and narrowly escaped being locked up for sedition. Because in the German States authority and opinion were less magnanimous and liberal, Hölderlin's family delivered him to the treatment that broke him. In that regard the case of John Clare would have been more apposite, though Clare's asylum years did not reduce him as utterly as Hölderlin was reduced, he being merely socially redundant, not a danger to the State. Though he reformulated his original assertion for the book publication, Auden would not correct its glibness. Could he possibly have thought that there is such a thing as a normal or sane mentality – in poetry or outside it? And assume that he himself was not 'mentally peculiar'? If so, for all his cleverness, he remained more self-deluded than Hölderlin ever was till he was 'alienated', self-estranged.

What meant more to me in my engagement with Hölderlin over the decades was his advocacy and practice of the 'modulation of tones' in longer poems, quite especially his inclusion of a 'naive tone' among those to be modulated. Earlier on he had called this tone 'the language of the heart', as distinct from the sublime, idealistic, idyllic and heroic modes. My versions began only with the poems for which he had found this tone, self-critical enough as he was from his early youth onwards to have discarded the vapid rhetoric to which he had been moved by his theological and philosophical aspirations. This naive tone must not be confused with dottiness. Hölderlin had once been the philosophical peer of his friends Hegel and Schelling, and remained anything but a simpleton in the critical prose I was too unphilosophical to translate, written in close proximity to his poetic concerns, up to the time of his Sophocles and Pindar versions and commentaries just before his self-alienation. Having begun as so intellectual a poet – or 'sentimental' one, in terms of Schiller's distinction between 'naive' and 'sentimental', that is, reflective poets – a deliberately placed 'naive tone' became central to his practice and to his understanding of the nature of all poetry. One instance of the naive tone in a poem otherwise sublime and visionary occurs in the poem 'Die Wanderung', in the lines

> Denn sagen hört' ich
> Noch heut in den Lüften:
> Frei sei'n, wie Schwalben, die Dichter.

A good deal of pondering was needed to translate this as

> For only today
> I heard it said in the breezes
> That free as swallows the poets are

rather than 'free, like the swallows'. A simile there would have been out of character, out of tone, because similes are a poetic and rhetorical artifice. (Wherever a simile occurs in poems, we can be pretty sure that the one thing is *not* like the other.) Hölderlin's words, so colloquial that they seem to spring from his native Swabian dialect – very appropriately, in a poem that takes off from Swabia on a flight through time and space – owe their effect to a daring simplicity and startling plainness. Here common sense and knowledge tells us that swallows are not free at all, only mobile by an instinctive compulsion to migrate. Hölderlin's words don't raise that doubt or 'suspension of disbelief': the poets' freedom becomes that of mobility, with the implication, left open, that this mobility, too, could be as compulsive as that of the swallows, and imaginative mobility is what characterizes not only this poem but all the poems and fragments of what ought to have become a single pan-historical, pan-mythical sequence. Like the Hölderlin of this phase, swallows have more than one home, so remote from one another that the migration between them becomes their greatest danger. So the naive analogy widens out into a whole complex of implications – even the danger incurred by Hölderlin in his strenuous imaginative flights and the price he had to pay for them, the plunge into a condition clinically classified as schizophrenia.

However, in recent decades readers have been attracted even to the last poems, written not by Hölderlin but by the self-estranged wreck of himself he called Scardanelli or 'something of the sort', since the identity had ceased to matter. Philippe Jaccottet is one of the excellent poets who have responded to their limpid naivety no longer deliberately arrived at by an effort of art, out of a self-conflict so intense that it could not be sustained for long. If there is dottiness, too, in some of these verses, it has a peculiar charm – almost as though the poet had been conscious enough of the dottiness to make fun of it – and some of Scardanelli's visitors believed that his madness was another deliberate resort, a downward flight into a childlike ingenuousness that could parody itself, much as it seems to parody the inane sentiments and stock pieties of poetasters who had never risked ambitions so high as to be not only heretical, but hubristic – in Hölderlin's own judgement, when he called himself a 'false priest', punished for that with a rigour more pre-Socratic Greek than Christian. Even if there was no method in his madness, then, it makes sense in the light of his own insights into the workings of Fate in Greek tragedy, the arc of ascent and fall or regression he had long known to be the inevitable course of his life.

Here it is relevant that in form and diction, too, most of Scardanelli's verse was a regression even beyond Hölderlin's earliest apprentice work, not included in this book; most conspicuous less in the return to rhymed iambic or trochaic stanzas no longer propelled by enthusiasm than in the generality of its images, when in the preceding stage Hölderlin had anticipated twentieth-century Imagist and Objectivist practices with images at once particular and evocative. In most of the doggerel on the seasons, dashed off as mementoes for visitors, the things of nature and human life once devoutly cherished by Hölderlin are so generalized and conventionalized that they become unreal; and in exceptional poems, probably written for his own satisfaction, such as 'The Walk', they can become surreal or subreal, properties of a life vaguely recollected or dreamed, rather than immediately apperceived. This makes some of them as remarkable in their way as the authentic poems of Hölderlin are in theirs – the nearest thing in poetry to work not only published but written after death. Perhaps that is why it was the poems of Scardanelli only that the composer Heinz Holliger chose for one of his major works, drawing much more from these jingles than their pathetic banality.

As for questions of how poetic texts can be or ought to be translated, they have come to weary me, and I have nothing to add to what I wrote in the past about my way of doing it. Had I not found it necessary, long ago, to reproduce Hölderlin's metres – with the single exception of one ode I transposed from Asclepiads into Alcaics, when the Asclepiads couldn't be made to work in English – many of my versions could have been made to run more smoothly and acceptably for English-language ears; but the exoticism of these metres, always at odds with the spontaneity of Hölderlin's 'language of the heart', struck me as indispensable in his case. Also, it was Hölderlin's example that impelled other English-language poets of my time, including Auden, to experiment again with those metres – as I did only once in a rejected juvenile poem.

My Hölderlin versions passed through many different stages, including the plain prose paraphrase I produced when I had no publisher for the verse translations, and a crib was needed. Yet some of the original rhythms pushed their way even into that. I don't find it in the least difficult to imagine the reverse of my procedure – a very different English Hölderlin whizzed into the twenty-first century with the benefit of electronics and a consumer-friendly idiom; but even if I had another sixty years for such an exercise, I can't see myself wishing to be its perpetrator. It's enough for me if these versions of mine remain accessories to the originals that face them in this book – or substitutes, as close to these as I could make them not only in sense or sense withheld, but in movement, structure, breath and tone, for readers with no access at all to the German texts.

M. H.

Suffolk, April 2003

Preface to the Third Edition

WITH THIS EDITION, corrected and enlarged once more, I come to
the end of half a century's work on the translations. If even this edition
cannot be definitive in any other regard, one reason is that no transla-
tion, as such, can be definitive. Another, that in Hölderlin's case quite a
number of the original texts never became definitive. Not only did he
never finish most of the poems drafted or merely planned in the last
years before his change of identity, but he continued to recast even
poems he had published in miscellanies or seemingly finalized in fair
copies. The critical and monumental edition of Hölderlin's works
known as the *Große Stuttgarter Ausgabe* had not been completed, after
decades of expert and minute work on it, when yet another edition, the
Frankfurter Ausgabe, was announced and initiated. The need for it arose
from the peculiar nature of Hölderlin's later texts, which cannot be
made readable without a degree of selection, if not reconstruction, so
that the emphasis in the latest edition fell on the facsimile reproduction
and exact transcription of manuscripts that were work sheets including
not only emendations but marginal *lemmata*, mere prose memoranda or
catchwords for further reworkings never carried out. By the time the
first book collection of poems by Hölderlin appeared, in 1826, their
author, though alive, was no longer related to his earlier writings and
had no part at all in the editing. This is the crux of the anomaly: a large
body of unprecedented poetry left for posthumous publication – in so
far as it is extant – but never prepared or only passed for publication by
the poet himself.

In an earlier preface, written in 1964, I tried to define and explain the
kind of Hölderlin translation I thought I had been doing ever since my
first, schoolboy, attempts. All I wish to say here is that it is too late for
me to change my ways, but that there are many possible ways of trans-
lating a poet so far removed from any poetic convention obtaining
either in German or English, in his lifetime or later. The way I chose –

or was impelled towards – was not that of free 'imitation', but one closer to Hölderlin's own practice as a translator: to get as much as possible of the original's quiddity into my versions, even if that meant grappling with metres and rhythms more refractory and alien in English than in German poetry, or with syntactic oddities which Hölderlin had derived from his 'colonization' of ancient Greece. Because for his Sophocles translations Hölderlin evolved a manner and diction not recognizable as German by his contemporaries, these unique translations were laughed at or dismissed as evidence of his 'madness', when it had been his lucid and considered intention not to germanize Sophocles, but to grecize and Sophoclize his German. What is usually meant by imitation in verse renderings is the very opposite of that procedure – the naturalization of a foreign text, its assimilation to established proprieties, when and where such were acknowledged, or to the poet-translator's own idiosyncrasies, in other eras, like our own.

Because the volume of the Frankfurt edition devoted to the most difficult and controversial texts, the 'hymns' (or cantos) and fragments, has not yet appeared, most of my translations are still based on the GSA readings: but the researches of D.E. Sattler and his assistants for the Frankfurt edition, and his editing of a facsimile edition of the Homburg Folio manuscript sheets, have not only provided me with a few variant readings but so drastically changed my understanding of Hölderlin's later work that a new Introduction to my versions was called for. It was D.E. Sattler's writings, too, that convinced me of the need to translate one of Hölderlin's translations – his late Pindar fragments – and his commentary on them, as essential complements and keys to his own poems written in the same critical years before his enforced hospitalization as a mental case. This translation alone, with its commentary, proves that Hölderlin was not 'mad' until he had been treated as a madman, and broken by that treatment; and that his later work has been wrongly dated to accord with assumptions about the progress of his change of personality. This change was not sudden. Nor was it complete by 1802, three years before the Pindar fragments and commentary were written.

Other additions to my versions fill little gaps left in my earlier selections – still only from Hölderlin's mature work, beginning in 1797. If most of the complements to my selection fall on the other side, his late and last phases, this has to do with my revaluation and new understanding of his so-called madness. I have added those poems written after 1806 which show that even his experiences in the mental clinic, gruelling and humiliating as they were, did not precipitate a total break in his identity as a man or poet. It was only after the confiscation of his manuscript sheets and years of adaptation to his life in the Tübingen tower that he came to deny any connection between Hölderlin and the very different person and poet – Scardanelli 'or something of the sort' – he had become.

A few minute changes in my text, as in my version of 'Hälfte des Lebens', are reinterpretations. My earlier title, 'The Middle of Life', for that poem goes back to my very first rendering of it at the age of 17, and it now strikes me as a rationalization of Hölderlin's title in the light of biographical concerns. I cannot justify my new reading of the word *hold* in the same poem as 'loving' rather than 'lovely' or 'beautiful', but the German word contains both meanings, and the one I have now opted for came to make better sense for me in the context. The flags or weather-vanes in the last line will also remain controversial. I have stuck to my 'weathercocks', and to 'clatter' rather than 'clang', less on semantic grounds than because I wanted harsher noises there and a feminine ending. In 'Colomb' I have incorporated a variant reading only because it contains a simile drawn from immediate observation – that of the bell 'put out of tune as by snow' – so vivid and so characteristic of Hölderlin's later vision that André du Bouchet chose to ring changes on that bell in his recently published meditations, '*désaccordée comme par la neige*'. This is one of many instances of how even Hölderlin's less than definitive texts have germinated in the minds of writers remote from him in place and time.

M.H.

Suffolk, October 1989

Introduction

JOHANN FRIEDRICH HÖLDERLIN was born in the small Swabian town Lauffen on the Neckar on March 20th, 1770. His father, the manager of estates belonging to the Lutheran Church, died soon after, in 1772. After his mother's remarriage in 1774, the family moved to Nürtingen, where her second husband was burgomaster. Hölderlin attended the local grammar school until 1784. His stepfather, too, had died in 1779, leaving Hölderlin uncommonly dependent on his mother.[1] He remained deeply, if ambivalently, attached to her; but also to his grandmother, his younger sister and his half-brother, Karl Gock. In 1784 Hölderlin became a boarder at the Lower Monastery School at Denkendorf, two years later at the Upper Monastery School at Maulbronn. (Despite the name, both were Protestant institutions.)

From 1788 to 1793 he studied for his ordination at the Theological Seminary at Tübingen, the 'Stift'. There he founded a Poetry Club together with his friends Neuffer and Magenau, who shared his enthusiasm for the French Revolution, and formed friendships with two other fellow students who were to become eminent philosophers, Hegel and Schelling. As early as 1787 he became engaged to Luise Nast, the cousin of a school friend, but broke off the engagement in 1790. At Tübingen he fell in love with Elise Lebret, but by this time he knew that he would not take up the career planned for him by his mother and might never be in a position to support a family. In the autumn of 1789 he had gone so far as to ask his mother's permission to leave the university, but was persuaded to stay on, wrote theses on the History of the Fine Arts in Greece and on Parallels between the Proverbs of Solomon and Hesiod's

---

1. Several biographers and psychologists have made much of that dependence, even tracing his later 'schizophrenia' to the emotional tensions of his childhood and adolescence. One Freudian study of that kind is Dr. Jean Laplanche's *Hölderlin et la Question du Père* (Paris, 1961).

Works and Days, as well as a great deal of poetry, obtained his degree of 'Magister' and passed his final examinations in theology.

Though Hölderlin was never to become a Lutheran minister, the kind of education he received has an immediate bearing on his poetry. The would-be harmonious blending of theological and classical studies that characterized the Denkendorf, Maulbronn and Tübingen institutions had a formative effect on his conception of poetry and of the poet's function, though it was not their blending but their incompatibility that was to preoccupy him. There may even be a vital connection between the peculiarities of Swabian religious traditions, such as the millenarian and mystical doctrines of Bengel and Oetinger, and some of Hölderlin's chiliastic visions. The French scholar Robert Minder wrote an ingenious summary of theological traditions which he traced not only to Hölderlin but also to Hegel and Karl Marx.[2]

Another critic, L. S. Salzberger,[3] argued that Hölderlin's was 'the typical Renaissance view of the *poeta theologus* or *sacer vates*' relating it to that of poets from Tasso, Ronsard and Sir Philip Sidney to Milton and Klopstock. The inner gate of the Tübingen Stift bore the inscription *Aedes Deo et Musis Sacrae*, and it was Hölderlin's privilege and burden to dedicate himself to the same dual service at a time when this Renaissance tradition was virtually extinct, religious allegiances harder and harder to reconcile with humanistic and aesthetic ones. The subject of the comparative study that Hölderlin wrote at Tübingen is also significant. Because of his essential syncretism, it could be said of Hölderlin, as Hazlitt said of Milton, that 'he had his thoughts constantly fixed on the contemplation of Hebrew theocracy, and of a perfect commonwealth', even though it was the theocracy of an idealized ancient Greece that Hölderlin much more often invoked until his 'return to the source' in middle life; and also that 'his religious zeal infused its character into his imagination, so that he devoted himself

2 *'Herrlichkeit' chez Hegel, ou le Monde des Pères Souabes.* In *Etudes Germaniques*, July–Dec. 1951, pages 225–290.

3. *The Sublime Art. Notes on Milton and Hölderlin.* In *Reason and Energy*, London, 1970.

with the same sense of duty to the cultivation of his genius, as he did to the exercise of virtue, or the good of his country'. Although there is no documentary evidence that Hölderlin ever read Milton, I have pointed to some striking concordances in the work of the two poets, especially Milton's *Samson Agonistes* and Hölderlin's *Empedocles* fragments. To Hazlitt's description of the *sacer vates* – with complications, in Hölderlin's case, due to his fervent pantheism, at one stage, and his need in early years to come to terms with the latest developments in German philosophy – we must add a radicalism and intransigence that prevented both Milton and Hölderlin from making a trade of their religious vocations. Both were deterred by 'a conscience that would retch', as Milton put it, though their reasons for preferring a 'blameless silence' may have been as different as the characters of the two men in other regards, their beliefs and their aspirations. The differences between Milton's England and Hölderlin's Württemberg in an era of post-Enlightenment, post-classicism, repressed revolutionary ferment and the Napoleonic wars, are so glaring that they need no comment here.

Even in his childhood Hölderlin had been moody, hyper-sensitive and subject to waves of extreme depression or elation. He was devoted not only to his friends but to a cult of friendship widespread in late eighteenth-century Germany and so effusive that twentieth-century biographers and critics, such as Pierre Berteaux, could mistake it for homosexuality; but he found it hard to be sociable in a more general way. His ode 'Mein Vorsaz' ('My Resolution'), written when he was seventeen, shows how acutely aware he was at this early time that his vocation and ambition set him apart even from his closest friends:

> O friends, my friends, who love me so loyally,
>> What can so dim, so trouble my lonely gaze?
>> What makes my wretched heart seek refuge
>> Here in this gloomy and deathly stillness?
>
> I flee the tender clasp of your hands, avoid
>> The soulful, happy touch of a brother's lips.

Oh, don't be angry, friends, forgive me! –
Look at my innermost self, then judge me! –

Is it hot thirst for manly perfection, then?
A craving, hushed, for fame and a hecatomb?
A feeble urge to Pindar's flight? Or
Strenuous striving for Klopstock's greatness?

Ah, friends, where can I hide, to what corner of
This earth escape, and wrapped in perpetual night,
Weep there? For never shall I know the
Flight of those men round the world, in no time.

And yet I will, I'll climb the most glorious path!
Climb on, climb on in ardent and reckless dreams
Of joining them; I will, though, dying,
Faintly I mutter, forget me, children!

Klopstock – acclaimed in his lifetime as 'the German Milton' – was Hölderlin's earliest model. Klopstock not only wrote his Christian epic *Der Messias* in classical hexameters, but imitated or adapted Greek and Latin ode forms, one of which, the Alcaic, Hölderlin chose for this early poem and returned to for his more mature work, after discarding the rhymed stanzas taken over from his second master, Schiller. As for Pindar, he outlasted both of Hölderlin's German masters, leading him to his most daring departures from all the conventions of German verse – structural, metric, and even syntactic. The Pindar translations I felt it necessary to re-translate from Hölderlin's German were the last piece of work completed by Hölderlin before the collapse of his poetic ambition.

His early ambition, a Hellenism more fervent and radical than any built into the educational system, and a political radicalism even less compatible with it, turned Hölderlin away from the career for which he had been trained since childhood, with subsidies from both Church and State. His alternative was the humble drudgery, but relative independence, of a private tutor. Despite pressure from his mother, who took care to keep him dependent on her financially throughout the crises that followed inevitably, Hölderlin refused again and again to take up the ministry for which he was qualified. With the help of friends and of Schiller, who became his hero and patron for a number of years, he obtained the position of private tutor to the son of Charlotte von Kalb, whose literary interests and connections made her a congenial employer. At her home in Waltershausen, where he lived from the winter of 1793 to the following summer, Hölderlin worked on a first version of his novel *Hyperion*. In the autumn he took his pupil to Jena, attended Fichte's philosophical lectures, saw a good deal of Schiller and met several other prominent German writers, including Goethe. An early fragment of the novel was published by Schiller in his periodical *Thalia*.

Meanwhile Hölderlin's pupil proved intractable. Charlotte von Kalb sent them both to Weimar, then made provision for Hölderlin to live independently in Jena and Nürtingen until the summer of 1795. He continued his work on *Hyperion*, on the philosophical and idealistic 'hymns' he was writing in those years – rhymed poems very close to Schiller's in manner and dedicated to 'the ideals of humanity' – and on a translation from Ovid.

In December 1795 he was appointed tutor to the children of J. F. Gontard, a wealthy banker in Frankfurt, whose wife Susette became the 'Diotima' of Hölderlin's poems. If, as research has suggested, at Waltershausen Hölderlin had entered into an affair with Wilhelmine Marianne Kirms, a young widow who acted as a companion to Charlotte von Kalb, and fathered her daughter born in July 1795 – to die of smallpox in the following year – nothing of this transpired in Hölderlin's extant letters of any period. Though Susette's social and marital status called for even greater discretion, no such reticence inhibited him from celebrating his love for Susette in letters, poems and the final version of *Hyperion*. Susette was more to him than a lover or mistress. She was the Platonic Diotima who transfigured Hölderlin's life and poetry. That is how he understood, explained and proclaimed the change; and his work bears it out. After the wordiness and stock metaphors of the rhymed 'hymns' propelled by enthusiasm without experience, in Frankfurt he found his true voice as a poet, the poise of the brief epigrams and almost epigrammatic odes with which my selection begins. The diffuse rhetoric of generalized enthusiasm had begun to crystallize.

In 1796 Susette, her four children, her mother-in-law and Hölderlin were forced to leave Frankfurt for Westphalia to escape the invading French army, while Gontard stayed behind to attend to his business. In Kassel they were joined by Wilhelm Heinse, the author of *Ardinghello*, a novel that influenced Hölderlin's view of ancient Greece by its penetration into what Nietzsche was to call the 'Dionysian' layers of the culture, as distinct from the Apollonian balance, symmetry and 'noble simplicity' which Winckelmann had emphasized. It was to Heinse that Hölderlin later addressed and dedicated his most explicitly Dionysian poem, the elegy 'Bread and Wine'. The relationship with Susette, who reciprocated Hölderlin's love, must have been easier during that emergency, in Gontard's absence.

After their return to Frankfurt in the following year, Hegel also became a tutor there. Hölderlin met Goethe once more, at Schiller's recommendation, but the rather formal interview was not to Hölderlin's advantage, and Goethe remained unaware or unappreciative of Hölderlin's best work. The first volume of *Hyperion* was published in 1797.

Hölderlin's novel has many of the peculiarities of his poems, especially the tendency towards a cyclic or spiralling progression that has been compared both to Hegel's dialectic in philosophy and to the sonata form in music. (Hölderlin was to make a structural principle of what he called 'the modulation of tones' in poetry.) This tendency may have something to do not only with aesthetics and philosophy – though at this period Hölderlin did keep up with the latest philosophical developments, also writing essays whose terminology is close to that of Fichte, Hegel and Schelling – but with Hölderlin's extreme vacillations of mood, which he summed up in his complaint, 'if only one were not so periodical!' In his tragic odes, as in his novel, Hölderlin's pantheism, his desire to be at one with the cosmos, continually comes up against his awareness not only of the differences between human and non-human nature, but of the isolation into which human beings are precipitated by their consciousness. This awareness, exacerbated by the philosophical preoccupations of Hölderlin's contemporaries and obsessions with the dichotomy of 'Nature' and 'Art', or nature and civilization, that had become acute in the writings of Rousseau, accounts for those moments in *Hyperion* which shock the reader by their bitterness, their sharp dualism and almost nihilistic despair.

'Man is a god when he dreams, a beggar when he reflects', Hyperion writes in the novel. Dreaming here is the state of mind that permits pantheistic communion; reflection, the self-consciousness that cuts off the individual from the rest of creation. It is the alternation of these states of mind, with characteristic modulations and variations more or less related to the hero's political and amorous experiences, and a gradual progression towards synthesis or reconciliation, that gives *Hyperion* a structure unlike that of any comparable novel. (Hölderlin also resorted to an astronomical term, the 'eccentric orbit', to describe his characteristic mode of progression.) Hyperion's dualism is elaborated in another passage:

> There is an oblivion of all existence, a silencing of all individual being, in which it seems that we have found all things.
>
> There is an oblivion of all existence, in which it seems that we have lost all things, a night of the soul in which not the faintest gleam of a star, not even the phosphorescence of rotten wood, can reach us.

When Hyperion is plunged into this negative state of mind – and all his experiences as a fighter for the liberation of Greece from the Turks, as of a lover and friend, are conducive to it – what had been 'all' before suddenly turns into 'nothing'. He becomes like one of those persons whom he pities for being 'in the grip of that Nothing which rules over us, who are thoroughly aware that we are born for Nothing, believe in a Nothing, work ourselves to the bone for a Nothing, until we gradually dissolve into Nothing . . .'.

Hölderlin's love for Susette, like his Hyperion's for the Diotima of the novel, was religious because it was a unifying principle and power, a binding together with Platonic extensions well beyond the personal sphere. As such it is celebrated not only in the poems to and about

Diotima and in *Hyperion* but in poems with no personal context at all. Hölderlin's departure from the Gontard household in the autumn of 1798, after an unpleasant confrontation with his employer, plunged Hölderlin back into the dichotomy, to the point of undermining his already precarious idealism. Both his idealism and his humanism rested on the One and All of antiquity, rather than on the rationalism of modern progressive creeds. Even before the enforced separation from Susette, Hölderlin's reflection told him that the relationship was socially impossible, if only because he was little more than a beggar in the husband's eyes. (Private tutors were only in the process of becoming more than servants.) Hölderlin was to apologize to Susette for letting the Diotima of the novel die – one instance of his extraordinary prescience in everything to do with his own deepest concerns. Premonitions of his own tragic 'course of life' never left him for long, even before the rupture. Now his work was to enter a distinctly tragic phase.

Very significantly, his own definition of tragedy hinged on the same antithesis of union and separation. 'A lyrical poem', he wrote, 'is the continuous metaphor of a feeling'. A tragic poem, on the other hand, 'is the metaphor of an intellectual point of view'; and this intellectual point of view 'can be no other than the awareness of being at one with all that lives'. The hero of Hölderlin's own unfinished tragedy, Empedocles, resembles Hölderlin in being a pantheist with a mission to inspire and unite a whole people; but in *The Death of Empedocles* the stress had to fall on the hero's total separation from all that he loves, not only from the Agrigentines and his favourite disciple but even from Nature and the gods, from the very cosmos with which he had felt at one. After his vain attempts to finish that play, in successive versions that could not keep pace with his precipitous development as a poet or his intense thinking about the grounds and requirements of tragedy, his pantheism itself became modified by a sense of *hubris*, as though the downfall of his hero had taught him that cosmic mysteries must remain unspoken, unrevealed. Here it is relevant to quote his later, profound and cryptic, definition of the tragic (from his commentary on his translation of the *Oedipus Tyrannus* of Sophocles): 'The representation of the tragic is mainly based on this, that what is monstrous and terrible in the coupling of god and man, in the total fusion of the power of Nature with the innermost depth of man, so that they are one at the moment of wrath, shall be made intelligible by showing how this total fusion into one is purged by their total separation.'

It was in 1797 that Hölderlin began work on his tragedy. An earlier dramatic project, *The Death of Socrates*, is mentioned in his letters, and several of his friends and contemporaries believed that he wrote a tragedy called *Agis*. Not a line remains of either work. The first version of *The Death of Empedocles*, mainly written in 1798, consists of an almost complete first act and the greater part of a second, though there are gaps and passages never finalized even in this largest of the fragments. (All three versions were conceived as a five-act tragedy.) The second version, mainly of 1799, differs both in plot and execution from the first. Unlike the earlier and later versions, it is written not in blank verse pentameters but in a shortened, predominantly iambic line that allows considerable rhythmic and metric variation, so much so that it has been described as free verse. Friedrich Beissner, editor of the GSA text, believed that Hölderlin may have completed more of the second version than the extant fragments.

Hölderlin did not publish so much as an extract from any of the three versions. Between the second and the third versions he wrote his reflections on this dramatic project and on tragedy in general, *Grund ʒum Empedokles*. The essay shows why the basic conception of the third version had to be totally different from that of the first and second. The planned introduction of a Chorus is only one feature of a much closer approximation in the last version to Hölderlin's Greek models, a shift that had begun in the second version, with its much greater stress on Empedocles' sin of *hubris*. As the essay confirms, in the process of writing the three versions Hölderlin grew more and more aware of the dramatist's need to remain partly detached from his hero – to be 'objective', as he called it, and able to place himself at one remove from that 'deepest inwardness' which the dramatic poem must convey even more dialectically than the tragic ode, Hölderlin's principle medium up to that time (apart from the novel, written in letter form, so as to permit the highest degree of subjectivity!)

Yet the main reason why Hölderlin finished no version of the play must be that he remained too closely identified with Empedocles, at the very period in his life when his own view of the poet as philosopher, prophet and priest — and as tragic hero — was subject to perpetual crisis and re-examination. The special significance for Hölderlin of Emped-ocles' mode of death — a physical fusion with the primal elements and return to the very womb of Earth — had already been intimated in his short ode 'Empedocles'; but the growing emphasis on his hero's guilt in the successive versions also has its parallels in later poems — most starkly and poignantly in the prose draft that breaks off his only strictly Pindaric hymn 'As on a holiday . . .', a poem written in the same year as the last version of the play, with many textual similarities. In the prose draft Hölderlin accuses himself of a *hubris* very much like that of which Manes accuses Empedocles:

> when of
> (a self-inflicted wound my heart is bleeding, and deeply lost
> is peace of mind, and freely modest contentment,
> And when unrest and deprivation drive me to
> the superabundance of the banqueting table of gods,
> when round about me . . .)

More remarkably still, Manes' characterization of the true saviour — as opposed to the hubristic, over-reaching pantheist, Empedocles — seems to point to that image of Christ which Hölderlin was to invoke in his elegies and hymns (or cantos) of the next years. Another way of putting it is that the play had to keep up with Hölderlin's own prodi-gious development in the years between 1797 and 1800 and that each version, therefore, ceased to be valid for him before it could be completed. It may even be that, just as Empedocles had displaced Socrates in his sympathy and imagination, another hero had displaced Empedocles by the time he had clarified his ideas about the nature and needs of tragedy; but here it is best to take up the biography again.

After his decision to leave the Gontard household in September 1798, Hölderlin settled nearby, at Homburg. He kept up a correspondence with Susette, mainly by hand delivery at secret meetings they were able to arrange until May 1800. At Homburg Hölderlin resumed relations with Isaak von Sinclair, whom he had first met in 1793, when Sinclair was a law student and ardent republican. Sinclair was to prove a most loyal and helpful friend to Hölderlin in the next few years. It was he who introduced Hölderlin to the Landgrave of Homburg, whose daughter Princess Auguste became an admirer of Hölderlin's works, to the point of being in love with their author, within the limits set by her piety and her rank. Apart from the ode addressed to her, she received the dedication of Hölderlin's last book publication, his translations of Sophocles' *Oedipus Tyrannus* and *Antigone*. It was to the Landgrave, Friedrich V, that Hölderlin was to dedicate his poem 'Patmos'. Its companion piece, 'The Rhine', was dedicated to Sinclair. The Princess of Dessau to whom he addressed another ode was Princess Auguste's married sister.

In November Sinclair invited Hölderlin to Rastatt, where Sinclair was the Landgrave's representative at the Congress that was to have settled questions of sovereignty arising from the shifting alliances and military occupations of the Napoleonic wars. Hölderlin's revolutionary hopes and his early admiration for Napoleon had already been shaken by Napoleon's imperial ambitions – very much like those of Hölderlin's coeval Beethoven. Sinclair's Republicanism or reformism was to precipitate another crisis for Hölderlin when his friend and patron was accused of a revolutionary conspiracy against the Prince Elector of Württemberg and tried for high treason in 1805. Although he was acquitted, Sinclair lost his function as a Minister to the Landgrave when the principality of Hessen-Homburg became part of the Grand Duchy of Hessen-Darmstadt in 1806.

1799 was a productive but critical year. For the first and last time Hölderlin tried desperately to establish himself as a self-supporting writer and find the place which he thought was due to him in the intellectual and cultural life of Germany. He planned a 'humanistic magazine', *Iduna*, to be devoted to the 'unification and reconciliation of the sciences with life, of art and good taste with genius, of the heart with the head, of the real with the ideal' – the very ends, in fact, that were his own most constant concern, basic to his view of the poet's religious and social function. His choice of contraries in the programme related his personal conflicts to a dichotomy widespread after the impact of Rousseau's thought, the cult of primitive genius in Herder and the literature of the *Sturm und Drang*, and the general tendency to posit an irreconcilable conflict between Nature and Art (or civilization). Schiller, too, was obsessed with it, as were the foremost German philosophers of Hölderlin's time. Goethe alone could claim to have overcome it, though, in its own way, Hölderlin's poetry achieved a fine balance of head and heart, of the real and the ideal, of 'Reason and Energy', as William Blake called two of his antinomies. The failure of Hölderlin's project – because of inadequate response from potential contributors, including Goethe – followed by that of his appeal to Schiller to find him an academic appointment, amounted to nothing less than his rejection by society. From now on Hölderlin felt himself to be a lonely outcast, like the Empedocles of his play or the Rousseau of his ode, and as a prophet without honour in his country. His poems of the next few years record the alienation, as do his letters of those years.

The second volume of *Hyperion* was published in 1799, and small batches of Hölderlin's poems continued to appear in yearbooks and miscellanies; but Hölderlin felt more and more isolated, more and more remote from the literature and culture of his time, which, in a letter, he was to describe as 'childlike'. Because of a growing impersonality and detachment in his work, there was a gradual transition from a predominantly tragic phase to a prophetic one, culminating in the visionary free verse poems and fragments on which he worked even after his breakdown of 1802. The transition can be followed in his later odes, such as 'Exhortation' or 'Nature and Art'; and even the last version of *The Death of Empedocles* almost transcends tragedy, since the hero seems to have undergone a profound catharsis before the opening scene. It was as though in the years of extreme loneliness, frustration and self-questioning that followed his departure from Frankfurt – and there was also the humiliation inflicted on Hölderlin as a lover powerless to assert any claim or right, but knowing that Susette could well be even less able to recover from their separation than he was – Hölderlin could preserve his faith only by renouncing all his ambitions and attachments, virtually giving up his own self and becoming a disembodied voice crying out to 'future ages'. In 1801 he wrote to his half-brother:

> I have struggled to the point of exhaustion to fix my faith and my vision upon that which is supreme in life; indeed, I had struggled amid sufferings which – to judge by all the evidence I know – were more overwhelming than any thing that men are capable of enduring, though they exert their utmost strength . . . At last, when my heart was already rent on more than one side, and yet held fast, I must also be led to embroil my thoughts in those evil doubts, that question so easily answered if only one's eyes are clear, namely what is more important, the eternal fountainhead of life or the temporal . . . But I continued to struggle till I found out the truth . . . There is only one quarrel in the world: which is more important, the whole or the individual part. And that quarrel, in every instance and application, is proved void in action, because the man who truly acts out of a sense of the whole is the more dedicated to peace for that very reason, more disposed to respect every individual person and thing, because his sense of humanity, the very quality that distinguishes him, will sooner permit him to fall into egoism – or whatever you choose to call it – than into pure generality.
>
> *A Deo principium.* Whoever understands this, and lives up to it . . . that person is free and strong and full of joy.

This renewed faith sustained Hölderlin's prophetic, and increasingly impersonal, poetry, but it could not alleviate his deepening solitude. Thanking his sister in 1800 for writing to remind him of their family bonds, he told her that 'this sustains my heart, which in the end too often loses its own voice in a solitude all too complete, and withdraws from one's very self.' The voice of the heart – words that also occur in one of Hölderlin's odes – was more than a sentimental trope in a poet who believed that the capacity to feel is a prerequisite even for religious dedication. It was the loss of that capacity – after the loss of the one woman he had loved religiously – that marks the poems written not by Hölderlin but by the person he became when his sufferings had broken him. Whether or not we call that condition 'catatonic stupor' – or 'schizophrenia', to use the later term – has little bearing on his poetry.

As far as his poetry is concerned, that quarrel between the whole and the part was truly resolved. If he had once been in acute danger of falling into 'pure generality' in his poems – the early poems not included here – because his youthful enthusiasm had shied away from particulars, the poetry of his prophetic phase became more and more physical, more and more sensuous, more and more concrete. Already in the successive drafts of his ode 'Des Morgens' (1799) we see how 'the leaves of the tree' becomes 'the poplar bends', then 'the birch tree bends', finally 'the beech tree bends'; but it is in the visionary landscapes of the free verse hymns and fragments – whether drawn from memory or from imagination and literary sources, as for the Greek landscapes he never saw – that he succeeded best in 'respecting every individual person and thing', just because each is imbued with a 'sense of the whole'. His turning away from an idealized ancient Greece to local, regional or national concerns and the interpretation of modern history was part of the same process.

At Homburg he took up his Greek studies in a more critical and methodical manner than before, and began to formulate his insights into the differences between ancient and modern cultures, as well as into the laws governing epic, dramatic and lyric poetry. In the spring of 1800 he went home to Nürtingen, as he had done repeatedly between attempts to make an independent life for himself, then stayed at Stuttgart as the guest of his friend Christian Landauer, to whom he dedicated an elegy I have not translated, 'Der Gang aufs Land'. The poems written there include the ode 'Das Ahnenbild', a longer poem, 'An eine Verlobte' and the tiny elegy 'Die Entschlafenen'. I had omitted all these poems from earlier selections because they struck me as untypical, if not freakish. Two of them are included now. All these Stuttgart poems differ from others written by Hölderlin at this period in being neither tragic nor prophetic. They are celebrations of those human affections and continuities denied to Hölderlin by his circumstances and vocation. They were also occasional poems, written in response to the friendship and hospitality offered to a homeless guest. The 'ancestral portrait' of the ode is one of Christian Landauer's father, who had died in August of that year, while Hölderlin was staying in the house. The boy of the poem was his friend's only son, four years old at the time. What Hölderlin's relative realism in this poem could not accommodate was that his friend's prosperity rested on a textile business founded by the same father, not on the agricultural and horticultural pursuits which the ode celebrates. Christian Landauer, though, would not have been Hölderlin's friend if he had not combined worldly astuteness with concerns more congenial to Hölderlin. If the ode stands out as the nearest thing to the domestic poetry, or the bucolics and idylls, otherwise beyond Hölderlin's range – 'Domestic Life' was a rejected title for the ode – his religious preoccupations were by no means in abeyance there. The dead father becomes a spirit – akin to the *lares* and *penates* of antiquity – in the penultimate strophe, by a construction so puzzling syntactically that I had to bridge it with guesswork; and a piety at once natural and spiritual informs the whole poem. The two strands intertwine in the child's drinking of his grandfather's wine – an image at once naively representational and fraught with religious symbolism. These attempts of Hölderlin's to merge his own preoccupations in those of 'ordinary' people are a prefiguration of his last, unrecognizable, phase and person. After the change he was to write two poems on the birth of a child.

From Stuttgart Hölderlin went to Nürtingen for Christmas, then set out for Hauptwyl in Switzerland to take up another engagement as a private tutor. As usual, Hölderlin travelled on foot most of the way, though it was January and he had to cross the Alps. He passed through Stuttgart again on the way, and his friends escorted him as far as Tübingen. By April his employer in Switzerland, Gonzenbach, whose two daughters were Hölderlin's pupils, terminated the engagement 'for family reasons'. Again, Hölderlin set out on one of his long walks, also rowing across Lake Constance, seeing the Danube, and revisiting his birthplace. His one Sapphic ode, 'Sung Beneath the Alps', and the elegy 'Homecoming' celebrate the landscapes through which he had passed and his return to his family in April. Many impressions of the journeys also entered into his hymns and fragments. For the rest of the year he remained at Nürtingen, with visits to Stuttgart.

In January 1802 he set out for his last appointment as a tutor, in Bordeaux. There, too, he spent only a few months, returning home – on foot once more – in a state of acute disturbance and distress. On his outward journey, which took more than a month, he is known to have stopped in Strasbourg and Lyon, where he had to report as an alien. The long itinerary of his return, including a visit to Paris, has been the subject of endless speculation and debate. Pierre Berteaux, who questioned the madness imputed to Hölderlin after his return, argued that Hölderlin could have passed through Frankfurt and learned of Susette's illness, possibly even have seen her, before arriving in Stuttgart in mid-June; but Susette died on June 22nd, by which time Hölderlin must have been back with his family. Berteaux also suggests that Hölderlin's mother found Susette's love letters to Hölderlin in the trunk he had sent home from Bordeaux, and that altercations about that precipitated Hölderlin's alleged rages. What is certain is that as soon as Hölderlin left his mother's house again for Stuttgart, after brief convalescence at home, he recovered sufficiently to work again. An estrangement from his whole family undoubtedly occurred at this time – and no wonder, in the light of what is now known of their behaviour towards him in later years, their petty squabbles about money up to and after his death, even over the monument to be placed on his grave.

After receiving the letter from Sinclair, written at the end of June, informing him of Susette's death, he took refuge again briefly at his mother's. Though Susette died of German measles caught from her children, her health had been in decline ever since her last meeting with Hölderlin in 1800.

There is a letter written by Hölderlin after his return from Bordeaux that tells us more about his state of mind at this time than all the biographical reconstructions or extant reports by acquaintances of his haggard appearance, his silences, unintelligible utterances and outbreaks of rage. The physical hardships of his travels, too, must have had something to do with the changes in his appearance. The letter, or draft of a letter, was to Casimir Ulrich Böhlendorff, written in November 1802:

Dear friend,

I have not written to you for a long time, and meanwhile have been in France and have seen the sad, lonely earth; the shepherds and shepherdesses of southern France and individual beauties, men and women, who grew up in the fear of political uncertainty and of hunger.

The mighty element, the fire of heaven and the silence of the people, their life in nature, their confinedness and their contentment, moved me continually, and as one says of heroes, I can well say of myself that Apollo has struck me.

In the regions bordering on the Vendée I was interested in a quality fiercely warlike, and purely masculine, to which the light of life becomes spontaneous, immediate in eye and limb, which experiences the sensation of death like a kind of virtuosity and satisfies its thirst for knowledge.

The athletic character of the southern peoples, in the ruins of the ancient spirit, made me more familiar with the true character of the Greeks; I came to understand their nature and their wisdom, their bodies, how they grew in their climate and the rule they used to preserve their exuberant genius from the violence of the element.

This determined their peculiarity as a people, their way of adopting foreign natures and of communicating with them, and it is from this that they derived their distinct individuality which seems alive, in so far as supreme understanding, to the Greeks, was the power to respond to reality; and this becomes comprehensible to us when we comprehend the heroic bodies of the Greeks; it is tenderness, like our own peculiarity as a people.

The contemplation of ancient statuary made an impression on me that brought me closer to an understanding not only of the Greeks, but of what is greatest in all art, which, even where movement is most intense, the conception most phenomenalized and the intention most serious, still preserves every detail intact and true to itself, so that assuredness, in this sense, is the supreme kind of representation.

After many shocks and disturbances of my mind it was necessary for me to settle down for a while, and for the time being I am staying in my home town.

Nature in these parts moves more powerfully, the more I study it. The thunder-storm, not only in its extreme manifestation, but precisely as a power and shape, among the other forms of the sky, light in its workings, nationally and as a principle that fashions a mode of fate, so that something is holy to us, its urgency in coming and going, what is characteristic in forests and the convergence in one region of different kinds of nature, so that all the holy places of the earth come together around one place, and the philosophic light around my window – these are now my joy; and may I bear in mind how I came here, as far as this place!

Dear friend, I think that we shall not gloss the poets up to our time, but that song altogether will assume a different character, and that we cannot make ourselves heard because we, after the Greeks, are beginning once more to sing nationally and naturally, that is, in a truly original way.

Please write to me soon. I need pure tones. Psyche among friends, the generation of thought in conversation and letters is necessary for artists . . . Otherwise we have no thought for ourselves; but it belongs to the holy image which we are shaping. A sincere farewell.

> Yours,
>
> Hölderlin

That autumn Hölderlin received medical treatment at Stuttgart, but was reported to have grown composed whenever the doctor's son read out passages from Homer to him. At the end of September Hölderlin travelled to Regensburg, where the Landgrave and his Minister, Sinclair, were trying to negotiate an enlargement of the Landgrave's territory. Soon after, Hölderlin submitted an early version of his Sophocles translations to a publisher and worked on his poem 'Patmos', sent to Sinclair in January 1803. In June of that year he set out on another walk, to Murhardt in Württemberg, where he called on his old friend Schelling. That year his Sophocles translations were accepted for book publication

– his first since the two volumes of *Hyperion*, and the only other he was to see into print.

Hölderlin's 'return to the source', his symbolic homecoming, is intimated in his dedication to Princess Auguste of his Sophocles book: 'Apart from these, if time permits, I will sing the forefathers of our princes, their seats, and the angels of our holy country.' It was in these years that he worked on his most ambitious project, a series of hymns or cantos that were to range over the cosmology, myths and history of ancient and modern times, from the revolt of the Titans to the discovery of America and Hölderlin's own era. The Virgin Mary and Columbus were the subject of extant drafts and fragments. Luther and Shakespeare were among the titles jotted down for poems never written or lost. Yet until the collapse of this endeavour he could not wholly renounce the Greek gods, and his last intense exertions were directed towards a visionary reconciliation of his Greek and Christian allegiances, even though this demanded an almost hopeless attempt to syncretize a pantheistic and polytheistic system with a higher monotheism.

In 1803, at Nürtingen, Hölderlin also prepared for publication the group of late short poems which appeared in a miscellany as 'Nachtgesänge' ('Canticles of Night') in 1804. They included the odes 'Chiron', 'Tears', 'To Hope', 'Vulcan', 'Timidness' and 'Ganymede', but also free verse poems that had originated as parts of his longer hymns, 'The Ages of Life', 'Half of Life' and 'The Nook at Hardt'. By recognizing that such fragments could be published as separate poems, Hölderlin won a last victory over the taste and conventions of his own time. Nearly a century had to pass before such poems came into their own, as anticipations of Symbolist, Imagist and even Surrealist practices. Yet these very fragments are closely akin to those that Hölderlin extracted from Pindar, with his comments, as late as 1805. By 'originality' Hölderlin meant something quite different from 'modernity' or personal idiosyncrasy; it had to do with 'going to the source'. If both his own poems and his Pindar versions strike us as 'modern', it is because they rely not on argument but on particulars charged with the most concentrated significance, on the mere naming of a person or thing or their invocation by signs, where less daring poets of Hölderlin's time or any other would have presented a sequence of arguments and metaphors. In the later versions of the hymns, too, there are instances not only of inverted or deliberately ambiguous syntax – justified by Hölderlin's insights into Greek poetry, especially Pindar's – but of a-syntactic sentences that serve as a poetic shorthand. The most astonishing contraction of all occurs in the later version of 'Patmos'. The later poems proceed by flashes of perception or allusion, true to the laws not of discourse or argument but of pre-articulate feeling and thought, a poetic 'architecture' which Hölderlin distinguished from the logical structure of expository prose.

In many cases it may well be that Hölderlin never got beyond drafts or sketches that would have been filled out at a later stage; and it is some of these that prefigure the work of twentieth-century poets like Ezra Pound, whose ambition and range in his *Cantos* are comparable to Hölderlin's in drafts like this one:

> So Mahomed,* Rinaldo,
> Barbarossa as a liberal spirit,
>
> The Emperor Heinrich.
> But we are mixing up
> the periods
>> Demetrius Poliorcetes
> Peter the Great
>>> Heinrich's
> crossing of the Alps, and that
> with his own hand he gave the people food
> and drink and his son Conrad died of poison
> Example of one who changes an age
> reformer
> Conradin etc.
>
> all as representative
> of conditions.

> * Hear the horn of the watchman by night
>   After midnight it is, at the fifth hour

Fortuitous as the resemblance may be, because Hölderlin's lines are only the nucleus of an unwritten poem, there is something about the quality of his historical imagination here that makes one think of Pound's *Cantos*; but also of Hölderlin's words in the letter to Böhlendorff about 'all the holy places of the earth coming together around one place', and the endeavour of a single mind, a single imagination, to embrace them all. Hölderlin put it more trenchantly still in the draft of one of his unfinished poems:

> And there I am
> All things at once

Another fragment of Hölderlin's contains hints of what he was trying to do before giving up his poetic ambition – perhaps, too, of the rages that alarmed his relatives and friends:

> But language –
> In thunder speaks the
> God.
> Often I have it, language
> anger, she said, was enough and approved by Apollo –
> If you have love enough, then, go on, rage out of love.
> Often I tried to sing, but they did not hear you. For that was holy
> Nature's will. For her you sang in your youth. Not singing
> You spoke to the deity,
> but what all of you have forgotten is that always the first-born
> belong not to mortals but to the gods.
> More common, more everyday
> the fruit must become, only then
> will mortals possess it.

Though far from becoming easier to grasp or to follow – the 'she' in the fifth line could be not a person but a noun feminine in German, like language itself – Hölderlin's language and imagery in the late poems did become more common, more everyday, often to the point of a colloquialism far removed from the sublime or abstract diction of his beginnings.

In July 1804 Sinclair took Hölderlin to Homburg, where he had obtained the hardly more than titular appointment of Court Librarian for his friend, paying the salary out of his own. In April the Sophocles book had appeared, with complimentary copies for Goethe, Hegel and Schelling, but not Schiller. Hölderlin's mother had resisted Sinclair's offer of the appointment, on the grounds that Hölderlin was unfit for it. In fact, Schelling and others thought that Hölderlin's condition had improved since the previous year, and Sinclair reported to Hölderlin's mother that in his opinion many of Hölderlin's oddities had been deliberately assumed. It was Hölderlin's failure to write to his mother at this period that made her anxious. In January 1805 Hölderlin came close to being implicated in the accusations raised against Sinclair, who was denounced for a plot not against his immediate sovereign the Landgrave, but against the Grand Duke of Württemberg. Hölderlin is reported to have protested vociferously more than once in public that he was no Jacobin – as indeed he had ceased to be, thanks to Napoleon's imperial conquests. The Landgrave protected Hölderlin, but believed that he was no longer capable of looking after himself. In new lodgings, in the absence of his friend and patron Sinclair, he is reported to have 'strummed wildly on his piano by day and by night'; but he was still capable of working on his Pindar translation and commentary when Sinclair returned to Homburg in July. In January 1806 Hölderlin's mother applied to the Consistory for an annual bounty for her son from the royal purse – the Grand Duke of Württemberg had assumed the title of King – on the grounds of his illness and 'exhaustion of his patrimony'. The bounty was awarded, although there is documentary evidence now that the substantial fortune Hölderlin had inherited from his father and an aunt, far from being 'exhausted', was withheld from him by his mother throughout his life. Not even the interest on his capital had been spent by him or on him when he died. In July of that year the Landgrave's territory was merged in a new Grand Duchy, so that Hölderlin's titular appointment was void.

In August Sinclair had to inform Hölderlin's mother that her son could not remain in Homburg and would have to be taken into care elsewhere, because he was in danger of being assaulted by the mob. In September Hölderlin, who resisted vehemently, was removed by force to the lately opened Autenrieth clinic in Tübingen. This was reputed to be the most 'advanced' mental home in Germany. There was drug treatment of a sort, belladonna and digitalis, but also the notorious Autenrieth mask, applied to stop patients from screaming, besides the straitjacket and long forcible immersions in cold water inside a cage. One of Hölderlin's fellow patients died of the treatment he received. Hölderlin was also treated for a physical condition, scabies. In the summer of 1807 he was discharged as an incurable case and given 'three years to live at the most'. He survived for another 36 years – just about half his lifetime.

At the clinic he was visited by the carpenter Ernst Zimmer, who had read *Hyperion*, and it was Zimmer who arranged with Autenrieth that private care would be a better alternative for Hölderlin. It was in Zimmer's house or 'tower' on the bank of the Neckar in Tübingen that Hölderlin was to spend the remainder of his life; and it was thanks to the kindness, understanding and care of the Zimmer family that this second half of Hölderlin's life was peaceful at least. Very soon Zimmer gave him not only the freedom of the house, but took him on those walks that were his consolation and the subject of verses not wholly void of personal responses and awareness, as the later ones became, when Hölderlin had ceased to exist as far as he was concerned, turning into 'Scardanelli, or something of the sort'.

The many reports by visitors in these later years, including those by the poet Wilhelm Waiblinger, who wrote a full account of his meetings, are of mainly pathological and sociological interest. I quote only Zimmer's account of the genesis of one little poem, 'The lines of life . . .', which shows that Hölderlin remained capable of at least one affection, though he kept most visitors at a distance with an excess of polite deference and forms of address like 'Your Highness' or 'Your Majesty'. In one of his periodic letters to Hölderlin's mother – who seems never to have visited her son in all the years up to her death in 1828 – the semi-literate carpenter informs her as follows of the writing of those lines: 'His poetic spirit still shows itself to be active, for instance in my house he saw the drawing of a temple. He told me to make one out of wood. I replied that I have to work for my living, that I am not so fortunate as to live in philosophic calm like him, immediately he replied, "Oh, I am a wretched creature", and in the same minute he wrote these verses on a wooden board with his pencil:

> The lines of life are various; they diverge and cease
> Like footpaths and the mountains' utmost ends.
> What here we are, elsewhere a God amends
> With harmonies, eternal recompense and peace.'

Almost all the later poems, usually on the seasons – with one or two exceptions in the years between 1823 and 1825 – were dashed off at the request of visitors, who wanted a memento or curio in exchange for little gifts of tobacco or the like. The poem 'Spring' ('When springtime from the depth . . .') is believed to have been written on Hölderlin's last birthday, in March 1843. He died suddenly of pulmonary congestion on June 7th of that year, at the age of 73.

It is useless to wonder what course Hölderlin's life might have taken if he had been granted some degree of financial independence at the age of 21, or even 25, but there can be little doubt that it would have been a rather less catastrophic one. At his death, in the absence of immediate heirs, his considerable inheritance passed to his sister and half-brother, without ever having been at his disposal. Even in the second half of his life, when there was no question of his earning a living, Zimmer had to make special appeals to Karl Gock, the half-brother, or to other legal guardians whenever Hölderlin's physical condition called for small additions to his frugal diet. Since Hölderlin's guardians also received the annual bounty for his maintenance out of royal funds, their treatment of him could not have been more callous or more mean. The piano that was Hölderlin's constant resort in those Tübingen years – he had come to prefer it to his first instrument, the flute – belonged not to him but to Zimmer, although Princess Auguste had given Hölderlin a piano in his Homburg years. It appears that, like most of his books, the piano was never moved into the room that was to be the nearest thing to a home ever occupied by him since his childhood.

In May or June 1807 Zimmer was also told to take away the loose-leaf folio manuscript sheaf in which Hölderlin had been drafting and rewriting his poems since the Homburg period, and deliver it to the family. The almost complete break in his work at this juncture may have a great deal to do with this confiscation of his work sheets – his only possible aid to continuity at the time. This is not to deny that there was a break and change in Hölderlin's personality both before and after his ordeal in the clinic. From his odes 'To the Fates' and 'The Course of Life' onwards he had predicted that his life would run an arc-shaped course, a sheer ascent and a sheer descent, a steep progression and a steep regression. In July 1799 he had written to his sister: 'And one day, when I am a grey-haired boy, may spring and the morning and the evening light rejuvenate me a little more each day, until I feel the last and sit down in the open air and from there go away, to eternal youth.'

Zimmer's comment on Hölderlin's 'madness' is as good as any: 'It's the too much he had in him that cracked his mind.' Another is by the poet Ernst Meister, one of a line of twentieth-century German poets, including Rilke, Trakl, Bobrowski and Celan, who were able to learn from Hölderlin in one way or another: 'Perhaps Hölderlin allowed himself to be "stricken" so as to make up for having missed the life of "ordinary" people, the provincial or parochial life, as it were, in the island's interior, against which the whole of being surges and breaks.'[4] According to Waiblinger's account, Hölderlin himself said: 'Only now do I understand human beings, now that I live far from them and in solitude.' In some of the later occasional verses there is such a degree of assent to the views and sentiments of 'ordinary' people that they read like mocking parodies of them, just as the letters Hölderlin was persuaded to write to his mother in those years read like mocking parodies of the filial sentiments he had long ceased to feel. That is why both contemporary and later commentators were able to suspect that his

---

4. Ernst Meister: *Prosa 1931 bis 1979*. Heidelberg, 1989.

'madness' was put on, that it served him as a means of deliberate non-communication. Other 'tower' poems, like 'The Walk' and 'The Merry Life', written out of a residual urge, rather than for casual visitors, hint at his own interpretation of his change of personality: peace at all costs, humble contentment, retraction as well as retirement, after unbearable endeavours, sufferings and defeats. Part of the cost, though, was loss of reality. Even the landscapes and townscapes of these poems have become scenery in more senses than one; they could be stage scenery, because there is nothing left in them of the breath, pulse and animation of Hölderlin's earlier responses to things seen, remembered or mythically evoked. What had gone out of them was conflict. 'Without Contraries there is no progression', Blake wrote. Hölderlin's last poems are poems of regression into a world ready-made for him and accepted, down to the tritest rhyming of one dead thing with another. Some of them do contain moments of unprecedented limpidity, just because the words used are impersonal and transparent. So in parts of the ode 'If from the distance . . .' in which Philippe Jaccottet found 'the most difficult and rarest thing of all, the moment when poetry, without seeming to do so, because it has been stripped of all brilliance, attains to what, to me, is the highest point'; but, in his *Paysages avec Figures Absentes* (1970), Jaccottet also found such moments in poems by Hölderlin written well before his years in the tower. In terms of Hölderlin's 'course of life' and its overall meaning, D.E. Sattler is not wrong in seeing 'childhood regained' in the best of the tower poems, but nor is David Constantine wrong in his judgement of these poems as a whole: 'Some of the Tübingen poems are beautiful and touching, and some have moments of the purest immanence such as the preceding poetry had always striven to achieve; but the inexorable trend is downwards and away.'

This selection now includes enough of the last verses for readers to judge for themselves – partly because I translated a batch of the Scardanelli poems for the first performance in England of Heinz Holliger's settings of them in his *Scardanelli Cycle* – one remarkable instance of the fascination the very unselfing in them can exercise. From his lifetime to its rediscovery and re-editing in the twentieth century, Hölderlin's work has given rise to so much disagreement, such diversity of judgement and interpretation, that I have tried hard here to confine myself to a sketching in of its background. It is in my selection and translations – reconsidered and enlarged over a period of fifty years – that my preferences are implicit; and though I have also tried hard not to rationalize the texts by ironing out their oddities, resolving their ambiguities and enigmas, texts like these cannot be translated at all without a modicum of interpretation. The controversies in the fifties about the newly discovered 'Friedensfeier', in which I took part briefly after identifying the manuscript in London, where it came to light, showed me that there could be no agreement even about the identity of the persons or powers invoked in the hymns, like the 'prince of the feast-day' in that poem, variously interpreted as Napoleon, as Christ, as a personification of peace itself, or as 'the genius of our people, . . . the long concealed "soul of the fatherland"'! Each of these interpretations was plausible and learnedly presented, each came to the conclusion most consonant with the interpreter's proclivities, beliefs and concerns. It became clear to me that what Hölderlin chose not to identify clearly in his poems – by circumscription, ambiguity or the withholding of names – should be left in suspense if at all possible. Nor, in Hölderlin's work, could a turn of speech or attribute in one poem necessarily serve as a key to its recurrence in another, because his progression was one through contraries, through conflicts strenuously fought out, and leaps into the unknown.

For Hölderlin, the need always to write in accordance with his latest insights and vision, even if these seemed to contradict earlier ones enacted with the same intensity, was more compelling still than the need for completeness and consistency. At the same time he believed in what, in an early letter, he called 'the aesthetic Church', demanding that everything done should come as close to artistic perfection as he could make it. That tension, as well as his precipitous career and the probable loss of many of his papers, goes far towards explaining the fragmentary state of much of his work. By producing later, much longer, versions of his brief Frankfurt odes, for instance, poems as artistically flawless as anything he produced, for himself he reduced these earlier odes to fragments, as it were, although the later, tragic or prophetic, elaborations of their themes made something quite different out of them, so that for his readers both versions are valid. On the other hand, for the last poems he sent out for periodical publication, he made poems of an unprecedented kind out of fragments.

Extreme antithesis and extreme synthesis make it hardly possible to separate aesthetic or stylistic considerations from religious and philosophical ones in Hölderlin's work, that of a poet who produced essentially classical work in a Romantic age. Yet one thing that is common to all of Hölderlin's work, not excluding the last poems, is what his coeval Wordsworth called 'natural piety'. It was in search of an all-pervading piety that Hölderlin turned to ancient Greece, away from a culture of which he wrote in *Hyperion*: 'Where you see nothing, there your gods dwell.' Because this ancient Greece could not be brought back, as Hölderlin came to acknowledge after daring plunges into its mysteries, the work up to his middle years is also distinguished by a powerful dynamic of aspiration – enacted not only by the enjambment of lines but the overflowing of whole strophes into the next – within strict forms and structures, a symmetry demanded by 'stillness of beauty'. (Even when he had abandoned the attempt to imitate the metrical correspondence in Pindar's odes, because the public function of their performance was missing, he kept to a basically triadic structure.) In the same way Hölderlin tried again and again to bridge what may well be unbridgeable antinomies between a pantheistic and polytheistic religion of nature and the 'solid letter' of Judaic-Christian monotheism, and to do so on the basis of his own epiphanies – up to the 'God of gods' of a late poem, a hierarchy that would embrace and justify the periodicity and alternation of divine revelation and retraction which he saw in successive eras. He himself was well aware that the language of his late hymns and fragments would be judged 'too unconventional' by contemporary readers, as his little preface to the 'Friedensfeier' attests. Some of the polysemies in such poems arose from his awareness that he was venturing on to forbidden ground, into mysteries that should be left unspoken; others from antinomies that he could not resolve, only bridge by a purely poetic structure and syntax or by images that are not metaphors reducible to a single meaning. One instance, not only 'too unconventional' but an affront to grammarians and logicians, if not to theologians, is the opening of his late 'Patmos' fragment:

> Voll Güt' ist; keiner aber fasset
> Allein Gott.

The syntactic preposterousness of those lines is heightened by an ambiguity which my translation could not render. Since the *allein* occurs in the second line, it could qualify either God or 'no one'; or both at once, just as 'God' is the elided subject of the first three words and the explicit object of the second clause. The lines could mean that no one can grasp God by himself, unaided, or that God cannot be grasped in Himself, alone; and the missing link in either case may or may not be the 'solid letter' of the earlier version of the poem, the tradition of scripture. It could also be the Trinity or unnamed agents of mediation. Poetically, though, these lines have the effect of a thunderclap and lightning flash — themselves the signs of the manifestation of God in antiquity and in Hölderlin's poems, and a physical phenomenon arising from the collision and fusion of disparate energies. This sentence explains why Ezra Pound liked to derive the German word *dichten*, to make poetry, from the adjective *dicht*, dense, so wresting a truth about poetry from an etymological error.

One way of dealing with such affronts offered by Hölderlin's poems is to ascribe them to his 'madness'. Yet already in his short ode of the Frankfurt years 'To the Sanctimonious Poets' — whose harshly sarcastic tone contrasts so starkly with that of his other poems of the period and makes it more like a satirical epigram — Hölderlin told the 'cold hypocrites' who were adorning their conventional poems with the names of Greek gods:

> You're rational! In Helios you don't believe,
> Nor in the Thunderer or the Sea-God;
> Dead is our Earth, so what fool would thank her?

'Dead is our Earth'. As far as I know, these – ironically intended – words of Hölderlin have never been promoted to the kind of actuality accorded to a comparable assertion by Nietzsche about the death of God. Yet, in spite of my reluctance to extract messages, let alone slogans, from Hölderlin's texts, I see a distinctly topical relevance in his faith in the powers of nature, as embodied in the ancient gods – *the* constant theme in his work inseparable from its poetic radicalism, not dependent on the concerns of his interpreters and not amenable to their ideological use by the selection of this or that quotation. Because Hölderlin's faith in the powers and processes of nature was an absolute and religious one, he could dissolve works of his own, just as organic nature dissolves its phenomena, so that new growth can develop from the dissolution. Unlike Goethe, whose metamorphoses, entelechies and evolutions, up to the 'die and become' of a late poem, are akin to Hölderlin's, he did not allow self-preservation to set a limit to that quest: no less than his works, to him the producers of poems, too, were only vessels that could be broken when they had served their purpose. Goethe wanted to preserve his person, and therefore left his contraries to run along parallel lines, sometimes making a game of them. Hölderlin had to enact his to the point of self-destruction. The confrontation of the antinomies Nature and Art, timeless Saturn and time-bound, historic Jupiter, then the growing concern with historical persons and eras, even with the historicity of 'the Only One', Christ, and of Christendom – all this was too much for mere 'natural piety'. Yet even in his apology for his later, 'too unconventional' mode of singing, it was on nature that Hölderlin based his appeal: 'and Nature, whence it originates, will also receive it again'.

There is no need to point to the present relevance of a dead earth. Even the spiritual and secular guardians of our civilization have had to concede that there is something wrong with a technology and an ethos that give human beings the right not only to rule the earth, sea and sky, but to damage them irreparably. More consistently than Goethe's, Hölderlin's 'natural piety' insisted on bounds set to the human urge to know and to exploit knowledge. So in the tragic ode 'The Poet's Vocation':

Too long now things divine have been cheaply used
And all the powers of heaven, the kindly, spent
In trifling waste by cold and cunning
Men without thanks, who when he, the Highest,

In person tills their field for them, think they know
The daylight and the Thunderer, and indeed
Their telescope may find them all, may
Count and may name every star of heaven.

Yet will the Father cover with holy night,
That we may last on earth, our too knowing eyes.
He loves no Titan! Never will our
Free-ranging power coerce his heaven.

Nor is it good to be all too wise . . .

Again, it would be idle to ask oneself whether Hölderlin could have preserved his faith that, ultimately, the universe cannot be 'coerced' or violated, if he had lived in this century. Every answer to that would be another profession of an interpreter's beliefs. I will only remark that the German text of the first of the strophes quoted does not run smoothly in metre, rhythm or grammar, so that, for once, the urgency of what Hölderlin had to say overruled his need for artistic perfection.

Hölderlin's 'love for Earth', which, in the fragment 'Home', is 'quenched' by picking berries, reached its fullest poetic enactment in poems he was unable to complete. It is in these fragments filled with immediate sensuous detail in which the phenomena of nature seem to be celebrated in their own right, rather than as symbols within a mythical, cosmological or eschatological system. So in 'For when the grape-vine's sap . . .' or 'On fallow foliage . . .'. These fragments are wholly unlike anything written by other European poets of Hölderlin's time. In a sense, they are also beyond interpretation, not so much because they are fragments whose larger context is missing as because anything read into them or out of them would so clearly fall short of doing justice to their immediacy. If there is anything to be regretted about the break that occurred in Hölderlin's middle years, it is that he did not salvage more of such fragments, completing them as short poems. Yet within a mere decade Hölderlin produced a poetic work so various, so rich in potentialities and possibilities for the 'future ages' in which he placed his hope, that regrets about it are out of place, as well as futile. Even his personal catastrophe is one that he foresaw at the start of that decade, willing to take the risk and pay the price; and, mad or not, even the verses he wrote in his decline, relapsing into generality and abstraction, can move us with faint echoes of his epiphanies, his verbal and visionary thunderclaps.

M. H.

Suffolk, October 1989

Bibliographical Note

The German texts reproduced here, and the translations, are mainly based on Friedrich Beissner's edition, *Hölderlin: Sämtliche Werke* (Große Stuttgarter Ausgabe, Stuttgart, 1943–1977), with a few emendations or variants taken from the facsimile editions of *Die Friedensfeier* by Wolfgang Binder and Alfred Kelletat (Tübingen, 1959) and of the *Homburger Folioheft* by D. E. Sattler and Emery E. George (Frankfurt, 1986), part of the current Frankfurt Edition of Hölderlin's works. The volume or volumes to be devoted to all the hymns and fragments in that edition had not appeared in time for my last revision of my work. Since for some of Hölderlin's poems there is no text that can be regarded as definitive, in one or two instances I have taken the liberty of producing a conflation of my own, so as to include those variants in the drafts that seemed most fully realized or most striking. Neither completeness in the presentation of variants nor elucidation could be attempted here. My notes are minimal and selective.

For the benefit of readers who wish to supplement the necessarily scanty material provided in my Introduction, I list a few publications in English that could prove helpful in different ways:

Marshall Montgomery: *Friedrich Hölderlin and the German Neo-Hellenic Movement*. Oxford, 1923
* E. M. Butler: *The Tyranny of Greece over Germany*. Cambridge, 1935
Ronald Peacock: *Hölderlin*. London, 1938
Agnes Stansfield: *Hölderlin*. Manchester, 1943
E. L. Stahl: *Hölderlin's Symbolism*. Oxford, 1945
* Edwin Muir: *Essays on Literature and Society*. London, 1949
L. S. Salzberger: *Hölderlin*. Cambridge, 1952
* C. M. Bowra: *Inspiration and Poetry*. London, 1955
Quarterly Review of Literature (Annandale-on-Hudson, N. Y.),
    Hölderlin Issue, Volume X, Numbers 1 & 2, 1959. (Contains essays

by Martin Heidegger, Erich Heller, Norbert von Hellingrath and Anthony Thorlby; and excerpts from Hölderlin's *Hyperion* in English.)

M. B. Benn: *Hölderlin and Pindar*. The Hague, 1962

* Michael Hamburger: *Reason and Energy*. Second edition, London, 1970

Richard Unger: *Hölderlin's Major Poetry*. Bloomington, Indiana and London, 1975

Eric L. Santer: *Friedrich Hölderlin. Narrative Vigilance and the Poetic Imagination*. New Brunswick & London, 1986

David Constantine: *Hölderlin*. Oxford, 1988

An English version by Willard R. Trask of Hölderlin's *Hyperion* was published in 1965 by Signet Classics, New York and London.

A selection from Hölderlin's letters, translated by Christopher Middleton, appeared in *The Poet's Vocation, Letters of Hölderlin, Rimbaud and Hart Crane*, Austin, Texas, n. d. 1967 (?).

Translations of two of Hölderlin's essays on tragedy, by Jeremy Adler, appeared in *Comparative Criticism*, Volume 7, Cambridge, 1985; his translation of Hölderlin's notes on the *Oedipus Tyrannus* and *Antigone* of Sophocles in Volume 6 of the same yearbook, 1983.

---

* These books contain chapters on Hölderlin.

Odes and Epigrams
(1797–1799)

Gebet für die Unheilbaren

Eil, o zaudernde Zeit, sie ans Ungereimte zu führen,
    Anders belehrest du sie nie wie verständig sie sind.
Eile, verderbe sie ganz, und führ' ans furchtbare Nichts sie,
    Anders glauben sie dir nie, wie verdorben sie sind.
Diese Thoren bekehren sich nie, wenn ihnen nicht schwindelt,
    Diese   sich nie, wenn sie Verwesung nicht sehn.

Prayer for the Incurable

Hurry, hesitant Time, and bring them up against nonsense,
    Else you'll warn them in vain what their good sense is about.
Hurry, denature them wholly, up against frightful non-being
    Bring them, or never they'll know just how denatured they are.
Never these fools will reform until they begin to feel giddy,
    Never [recover their health] save in the stench of decay.

Guter Rath

Hast du Verstand und ein Herz, so zeige nur eines von beiden,
  Beides verdammen sie dir, zeigest du beides zugleich.

Advocatus Diaboli

Tief im Herzen haß ich den Troß der Despoten und Pfaffen
  Aber noch mehr das Genie, macht es gemein sich damit.

Die Vortreflichen

Lieben Brüder! versucht es nur nicht, vortreflich zu werden
  Ehrt das Schiksaal und tragts, Stümper auf Erden zu seyn
Denn ist Einmal der Kopf voran, so folget der Schweif auch
  Und die klassische Zeit deutscher Poëten ist aus.

Die beschreibende Poësie

Wißt! Apoll ist der Gott der Zeitungsschreiber geworden
  Und sein Mann ist, wer ihm treulich das Factum erzählt.

Falsche Popularität

O der Menschenkenner! er stellt sich kindisch mit Kindern
  Aber der Baum und das Kind suchet, was über ihm ist.

Epigrams (1797)

Good Advice

You've a head *and* a heart? Reveal only one of them, I say;
　　If you reveal both at once, doubly they'll damn you, for both.

Advocatus Diaboli

Deep in my heart I abhor the nexus of rulers and clerics,
　　Yet more deeply I loathe genius in league with that gang.

The Excellent

Dearest brothers, whatever you do, never try to be excellent writers;
　　Honour fate, and accept that it's human to bungle your trade.
For if once the head ventures forth, the tail will certainly follow,
　　And our classical age, Germans, is over for good.

Descriptive Poetry

Latest news: Apollo's become the god of journalists, press men,
　　And his blue-eyed boy he who reports all the facts.

False Popularity

O the worldly-wise man! With children his manner is childish;
　　But the tree and the child seek what is higher than they.

An Diotima

Schönes Leben! du lebst, wie die zarten Blüthen im Winter,
    In der gealterten Welt blühst du verschlossen, allein.
Liebend strebst du hinaus, dich zu sonnen am Lichte des Frühlings,
    Zu erwarmen an ihr suchst du die Jugend der Welt.
Deine Sonne, die schönere Zeit, ist untergegangen
    Und in frostiger Nacht zanken Orkane sich nun.

To Diotima

Beautiful being, you live as do delicate blossoms in winter,
    In a world that's grown old hidden you blossom, alone.
Lovingly outward you press to bask in the light of the springtime,
    To be warmed by it still, look for the youth of the world.
But your sun, the lovelier world, has gone down now,
    And the quarrelling gales rage in an icy bleak night.

Diotima

Komm und besänftige mir, die du einst Elemente versöhntest
    Wonne der himmlischen Muse das Chaos der Zeit,
Ordne den tobenden Kampf mit Friedenstönen des Himmels
    Bis in der sterblichen Brust sich das entzweite vereint,
Bis der Menschen alte Natur die ruhige große,
    Aus der gährenden Zeit, mächtig und heiter sich hebt.
Kehr' in die dürftigen Herzen des Volks, lebendige Schönheit!
    Kehr an den gastlichen Tisch, kehr in die Tempel zurük!
Denn Diotima lebt, wie die zarten Blüthen im Winter,
    Reich an eigenem Geist sucht sie die Sonne doch auch.
Aber die Sonne des Geists, die schönere Welt ist hinunter
    Und in frostiger Nacht zanken Orkane sich nur.

Diotima

Bliss of the heavenly Muse who on elements once imposed order,
    Come, and for me now assuage the chaos come back in our time,
Temper the furious war with peace-giving, heavenly music
    Till in the mortal heart all that's divided unites,
Till the former nature of men, the calm, the majestic,
    From our turbulent age rises, restored to its prime.
Living beauty, return to the destitute hearts of the people,
    To the banqueting table return, enter the temples once more!
For Diotima lives as do delicate blossoms in winter,
    Blessed with a soul of her own, yet needing and seeking the sun.
But the lovelier world, the sun of the spirit is darkened,
    Only quarrelling gales rage in an icy bleak night.

Buonaparte

Heilige Gefäße sind die Dichter,
    Worinn des Lebens Wein, der Geist
      Der Helden sich aufbewahrt,

Aber der Geist dieses Jünglings
    Der schnelle, müßt' er es nicht zersprengen
      Wo es ihn fassen wollte, das Gefäß?

Der Dichter laß ihn unberührt wie den Geist der Natur,
    An solchem Stoffe wird zum Knaben der Meister.

Er kann im Gedichte nicht leben und bleiben,
    Er lebt und bleibt in der Welt.

Bonaparte

Poets are holy vessels
   In which the wine of life,
      The spirit of heroes is preserved;

But this young man's spirit,
   The quick – would it not burst
      Any vessel that tried to contain it?

Let the poet leave him untouched like the spirit of Nature,
   For both reduce to a bungling boy the masterly craftsman.

In the poem he cannot live and last;
   He lives and lasts in the world.

Empedokles

Das Leben suchst du, suchst, und es quillt und glänzt
   Ein göttlich Feuer tief aus der Erde dir,
     Und du in schauderndem Verlangen
       Wirfst dich hinab, in des Aetna Flammen.

So schmelzt' im Weine Perlen der Übermuth
   Der Königin; und mochte sie doch! hättst du
     Nur deinen Reichtum nicht, o Dichter
       Hin in den gährenden Kelch geopfert!

Doch heilig bist du mir, wie der Erde Macht,
   Die dich hinwegnahm, kühner Getödteter!
     Und folgen möcht' ich in die Tiefe,
       Hielte die Liebe mich nicht, dem Helden.

Empedocles

You look for life, you look and from deeps of Earth
   A fire, divinely gleaming wells up for you,
      And quick, aquiver with desire, you
         Hurl yourself down into Etna's furnace.

So did the Queen's exuberance once dissolve
   Rare pearls in wine; and why should she not? But you,
      If only you, O poet, had not
         Offered your wealth to the seething chalice!

Yet you are holy to me as is the power
   Of Earth that took you from us, the boldly killed!
      And gladly, did not love restrain me,
         Deep as the hero plunged down I'd follow.

An die Parzen

Nur Einen Sommer gönnt, ihr Gewaltigen!
    Und einen Herbst zu reifem Gesange mir,
        Daß williger mein Herz, vom süßen
           Spiele gesättiget, dann mir sterbe.

Die Seele, der im Leben ihr göttlich Recht
    Nicht ward, sie ruht auch drunten im Orkus nicht;
        Doch ist mir einst das Heil'ge, das am
           Herzen mir liegt, das Gedicht gelungen,

Willkommen dann, o Stille der Schattenwelt!
    Zufrieden bin ich, wenn auch mein Saitenspiel
        Mich nicht hinab geleitet; Einmal
           Lebt ich, wie Götter, und mehr bedarfs nicht.

•To the Fates

One summer only grant me, you powerful Fates,
   And one more autumn only for mellow song,
      So that more willingly, replete with
         Music's late sweetness, my heart may die then.

The soul in life denied its god-given right
   Down there in Orcus also will find no peace;
      But when what's holy, dear to me, the
         Poem's accomplished, my art perfected,

Then welcome, silence, welcome cold world of shades!
   I'll be content, though here I must leave my lyre
      And songless travel down; for *once* I
         Lived like the gods, and no more is needed.

Diotima

Du schweigst und duldest, und sie versteh'n dich nicht,
    Du heilig Leben! welkest hinweg und schweigst,
        Denn ach, vergebens bei Barbaren
            Suchst du die Deinen im Sonnenlichte,

Die zärtlichgroßen Seelen, die nimmer sind!
    Doch eilt die Zeit. Noch siehet mein sterblich Lied
        Den Tag, der, Diotima! nächst den
            Göttern mit Helden dich nennt, und dir gleicht.

Diotima

You suffer and keep silent and, strange to them,
   You holy being, silently wilt away;
      For, ah, in vain among barbarians
         Here in the sunlight you seek your kindred,

The nobly tender spirits that are no more!
   Yet time speeds on. Though mortal, my song will live
      To see the day which next to gods, with
         Heroes will name you, itself be like you.

An ihren Genius

Send' ihr Blumen und Frücht' aus nieversiegender Fülle,
    Send' ihr, freundlicher Geist, ewige Jugend herab!
Hüll' in deine Wonnen sie ein und laß sie die Zeit nicht
    Sehn, wo einsam und fremd sie , die Athenerin, lebt,
Bis sie im Lande der Seeligen einst die fröhlichen Schwestern,
    Die zu Phidias Zeit herrschten und liebten, umfängt.

To Her Genius

Send her flowers and fruit from inexhaustible fulness,
    Send her, tutelar spirit, deathless youth from above!
Wrap her up in your joys and never let her experience
    Years when lonely, estranged, she, the Athenian, must live,
Till in the land of the blessed one day she fondly embraces
    Happy sisters who ruled, loved when Phidias was young.

Abbitte

Heilig Wesen! gestört hab' ich die goldene
    Götterruhe dir oft, und der geheimeren,
        Tiefern Schmerzen des Lebens
            Hast du manche gelernt von mir.

O vergiß es, vergieb! gleich dem Gewölke dort
    Vor dem friedlichen Mond, geh' ich dahin, und du
        Ruhst und glänzest in deiner
            Schöne wieder, du süßes Licht!

Plea for Forgiveness

Holy being, I know, often I've troubled your
    Golden, godlike repose, so that you learned from me
        Much that might have been spared you,
            Life's more hidden, obscurer griefs.

O forgive me, forget! Look, as the clouds up there
    Veil with black the slow moon, I drift away, while you
        Stay and shine in your beauty,
            Gentle light, as you shone before.

Ehmals und Jezt

In jüngern Tagen war ich des Morgens froh,
    Des Abends weint' ich; jezt, da ich älter bin,
        Beginn ich zweifelnd meinen Tag, doch
            Heilig und heiter ist mir sein Ende.

Then and Now ✿

In younger days each morning I rose with joy,
    To weep at nightfall; now, in my later years,
      Though doubting I begin my day, yet
        Always its end is serene and holy.

Lebenslauf

Hoch auf strebte mein Geist, aber die Liebe zog
   Schön ihn nieder; das Laid beugt ihn gewaltiger;
     So durchlauf ich des Lebens
       Bogen und kehre, woher ich kam.

The Course of Life

High my spirit aspired, truly, however, love
    Pulled it earthward; and grief lower still bows it down.
        So I follow the arc of
            Life and return to my starting-place.

Die Kürze

»Warum bist du so kurz? liebst du, wie vormals, denn
　　»Nun nicht mehr den Gesang? fandst du, als Jüngling, doch,
　　　　»In den Tagen der Hoffnung,
　　　　　　»Wenn du sangest, das Ende nie!

Wie mein Glük, ist mein Lied. – Willst du im Abendroth
　　Froh dich baden? hinweg ists! und die Erd’ ist kalt,
　　　　Und der Vogel der Nacht schwirrt
　　　　　　Unbequem vor das Auge dir.

Brevity

'Why so brief now, so curt? Do you no longer, then,
    Love your art as you did? When in your younger days,
        Hopeful days, in your singing
            What you loathed was to make an end!'

Like my joy is my song. – Who in the sundown's red
    Glow would happily bathe? Gone it is, cold the earth,
        And the bird of the night whirs
            Down, so close that you shield your eyes.

Menschenbeifall

Ist nicht heilig mein Herz, schöneren Lebens voll,
  Seit ich liebe? warum achtetet ihr mich mehr,
    Da ich stolzer und wilder,
      Wortereicher und leerer war?

Ach! der Menge gefällt, was auf den Marktplaz taugt,
  Und es ehret der Knecht nur den Gewaltsamen;
    An das Göttliche glauben
      Die allein, die es selber sind.

Human Applause

Has love not hallowed, filled with new life my heart,
　　With lovelier life? Then why did you prize me more
　　　　When I was proud and wild and frantic,
　　　　　　Lavish of words, yet in substance empty?

The crowd likes best what sells in the market-place,
　　And loud-mouthed force alone wins a slave's respect.
　　　　In gods and godhead only he can
　　　　　　Truly believe who himself is godlike.

Die Heimath

Froh kehrt der Schiffer heim an den stillen Strom
   Von fernen Inseln, wo er geerndtet hat;
      Wohl möcht' auch ich zur Heimath wieder;
         Aber was hab' ich, wie Laid, geerndtet? –

Ihr holden Ufer, die ihr mich auferzogt,
   Stillt ihr der Liebe Laiden? ach! gebt ihr mir,
      Ihr Wälder meiner Kindheit, wann ich
         Komme, die Ruhe noch Einmal wieder?

• Home

Content the boatman turns to the river's calm
   From distant isles, his harvest all gathered in;
     I too would gladly now turn homeward
       Only, what harvest but pain have I reaped?

Kind river-banks that tended and brought me up,
   Can you allay love's sufferings, give me back,
     You forests of my childhood, should I
       Come to you now, the same peace as ever?

Der gute Glaube

Schönes Leben! du liegst krank, und das Herz ist mir
  Müd vom Weinen und schon dämmert die Furcht in mir,
    Doch, doch kann ich nicht glauben,
      Daß du sterbest, so lang du liebst.

Good Faith

Dearest one, you lie sick, so that with weeping my
  Heart is weary, and fear almost takes root in me;
    Yet I cannot believe that
      You could die when you still can love.

Ihre Genesung

Deine Freundin, Natur! leidet und schläft und du
   Allbelebende, säumst? ach! und ihr heilt sie nicht,
      Mächt'ge Lüfte des Aethers,
         Nicht ihr Quellen des Sonnenlichts?

Alle Blumen der Erd', alle die fröhlichen,
   Schönen Früchte des Hains, heitern sie alle nicht
      Dieses Leben, ihr Götter!
         Das ihr selber in Lieb' erzogt? –

Ach! schon athmet und tönt heilige Lebenslust
   Ihr im reizenden Wort wieder wie sonst und schon
      Glänzt das Auge des Lieblings
         Freundlichoffen, Natur! dich an.

Her Recovery

Nature, she who's your friend drowses and ails, and you
    Dally, giver of life? Cannot you heal her, then,
        Potent breezes of Aether,
            Sunlight's well-springs, will you not help?

All the flowers of the earth, all the good ripening
    Happy fruits of the grove, how can it be that all
        Fail to cheer this one life which,
            Gods, yourselves you raised up with love?

Ah, already restored, holy desire to live
    Breathes and sounds in her talk, charming as ever, and
        Fondly, Nature, your darling
            Open-eyed to your beam responds.

Das Unverzeihliche

Wenn ihr Freunde vergeßt, wenn ihr den Künstler höhnt,
   Und den tieferen Geist klein und gemein versteht,
      Gott vergiebt es, doch stört nur
        Nie den Frieden der Liebenden.

ˋ The Unpardonable

If you drop an old friend, laugh at the artist and
    Meanly, vulgarly judge, wronging the deeper mind,
        God forgives you; but never
            Break the quiet that lovers know.

An die jungen Dichter

Lieben Brüder! es reift unsere Kunst vieleicht,
　　Da, dem Jünglinge gleich, lange sie schon gegährt,
　　　　Bald zur Stille der Schönheit;
　　　　　　Seid nur fromm, wie der Grieche war!

Liebt die Götter und denkt freundlich der Sterblichen!
　　Haßt den Rausch, wie den Frost! lehrt und beschreibet nicht!
　　　　Wenn der Meister euch ängstigt,
　　　　　　Fragt die große Natur um Rath.

To the Young Poets

Quite soon, dear brothers, perhaps our art,
    So long in youth-like ferment, will now mature
        To beauty's plenitude, to stillness;
            Only be pious, like Grecian poets!

Of mortal men think kindly, but love the gods!
    Loathe drunkenness like frost! Don't describe or teach!
        And if you fear your master's bluntness,
            Go to great Nature, let her advise you!

An die Deutschen

Spottet ja nicht des Kinds, wenn es mit Peitsch' und Sporn
    Auf dem Rosse von Holz muthig und groß sich dünkt,
        Denn, ihr Deutschen, auch ihr seyd
           Thatenarm und gedankenvoll.

Oder kömmt, wie der Stral aus dem Gewölke kömmt,
    Aus Gedanken die That? Leben die Bücher bald?
        O ihr Lieben, so nimmt mich
           Daß ich büße die Lästerung.

To the Germans

Do not laugh at the child when with his whip and spurs
    Brave and mighty he feels up on his rocking-horse,
        For, you Germans, you too are
            Poor in deeds though you've thoughts enough!

Or, as lightning from clouds, out of mere thoughts will deeds,
    Potent, come leaping out? Books now begin to live?
        O, my dear ones, then seize me,
            Make me pay for my slanderous words.

Die scheinheiligen Dichter

Ihr kalten Heuchler, sprecht von den Göttern nicht!
    Ihr habt Verstand! ihr glaubt nicht an Helios,
        Noch an den Donnerer und Meergott;
            Todt ist die Erde, wer mag ihr danken? –

Getrost ihr Götter! zieret ihr doch das Lied,
    Wenn schon aus euren Nahmen die Seele schwand,
        Und ist ein großes Wort vonnöthen,
            Mutter Natur! so gedenkt man deiner.

The Sanctimonious Poets

Cold hypocrites, of gods do not dare to speak!
   You're rational! In Helios you don't believe,
      Nor in the Thunderer or the Sea-God;
         Dead is our Earth, so what fool would thank her? –

Take comfort, gods! For yet you adorn their verse
   Though now the soul's gone out of your pilfered names;
      And if some high-flown word is needed,
         You, Mother Nature, they still remember.

Dem Sonnengott

Wo bist du? trunken dämmert die Seele mir
  Von aller deiner Wonne; denn eben ists,
    Daß ich gesehn, wie, müde seiner
      Fahrt, der entzükende Götterjüngling

Die jungen Loken badet' im Goldgewölk';
  Und jezt noch blikt mein Auge von selbst nach ihm;
    Doch fern ist er zu frommen Völkern,
      Die ihn noch ehren, hinweggegangen.

Dich lieb' ich, Erde! trauerst du doch mit mir!
  Und unsre Trauer wandelt, wie Kinderschmerz,
    In Schlummer sich, und wie die Winde
      Flattern und flüstern im Saitenspiele,

Bis ihm des Meisters Finger den schönern Ton
  Entlokt, so spielen Nebel und Träum' um uns
    Bis der Geliebte wiederkömt und
      Leben und Geist sich in uns entzündet.

To the Sun-God

Where are you? Dazzled, drunken my soul grows faint
    And dark with so much gladness; for only now
        It was I watched while weary with his
            Course, the enrapturing sun-god lingered

To bathe his youthful locks in the golden clouds;
    And, full of him, my eyes of themselves gaze on,
        Though far from here, to pious nations
            Who still revere him, by now he's journeyed.

You, Earth, I love who join me in mourning him,
    And like the griefs of children our mourning turns
        To sleep and, much as in the lyre-strings
            Fluttering winds will run wild and whisper

Until the master's finger lures forth a tone
    More pure, so dreams and mist all around us play
        Until the loved one comes again and
            Kindles new life in our minds, new vigour.

Sonnenuntergang

Wo bist du? trunken dämmert die Seele mir
  Von aller deiner Wonne; denn eben ist's,
    Daß ich gelauscht, wie, goldner Töne
      Voll der entzükende Sonnenjüngling

Sein Abendlied auf himmlischer Leyer spielt';
  Es tönten rings die Wälder und Hügel nach.
    Doch fern ist er zu frommen Völkern,
      Die ihn noch ehren, hinweggegangen.

Sunset

Where are you? Dazzled, drunken my soul grows faint
  And dark with so much gladness; for even now
    I listened while, too rich in golden
      Sounds, the enrapturing youth, the sun-god

Intoned his evening hymn on a heavenly lyre;
  All round the hills and forests re-echoed it,
    Though far from here – to pious nations
      Who still revere him – by now he's journeyed.

Sokrates und Alcibiades

»Warum huldigest du, heiliger Sokrates,
   »Diesem Jünglinge stets? kennest du Größers nicht?
      »Warum siehet mit Liebe,
         »Wie auf Götter, dein Aug' auf ihn?

Wer das Tiefste gedacht, liebt das Lebendigste,
   Hohe Jugend versteht, wer in die Welt geblikt
      Und es neigen die Weisen
         Oft am Ende zu Schönem sich.

Socrates and Alcibiades

'Holy Socrates, why always with deference
    Do you treat this young man? Don't you know greater things?
      Why so lovingly, raptly,
        As on gods, do you gaze on him?'

Who the deepest has thought loves what is most alive,
    Wide experience may well turn to what's best in youth,
      And the wise in the end will
        Often bow to the beautiful.

An unsre grossen Dichter

Des Ganges Ufer hörten des Freudengotts
    Triumph, als allerobernd vom Indus her
        Der junge Bacchus kam, mit heilgem
            Weine vom Schlafe die Völker wekend.

O wekt, ihr Dichter! wekt sie vom Schlummer auch,
    Die jezt noch schlafen, gebt die Geseze, gebt
        Uns Leben, siegt, Heroën! ihr nur
            Habt der Eroberung Recht, wie Bacchus.

To our Great Poets

The banks of Ganges heard how the god of joy
   Was hailed when conquering all from far Indus came
     The youthful Bacchus, and with holy
       Wine from their drowsiness woke the peoples.

You also, poets, rouse them, awaken those
   Who still are sleepy, give us the laws, and give
     Us life! Make known your triumph! Only
       You, like that god, have the right to conquer.

Πρὸς Ἑαυτὸν

Lern im Leben die Kunst, im Kunstwerk lerne das Leben,
  Siehst du das Eine recht, siehst du das andere auch.

Sophokles

Viele versuchten umsonst das Freudigste freudig zu sagen
  Hier spricht endlich es mir, hier in der Trauer sich aus.

Der zürnende Dichter

Fürchtet den Dichter nicht, wenn er edel zürnet, sein Buchstab
  Tödtet, aber es macht Geister lebendig der Geist.

Die Scherzhaften

Immer spielt ihr und scherzt? ihr müßt! o Freunde! mir geht diß
  In die Seele, denn diß müssen Verzweifelte nur.

Wurzel alles Übels

Einig zu seyn, ist göttlich und gut; woher ist die Sucht denn
  Unter den Menschen, daß nur Einer und Eines nur sei?

Epigrams (1799)

Πρὸς Ἑαυτὸν
(TO HIMSELF)

Living, in life, learn your art, in art works learn about living;
    If the one you see clearly, aright, likewise the other you'll see.

Sophocles

Many have tried, but in vain, with joy to express the most joyful;
    Here at last, in grave sadness, wholly I find it expressed.

The Angry Poet

Never fear the poet when nobly he rages; his letter
    Kills, but his spirit to spirits gives new vigour, new life.

The Jokers

Always you trifle and joke? You have to? O friends, how my very
    Soul responds to your plight: No one has to but those in despair.

The Root of All Evil

Being at one is godlike and good, but human, too human, the mania
    Which insists there is only the One, one country, one truth and
                                      [one way.

Palingenesie

Mit der Sonne sehn' ich mich oft vom Aufgang bis zum Niedergang
den weiten Bogen schnell hineilend zu wandeln, oft, mit Gesang zu
folgen dem großen dem Vollendungsgange der alten Natur,
Und, wie der Feldherr auf dem Helme den Adler trägt in Kampf
und Triumph, so möcht ich daß sie mich trüge
Mächtig das Sehnen der Sterblichen.
Aber es wohnet auch ein Gott in dem Menschen daß er Vergangenes
und Zukünftiges sieht und wie vom Strom ins Gebirg hinauf an die
Quelle lustwandelt er durch Zeiten
Aus ihrer Thaten stillem Buch ist Vergangenem bekannt er durch
– – die goldenes beut

Palingenesis

Together with the sun I often yearn to run the wide arc from its rising to its going down, speeding on, often with song to follow ancient Nature's great course of perfection,
And, as the general bears on his helmet the eagle in battle and triumph, I wish that the sun might bear me
Mighty the yearning of mortals.
Yet in the man a god has his dwelling, too, so that he sees what is past and to come and as from the river up into the mountain range he rambles to the source through the ages
From the silent book of the sun's deeds he is familiar with the past through
– – that offers golden treasure

The Later Odes
(1798–1803)

Vanini

Den Gottverächter schalten sie dich? mit Fluch
   Beschwerten sie dein Herz dir und banden dich
      Und übergaben dich den Flammen,
         Heiliger Mann! o warum nicht kamst du

Vom Himmel her in Flammen zurük, das Haupt
   Der Lästerer zu treffen und riefst dem Sturm;
      Daß er die Asche der Barbaren
         Fort aus der Erd', aus der Heimath werfe!

Doch die du lebend liebtest, die dich empfieng,
   Den Sterbenden, die heil'ge Natur vergißt
      Der Menschen Thun und deine Feinde
         Kehrten, wie du, in den alten Frieden.

Vanini

God's enemy, despiser, they called you, heaped
    Their curses on your heart and then bound you fast
      And left you to the flames, you holy
        Man! O but why did you not come back then

In flames from Heaven, blazing, to strike the heads
    Of those blasphemers, call on the gales to sweep
      The ashes of those cold barbarians
        Out of this earth, of the sullied homeland!

Yet she who had your love while you lived, received
    You dying – holy Nature, I know, forgets
      Our human acts and, as to you, gave
        Back the old peace to your persecutors.

Der Mensch

Kaum sproßten aus den Wassern, o Erde, dir
   Der jungen Berge Gipfel und dufteten
     Lustathmend, immergrüner Haine
       Voll, in des Oceans grauer Wildniß

Die ersten holden Inseln; und freudig sah
   Des Sonnengottes Auge die Neulinge
     Die Pflanzen, seiner ew'gen Jugend
       Lächelnde Kinder, aus dir geboren.

Da auf der Inseln schönster, wo immerhin
   Den Hain in zarter Ruhe die Luft umfloß,
     Lag unter Trauben einst, nach lauer
       Nacht, in der dämmernden Morgenstunde

Geboren, Mutter Erde! dein schönstes Kind; –
   Und auf zum Vater Helios sieht bekannt
     Der Knab', und wacht und wählt die süßen
       Beere versuchend, die heil'ge Rebe

Zur Amme sich; und bald ist er groß; ihn scheun
   Die Thiere, denn ein anderer ist, wie sie
     Der Mensch; nicht dir und nicht dem Vater
       Gleicht er, denn kühn ist in ihm und einzig

Des Vaters hohe Seele mit deiner Lust,
   O Erd'! und deiner Trauer von je vereint;
     Der Göttermutter, der Natur, der
       Allesumfassenden möcht' er gleichen!

9 Man

When scarcely from the waters, O Earth, for you
　　Young mountain peaks had sprouted and, breathing joy,
　　　　The first delightful islands, full of
　　　　　　Evergreen copses, gave out their fragrance

Amid the sea's grey desert; and glad of them
　　The Sun-God's eye looked down at the newly raised,
　　　　The plants, the smiling children of his
　　　　　　Weariless youth, and of you, their mother –

Then on the loveliest island where delicate
　　And calm the air flowed ceaselessly round the copse,
　　　　One morning, born in early half-light
　　　　　　After a temperate night, and bedded

Beneath the clustered grapes, lay your loveliest child; –
　　And up to Father Helios now the boy
　　　　Turns eyes that know him, wakes and, tasting
　　　　　　Berries for sweetness, as nurse he chooses

The holy vine; and soon is grown up. He's shunned
　　By animals, for different from them is Man.
　　　　Not you, his mother, nor his father
　　　　　　Does he resemble, for in him, boldly

Uniquely blended, live both his father's soul
　　And, Earth, your joy, your sadness, inveterate;
　　　　He longs to be like her, like Nature,
　　　　　　Mother of gods and the all-embracing!

Ach! darum treibt ihn, Erde! vom Herzen dir
  Sein Übermuth, und deine Geschenke sind
    Umsonst und deine zarten Bande;
      Sucht er ein Besseres doch, der Wilde!

Von seines Ufers duftender Wiese muß
  Ins blüthenlose Wasser hinaus der Mensch,
    Und glänzt auch, wie die Sternenacht, von
      Goldenen Früchten sein Hain, doch gräbt er

Sich Höhlen in den Bergen und späht im Schacht
  Von seines Vaters heiterem Lichte fern,
    Dem Sonnengott auch ungetreu, der
      Knechte nicht liebt und der Sorge spottet.

Denn freier athmen Vögel des Walds, wenn schon
  Des Menschen Brust sich herrlicher hebt, und der
    Die dunkle Zukunft sieht, er muß auch
      Sehen den Tod und allein ihn fürchten.

Und Waffen wider alle, die athmen, trägt
  In ewigbangem Stolze der Mensch; im Zwist
    Verzehrt er sich und seines Friedens
      Blume, die zärtliche, blüht nicht lange.

Ist er von allen Lebensgenossen nicht
  Der seeligste? Doch tiefer und reißender
    Ergreift das Schiksaal, allausgleichend,
      Auch die entzündbare Brust dem Starken.

O that is why his arrogance drives him far
 From your safe-keeping, Earth, and in vain are all
  Your gifts and all your gentle fetters –
   Little to him, who wants more, the wild one!

Beyond his fragrant river-side meadows, out
 Into the flowerless water is Man impelled
  And though with golden fruit his orchard
   Gleams like the star-jewelled night, yet caves for

Himself he digs in mountains and scans the shaft,
 Remote from his great father's untroubled light,
  Disloyal also to the Sun-God,
   Scorner of cares never fond of drudges.

For woodland birds more freely draw breath, and though
 Man's breast more grandly, proudly expands, his gaze
  Can penetrate the future's darkness,
   Death he sees too and alone must fear it.

And arms against all creatures that live and stir
 In pride for ever anxious he bears consumes
  Himself in discord; and not long the
   Delicate bloom of his peace contents him.

Is Man not blessed, not blissful compared to all
 His fellow creatures? Yet with a tighter hold,
  More deeply Fate, all-levelling, grips the
   Strong one's inflammable heart to wrench it.

Hyperions Schiksaalslied

Ihr wandelt droben im Licht
  Auf weichem Boden, seelige Genien!
    Glänzende Götterlüfte
     Rühren euch leicht,
       Wie die Finger der Künstlerin
       Heilige Saiten.

Schiksaallos, wie der schlafende
  Säugling, athmen die Himmlischen;
   Keusch bewahrt
    In bescheidener Knospe,
     Blühet ewig
      Ihnen der Geist,
       Und die seeligen Augen
       Bliken in stiller
        Ewiger Klarheit.

Doch uns ist gegeben,
  Auf keiner Stätte zu ruhn,
   Es schwinden, es fallen
    Die leidenden Menschen
    Blindlings von einer
    Stunde zur andern
      Wie Wasser von Klippe
      Zu Klippe geworfen,
        Jahr lang ins Ungewisse hinab.

Hyperion's Song of Fate

You walk above in the light,
   Weightless tread a soft floor, blessed genii!
    Radiant the gods' mild breezes
     Gently play on you
      As the girl artist's fingers
      On holy strings.

Fateless the Heavenly breathe
   Like an unweaned infant asleep;
    Chastely preserved
     In modest bud
      For ever their minds
       Are in flower
        And their blissful eyes
         Eternally tranquil gaze,
         Eternally clear.

But we are fated
   To find no foothold, no rest,
    And suffering mortals
     Dwindle and fall
      Headlong from one
       Hour to the next,
        Hurled like water
         From ledge to ledge
          Downward for years to the vague abyss.

Da ich ein Knabe war . . .

Da ich ein Knabe war,
  Rettet' ein Gott mich oft
    Vom Geschrei und der Ruthe der Menschen,
      Da spielt' ich sicher und gut
        Mit den Blumen des Hains,
          Und die Lüftchen des Himmels
            Spielten mit mir.

Und wie du das Herz
Der Pflanzen erfreust,
Wenn sie entgegen dir
Die zarten Arme streken,

So hast du mein Herz erfreut
Vater Helios! und, wie Endymion,
War ich dein Liehling,
Heilige Luna!

O all ihr treuen
Freundlichen Götter!
Daß ihr wüßtet,
Wie euch meine Seele geliebt!

Zwar damals rieff ich noch nicht
Euch mit Nahmen, auch ihr
Nanntet mich nie, wie die Menschen sich nennen
Als kennten sie sich.

Doch kannt' ich euch besser,
Als ich je die Menschen gekannt,

In my boyhood days . . .

In my boyhood days
Often a god would save me
From the shouts and the rod of men;
Safe and good then I played
With the orchard flowers
And the breezes of heaven
Played with me.

And as you make glad
The hearts of the plants
When toward you they stretch
Their delicate arms,

So you made glad my heart,
Father Helios, and like Endymion
I was your darling,
Holy Luna.

O all you loyal,
Kindly gods!
Would that you knew how
My soul loved you then.

True, at that time I did not
Evoke you by name yet, and you
Never named me, as men use names,
As though they knew one another.

Yet I knew you better
Than ever I have known men,

Ich verstand die Stille des Aethers
Der Menschen Worte verstand ich nie.

Mich erzog der Wohllaut
Des säuselnden Hains
Und lieben lernt' ich
Unter den Blumen.

Im Arme der Götter wuchs ich groß.

I understood the silence of Aether,
But human words I've never understood.

I was reared by the euphony
Of the rustling copse
And learned to love
Amid the flowers.

I grew up in the arms of the gods.

Hört' ich die Warnenden izt . . .

Hört' ich die Warnenden izt, sie lächelten meiner und dächten,
   Früher anheim uns fiel, weil er uns scheute, der Thor.
Und sie achtetens keinen Gewinn,

Singt, o singet mir nur, unglükweissagend, ihr Furchtbarn
   Schiksaalsgötter das Lied immer und immer ums Ohr
Euer bin ich zulezt, ich weiß es, doch will zuvor ich
   Mir gehören und mir Leben erbeuten und Ruhm.

If to those warning ones . . .

If to those warning ones now I listened, they'd smile at me, thinking,
    Sooner we got him because always he shunned us, the fool;
Yet they'd count it no gain,

Sing then, sing your old song foretelling my doom, and repeat it,
    Terrible Gods of Fate, ceaselessly drone in my ears.
Yours I shall be in the end, I know, but first I'll belong to
    None but myself and secure life for myself and a name.

Die Launischen

Hör' ich ferne nur her, wenn ich für mich geklagt,
    Saitenspiel und Gesang, schweigt mir das Herz doch gleich;
       Bald auch bin ich verwandelt,
          Blinkst du, purpurner Wein! mich an

Unter Schatten des Walds, wo die gewaltige
    Mittagssonne mir sanft über dem Laube glänzt;
       Ruhig siz' ich daselbst, wenn
          Zürnend schwerer Belaidigung

Ich im Felde geirrt – Zürnen zu gerne doch
    Deine Dichter, Natur! trauern und weinen leicht,
       Die Beglükten; wie Kinder,
          Die zu zärtlich die Mutter hält,

Sind sie mürrisch und voll herrischen Eigensinns;
    Wandeln still sie des Wegs, irret Geringes doch
       Bald sie wieder; sie reißen
          Aus dem Gleise sich sträubend dir.

Doch du rührest sie kaum, Liebende! freundlich an,
    Sind sie friedlich und fromm; fröhlich gehorchen sie;
       Du lenkst, Meisterinn! sie mit
          Weichem Zügel, wohin du willst.

The Capricious

From afar let me hear music of strings or song
    When alone I've complained – peace fills my heart at once;
        Likewise soon I'm transformed when,
            Purple vine, you appear to me

In the shade of the wood where the strong noonday sun
    Mildly gleams up above, gilding the summer leaves;
        Quiet there I will sit, though
            Until then I had roamed the fields

Angry, grievously wronged – that's how your poets are,
    Nature, too prone to rage, ready to mourn and weep,
        Pampered fellows; like children
            Spoilt by mothers too lax, too fond,

Always moody they are, stubborn and arrogant;
    If contented they walk, yet will some little thing
        Soon confuse them; and wildly
            From your path they will rush, astray.

Scarcely touched, though, by you, fond one, with tenderness,
    Now they're docile and good, gladly obey your word;
        You, their goddess, can lead them
            Where you choose with your gentle reins.

Der Zeitgeist

Zu lang schon waltest über dem Haupte mir
   Du in der dunkeln Wolke, du Gott der Zeit!
     Zu wild, zu bang ist's ringsum, und es
       Trümmert und wankt ja, wohin ich blike.

Ach! wie ein Knabe, seh' ich zu Boden oft,
   Such' in der Höhle Rettung von dir, und möcht'
     Ich Blöder, eine Stelle finden,
       Alleserschütt'rer! wo du nicht wärest.

Lass' endlich, Vater! offenen Aug's mich dir
   Begegnen! hast denn du nicht zuerst den Geist
     Mit deinem Stral aus mir gewekt? mich
       Herrlich an's Leben gebracht, o Vater! –

Wohl keimt aus jungen Reben uns heil'ge Kraft;
   In milder Luft begegnet den Sterblichen,
     Und wenn sie still im Haine wandeln,
       Heiternd ein Gott; doch allmächt'ger wekst du

Die reine Seele Jünglingen auf, und lehrst
   Die Alten weise Künste; der Schlimme nur
     Wird schlimmer, daß er bälder ende,
       Wenn du, Erschütterer! ihn ergreiffest.

The Spirit of the Age

Too long above my head you have governed there,
    Wrapped in the thunder cloud, you the God of Time!
        Too desolate and awed the land lies,
            All that I look at breaks up and totters.

O like a boy at times I cast down my eyes,
    Seek refuge from you in some deep cave, and search,
        Poor craven, for a single place where
            You, the all-shattering, might be absent.

But, Father, open-eyed let me meet at last
    Your face! Was it not you with your beam who first
        Drew out the mind in me, awakened,
            Gloriously brought me to life, O Father? –

True, from young vines we gather a holy strength;
    In mild spring air, or when they are wandering
        In orchards calmly, men will meet a
            Brightening god; yet with powers more far-flung

You rouse the souls of youths, and to older men
    Impart wise arts; the bad man alone grows worse,
        So that his end will come the sooner,
            When with your world-shaking might you seize him.

Abendphantasie

Vor seiner Hütte ruhig im Schatten sizt
 Der Pflüger, dem Genügsamen raucht sein Heerd.
  Gastfreundlich tönt dem Wanderer im
   Friedlichen Dorfe die Abendgloke.

Wohl kehren izt die Schiffer zum Hafen auch,
 In fernen Städten, fröhlich verrauscht des Markts
  Geschäfft' ger Lärm; in stiller Laube
   Glänzt das gesellige Mahl den Freunden.

Wohin denn ich? Es leben die Sterblichen
 Von Lohn und Arbeit; wechselnd in Müh' und Ruh'
  Ist alles freudig; warum schläft denn
   Nimmer nur mir in der Brust der Stachel?

Am Abendhimmel blühet ein Frühling auf;
 Unzählig blühn die Rosen und ruhig scheint
  Die goldne Welt; o dorthin nimmt mich
   Purpurne Wolken! und möge droben

In Licht und Luft zerrinnen mir Lieb' und Laid! –
 Doch, wie verscheucht von thöriger Bitte, flieht
  Der Zauber; dunkel wirds und einsam
   Unter dem Himmel, wie immer, bin ich –

Komm du nun, sanfter Schlummer! zu viel begehrt
 Das Herz; doch endlich, Jugend! verglühst du ja,
  Du ruhelose, träumerische!
   Friedlich und heiter ist dann das Alter.

Evening Fantasy

At peace the ploughman sits in the shade outside
   His cottage; smoke curls up from his modest hearth.
      A traveller hears the bell for vespers
         Welcome him in to a quiet village.

Now too the boatmen make for the harbour pool,
   In distant towns the market's gay noise and throng
      Subside; a glittering meal awaits the
         Friends in the garden's most hidden arbour.

But where shall I go? Does not a mortal live
   By work and wages? Balancing toil with rest
      All makes him glad. Must I alone then
         Find no relief from the thorn that goads me?

A springtime buds high up in the evening sky,
   There countless roses bloom, and the golden world
      Seems calm, fulfilled; O there now take me,
         Crimson-edged clouds, and up there at last let

My love and sorrow melt into light and air! –
   As if that foolish plea had dispersed it, though,
      The spell breaks; darkness falls, and lonely
         Under the heavens I stand as always. –

Now you come, gentle sleep! For the heart demands
   Too much; but youth at last, you the dreamy, wild,
      Unquiet, will burn out, and leave me
         All my late years for serene contentment.

Des Morgens

Vom Thaue glänzt der Rasen; beweglicher
    Eilt schon die wache Quelle; die Buche neigt
        Ihr schwankes Haupt und im Geblätter
            Rauscht es und schimmert; und um die grauen

Gewölke streifen röthliche flammen dort,
    Verkündende, sie wallen geräuschlos auf;
        Wie Fluthen am Gestade, woogen
            Höher und höher die Wandelbaren.

Komm nun, o komm, und eile mir nicht zu schnell,
    Du goldner Tag, zum Gipfel des Himmels fort!
        Denn offner fliegt, vertrauter dir mein
            Auge, du Freudiger! zu, so lang du

In deiner Schöne jugendlich blikst und noch
    Zu herrlich nicht, zu stolz mir geworden bist;
        Du möchtest immer eilen, könnt ich,
            Göttlicher Wandrer, mit dir! – doch lächelst

Des frohen übermüthigen du, daß er
    Dir gleichen möchte; seegne mir lieber dann
        Mein sterblich Thun und heitre wieder
            Gütiger! heute den stillen Pfad mir.

✦ In the Morning

With dew the lawn is glistening; more nimbly now,
    Awake, the stream speeds onward; the beech inclines
        Her limber head and in the leaves a
            Rustle, a glitter begins; and round the

Grey cloud-banks there a flicker of reddish flames,
    Prophetic ones, flares up and in silence plays;
        Like breakers by the shore they billow
            Higher and higher, the ever-changing.

Now come, O come, and not too impatiently,
    You golden day, speed on to the peaks of heaven!
        For more familiar and more open,
            Glad one, my vision flies up towards you

While youthful in your beauty you gaze and have
    Not grown too glorious, dazzling and proud for me;
        Speed as you will, I'd say, if only
            I could go with you, divinely ranging!

But at my happy arrogance now you smile,
    That would be like you; rather, then, rambler, bless
        My mortal acts, and this day also,
            Kindly one, brighten my quiet pathway.

Der Main

Wohl manches Land der lebenden Erde möcht'
  Ich sehn, und öfters über die Berg' enteilt
    Das Herz mir, und die Wünsche wandern
      Über das Meer, zu den Ufern, die mir

Vor andern, so ich kenne, gepriesen sind;
  Doch lieb ist in der Ferne nicht Eines mir,
    Wie jenes, wo die Göttersöhne
      Schlafen, das trauernde Land der Griechen.

Ach! einmal dort an Suniums Küste möcht'
  Ich landen, deine Säulen, Olympion!
    Erfragen, dort, noch eh der Nordsturm
      Hin in den Schutt der Athenertempel

Und ihrer Götterbilder auch dich begräbt;
  Denn lang schon einsam stehst du, o Stolz der Welt,
    Die nicht mehr ist! – und o ihr schönen
      Inseln Joniens, wo die Lüfte

Vom Meere kühl an warme Gestade wehn,
  Wenn unter kräft' ger Sonne die Traube reift,
    Ach! wo ein goldner Herbst dem armen
      Volk in Gesänge die Seufzer wandelt,

Wenn die Betrübten izt ihr Limonenwald
  Und ihr Granatbaum, purpurner Äpfel voll
    Und süßer Wein und Pauk' und Zithar
      Zum labyrintischen Tanze ladet –

The River Main

True, on this living earth there are many lands
   I long to see, and over the hills at times
      My heart runs off, my wishes wander
         Seaward, and on to those shores which more than

All others that I know have been glorified;
   But far away not one is as dear to me
      As that where now the sons of gods lie
         Sleeping, the mournful, the Hellenes' country.

O once I long to land there, on Sunium's coast,
   Once ask my way to your columns, Olympion,
      And soon, before the northern gale can
         Bury you too in the scattered rubble

Of temples Athens raised, and their imaged gods;
   For long now desolate you have stood, O pride
      Of worlds that are no more! And O you
         Lovely Ionian isles, where breezes

Waft coolness to warm shores from the open sea
   While under potent sunbeams the grape matures,
      And, oh, where still a golden autumn
         Turns into songs the poor people's sighing,

Now that their lemon grove, their pomegranate tree
   That bends with purple fruit, and sweet wine and drum
      And zither to the labyrinthine
         Dance have allured them, however troubled –

Zu euch vieleicht, ihr Inseln! geräth noch einst
  Ein heimathloser Sänger; denn wandern muß
    Von Fremden er zu Fremden, und die
      Erde, die freie, sie muß ja leider!

Statt Vaterlands ihm dienen, so lang er lebt,
  Und wenn er stirbt – doch nimmer vergeß ich dich,
    So fern ich wandre, schöner Main! und
      Deine Gestade, die vielbeglükten.

Gastfreundlich nahmst du Stolzer! bei dir mich auf
  Und heitertest das Auge dem Fremdlinge,
    Und still hingleitende Gesänge
      Lehrtest du mich und geräuschlos Leben.

O ruhig mit den Sternen, du Glüklicher!
  Wallst du von deinem Morgen zum Abend fort,
    Dem Bruder zu, dem Rhein; und dann mit
      Ihm in den Ocean freudig nieder!

To you, perhaps, you islands, yet one day shall
    A homeless singer come; for he's driven on
        From stranger still to stranger, and the
            Earth, the unbounded, alas, must serve him

In place of home and nation his whole life long,
    And when he dies – but never, delightful Main,
        Shall I forget you or your banks, the
            Variously blessed, on my farthest travels.

Hospitably, though proud, you admitted me,
    And, smoothly flowing, brightened the stranger's eye
        And taught me gently gliding songs, and
            Taught me the strength that's alive in silence.

O calmly as the stars move, you happy one,
    You travel from your morning to evening,
        Towards your brother, Rhine; then, with him,
            Joyfully down to the greater ocean.

Mein Eigentum

In seiner Fülle ruhet der Herbsttag nun,
    Geläutert ist die Traub und der Hain ist roth
        Vom Obst, wenn schon der holden Blüthen
            Manche der Erde zum Danke fielen.

Und rings im Felde, wo ich den Pfad hinaus
    Den stillen wandle, ist den Zufriedenen
        Ihr Gut gereift und viel der frohen
            Mühe gewähret der Reichtum ihnen.

Vom Himmel bliket zu den Geschäfftigen
    Durch ihre Bäume milde das Licht herab,
        Die Freude theilend, denn es wuchs durch
            Hände der Menschen allein die Frucht nicht.

Und leuchtest du, o Goldnes, auch mir, und wehst
    Auch du mir wieder, Lüftchen, als seegnetest
        Du eine Freude mir, wie einst, und
            Irrst, wie um Glükliche, mir am Busen?

Einst war ichs, doch wie Rosen, vergänglich war
    Das fromme Leben, ach! und es mahnen noch,
        Die blühend mir geblieben sind, die
            Holden Gestirne zu oft mich dessen.

Beglükt, wer, ruhig liebend ein frommes Weib,
    Am eignen Heerd in rühmlicher Heimath lebt,
        Es leuchtet über vestem Boden
            Schöner dem sicheren Mann sein Himmel.

My Possessions

At rest in fulness, calm lies the autumn day,
    The mellow grape is clear and the orchard red
        With fruit, though many treasured blossoms
            Long ago fell to the Earth in tribute.

And all around where now by the quiet path
    I cross the field, for satisfied men their crops
        Have ripened, and their riches grant them
            Hour after hour of rewarding labour.

From heaven through leafy boughs on the busy ones
    A light subdued and temperate glances down
        To share their pleasure; for not human
            Hands by themselves made the cornfield prosper.

And, golden light, for me will you also shine,
    And, breeze, once more for me will you waft, as though
        To bless a joy, and still around me
            Flutter and play, as for happy mortals?

I too was one, but brief as the full-blown rose
    My good life passed, and they that alone are left
        In flower for me, the constellations,
            Often, too often, remind me of it.

Blessed he who calmly loving a gentle wife
    Can call a worthy homeland and hearth his own;
        Above firm ground more brightly for the
            Settled man shines his own sky's effulgence.

Denn, wie die Pflanze, wurzelt auf eignem Grund
    Sie nicht, verglüht die Seele des Sterblichen,
        Der mit dem Tageslichte nur, ein
            Armer, auf heiliger Erde wandelt.

Zu mächtig ach! ihr himmlischen Höhen zieht
    Ihr mich empor, bei Stürmen, am heitern Tag
        Fühl ich verzehrend euch im Busen
            Wechseln, ihr wandelnden Götterkräfte.

Doch heute laß mich stille den trauten Pfad
    Zum Haine gehn, dem golden die Wipfel schmükt
        Sein sterbend Laub, und kränzt auch mir die
            Stirne, ihr holden Erinnerungen!

Und daß mir auch zu retten mein sterblich Herz,
    Wie andern eine bleibende Stätte sei,
        Und heimathlos die Seele mir nicht
            Über das Leben hinweg sich sehne,

Sei du, Gesang, mein freundlich Asyl! sei du
    Beglükender! mit sorgender Liebe mir
        Gepflegt, der Garten, wo ich, wandelnd
            Unter den Blüthen, den immerjungen,

In sichrer Einfalt wohne, wenn draußen mir
    Mit ihren Wellen allen die mächtge Zeit
        Die Wandelbare fern rauscht und die
            Stillere Sonne mein Wirken fördert.

Ihr seegnet gütig über den Sterblichen
    Ihr Himmelskräfte! jedem sein Eigentum,
        O seegnet meines auch und daß zu
            Frühe die Parze den Traum nicht ende.

• For like the plant that fails to take root within
    Its native ground, the soul of that mortal wilts
        Who with the daylight only roams, a
            Pauper astray on our Earth, the hallowed.

• Too strongly always, heavenly heights, you pull
    Me upward; gales that rage on a sunny day
        Bring home to me your clashing powers,
            Mutable gods, and they rend, destroy me.

Today, though, let me walk the familiar path
    In silence to the copse that is crowned with gold
        Of dying leaves; and my brow also
            Garland with gold now, dear recollections!

And that my mortal heart nonetheless may last,
    A quiet, sure retreat, as are other men's,
        And that my soul may not outfly this
            Life in its longing, for ever homeless,

You be my gracious refuge now, song, and you,
    Joy-giver, now be tended with loving care,
        The garden where intently walking
            Under the blossoms that do not wither,

I live in safe ingenuousness while outside
    With all its waves the changeable, mighty Time,
        Roars far away, and to my labours
            Only the quieter sun contributes.

Above us mortals, heavenly powers, you bless
    Each man's possessions, kindly disposed to all;
        O bless mine also, lest too soon the
            Fate put an end to my earthly dreaming.

Palinodie

Was dämmert um mich, Erde! dein freundlich Grün?
  Was wehst du wieder, Lüftchen, wie einst, mich an?
    In allen Wipfeln rauschts,

Was wekt ihr mir die Seele? was regt ihr mir
  Vergangnes auf, ihr Guten! o schonet mein
    Und laßt sie ruhn, die Asche meiner
      Freuden, ihr spottetet nur! o wandelt,

Ihr schiksaallosen Götter, vorbei und blüht
  In eurer Jugend über den Alternden
    Und wollt ihr zu den Sterblichen euch
      Gerne gesellen, so blühn der Jungfraun

Euch viel, der jungen Helden, und schöner spielt
  Der Morgen um die Wange der Glüklichen
    Denn um ein trübes Aug' und lieblich
      Tönen die Sänge der Mühelosen.

Ach! vormals rauschte leicht des Gesanges Quell
  Auch mir vom Busen, da noch die Freude mir
    Die himmlische vom Auge glänzte

Versöhnung o Versöhnung, ihr gütigen
  Ihr immergleichen Götter und haltet ein
    Weil ihr die reinen Quellen liebt

 ›Palinode

Why, Earth, around me glimmer your friendly leaves?
    Why, little wind, as once do you breathe on me?
       In all the tree-tops there's a rustling,

Why do you rouse my soul and stir up the past
    In me, you kindly ones? O be kinder still
       And let them be, the embers of my
          Joys! You were mocking me! Travel on, then,

You fateless gods, pass by, while high up you flower
    In ever-youthful prime, this decrepit man,
       And if you seek the company of
          Mortals, young virgins enough like blossoms

Await you, and young heroes, and morning plays
    More sweetly on the cheeks of the fortunate
       Than on an eye that's dim, and pleasing
          Sound all the songs of the blithely carefree.

Ah, easy once the well-spring of song flowed out
    Of my breast also, purling, when still pure joy,
       The heavenly, glittered in my eyes and

 • Be merciful, make peace, you benevolent,
    You never-changing gods, and desist, desist,
       Because you love pure sources

An eine Fürstin von Dessau

Aus stillem Haußе senden die Götter oft
  Auf kurze Zeit zu Fremden die Lieblinge
    Damit, erinnert, sich am edlen
      Bilde der Sterblichen Herz erfreue.

So kommst du aus Luisiums Hainen auch
  Aus heilger Schwelle dort, wo geräuschlos rings
    Die Lüfte sind und friedlich um dein
      Dach die geselligen Bäume spielen,

Aus deines Tempels Freuden, o Priesterin!
  Zu uns, wenn schon die Wolke das Haupt uns beugt
    Und längst ein göttlich Ungewitter
      über dem Haupt uns wandelt.

O theuer warst du, Priesterin! da du dort
  Im Stillen göttlich Feuer behütetest,
    Doch theurer heute, da du Zeiten
      Unter den Zeitlichen seegnend feierst.

Denn wo die Reinen wandeln, vernehmlicher
  Ist da der Geist, und offen und heiter blühn
    Des Lebens dämmernde Gestalten
      Da, wo ein sicheres Licht erscheinet.

Und wie auf dunkler Wolke der schweigende
  Der schöne Bogen blühet, ein Zeichen ist
    Er künftger Zeit, ein Angedenken
      Seeliger Tage, die einst gewesen,

To a Princess of Dessau

The gods will often send from a quiet house
    To strangers briefly those whom their love prefers,
        So that, reminded, by that noble
            Image the hearts of us men are gladdened.

So from Luisium's groves now you too have come
    Across a holy threshold where breezes play
        In silence, peacefully around your
            Gables the sociable fruit trees whisper,

To us, O priestess, out of your temple's joys,
    Although the cloud hangs heavy above our heads
        And long a God-sent thunder-storm has
            Drifted towards us, remotely rumbling.

How dear to us you were when in silence there
    You, priestess, lived and guarded the sacred flame,
        Yet dearer now, amid the time-bound
            Blessing the times by your celebration.

For where the pure are present, more palpable
    The spirit is, and, flower-like, more open, clear
        The dimly glimmering shapes of life grow
            Where they are lit by a steady radiance,

And as on dark clouds blossoms the beautiful,
    The silent rainbow, gleaming to signify
        A future time or else recall the
            Happier days of a former season,

So ist dein Leben, heilige Fremdlingin!
　　Wenn du Vergangnes über Italiens
　　　　Zerbrochnen Säulen, wenn du neues
　　　　　　Grünen aus stürmischer Zeit betrachtest.

So *your* life, holy foreigner, must appear
    When over broken pillars in Italy
        You contemplate things past, or else new
            Leaves on the trees which today's gale lashes.

Der Prinzessin Auguste von Homburg

DEN 28TEN NOV. 1799

Noch freundlichzögernd scheidet vom Auge dir
   Das Jahr, und in hesperischer Milde glänzt
      Der Winterhimmel über deinen
         Gärten, den dichtrischen, immergrünen.

Und da ich deines Festes gedacht' und sann,
   Was ich dir dankend reichte, da weilten noch
      Am Pfade Blumen, daß sie dir zur
         Blühenden Krone, du Edle, würden.

Doch Andres beut dir, Größeres, hoher Geist!
   Die festlichere Zeit, denn es hallt hinab
      Am Berge das Gewitter, sieh! und
         Klar, wie die ruhigen Sterne, gehen

Aus langem Zweifel reine Gestalten auf;
   So dünkt es mir; und einsam, o Fürstin! ist
      Das Herz der Freigebornen wohl nicht
         Länger im eigenen Glük; denn würdig

Gesellt im Lorbeer ihm der Heroë sich,
   Der schöngereifte, ächte; die Weisen auch,
      Die Unsern sind es werth; sie bliken
         Still aus der Höhe des Lebens, die ernsten Alten.

Geringe dünkt der träumende Sänger sich,
   Und Kindern gleich am müßigen Saitenspiel,
      Wenn ihn der Edlen Glük, wenn ihn die
         That und der Ernst der Gewalt'gen aufwekt.

To Princess Augusta of Homburg

28 NOVEMBER 1799

Still kindly lingering the year from your eye departs,
    And in hesperian mildness now faintly gleams
        The winter sky above your gardens,
            Evergreen arbours, poetic orchards.

And as I pondered here on your birthday, thought
    What, thankful, I might offer, there still remained
        Late flowers beside the pathway, fit to
            Make you a crown that's alive, Augusta.

Yet, lofty spirit, other and greater things
    A time more festive yields you; the thunder rolls
        Away down mountain-sides and, look, as
            Tranquil and clear as the constellations

Pure shapes, pure signs arise from protracted doubt;
    So now it seems to me; and no longer shall
        The hearts of free-born men be lonely
            In their own triumph, Princess; for worthy,

The hero in his laurel consorts with them,
    The well-matured, the true one; and wise men too,
        Our own, deserve to join them; calmly
            Down from life's summit they gaze, those grave ones.

How small the dreaming singer must think himself,
    How like a child who randomly plucks the strings,
        When roused by triumph of the noble,
            Deeds, and decisions of mighty rulers.

Doch herrlicht mir dein Nahme das Lied; dein Fest
    Augusta! durft' ich feiern; Beruf ist mirs,
        Zu rühmen Höhers, darum gab die
            Sprache der Gott und den Dank ins Herz mir.

O daß von diesem freudigen Tage mir
    Auch meine Zeit beginne, daß endlich auch
        Mir ein Gesang in deinen Hainen,
            Edle! gedeihe, der deiner werth sei.

Yet by your name my song is enhanced for me;
    Allowed to mark your day, my own call I serve,
        To praise what's higher: for this the
            God gave me speech and a heart that's grateful.

O that this joyful day would initiate
    For me a new time also, one song of mine
        Within your groves at last would prosper,
        Noble as you are and worthy of you.

Wohl geh' ich Täglich . . .

Wohl geh' ich täglich andere Pfade, bald
   Ins grüne Laub im Walde, zur Quelle bald,
     Zum Felsen, wo die Rosen blühen,
       Blike vom Hügel ins Land, doch nirgend

Du Holde, nirgend find ich im Lichte dich
   Und in die Lüfte schwinden die Worte mir
     Die frommen, die bei dir ich ehmals

Ja, ferne bist du, seeliges Angesicht!
   Und deines Lebens Wohllaut verhallt von mir
     Nicht mehr belauscht, und ach! wo seid ihr
       Zaubergesänge, die einst das Herz mir

Besänftiget mit Ruhe der Himmlischen?
   Wie lang ist's! o wie lange! der Jüngling ist
     Gealtert, selbst die Erde, die mir
       Damals gelächelt, ist anders worden.

Leb immer wohl! es scheidet und kehrt zu dir
   Die Seele jeden Tag, und es weint um dich
     Das Auge, daß es helle wieder
       Dort wo du säumest, hinüberblike.

Though every day I follow . . .

Though every day I follow a different path,
    Now deep into green leaves in the wood, and now
        Towards the spring, the rock where roses
            Bloom, from the hilltop look out, yet nowhere

I can find you, my love, in the light of day,
    And into air dissolve all the words I learned,
        Devout ones, when with you I

Yes, you are far indeed from me, blessèd face,
    And now the euphony of your life is lost
        To me, your listener, and where are you,
            Magical songs that would once make gentle

My heart with quiet known to the Heavenly?
    How long ago, how long! That young man has aged,
        And Earth, the very Earth that seemed to
            Smile on me then, now is changed and shrunken.

Farewell, then, always. Daily the soul takes leave
    Of you, returns to you, and the eye will weep
        For you each day, to look more keenly
            Into the distance where you are staying.

Geh unter, schöne Sonne . . .

Geh unter, schöne Sonne, sie achteten
  Nur wenig dein, sie kannten dich, Heilge, nicht,
    Denn mühelos und stille bist du
      Über den mühsamen aufgegangen.

Mir gehst du freundlich unter und auf, o Licht!
  Und wohl erkennt mein Auge dich, herrliches!
    Denn göttlich stille ehren lernt' ich
      Da Diotima den Sinn mir heilte.

O du des Himmels Botin! wie lauscht ich dir!
  Dir, Diotima! Liebe! wie sah von dir
    Zum goldnen Tage dieses Auge
      Glänzend und dankend empor. Da rauschten

Lebendiger die Quellen, es athmeten
  Der dunkeln Erde Blüthen mich liebend an,
    Und lächelnd über Silberwolken
      Neigte sich seegnend herab der Aether.

Go down, then, lovely sun . . .

Go down, then, lovely sun, for but little they
    Regarded you, nor, holy one, knew your worth,
        Since without toil you rose, and quiet,
            Over a people for ever toiling.

To me, however, kindly you rise and set,
    O glorious light, and brightly my eyes respond,
        For godly, silent reverence I
            Learned when Diótima soothed my frenzy.

O how I listened, Heaven's own messenger,
    To you, my teacher! Love! How to the golden day
        These eyes transfused with thanks looked up from
            Gazing at you. And at once more living

The brooks began to murmur, more lovingly
    The blossoms of dark Earth breathed their scent at me
        And through the silver clouds a smiling
            Aether bowed down to bestow his blessing.

Und wenig Wissen . . .

Und wenig Wissen, aber der Freude viel
  Ist Sterblichen gegeben,

Warum, o schöne Sonne, genügst du mir
  Du Blüthe meiner Blühten! am Maitag nicht?
    Was weiß ich höhers denn?

O daß ich lieber wäre, wie Kinder sind!
  Daß ich, wie Nachtigallen, ein sorglos Lied
    Von meiner Wonne sänge!

And little knowledge . . .

And little knowledge only, but joy enough
    Is granted to us mortals,

Then why, O lovely sun, do you not suffice,
    You blossom of my blossoms, for me, in May?
        What do I know that's higher?

Oh that like children rather I could become!
    That, like the nightingales, I could sing a song
        Quite free of care, all rapture!

Gesang des Deutschen

O heilig Herz der Völker, o Vaterland!
  Allduldend, gleich der schweigenden Mutter Erd',
    Und allverkannt, wenn schon aus deiner
      Tiefe die Fremden ihr Bestes haben!

Sie erndten den Gedanken, den Geist von dir,
  Sie pflüken gern die Traube, doch höhnen sie
    Dich, ungestalte Rebe! daß du
      Schwankend den Boden und wild umirrest.

Du Land des hohen ernsteren Genius!
  Du Land der Liebe! bin ich der deine schon,
    Oft zürnt' ich weinend, daß du immer
      Blöde die eigene Seele läugnest.

Doch magst du manches Schöne nicht bergen mir;
  Oft stand ich überschauend das holde Grün,
    Den weiten Garten hoch in deinen
      Lüften auf hellem Gebirg' und sah dich.

An deinen Strömen gieng ich und dachte dich,
  Indeß die Töne schüchtern die Nachtigall
    Auf schwanker Weide sang, und still auf
      Dämmerndem Grunde die Welle weilte.

Und an den Ufern sah ich die Städte blühn,
  Die Edlen, wo der Fleiß in der Werkstatt schweigt,
    Die Wissenschaft, wo deine Sonne
      Milde dem Künstler zum Ernste leuchtet.

The German's Song

You holy heart of peoples, my fatherland,
   All-suffering in silence like Mother Earth
      And all-unrecognized, though strangers
         Draw from your depth their supreme possessions.

From you they harvest spirit, from you the thought,
   And gladly pluck the grape while they slight and mock
      The shapeless vine, because unstable
         Wildly you roam on the ground, a straggler.

You land of graver genius, of the high,
   You land of love, though yours I am utterly,
      I've raged at you, and wept, deploring
         How you deny your own soul for ever.

Yet much that's beautiful you can't hide from me;
   I've often stood surveying the dear expanse
      Of green, those gardens, from your airy
         Heights, on the mountains all bright, and seen you.

Beside your rivers often I've walked and thought,
   While shy the nightingale would send out her song
      From swaying willow boughs, and quiet
         Wavelets would rest on the darkling pebbles.

And by the banks I saw the fine cities flower,
   Within whose workshops industry makes no noise,
      Nor science either, where your sun shines
         Mildly on artists for deep endeavours.

Kennst du Minervas Kinder? sie wählten sich
  Den Oelbaum früh zum Lieblinge; kennst du sie?
    Noch lebt, noch waltet der Athener
      Seele, die sinnende, still bei Menschen,

Wenn Platons frommer Garten auch schon nicht mehr
  Am alten Strome grünt und der dürftge Mann
    Die Heldenasche pflügt, und scheu der
      Vogel der Nacht auf der Säule trauert.

O heilger Wald! o Attika! traf Er doch
  Mit seinem furchtbarn Strale dich auch, so bald,
    Und eilten sie, die dich belebt, die
      Flammen entbunden zum Aether über?

Doch, wie der Frühling, wandelt der Genius
  Von Land zu Land. Und wir? ist denn Einer auch
    Von unsern Jünglingen, der nicht ein
      Ahnden, ein Räthsel der Brust, verschwiege?

Den deutschen Frauen danket! sie haben uns
  Der Götterbilder freundlichen Geist bewahrt,
    Und täglich sühnt der holde klare
      Friede das böse Gewirre wieder.

Wo sind jezt Dichter, denen der Gott es gab,
  Wie unsern Alten, freudig und fromm zu seyn,
    Wo Weise, wie die unsre sind? die
      Kalten and Kühnen, die Unbestechbarn!

Nun! sei gegrüßt in deinem Adel, mein Vaterland
  Mit neuem Nahmen, reifeste Frucht der Zeit!
    Du lezte und du erste aller
      Musen, Urania, sei gegrüßt mir!

Recall Minerva's children. They early made
  The olive tree their favourite. Think of them.
    For still the Athenian soul, the pensive,
      Lives and in silence prevails where men are,

Though Plato's pious garden no longer blooms
  Beside the ancient river, a needy man
    Ploughs up the hero's ash, and shyly,
      Perched on the pillar, a nightbird mourns them.

You holy woods! O Attica! Then, so soon
  He struck you, even you, with the dreadful ray,
    And it, the fire that once infused you,
      Loosed, leapt away and was merged in Aether?

And yet, like springtime, genius always roams
  From land to land. And we? Is there only one
    Among our youths who does not hide a
      Heart-premonition, a dark foreknowing?

Give thanks to German women. It's they who kept
  Alive the kindly spirit of imaged gods,
    And daily still their dear and lucid
      Quiet assuages our rank confusion.

Where now are poets blessed by the God to be,
  Like ours, the old ones, pious and full of joy,
    Where wise men to compare with ours, the
      Cold, incorruptible, never daunted!

What's best in you I'll greet, then, my fatherland,
  With names all new, the mellowest fruit of time,
    You that are last and first among the
      Muses, Urania, let me greet you.

Noch säumst und schweigst du, sinnest ein freudig Werk,
   Das von dir zeuge, sinnest ein neu Gebild,
     Das einzig, wie du selber, das aus
       Liebe geboren und gut, wie du, sei –

Wo ist dein Delos, wo dein Olympia,
   Daß wir uns alle finden am höchsten Fest? –
     Doch wie erräth der Sohn, was du den
       Deinen, Unsterbliche, längst bereitest?

In silence yet you ponder a joyous work
    To testify of you, and withhold its shape
        That, like you, will be new, uniquely
            Born out of love and as good as you are –

Where is your Delos, where your Olympia,
    For celebration that would conjoin us all? –
        How shall your son divine the gift that,
            Deathless one, long you have darkly fashioned?

Der Frieden

Wie wenn die alten Wasser, die
        in andern Zorn
    In schröklichern verwandelt wieder
      Kämen, zu reinigen, da es noth war,

So gählt und wuchs und woogte von Jahr zu Jahr
    Rastlos und überschwemmte das bange Land
      Die unerhörte Schlacht, daß weit hüllt
        Dunkel und Blässe das Haupt der Menschen.

Die Heldenkräfte flogen, wie Wellen, auf
    Und schwanden weg, du kürztest o Rächerin!
      Den Dienern oft die Arbeit schnell und
        Brachtest in Ruhe sie heim, die Streiter.

O du die unerbittlich und unbesiegt
    Den Feigern und den Übergewaltgen trift,
      Daß bis ins lezte Glied hinab vom
        Schlage sein armes Geschlecht erzittert,

Die du geheim den Stachel und Zügel hältst
    Zu hemmen und zu fördern, o Nemesis,
      Strafst du die Todten noch, es schliefen
        Unter Italiens Lorbeergärten

Sonst ungestört die alten Eroberer.
    Und schonst du auch des müßigen Hirten nicht,
      Und haben endlich wohl genug den
        Üppigen Schlummer gebüßt die Völker?

Peace

As though the old flood waters, which

        wilder still,

   Whipped up to new, more dreadful fury,

    Now were returning, to cleanse, as needed,

So grew and swelled and billowed from year to year

   This battle like no other and overflowed

    The awe-struck land, till far and wide in

     Darkness and pallor men's heads were shrouded.

The strength of heroes rose like the wind-lashed waves

   And then died down, Avenger, for often you

    Cut short your servants' work and quickly

     Brought them back home to their rest, those fighters.

O you the unrelenting, unvanquished, who

   Strike both the coward and the too violent

    That down to the last limb his wretched

     Lineage will feel the reverberation,

Who, hidden, hold the spur and the rein as well,

   To further and restrain us, O Nemesis,

    The very dead you punish – under

     Italy's laurel-dark gardens nothing

Disturbed the ancient conquerors where they slept.

   And now the idle shepherds you do not spare?

    And still have not the nations done you

     Penance enough for luxurious slumber?

Wer hub es an? wer brachte den Fluch? von heut
   Ists nicht und nicht von gestern, und die zuerst
      Das Maas verloren, unsre Väter
         Wußten es nicht, und es trieb ihr Geist sie.

Zu lang, zu lang schon treten die Sterblichen
   Sich gern aufs Haupt, und zanken um Herrschaft sich,
      Den Nachbar fürchtend, und es hat auf
         Eigenem Boden der Mann nicht Seegen.

Und unstät wehn und irren, dem Chaos gleich,
   Dem gährenden Geschlechte die Wünsche noch
      Umher und wild ist und verzagt und kalt von
         Sorgen das Leben der Armen immer.

Du aber wandelst ruhig die sichre Bahn
   O Mutter Erd im Lichte. Dein Frühling blüht,
      Melodischwechselnd gehn dir hin die
         Wachsenden Zeiten, du Lebensreiche!

Komm du nun, du der heiligen Musen all,
   Und der Gestirne Liebling, verjüngender
      Ersehnter Friede, komm und gieb ein
         Bleiben im Leben, ein Herz uns wieder.

Unschuldiger! sind klüger die Kinder doch
   Beinahe, denn wir Alten; es irrt der Zwist
      Den Guten nicht den Sinn, und klar und
         Freudig ist ihnen ihr Auge blieben.

Und wie mit andern Schauenden lächelnd ernst
   Der Richter auf der Jünglinge Rennbahn sieht,
      Wo glühender die Kämpfenden die
         Wagen in stäubende Wolken treiben,

Who started it? Who brought us the curse? Not from
   Today, nor yesterday does it spring, and those
      Who first transgressed the bounds, our forbears,
         Did it unknowing, their daemons drove them.

Too long, too long now mortals have liked to tread
   On others' heads, and bickered for mastery,
      In fear of neighbours, and no man on
         Soil that's his own ever finds contentment.

And chaos-like, inconstant, the wishes of
   This race in ferment waver and flutter still,
      And always wild and awed and cold with
         Care is the life of these wretched beings.

But you, O Mother Earth, in the light pursue
   Your steady course. Your springtime as ever flowers,
      Melodious in their modulations,
         Seasons go by but leave you more living.

Now come, best loved by all the nine Muses and
   The circling constellations, you long desired
      Rejuvenator, Peace, and give us
         Back a firm foothold in life, a centre.

You innocent! But almost, it seems, a child
   Is wiser than we old ones; no conflict tears
      His mind or heart, and still untroubled,
         Joyful and clear are the eyes of children.

And as the umpire, smilingly earnest, looks
   Upon the young men's racecourse with other guests
      And sees the combatants more hotly
         Drive into clouds their dust-whirling chariots,

So steht und lächelt Helios über uns
    Und einsam ist der Göttliche, Frohe nie,
        Denn ewig wohnen sie, des Aethers
            Blühende Sterne, die Heiligfreien.

So up above us Helios stands and smiles,
　　The glad, divine, and never is lonely there,
　　　　For without end they dwell there, Aether's
　　　　　　Blossoming stars, in their holy freedom.

An die Deutschen

Spottet nimmer des Kinds, wenn noch das albernne
    Auf dem Rosse von Holz herrlich und viel sich dünkt,
        O ihr Guten! auch wir sind
            Thatenarm und gedankenvoll!

Aber kommt, wie der Stral aus dem Gewölke kommt,
    Aus Gedanken vieleicht, geistig und reif die That?
        Folgt die Frucht, wie des Haines
            Dunklem Blatte, der stillen Schrift?

Und das Schweigen im Volk, ist es die Feier schon
    Vor dem Feste? die Furcht, welche den Gott ansagt?
        O dann nimmt mich, ihr Lieben!
            Daß ich büße die Lästerung.

Schon zu lange, zu lang irr ich, dem Laien gleich,
    In des bildenden Geists werdender Werkstatt hier,
        Nur was blühet, erkenn ich,
            Was er sinnet, erkenn ich nicht.

Und zu ahnen ist süß, aber ein Leiden auch
    Und schon Jahre genug leb' ich in sterblicher
        Unverständiger Liebe
            Zweifelnd, immer bewegt vor ihm,

Der das stetige Werk immer aus liebender
    Seele näher mir bringt, lächelnd dem Sterblichen
        Wo ich zage, des Lebens
            Reine Tiefe zu Reife bringt.

To the Germans

Never laugh at the child, seeing the silly one
    Feel important and great up on his rocking-horse;
        O my brothers, we too are
            Poor in deeds though we've thoughts enough!

But as lightning from clouds, out of mere thoughts perhaps
    Will the deed in the end, lucid, mature, leap out?
        As from dark orchard leaves, from
            Quiet scripts does the fruit ensue?

And this hush in the crowd, is it the joy before
    Joy's occasion? The awe marking the god's approach?
        O then seize me, my dear ones
            Make me pay for my slanderous words.

Far too long now, too long like a poor layman I
    In the shaping Spirit's workshop have roamed perplexed;
        Things half-grown I can see there,
            What he schemes I can not make out.

Sweet it is to divine, but an affliction too,
    And enough years I've spent loving as mortals do,
        Doubting, uncomprehending,
            Ever moved in his presence who

Ever closer to me out of his loving soul
    Brings the constant great work, smiles at the mortal man
        Where I falter, and to its
            Ripeness brings the pure depth of life.

Schöpferischer, o wann, Genius unsers Volks,
  Wann erscheinest du ganz, Seele des Vaterlands,
    Daß ich tiefer mich beuge,
      Daß die leiseste Saite selbst

Mir verstumme vor dir, daß ich beschämt
  Eine Blume der Nacht, himmlischer Tag, vor dir
    Enden möge mit Freuden,
      Wenn sie alle, mit denen ich

Vormals trauerte, wenn unsere Städte nun
  Hell und offen und wach, reineren Feuers voll
    Und die Berge des deutschen
      Landes Berge der Musen sind,

Wie die herrlichen einst, Pindos und Helikon
  Und Parnassos, und rings unter des Vaterlands
    Goldnem Himmel die freie,
      Klare, geistige Freude glänzt.

Wohl ist enge begränzt unsere Lebenszeit,
  Unserer Jahre Zahl sehen und zählen wir,
    Doch die Jahre der Völker,
      Sah ein sterbliches Auge sie?

Wenn die Seele dir auch über die eigne Zeit
  Sich die sehnende schwingt, trauernd verweilest du
    Dann am kalten Gestade
      Bei den Deinen und kennst sie nie,

Und die Künftigen auch, sie, die Verheißenen
  Wo, wo siehest du sie, daß du an Freundeshand
    Einmal wieder erwarmest,
      Einer Seele vernehmlich seist?

O creative one, when, genius innate in us,
   Wholly will you appear, soul of our fatherland?
      So that lower I bow then,
         Of my strings the most muted then

Dare not sound, and ashamed, dumb before you I droop
   Like a flower of the night, heavenly day, and long
      But to wither with gladness,
         When all those in whose midst I could

Only mourn – when our towns, brightened now, are awake,
   Open and communal, full of a purer fire,
      And the mountains of German
         Lands are mountains the Muses haunt

Like those glorious ones then, Pindos and Helicon
   And Parnassus, and here under the fatherland's
      Golden sky the pellucid,
         Free and enlightened gladness gleams.

True, the span of our lives briefly extends; we can
   See and count the few years granted to us on earth,
      But the years of the peoples,
         These what mortal man's eye has seen?

Though your soul roams away, winged with its yearning soars
   Far beyond your own time, mournful you linger here,
      Cold on desolate shores, with
         Your own kind, but estranged from them;

And those others to come, those for whose advent we wait,
   Where, O where can you see them, that once more you'll be
      Warmed by one hand that's friendly,
         Audible to one living soul?

Klanglos,   ists in der Halle längst,
   Armer Seher! bei dir, sehnend verlischt dein Aug
      Und du schlummerst hinunter
         Ohne Namen und unbeweint.

Without resonance, long empty for you it's been
   In your hall, poor seer, now; yearning your eye grows dim,
      And you drowse away, vanish
         Never noticed, unnamed, unwept.

Rousseau

Wie eng begränzt ist unsere Tageszeit.
 Du warst und sahst und stauntest, schon Abend ists,
  Nun schlafe, wo unendlich ferne
   Ziehen vorüber der Völker Jahre.

Und mancher siehet über die eigne Zeit
 Ihm zeigt ein Gott ins Freie, doch sehnend stehst
  Am Ufer du, ein Ärgerniß den
   Deinen, ein Schatten, und liebst sie nimmer,

Und jene, die du nennst, die Verheißenen,
 Wo sind die Neuen, daß du an Freundeshand
  Erwarmst, wo nahn sie, daß du einmal
   Einsame Rede, vernehmlich seiest?

Klanglos ists, armer Mann, in der Halle dir,
 Und gleich den Unbegrabenen, irrest du
  Unstät und suchest Ruh und niemand
   Weiß den beschiedenen Weg zu weisen.

Sei denn zufrieden!   der Baum entwächst
 Dem heimatlichen Boden, aber es sinken ihm
  Die liebenden, die jugendlichen
   Arme, und trauernd neigt er sein Haupt.

Des Lebens Überfluß, das Unendliche,
 Das um ihn   und dämmert, er faßt es nie.
  Doch lebts in ihm und gegenwärtig,
   Wärmend und wirkend, die Frucht entquillt ihm.

Rousseau

How narrowly confined is our day-time here.
    You were and saw and wondered, and darkness falls;
        Now sleep, where infinitely far the
            Years of the peoples go drifting past you.

And some there are whose vision outflies their time;
    Abroad a god directs them, but, yearning, you
        Must haunt the shore, a shade, an outcast
            Cursed by your kin, and no longer love them,

And those you name, whose coming is promised us,
    Where are those new ones, that by a friendly hand
        You may be warmed, where drawing near, that
            Audibly, you, lonely speech, may sound then?

The ball yields no response to your voice, poor man;
    And like the unburied dead you must roam about
        Unquiet, seeking rest, and no one
            To the allotted way can direct you.

So be content!   the tree outgrows
    His native soil, but soon will his branching arms
        The loving, youthful, then begin to
            Droop, and his head he will bow in sadness.

Life's superfluity, the immensely rich
    That teems and glimmers round him, he'll never grasp.
        And yet it lives in him, and present,
            Warming, effective, his fruit contains it.

Du hast gelebt!   auch dir, auch dir
   Erfreuet die ferne Sonne dein Haupt,
      Und Stralen aus der schönern Zeit. Es
         Haben die Boten dein Herz gefunden.

Vernommen hast du sie, verstanden die Sprache der Fremdlinge,
   Gedeutet ihre Seele! Dem Sehnenden war
      Der Wink genug, und Winke sind
         Von Alters her die Sprache der Götter.

Und wunderbar, als hätte von Anbeginn
   Des Menschen Geist das Werden und Wirken all,
      Des Lebens Weise schon erfahren

Kennt er im ersten Zeichen Vollendetes schon,
   Und fliegt, der kühne Geist, wie Adler den
      Gewittern, weissagend seinen
         Kommenden Göttern voraus

You lived! and *your* crest too, though but once, yours too
   Is gladdened by the light of a distant sun,
      The radiance of a better age. The
         Heralds who looked for your heart have found it.

You've heard and comprehended the strangers' tongue,
   Interpreted their soul! For the yearning man
      The hint sufficed, because in hints from
         Time immemorial the gods have spoken.

And marvellous, as though from the very first
   The human mind had known all that grows and moves,
      Foreknown life's melody and rhythm,

In seed grains he can measure the full-grown plant;
   And flies, bold spirit, flies as the eagles do
      Ahead of thunder-storms, preceding
         Gods, his own gods, to announce their coming.

Heidelberg

Lange lieb' ich dich schon, möchte dich, mir zur Lust,
   Mutter nennen, und dir schenken ein kunstlos Lied,
      Du, der Vaterlandsstädte
         Ländlichschönste, so viel ich sah.

Wie der Vogel des Walds über die Gipfel fliegt,
   Schwingt sich über den Strom, wo er vorbei dir glänzt,
      Leicht und kräftig die Brüke,
         Die von Wagen und Menschen tönt.

Wie von Göttern gesandt, fesselt' ein Zauber einst
   Auf die Brüke mich an, da ich vorüber gieng,
      Und herein in die Berge
         Mir die reizende Ferne schien

Und der Jüngling, der Strom, fort in die Ebne zog,
   Traurigfroh, wie das Herz, wenn es, sich selbst zu schön,
      Liebend unterzugehen,
         In die Fluthen der Zeit sich wirft.

Quellen hattest du ihm, hattest dem Flüchtigen
   Kühle Schatten geschenkt, und die Gestade sahn
      All' ihm nach, und es bebte
         Aus den Wellen ihr lieblich Bild.

Aber schwer in das Thal hieng die gigantische,
   Schiksaalskundige Burg nieder bis auf den Grund,
      Von den Wettern zerrissen
         Doch die ewige Sonne goß

Heidelberg

Long I have loved you and wish, for my own delight,
  I could call you Mother and give you an artless song,
    You of my native land's cities
      Known to me, the most rurally beautiful.

As the bird of the forest does over mountain peaks –
  Over the river, where gleaming it passes your site
    Lightly and strongly the bridge vaults,
      Noisy with coaches and men.

As though sent by gods, once an enchantment transfixed
  Me upon that bridge as I was walking by,
    And the alluring distance
      Shone for me into the hills,

And that youth, the river, travelled on to the plain,
  Sadly glad, like the heart when, too full of itself,
    To perish lovingly
      It casts itself into the currents of time.

To that fugitive one you had given sources,
  Had given him cool shadows, and all the banks
    Gazed after him, from the wavelets
      Their charming image, tremulous, rose.

But heavily into the valley hung the gigantic
  Castle acquainted with fate, to its very foundations
    Blasted and torn by all weathers;
      Yet the eternal sun poured down

Ihr verjüngendes Licht über das alternde
  Riesenbild, und umher grünte lebendiger
    Epheu; freundliche Wälder
      Rauschten über die Burg herab.

Sträuche blühten herab, bis wo im heitern Thal,
  An den Hügel gelehnt, oder dem Ufer hold,
    Deine fröhlichen Gassen
      Unter duftenden Gärten ruhn.

His rejuvenating light, even over the aging
    Giant hulk, and round about it living ivy
        Greenly grew; benevolent copses
            Rustled down to the castle walls,

Shrubs came blossoming down to where in the bright, calm valley,
    Leaning against the hill or loving the river bank,
        Your cheerful streets and pathways
            Under fragrant gardens repose.

Heidelberg

Alcaic Version

Long I have loved you, and now for my own delight
    Would call you Mother, offer an artless song
        To you, of all the homeland cities
            Which I have seen the most lapped in beauty.

As over hilltops birds of the forest fly,
    Across the river gleaming past you the bridge
        Vaults over, sturdily and lightly,
            Loud with the traffic of feet and coachwheels.

As though divinely sent, an enchantment once
    Transfixed me on the bridge as I walked that way
        And right into the hills there came the
            Radiance and lure of far-distant places

And he, the youth, the river sought out the plains
    As sadly glad as hearts that, too full for ease,
        To perish out of love's abundance
            Hurl themselves down into time's quick torrents.

To him, the fleeting, well-springs you'd given, and
    Cool shade enough, and after him all the banks
        Now gazed, and from the rippled water
            Quivered their beautiful mirror image.

But heavy, hulking into the valley hung
    The fate-acquainted castle, the vast, all torn
        And battered down to its foundations;
            Nevertheless even there the sun now

Poured out renewing, youth-giving light upon
    That aging bastion's bulk, and around it bloomed
        The living ivy; kindly forests
            Breathed their soft murmur on brittle stonework.

Shrubs blossomed down to where in the valley's calm,
    Close to the hillside, leaning or fondly pressed
        Against the river-bank, your cheerful
            Streets are at rest beneath fragrant gardens.

Die Götter

Du stiller Aether! immer bewahrst du schön
   Die Seele mir im Schmerz, und es adelt sich
      Zur Tapferkeit vor deinen Stralen,
         Helios! oft die empörte Brust mir.

Ihr guten Götter! arm ist, wer euch nicht kennt,
   Im rohen Busen ruhet der Zwist ihm nie,
      Und Nacht ist ihm die Welt und keine
         Freude gedeihet und kein Gesang ihm.

Nur ihr, mit eurer ewigen Jugend, nährt
   In Herzen die euch lieben, den Kindersinn,
      Und laßt in Sorgen und in Irren
         Nimmer den Genius sich vertrauern.

The Gods

You silent Aether, always in pain or grief
    You keep my soul untouched, and when, hurt, I rage,
        Yet often I take heart, ennobled,
            Helios, in face of your nobler brightness.

You kindly gods, not knowing you men are poor,
    Their coarse hearts rent by war that will not abate;
        The world is night to them, no pleasure
            Prospers for them and no song grows mellow.

But you alone can feed with your deathless youth,
    In those that truly love you, the childlike mind,
        And never, when they stray or suffer,
            Wholly let sadness becloud their genius.

Der Nekar

In deinen Thälern wachte mein Herz mir auf
  Zum Leben, deineWellen umspielten mich,
    Und all der holden Hügel, die dich
      Wanderer! kennen, ist keiner fremd mir.

Auf ihren Gipfeln löste des Himmels Luft
  Mir oft der Knechtschaft Schmerzen; und aus dem Thal,
  Wie Leben aus dem Freudebecher,
    Glänzte die bläuliche Silberwelle.

Der Berge Quellen eilten hinab zu dir,
  Mit ihnen auch mein Herz und du nahmst uns mit,
  Zum stillerhahnen Rhein, zu seinen
    Städten hinunter und lustgen Inseln.

Noch dünkt die Welt mir schön, und das Aug entflieht
  Verlangend nach den Reizen der Erde mir,
    Zum goldenen Paktol, zu Smirnas
    Ufer, zu Ilions Wald. Auch möcht ich

Bei Sunium oft landen, den stummen Pfad
  Nach deinen Säulen fragen, Olympion!
    Noch eh der Sturmwind und das Alter
    Hin in den Schutt der Athenertempel

Und ihrer Gottesbilder auch dich begräbt,
  Denn lang schon einsam stehst du, o Stolz der Welt,
    Die nicht mehr ist. Und o ihr schönen
    Inseln Ioniens! wo die Meerluft

The Neckar

Your banks and dells awakened my heart to life,
   Your wavelets played, their rippling my music then;
      Of all the lovely hills that know you,
         Rambler, not one is unknown to me there.

Up on their tops quite often the heavens' air
   Allayed the pangs of servitude; from the vale,
      As from the wine-cup life and gladness,
         Glittered the bluish and silver wavelet.

The mountain brooks came hurrying down to you,
   And with them came my heart, and you carried us
      To calm, exalted Rhine, conveyed us
         Down to his cities and pleasant islets.

The world seems lovely still, and my vision flees
   From me, allured by Earth and her various charms,
      To golden Pactolus, to Smyrna's
         Coast or to Ilium's woods. And often

I long to land at Sunium and ask the path,
   The dumb, where are your pillars, Olympion,
      And soon, before the gales and age can
         Bury you too in the scattered rubble

Of temples Athens raised, and her imaged gods,
   For long now desolate you have stood, O pride
      Of worlds that are no more. And O you
         Lovely Ionian isles where the sea breeze

Die heißen Ufer kühlt und den Lorbeerwald
　　Durchsäuselt, wenn die Sonne den Weinstok wärmt,
　　　　Ach! wo ein goldner Herbst dem armen
　　　　　　Volk in Gesänge die Seufzer wandelt,

Wenn sein Granatbaum reift, wenn aus grüner Nacht
　　Die Pomeranze blinkt, und der Mastyxbaum
　　　　Von Harze träuft und Pauk und Cymbel
　　　　　　Zum labyrintischen Tanze klingen.

Zu euch, ihr Inseln! bringt mich vielleicht, zu euch
　　Mein Schuzgott einst; doch weicht mir aus treuem Sinn
　　　　Auch da mein Nekar nicht mit seinen
　　　　　　Lieblichen Wiesen und Uferweiden.

Wafts coolness on hot shores and runs rustling through
    The laurel wood, when sunbeams caress the vine,
        And oh, where still a golden autumn
            Turns into songs the poor people's sighing,

When their pomegranate ripens, the orange glints
    In a green night and richly the resin drips
        From mastic trees and drum and cymbal
            Beat to the wild labyrinthine dances.

To you, perhaps, you islands, my guardian god
    One day will take me; yet even then I should
        Recall my Neckar, loyal to his
            Amiable meadows and bankside willows.

Die Heimath

Froh kehrt der Schiffer heim an den stillen Strom,
   Von Inseln fernher, wenn er geerndtet hat;
     So käm' auch ich zur Heimath hätt' ich
       Güter so viele, wie Laid, geerndtet.

Ihr theuern Ufer, die mich erzogen einst,
   Stillt ihr der Liebe Leiden, versprecht ihr mir,
     Ihr Wälder meiner Jugend, wenn ich
       Komme, die Ruhe noch einmal wieder?

Am kühlen Bache, wo ich der Wellen Spiel,
   Am Strome, wo ich gleiten die Schiffe sah,
     Dort bin ich bald; euch traute Berge,
       Die mich behüteten einst, der Heimath

Verehrte sichre Grenzen, der Mutter Haus
   Und liebender Geschwister Umarmungen
     Begrüß' ich bald und ihr umschließt mich,
       Daß, wie in Banden, das Herz mir heile,

Ihr treugebliehnen! aber ich weiß, ich weiß,
   Der Liebe Laid, diß heilet so bald mir nicht,
     Diß singt kein Wiegensang, den tröstend
       Sterbliche singen, mir aus dem Busen.

Denn sie, die uns das himmlische Feuer leihn,
   Die Götter schenken heiliges Laid uns auch,
     Drum bleibe diß. Ein Sohn der Erde
       Schein' ich; zu lieben gemacht, zu leiden.

Home

Content the boatman turns to the river's calm
   From distant isles, his harvest all gathered in;
      So too would I go home now, had I
         Reaped as much wealth as I've gathered sorrow.

Dear river-banks that reared me and taught me once,
   Do you allay love's sufferings, promise me
      You forests of my childhood, should I
         Come to you now, the same peace as ever?

Where by the stream, the cool, I saw wavelets play
   And on the river's meadow watched boats glide past,
      There soon I'll be; you long-loved mountains,
         Once my protectors, and still the homeland's

Revered and certain frontiers, my mother's house,
   Embrace of loving brother and sister there
      I'll welcome soon, and you'll enclose me,
         Healing my heart like a gentle bandage,

You ever loyal ones; but I know, I know,
   This grief, the grief of love, will be slow to heal,
      Of this no lullaby that mortals
         Chant to give comfort will now relieve me.

For they who lend us heavenly light and fire,
   The gods, with holy sorrow endow us too.
      So be it, then. A son of Earth I
         Seem; and was fashioned to love, to suffer.

Die Liebe

Wenn ihr Freunde vergeßt, wenn ihr die Euern all,
   O ihr Dankbaren, sie, euere Dichter schmäht,
      Gott vergeb' es, doch ehret
         Nur die Seele der Liebenden.

Denn o saget, wo lebt menschliches Leben sonst
   Da die knechtische jezt alles, die Sorge zwingt?
      Darum wandelt der Gott auch
         Sorglos über dem Haupt uns längst.

Doch, wie immer das Jahr kalt und gesanglos ist
   Zur beschiedenen Zeit, aber aus weißem Feld
      Grüne Halme doch sprossen,
         Oft ein einsamer Vogel singt,

Wenn sich mälig der Wald dehnet, der Strom sich regt,
   Schon die mildere Luft leise von Mittag weht
      Zur erlesenen Stunde,
         So ein Zeichen der schönern Zeit,

Die wir glauben, erwächst einziggenügsam noch,
   Einzig edel und fromm über dem ehernen,
      Wilden Boden die Liebe,
         Gottes Tochter, von ihm allein.

Sei geseegnet, o sei, himmlische Pflanze, mir
   Mit Gesange gepflegt, wenn des ätherischen
      Nektars Kräfte dich nähren,
         Und der schöpfrische Stral dich reift.

Love

If you drop an old friend, if, O you grateful ones,
   Your own poets you slight, slander and cheapen, may
      God forgive you, but always
         Honour lovers, respect their soul.

For, I ask you, where else humanly do men live
   Now that slavish one, Care, rules and compels us all?
      Therefore too has the God long
         Moved uncaring above our heads.

Yet no matter how cold, songless the year may be,
   When the season is due still from the field all white
      New green blades will be sprouting,
         Often one lonely small bird will sing,

When the woods all expand, slowly, the river stirs
   Milder breezes at last tenderly blow from the south,
      At the hour pre-elected,
         So, a sign of the better age

We believe in, unique thanks to her self-content,
   Noble, pious, on soil hard as iron and waste,
      Love, the daughter of God, comes,
         Only his and from him alone.

You, then, heavenly plant, now let me bless, and be
   Ever tended with song, when the aetherial
      Nectar's energies feed you,
         Ripened by the creative ray.

Wachs und werde zum Wald! eine beseeltere,
   Vollentblühende Welt! Sprache der Liebenden
      Sei die Sprache des Landes,
         Ihre Seele der Laut des Volks!

Grow and be a whole wood! Be a more soul-inspired,
   Fully blossoming world! Language of lovers now
      Be the language our land speaks,
         And their soul be the people's lilt!

Lebenslauf

Größers wolltest auch du, aber die Liebe zwingt
    All uns nieder, das Laid beuget gewaltiger,
        Doch es kehret umsonst nicht
            Unser Bogen, woher er kommt.

Aufwärts oder hinab! herrschet in heil'ger Nacht,
    Wo die stumme Natur werdende Tage sinnt,
        Herrscht im schiefesten Orkus
            Nicht ein Grades, ein Recht noch auch?

Diß erfuhr ich. Denn nie, sterblichen Meistern gleich,
    Habt ihr Himmlischen, ihr Alleserhaltenden,
        Daß ich wüßte, mit Vorsicht
            Mich des ebenen Pfads geführt.

Alles prüfe der Mensch, sagen die Himmlischen,
    Daß er, kräftig genährt, danken für Alles lern',
        Und verstehe die Freiheit,
            Aufzubrechen, wohin er will.

The Course of Life

More you also desired, but every one of us
    Love draws earthward, and grief bends with still greater power;
        Yet our arc not for nothing
            Brings us back to our starting-place.

Whether upward or down – does not in holy night
    Where mute Nature thinks out days that are still to come,
        Though in crookedest Orcus,
            Yet a straightness, a law prevail?

This I learned. For not once, as mortal masters do,
    Did you heavenly ones, wise preservers of all,
        To my knowledge, with foresight
            Lead me on by a level path.

All a man shall try out, thus say the heavenly,
    So that strongly sustained he shall give thanks for all,
        Learn to grasp his own freedom
            To be gone where he's moved to go.

Ihre Genesung

Sieh! dein Liebstes, Natur, leidet und schläft und du
    Allesheilende, säumst? oder ihr seids nicht mehr,
        Zarte Lüfte des Aethers,
            Und ihr Quellen des Morgenlichts?

Alle Blumen der Erd, alle die goldenen
    Frohen Früchte des Hains, alle sie heilen nicht
        Dieses Leben, ihr Götter,
            Das ihr selber doch euch erzogt?

Ach! schon athmet und tönt heilige Lebenslust
    Ihr im reizenden Wort wieder, wie sonst und schon
        Glänzt in zärtlicher Jugend
            Deine Blume, wie sonst, dich an,

Heilge Natur, o du, welche zu oft, zu oft,
    Wenn ich trauernd versank, lächelnd das zweifelnde
        Haupt mit Gaaben umkränzte,
            Jugendliche, nun auch, wie sonst!

Wenn ich altre dereinst, siehe so geb ich dir,
    Die mich täglich verjüngt, Allesverwandelnde,
        Deiner Flamme die Schlaken,
            Und ein anderer leb ich auf.

Her Recovery

Nature, look, your most loved drowses and ails, and you
    Dally, healer of all? Have you grown weak, then, tired,
        Gentle breezes of Aether,
            Limpid sources of morning light?

All the flowers of the earth, all the deep golden-hued
    Happy fruits of the grove, how can it be that all
        Fail to cure this one life which,
            Gods, you raised for your own delight?

Ah, already restored, holy desire to live
    Breathes and sounds in her talk, charming as ever, and
        Tenderly youthful your flower
            Gleams at you as she did before,

Holy Nature, the same who all too often when
    Sadness made me sink down, smiling would garland my
        Head with gifts, with your riches,
            Youthful Nature, now too restored!

Look, one day when I'm old, you that transmute all things,
    And now daily renew youth in me, I will give
        To your flame the dead cinders
            And revive as a different man.

Der Abschied

Zweite Fassung

Trennen wollten wir uns? wähnten es gut und klug?
    Da wirs thaten, warum schrökte, wie Mord, die That?
        Ach! wir kennen uns wenig,
            Denn es waltet ein Gott in uns.

Den verrathen? ach ihn, welcher uns alles erst,
    Sinn und Leben erschuff, ihn, den beseelenden
        Schuzgott unserer Liebe,
            Diß, diß Eine vermag ich nicht.

Aber anderen Fehl denket der Weltsinn sich,
    Andern ehernen Dienst übt er und anders Recht,
        Und es listet die Seele
            Tag für Tag der Gebrauch uns ab.

Wohl! ich wußt' es zuvor. Seit die gewurzelte
    Ungestalte die Furcht Götter und Menschen trennt,
        Muß, mit Blut sie zu sühnen,
            Muß der Liebenden Herz vergehn.

Laß mich schweigen! o laß nimmer von nun an mich
    Dieses Tödtliche sehn, daß ich im Frieden doch
        Hin ins Einsame ziehe,
            Und noch unser der Abschied sei!

Reich die Schaale mir selbst, daß ich des rettenden
    Heilgen Giftes genug, daß ich des Lethetranks
        Mit dir trinke, daß alles
            Haß und Liebe vergessen sei!

The Farewell

Second Version

So we wanted to part? Thought it both good and wise?
    Why, then, why did the act shock us as murder would?
        Ab, ourselves we know little,
            For within us a god commands.

Wrong that god? And betray him who created for us
    Meaning, life, all we had, him who inspired and moved,
        Who protected our loving,
            This, this one thing I cannot do.

But a different wrong, different slavery
    Now the world's mind invents, threatens with other laws,
        And, by cunning, convention
            Day by day steals away our souls.

Oh, I knew it before. Ever since deep-rooted Fear,
    Ugly, crippled, estranged mortals from heaven's gods
        To appease them with bloodshed
            Lovers' hearts must be sacrificed.

Silent now let me be! Never henceforth let me know
    This, my deadly disgrace, so that in peace I may
        Hide myself where it's lonely
            And the parting at least be ours.

Pass the cup, then, yourself, that of the rescuing,
    Holy poison enough, that of the lethal draught
        I may drink with you, all things,
            Hate and love be forgotten then.

Hingehn will ich. Vieleicht seh' ich in langer Zeit
    Diotima! dich hier. Aber verblutet ist
        Dann das Wünschen und friedlich
            Gleich den Seeligen, fremde gehn

Wir umher, ein Gespräch führet uns ab und auf,
    Sinnend, zögernd, doch izt mahnt die Vergessenen
        Hier die Stelle des Abschieds,
            Es erwarmet ein Herz in uns,

Staunend seh' ich dich an, Stimmen und süßen Sang,
    Wie aus voriger Zeit hör' ich und Saitenspiel,
        Und die Lilie duftet
            Golden über dem Bach uns auf.

To be gone is my wish. Later perhaps one day,
    Diotima, we'll meet – here, but desire by then
        Will have bled away, peaceful
            Like the blessed, and like strangers we'll

Walk about, as our talk leads us now here, now there,
    Musing, hesitant, but then the oblivious ones
        See the place where they parted,
            And a heart newly warms in us,

Wondering I look at you, voices and lovely song
    As from distant times, music of strings, I hear
        And the lily unfolds her
            Fragrance, golden above the brook.

Diotima

Du schweigst und duldest, denn sie verstehn dich nicht,
  Du edles Leben! siehest zur Erd' und schweigst
    Am schönen Tag, denn ach! umsonst nur
      Suchst du die Deinen im Sonnenlichte,

Die Königlichen, welche, wie Brüder doch,
  Wie eines Hains gesellige Gipfel sonst
    Der Lieb' und Heimath sich und ihres
      Immerumfangenden Himmels freuten,

Des Ursprungs noch in tönender Brust gedenk;
  Die Dankbarn, sie, sie mein ich, die einzigtreu
    Bis in den Tartarus hinab die Freude
      Brachten, die Freien, die Göttermenschen,

Die zärtlichgroßen Seelen, die nimmer sind;
  Denn sie beweint, so lange das Trauerjahr
    Schon dauert, von den vor'gen Sternen
      Täglich gemahnet, das Herz noch immer

Und diese Todtenklage, sie ruht nicht aus.
  Die Zeit doch heilt. Die Himmlischen sind jezt stark,
    Sind schnell. Nimmt denn nicht schon ihr altes
      Freudiges Recht die Natur sich wieder?

Sieh! eh noch unser Hügel, o Liebe, sinkt,
  Geschiehts, und ja! noch siehet mein sterblich Lied
    Den Tag, der, Diotima! nächst den
      Göttern mit Helden dich nennt, und dir gleicht.

Diotima

You suffer and keep silent, unknown to them,
    You noble being, silently earthward gaze
        At brightest noon, for it's in vain that
            Here in the sunlight you seek your kindred,

Those regal ones who truly like brothers once,
    Like crests of one companionable grove were glad
        Of love and of their homeland and the
            Heaven that ever enfolded, blessed them,

Their tuneful bosoms true to their origin;
    Those grateful ones, I mean, who unmatched in faith
        As far as deepest Tartarus proffered
            Gladness, untrammelled as gods, though human,

Those tender noble spirits that are no more;
    For these, though long already our time of loss
        Has lasted, by the former planets
            Daily reminded, the heart still weeps, and

This keening for the dead does not flag or rest.
    Yet time heals all. The Heavenly now are strong,
        Are quick. Already does not Nature
            Claim her old joy-giving rights, reclaim them?

Look, Diotima, dear one, before our mound
    Subsides that age will come, and my mortal song
        Yet see the day which next to gods, with
            Heroes will name you, itself be like you.

Rükkehr in die Heimath

Ihr milden Lüfte! Boten Italiens!
   Und du mit deinen Pappeln, geliebter Strom!
     Ihr woogenden Gebirg! o all ihr
       Sonnigen Gipfel, so seid ihrs wieder?

Du stiller Ort! in Träumen erschienst du fern
   Nach hoffnungslosem Tage dem Sehnenden,
     Und du mein Haus, und ihr Gespielen,
       Bäume des Hügels, ihr wohlbekannten!

Wie lang ists, o wie lange! des Kindes Ruh
   Ist hin, und hin ist Jugend und Lieb' und Lust;
     Doch du, mein Vaterland! du heilig-
       Duldendes! siehe, du bist geblieben.

Und darum, daß sie dulden mit dir, mit dir
   Sich freun, erziehst du, theures! die Deinen auch
     Und mahnst in Träumen, wenn sie ferne
       Schweifen und irren, die Ungetreuen.

Und wenn im heißen Busen dem Jünglinge
   Die eigenmächt'gen Wünsche besänftiget
     Und stille vor dem Schiksaal sind, dann
       Giebt der Geläuterte dir sich lieber.

Lebt wohl dann, Jugendtage, du Rosenpfad
   Der Lieb', und all' ihr Pfade des Wanderers,
     Lebt wohl! und nimm und seegne du mein
       Leben, o Himmel der Heimath, wieder!

Return to the Homeland

You gentle breezes, heralds of Italy,
    And you with all your poplars, dear river-banks,
        You billowing mountain range, and sunny
            Peaks – can it be, is it really you, then?

You quiet place, in dreams after hopeless days
    You taunted me, the homesick, but stayed remote,
        And you, my house, and you, my playmates,
            Trees of the hillside, my old companions!

How long ago, how long! Now the child's calm trust
    Is gone, and gone are youth and delight and love;
        But you, the suffering, the holy,
            Look, you alone have remained, my homeland.

And it's for that, to suffer with you, with you
    To share their joys that, dear one, you raise your sons,
        And when, unfaithful, far from you they
            Wander astray, in their dreams remind them.

And when at last the youth in his fervid heart
    Feels autocratic wishes abate, grow still
        In face of destiny, to you more
            Readily too will the mellowed yield then.

Good-bye, then, days of youth, and you rose-lined path
    Of love, and all you paths of the roaming man,
        Good-bye! And you, my homeland's heaven,
            Take back this life that was yours, and bless it.

Das Ahnenbild

Ne virtus ulla pereat!

Alter Vater! Du blikst immer, wie ehmals, noch,
　　Da du gerne gelebt unter den Sterblichen,
　　　　Aber ruhiger nur, und
　　　　　　Wie die Seeligen, heiterer

In die Wohnung, wo doch, Vater! das Söhnlein nennt,
　　Wo es lächelnd vor dir spielt und den Muthwill übt,
　　　　Wie die Lämmer im Feld', auf
　　　　　　Grünem Teppiche, den zur Lust

Ihm die Mutter gegönnt. Ferne sich haltend, sieht
　　Ihm die Liebende zu, wundert der Sprache sich
　　　　Und des jungen Verstandes
　　　　　　Und des blühenden Auges schon.

Und an andere Zeit mahnt sie der Mann, dein Sohn;
　　An die Lüfte des Mais, da er geseufzt um sie,
　　　　An die Bräutigamstage,
　　　　　　Da der Stolze die Demuth lernt.

Doch es wandte sich bald: Sicherer, denn er war,
　　Ist er, herrlicher ist unter den Seinigen
　　　　Nun der Zweifachgeliebte,
　　　　　　Und ihm gehet sein Tagewerk.

Stiller Vater! auch du lebtest und liebtest so:
　　Darum wohnest du nun, als ein Unsterblicher,
　　　　Bei den Kindern, und Leben,
　　　　　　Wie vom schweigenden Aether, kommt

The Ancestral Portrait

Ne virtus ulla pereat!

Agèd father, you gaze now as you did before
    When it pleased you to live here among mortal kin,
        Yet more quietly now and,
            Like the blessed, more serenely too,

On the room where a boy, father, still speaks your name,
    Where he smiles as he plays, frolics in front of you
        Like the lambs in the field, on
            His green carpet, laid out for him

By his mother, for joy. Keeping her distance, she
    Raptly loving, looks on, marvels at words he tries,
        At his young comprehension,
            At the light that shines from his eyes.

And her husband, your son, turns her fond musing back:
    May-time breezes in which only for her he sighed,
        Testing days of his courtship,
            When the proud one must learn to bow.

But quite soon that was changed: surer than once he'd been
    He has grown, more secure, lordly amid his own,
        Now the doubly belovèd,
            And his labour goes well for him.

Tranquil father, so too you once would live and love;
    That is why you can dwell, now an immortal, here
        With your children, a life like
            That of Aether, the silent, comes

Öfters über das Haus, ruhiger Mann! von dir,
   Und es mehrt sich, es reift, edler von Jahr zu Jahr,
      In bescheidenem Glüke,
         Was mit Hofnungen du gepflanzt.

Die du liebend erzogst, siehe! sie grünen dir,
   Deine Bäume, wie sonst, breiten ums Haus den Arm,
      Voll von dankenden Gaaben;
         Sichrer stehen die Stämme schon;

Und am Hügel hinab, wo du den sonnigen
   Boden ihnen gebaut, neigen und schwingen sich
      Deine freudigen Reben,
         Trunken, purpurner Trauben voll.

Aber unten im Haus ruhet, besorgt von dir,
   Der gekelterte Wein. Theuer ist der dem Sohn',
      Und er sparet zum Fest das
         Alte, lautere Feuer sich.

Dann beim nächtlichen Mahl, wenn er, in Lust und Ernst,
   Von Vergangenem viel, vieles von Künftigem
      Mit den Freunden gesprochen,
         Und der lezte Gesang noch hallt,

Hält er höher den Kelch, siehet dein Bild und spricht:
   Deiner denken wir nun, dein, und so werd' und bleib'
      Ihre Ehre des Haußes
         Guten Genien, hier und sonst!

Und es tönen zum Dank hell die Krystalle dir;
   Und die Mutter, sie reicht, heute zum erstenmal,
      Daß es wisse vom Feste,
         Auch dem Kinde von deinem Trank.

To the house at times, calm of your calm, from you
  And, more noble each year, all that your hopes could plant
    Thrives, matures and increases
      In their modest, their frugal bliss.

Those that loving you reared, look! they grow green for you,
  These your trees, as before, spreading around the house
    Grateful gifts by the armful;
      Firmer, stronger their trunks have grown;

On the slope of this hill, where you had cut for them
  Sunny tracts, now there sway, bend in the autumn winds
    Happy grapevines you planted,
      Drunken, laden with purple fruit.

Down below, in the house, thanks to your work and care,
  Lies the wine that you pressed. Dear it is to your son,
    And he saves for the feast-day
      Yours, the older, more mellow fire.

Then, at table by night, when, at once glad and grave,
  Much of days that have passed, much of the days to come
    With his friends he has spoken,
      And the last of their songs subsides,

High he raises his glass, looks at your portrait, says:
  Now our thought be of you, yours be the name that guards
    This our household, its honour,
      Now and ever, within, without!

And for you, giving thanks, brightly the crystals clink;
  And the mother for once, so that he too may share,
    Know the festive occasion,
      Lets the child even taste your wine.

Die Entschlafenen

Einen vergänglichen Tag lebt' ich und wuchs mit den Meinen,
    Eins um's andere schon schläft mir und fliehet dahin.
Doch ihr Schlafenden wacht am Herzen mir, in verwandter
    Seele ruhet von euch mir das entfliehende Bild.
Und lebendiger lebt ihr dort, wo des göttlichen Geistes
    Freude die Alternden all, alle die Todten verjüngt.

The Departed

With my own kind I lived and could grow for a day that was fleeting,
    One by one they depart, gone from me into their sleep.
Yet you sleepers within me are wakeful, and in my related
    Soul an image of each, fugitive, lingers and rests.
And more living there you live on where the god-given spirit's
    Joy rejuvenates all, all who have aged, and the dead.

Ermunterung

Zweite Fassung

Echo des Himmels! heiliges Herz! warum,
   Warum verstummst du unter den Lebenden,
     Schläfst, freies! von den Götterlosen
       Ewig hinab in die Nacht verwiesen?

Wacht denn, wie vormals, nimmer des Aethers Licht?
   Und blüht die alte Mutter, die Erde nicht?
     Und übt der Geist nicht da und dort, nicht
       Lächelnd die Liebe das Recht noch immer?

Nur du nicht mehr! doch mahnen die Himmlischen,
   Und stillebildend weht, wie ein kahl Gefild,
     Der Othem der Natur dich an, der
       Alleserheiternde, seelenvolle.

O Hoffnung! bald, bald singen die Haine nicht
   Des Lebens Lob allein, denn es ist die Zeit,
     Daß aus der Menschen Munde sie, die
       Schönere Seele sich neuverkündet,

Dann liebender im Bunde mit Sterblichen
   Das Element sich bildet, und dann erst reich,
     Bei frommer Kinder Dank, der Erde
       Brust, die unendliche, sich entfaltet

Und unsre Tage wieder, wie Blumen, sind,
   Wo sie, des Himmels Sonne sich ausgetheilt
     Im stillen Wechsel sieht und wieder
       Froh in den Frohen das Licht sich findet,

Exhortation

Second Version

Echo of Heaven, heart that is hallowed, why,
    Why do you now fall silent, though living still,
        And sleep, you free one, by the godless
            Banished for ever to Night's deep dungeons?

Does not the light of Aether, as always, wake?
    And Earth, our ancient mother, still thrive and flower?
        And here and there does not the spirit,
            Love, with a smile wield her laws as ever?

You only fail! Yet heavenly powers exhort,
    And silently at work, like a stubble field,
        The breath of Nature blows upon you,
            She the all-brightening, soul-inspiring.

O hope, now soon, now soon not the groves alone
    Shall sing life's praise, for almost the time is come
        When through the mouths of mortals, this, the
            Lovelier soul will make known her coming,

Allied with men more lovingly then once more
    The element will form, and not rich or full
        But when her pious children thank her,
            Endless the breast of our Earth unfold then,

And once again like blossoms our days will be
    Where heavenly Helios sees his own light shared out
        In quiet alternation, finding
            Joy in the joy of those mortal mirrors,

Und er, der sprachlos waltet und unbekannt
   Zukünftiges bereitet, der Gott, der Geist
     Im Menschenwort, am schönen Tage
       Kommenden Jahren, wie einst, sich ausspricht.

And he who silent rules and in secret plans
    Things yet to come, the Godhead, the Spirit housed
      In human words, once more, at noontide,
        Clearly will speak to the future ages.

Natur und Kunst
ODER
Saturn und Jupiter

Du waltest hoch am Tag' und es blühet dein
   Gesez, du hältst die Waage, Saturnus Sohn!
     Und theilst die Loos' und ruhest froh im
       Ruhm der unsterblichen Herrscherkünste.

Doch in den Abgrund, sagen die Sänger sich,
   Habst du den heil'gen Vater, den eignen, einst
     Verwiesen und es jammre drunten,
       Da, wo die Wilden vor dir mit Recht sind,

Schuldlos der Gott der goldenen Zeit schon längst:
   Einst mühelos, und größer, wie du, wenn schon
     Er kein Gebot aussprach und ihn der
       Sterblichen keiner mit Nahmen nannte.

Herab denn! oder schäme des Danks dich nicht!
   Und willst du bleiben, diene dem Älteren,
     Und gönn' es ihm, daß ihn vor Allen,
       Göttern und Menschen, der Sänger nenne!

Denn, wie aus dem Gewölke dein Bliz, so kömmt
   Von ihm, was dein ist, siehe! so zeugt von ihm,
     Was du gebeutst, und aus Saturnus
       Frieden ist jegliche Macht erwachsen.

Nature and Art

OR

Saturn and Jupiter

High up in day you govern, your law prevails,
    You hold the scales of judgement, O Saturn's son,
        Hand out our lots and well-contented
            Rest on the fame of immortal kingship.

Yet, singers know it, down the abyss you hurled
    The holy father once, your own parent, who
        Long now has lain lamenting where the
            Wild ones before you more justly languish,

Quite guiltless he, the god of the golden age:
    Once effortless and greater than you, although
        He uttered no commandment, and no
            Mortal on earth ever named his presence.

So down with you! Or cease to withhold your thanks!
    And if you'll stay, defer to the older god
        And grant him that above all others,
            Gods and great mortals, the singer name him!

For as from clouds your lightning, from him has come
    What you call yours. And, look, the commands you speak
        To him bear witness, and from Saturn's
            Primitive peace every power developed.

Und hab' ich erst am Herzen Lebendiges
   Gefühlt und dämmert, was du gestaltetest
    Und war in ihrer Wiege mir in
      Wonne die wechselnde Zeit entschlummert:

Dann kenn' ich dich, Kronion! dann hör' ich dich,
   Den weisen Meister, welcher, wie wir, ein Sohn
    Der Zeit, Geseze giebt und, was die
      Heilige Dämmerung birgt, verkündet.

And once my heart can feel and contain that life
　　Most living, his, and things that you shaped grow dim,
　　　　And in his cradle changing Time has
　　　　　　Fallen asleep and sweet quiet lulls me –

I'll know you then, Kronion, and hear you then,
　　The one wise master who, like ourselves, a son
　　　　Of Time, gives laws to us, uncovers
　　　　　　That which lies hidden in holy twilight.

Die Dioskuren

Ihr edeln Brüder droben, unsterbliches
  Gestirn, euch frag ich Helden woher es ist,
    Daß ich so unterthan ihm bin und
      So der Gewaltige sein mich nennet?

Denn wenig, aber Eines hab ich daheim, das ich
  Da niemand mag soll tauschen, ein gutes Glük
    Ein lichtes, reines, zum Gedächtniß
      Lebender Tage zurükgeblieben.

So aber er gebietet, diß Eine doch
  Wohin ers wollte, wagt' ich mein Saitenspiel
    Samt dem Gesange folgt ich, selbst ins
      Dunkel der Tapferen ihm hinunter.

Mit Wolken, säng ich, tränkt das Gewitter dich
  Du spöttischer Boden, aber mit Blut der Mensch
    So schweigt, so heiligt, der sein Gleiches
      Droben und drunten umsonst erfragte.

The Dioscuri

You brothers, always noble, immortal now
    Among the stars, you heroes up there I ask
        How can he so compel me, make me
            So much submit to his power's persuasion?

For little, yet one thing I've at home which I,
    Since no one else, shall barter, a happiness
        That's bright and pure, bequeathed to me as
            Constant reminder of days more living.

Yet if he were to order this one thing where
    He wanted it, I'd place it at risk, my lyre,
        And with it all my song, and follow
            Him down myself, to the dark of brave men.

With clouds, I'd sing, thunder-storms drench you through,
    Derisive soil, with blood you are drenched by men.
        So he who high and low has sought his
            Equal, in vain, by his silence hallows.

Unter den Alpen gesungen

Heilige Unschuld, du der Menschen und der
Götter liebste vertrauteste! du magst im
Haußе oder draußen ihnen zu Füßen
        Sizen, den Alten,

Immerzufriedner Weisheit voll; denn manches
Gute kennet der Mann, doch staunet er, dem
Wild gleich, oft zum Himmel, aber wie rein ist
        Reine, dir alles!

Siehe! das rauhe Thier des Feldes, gerne
Dient und trauet es dir, der stumme Wald spricht
Wie vor Alters, seine Sprüche zu dir, es
        Lehren die Berge

Heil'ge Geseze dich, und was noch jezt uns
Vielerfahrenen offenbar der große
Vater werden heißt, du darfst es allein uns
        Helle verkünden.

So mit den Himmlischen allein zu seyn, und
Geht vorüber das Licht, und Strom und Wind, und
Zeit eilt hin zum Ort, vor ihnen ein stetes
        Auge zu haben,

Seeliger weiß und wünsch' ich nichts, so lange
Nicht auch mich, wie die Weide, fort die Fluth nimmt,
Daß wohl aufgehoben, schlafend dahin ich
        Muß in den Woogen;

Sung Beneath the Alps

Innocence, you the holy, dearest and nearest
Both to men and to gods! In the house or
Out of doors alike to sit at the ancients'
                Feet it behoves you,

Ever contented wisdom yours; for men know
Much that's good, yet like animals often
Scan the heavens perplexed; to you, though, how pure are
                All things, you pure one!

Look, the rough grassland beast is glad to serve and
Trust you; mute though it be, yet the forest
Now as ever yields its oracles up, the
                Mountains still teach you

God-hallowed laws, and that which even now the
Mighty Father desires to make known to
Us the much experienced, you, and you only
                Clearly may tell us.

Being alone with heavenly powers, and when the
Light begins to pass by, and swiftly river,
Wind and time seek out the place, with a constant
                Eye then to face them –

Nothing more blessed I know, nor want, as long as
Not like willows me too the flood sweeps on, and
Well looked after, sleeping, down I must travel,
                Waves for my bedding;

Aber es bleibt daheim gern, wer in treuem
Busen Göttliches hält, und frei will ich, so
Lang ich darf, euch all', ihr Sprachen des Himmels!
                              Deuten und singen.

Gladly, though, he will stay at home who harbours
Things divine in his heart; and you, all Heaven's
Languages, freely, as long as I may, I'll
                              Sing and interpret.

Dichterberuf

Des Ganges Ufer hörten des Freudengotts
    Triumph, als allerobernd vom Indus her
       Der junge Bacchus kam, mit heilgem
          Weine vom Schlafe die Völker wekend.

Und du, des Tages Engel! erwekst sie nicht,
    Die jezt noch schlafen? gieb die Geseze, gieb
       Uns Leben, siege, Meister, du nur
          Hast der Eroberung Recht, wie Bacchus.

Nicht, was wohl sonst des Menschen Geschik und Sorg'
    Im Haus und unter offenem Himmel ist,
       Wenn edler, denn das Wild, der Mann sich
          Wehret und nährt! denn es gilt ein anders

Zu Sorg' und Dienst den Dichtenden anvertraut!
    Der Höchste, der ists, dem wir geeignet sind,
       Daß näher, immerneu besungen
          Ihn die befreundete Brust vernehme.

Und dennoch, o ihr Himmlischen all, und all
    Ihr Quellen und ihr Ufer und Hain' und Höhn,
       Wo wunderbar zuerst, als du die
          Loken ergriffen, und unvergeßlich

Der unverhoffte Genius über uns
    Der schöpferische, göttliche kam, daß stumm
       Der Sinn uns ward und, wie vom
          Strale gerührt das Gebein erbebte,

The Poet's Vocation

The banks of Ganges heard how the god of joy
   Was hailed when conquering all from far Indus came
      The youthful Bacchus, and with holy
         Wine from their drowsiness woke the peoples.

And you, our own day's angel, do not awake
   Those drowsing still? O give us the laws, and give
      Us life. You, Master, triumph! Only
         You, like that god, have the right to conquer.

Not that which else is human kind's care and skill
   Both in the house and under the open sky
      When, nobler than wild beasts, men work to
         Fend, to provide for themselves – to poets

A different task and calling have been assigned.
   The Highest, he it is whom alone we serve,
      So that more closely, ever newly
         Sung, he will meet with a friendly echo.

And yet, you heavenly powers, you all, and all
   You fountains, all you banks and you groves and peaks
      Where marvellous at first when by the
         Forelock you seized us, and unforeseen the

Divine, creative Genius came over us,
   Dumbfounding mind and sense, unforgettably,
      And left us as though struck by lightning
         Down to our bones that were still aquiver,

Ihr ruhelosen Thaten in weiter Welt!
  Ihr Schiksaalstag', ihr reißenden, wenn der Gott
    Stillsinnend lenkt, wohin zorntrunken
      Ihn die gigantischen Rosse bringen,

Euch sollten wir verschweigen, und wenn in uns
  Vom stetigstillen Jahre der Wohllaut tönt,
    So sollt' es klingen, gleich als hätte
      Muthig und müßig ein Kind des Meisters

Geweihte, reine Saiten im Scherz gerührt?
  Und darum hast du, Dichter! des Orients
    Propheten und den Griechensang und
      Neulich die Donner gehört, damit du

Den Geist zu Diensten brauchst und die Gegenwart
  Des Guten übereilest, in Spott, und den Albernen
    Verläugnest, herzlos, und zum Spiele
      Feil, wie gefangenes Wild, ihn treibest?

Bis aufgereizt vom Stachel im Grimme der
  Des Ursprungs sich erinnert und ruft, daß selbst
    Der Meister kommt, dann unter heißen
      Todesgeschossen entseelt dich lässet.

Zu lang ist alles Göttliche dienstbar schon
  Und alle Himmelskräfte verscherzt, verbraucht
    Die Gütigen, zur Lust, danklos, ein
      Schlaues Geschlecht und zu kennen wähnt es,

Wenn ihnen der Erhabne den Aker baut,
  Das Tagslicht und den Donnerer, und es späht
    Das Sehrohr wohl sie all und zählt und
      Nennet mit Nahmen des Himmels Sterne.

You restless deeds at large in a boundless world!
    You fateful days, you sweeping ones, when the God
        Drives calmly pondering where, drunk with
           Rage, the gigantic horses take him –

Of you should we keep silent, and when in us
    Euphonious peals the constant, the quiet year,
        Then should it sound as though capricious,
           Curious, a child had been idly twanging

The Master's lyre, the hallowed, the pure, in jest?
    And for that only, poet, you heard the East's
        Great prophets, heard Greek song, and lately
           Heard divine thunder ring out – to make a

Vile trade of it, exploiting the Spirit, presume
    On his kind presence, mocking him, heartlessly
        Deny the simple one and drive him
           Round like a captured wild beast for pennies?

Till by that prodding roused in fierce anger he
    Recalls his origin and cries out, so that
        The Master comes himself, to leave you
           Lifeless and seared by his lethal missiles.

Too long now things divine have been cheaply used
    And all the powers of heaven, the kindly, spent
        In trifling waste by cold and cunning
           Men without thanks, who when he, the Highest,

In person tills their field for them, think they know
    The daylight and the Thunderer, and indeed
        Their telescope may find them all, may
           Count and may name every star of heaven.

Der Vater aber deket mit heilger Nacht,
   Damit wir bleiben mögen, die Augen zu.
      Nicht liebt er Wildes! Doch es zwinget
         Nimmer die weite Gewalt den Himmel.

Noch ists auch gut, zu weise zu seyn. Ihn kennt
   Der Dank. Doch nicht behält er es leicht allein,
      Und gern gesellt, damit verstehn sie
         Helfen, zu anderen sich ein Dichter.

Furchtlos bleibt aber, so er es muß, der Mann
   Einsam vor Gott, es schüzet die Einfalt ihn,
      Und keiner Waffen brauchts und keiner
         Listen, so lange, bis Gottes Fehl hilft.

Yet will the Father cover with holy night,
    That we may last on earth, our too knowing eyes.
        He loves no Titan! Never will our
            Free-ranging power coerce his heaven.

Nor is it good to be all too wise. Our thanks
    Know God. Yet never gladly the poet keeps
        His lore unshared, but likes to join with
            Others who help him to understand it.

But, if he must, undaunted the man remains
    Alone with God – ingenuousness keeps him safe –
        And needs no weapon and no wile till
            God's being missed in the end will help him.

Stimme des Volks

Zweite Fassung

Du seiest Gottes Stimme, so glaubt' ich sonst
   In heil'ger Jugend; ja, und ich sag' es noch!
     Um unsre Weisheit unbekümmert
       Rauschen die Ströme doch auch, und dennoch,

Wer liebt sie nicht? und immer bewegen sie
   Das Herz mir, hör' ich ferne die Schwindenden,
     Die Ahnungsvollen meine Bahn nicht,
       Aber gewisser ins Meer hin eilen.

Denn selbstvergessen, allzubereit den Wunsch
   Der Götter zu erfüllen, ergreift zu gern
     Was sterblich ist, wenn offnen Augs auf
       Eigenen Pfaden es einmal wandelt,

Ins All zurük die kürzeste Bahn; so stürzt
   Der Strom hinab, er suchet die Ruh, es reißt,
     Es ziehet wider Willen ihn, von
       Klippe zu Klippe den Steuerlosen

Das wunderbare Sehnen dem Abgrund zu;
   Das Ungebundne reizet und Völker auch
     Ergreifft die Todeslust und kühne
       Städte, nachdem sie versucht das Beste,

Von Jahr zu Jahr forttreibend das Werk, sie hat
   Ein heilig Ende troffen; die Erde grünt
     Und stille vor den Sternen liegt, den
       Betenden gleich, in den Sand geworfen

Voice of the People

Second Version

The voice of God I called you and thought you once,
   In holy youth; and still I do not recant!
      No less indifferent to our wisdom
         Likewise the rivers rush on, but who does

Not love them? Always too my own heart is moved
   When far away I hear those foreknowing ones,
      The fleeting, by a route not mine but
         Surer than mine, and more swift, roar seaward,

For once they travel down their allotted paths
   With open eyes, self-oblivious, too ready to
      Comply with what the gods have wished them,
         Only too gladly will mortal beings

Speed back into the All by the shortest way;
   So rivers plunge – not movement, but rest they seek –
      Drawn on, pulled down against their will from
         Boulder to boulder – abandoned, helmless –

By that mysterious yearning toward the chasm;
   Chaotic deeps attract, and whole peoples too
      May come to long for death, and valiant
         Towns that have striven to do the best thing,

Year in, year out pursuing their task – these too
   A holy end has stricken; the earth grows green,
      And there beneath the stars, like mortals
         Deep in their prayers, quite still, prostrated

Freiwillig überwunden die lange Kunst
   Vor jenen Unnachahmbaren da; er selbst,
      Der Mensch, mit eigner Hand zerbrach, die
         Hohen zu ehren, sein Werk der Künstler.

Doch minder nicht sind jene den Menschen hold,
   Sie lieben wieder, so wie geliebt sie sind,
      Und hemmen öfters, daß er lang im
         Lichte sich freue, die Bahn des Menschen.

Und, nicht des Adlers Jungen allein, sie wirft
   Der Vater aus dem Neste, damit sie nicht
      Zu lang' ihm bleiben, uns auch treibt mit
         Richtigem Stachel hinaus der Herrscher.

Wohl jenen, die zur Ruhe gegangen sind,
   Und vor der Zeit gefallen, auch die, auch die
      Geopfert, gleich den Erstlingen der
         Erndte, sie haben ein Theil gefunden.

Am Xanthos lag, in griechischer Zeit, die Stadt,
   Jezt aber, gleich den größeren die dort ruhn
      Ist durch ein Schiksaal sie dem heilgen
         Lichte des Tages hinweggekommen.

Sie kamen aber nicht in der offnen Schlacht
   Durch eigne Hand um. Fürchterlich ist davon,
      Was dort geschehn, die wunderbare
         Sage von Osten zu uns gelanget.

Es reizte sie die Güte von Brutus. Denn
   Als Feuer ausgegangen, so bot er sich
      Zu helfen ihnen, ob er gleich, als Feldherr
         Stand in Belagerung vor den Thoren.

On sand, outgrown, and willingly, lies long art
    Flung down before the Matchless; and he himself,
        The man, the artist with his own two
            Hands broke his work for their sake, in homage.

Yet they, the Heavenly, to men remain well-disposed,
    As we love them so they will return our love
        And lest too briefly he enjoy the
            Light, will obstruct a man's course to ruin.

And not the eagle's fledgelings alone their sire
    Throws out of eyries, knowing that else too long
        They'd idle – us the Ruler also
            Goads into flight with a prong that's fitting.

Those men I praise who early lay down to rest,
    Who fell before their time, and those also, those
        Like first-fruits of the harvest offered
            Up – they were granted a part, a portion.

By Xanthos once, in Grecian times, there stood
    The town, but now, like greater ones resting there,
        Because a destiny ordained it
            Xanthos is lost to our holy daylight.

But not in open battle, by their own hands
    Her people perished. Dreadful and marvellous
        The legend of that town's destruction,
            Travelling on from the East, has reached us.

The kindliness of Brutus provoked them. For
    When fire broke out, most nobly he offered them
        His help, although he led those troops which
            Stood at their gates to besiege the township.

Doch von den Mauern warfen die Diener sie
    Die er gesandt. Lebendiger ward darauf
        Das Feuer und sie freuten sich und ihnen
            Streket' entgegen die Hände Brutus

Und alle waren außer sich selbst. Geschrei
    Entstand und Jauchzen. Drauf in die Flamme warf
        Sich Mann undWeib, von Knaben stürzt' auch
            Der von dem Dach, in der Väter Schwerdt der.

Nicht räthlich ist es, Helden zu trozen. Längst
    Wars aber vorbereitet. Die Väter auch
        Da sie ergriffen waren, einst, und
            Heftig die persischen Feinde drängten,

Entzündeten, ergreiffend des Stromes Rohr,
    Daß sie das Freie fänden, die Stadt. Und Haus
        Und Tempel nahm, zum heilgen Aether
            Fliegend, und Menschen hinweg die Flamme.

So hatten es die Kinder gehört, und wohl
    Sind gut die Sagen, denn ein Gedächtniß sind
        Dem Höchsten sie, doch auch bedarf es
            Eines, die heiligen auszulegen.

Yet from the walls they threw all the servants down
    Whom he had sent. Much livelier then at once
        The fire flared up, and they rejoiced, and
            Brutus extended his arms towards them,

All were beside themselves. And great crying there,
    Great jubilation sounded. Then into flames
        Leapt man and woman; boys came hurtling
            Down from the roofs or their fathers stabbed them.

It is not wise to fight against heroes. But
    Events long past prepared it. Their ancestors
        When they were quite encircled once and
            Strongly the Persian forces pressed them,

Took rushes from the rivers and, that their foes
    Might find a desert there, set ablaze their town;
        And house and temple – breathed to holy
            Aether – and men did the flame carry off there.

So their descendants heard, and no doubt such lore
    Is good, because it serves to remind us of
        The Highest; yet there's also need of
            One to interpret these holy legends.

Der blinde Sänger

ἔλυσεν αἰνὸν ἄχος ἀπ'ὀμμάτων Ἄρης – SOPHOKLES

Wo bist du, Jugendliches! das immer mich
　Zur Stunde wekt des Morgens, wo bist du, Licht!
　　Das Herz ist wach, doch bannt und hält in
　　　Heiligem Zauber die Nacht mich immer.

Sonst lauscht' ich um die Dämmerung gern, sonst harrt'
　Ich gerne dein am Hügel, und nie umsonst!
　　Nie täuschten mich, du Holdes, deine
　　　Boten, die Lüfte, denn immer kamst du,

Kamst allbeseeligend den gewohnten Pfad
　Herein in deiner Schöne, wo bist du, Licht!
　　Das Herz ist wieder wach, doch bannt und
　　　Hemmt die unendliche Nacht mich immer.

Mir grünten sonst die Lauben; es leuchteten
　Die Blumen, wie die eigenen Augen, mir;
　　Nicht ferne war das Angesicht der
　　　Meinen und leuchtete mir und droben

Und um die Wälder sah ich die Fittige
　Des Himmels wandern, da ich ein Jüngling war;
　　Nun siz ich still allein, von einer
　　　Stunde zur anderen und Gestalten

Aus Lieb und Laid der helleren Tage schafft
　Zur eignen Freude nun mein Gedanke sich,
　　Und ferne lausch' ich hin, ob nicht ein
　　　Freundlicher Retter vieleicht mir komme.

The Blind Singer

ἔλυσεν αἰνὸν ἄχος ἀπ᾽ὀμμάτων Ἄρης — SOPHOCLES

Where are you, youthful herald who always once
    Would waken me at daybreak, where are you, light?
        The heart's awake, but always Night now
            Holds me and binds me with holy magic.

Once towards dawn I'd listen, was glad to wait
    For you upon your hillside, and never in vain!
        Nor ever did your messengers, the
            Breezes, deceive me, for always, dear one,

You came, delighting all, in your loveliness,
    Came down the usual pathway; where are you, light?
        The heart's awake once more, but always
            Infinite Night now constricts me, binds me.

Once green the bowers would beckon to me; the flowers
    Would shine for me, would gleam like my own two eyes;
        Not distant from me were my loved ones'
            Faces and shone for me, up above me

And round the woods I saw, as they travelled on,
    The wings of heaven – then, in the time of youth;
        Now here I sit alone in silence
            Hour after hour and for only comfort

My mind devises shapes for itself, made up
    Of love and grief remembered from brighter days,
        And far I strain my hearing lest a
            Kindly deliverer perhaps is coming.

Dann hör ich oft die Stimme des Donnerers
   Am Mittag, wenn der eherne nahe kommt,
      Wenn ihm das Haus hebt und der Boden
         Unter ihm dröhnt und der Berg es nachhallt.

Den Retter hör' ich dann in der Nacht, ich hör'
   Ihn tödtend, den Befreier, belebend ihn,
      Den Donnerer vom Untergang zum
         Orient eilen und ihm nach tönt ihr,

Ihm nach, ihr meine Saiten! es lebt mit ihm
   Mein Lied und wie die Quelle dem Strome folgt,
      Wohin er denkt, so muß ich fort und
         Folge dem Sicheren auf der Irrbahn.

Wohin? wohin? ich höre dich da und dort
   Du Herrlicher! und rings um die Erde tönts.
      Wo endest du? und was, was ist es
         lJber den Wolken und o wie wird mir?

Tag! Tag! du über stürzenden Wolken! sei
   Willkommen mir! es blühet mein Auge dir.
      O Jugendlicht! o Glük! das alte
         Wieder! doch geistiger rinnst du nieder

Du goldner Quell aus heiligem Kelch! und du,
   Du grüner Boden, friedliche Wieg'! und du,
      Haus meiner Väter! und ihr Lieben,
         Die mir begegneten einst, o nahet,

O kommt, daß euer, euer die Freude sei,
   Ihr alle, daß euch seegne der Sehende!
      O nimmt, daß ichs ertrage, mir das
         Leben, das Göttliche mir vom Herzen.

Then often I can hear the great Thunderer's voice,
　　At noon when he, the brazen one, draws most near,
　　　　When his own house quakes, the foundations
　　　　　　Under him boom and the hill repeats it.

The saviour then I hear in the night, I hear
　　Him kill, the liberator, and give new life,
　　　　From West to East I hear the Thunderer
　　　　　　Quickly sweep on, and it's him you echo,

My strings! With him, with him does my poem live,
　　And as the stream must follow the river's course,
　　　　Where his thought goes I'm drawn, impelled to
　　　　　　Follow the sure one through devious orbits.

Where to? where to? I hear you now here now there,
　　You glorious one! And all round the earth it sounds.
　　　　Where do you end? And what, what is it
　　　　　　Lurks above clouds there, and what befalls me?

Day! Day! Above the tottering clouds, it's you
　　I welcome back! My eyes are in flower for you.
　　　　O light of youth! And joy, the same as
　　　　　　Once! Yet more spiritual now you pour from

A holy chalice, pure golden source! And you,
　　You verdant earth, our cradle of peace, and you,
　　　　Ancestral house, and all you dear ones
　　　　　　Met in the past, O draw near, assemble,

O come that yours, that yours be the joy, return
　　And all receive the seeing man's blessing now!
　　　　O take, that I may bear it, take this
　　　　　　Life, the divine, from my heart too burdened.

Chiron

Wo bist du, Nachdenkliches! das immer muß
    Zur Seite gehn, zu Zeiten, wo bist du, Licht?
        Wohl ist das Herz wach, doch mir zürnt, mich
           Hemmt die erstaunende Nacht nun immer.

Sonst nemlich folgt' ich Kräutern des Walds und lauscht'
    Ein waiches Wild am Hügel; und nie umsonst.
        Nie täuschten, auch nicht einmal deine
           Vögel; denn allzubereit fast kamst du,

So Füllen oder Garten dir labend ward,
    Rathschlagend, Herzens wegen; wo bist du, Licht?
        Das Herz ist wieder wach, doch herzlos
           Zieht die gewaltige Nacht mich immer.

Ich war's wohl. Und von Krokus und Thymian
    Und Korn gab mir die Erde den ersten Straus.
        Und bei der Sterne Kühle lernt' ich,
           Aber das Nennbare nur. Und bei mir

Das wilde Feld entzaubernd, das traur'ge, zog
    Der Halbgott, Zevs Knecht, ein, der gerade Mann;
        Nun siz' ich still allein von einer
           Stunde zur anderen, und Gestalten

Aus frischer Erd' und Wolken der Liebe schafft,
    Weil Gift ist zwischen uns, mein Gedanke nun;
        Und ferne lausch' ich hin, ob nicht ein
           Freundlicher Retter vieleicht mir komme.

Chiron

Where are you, thought-infusing, which at this time
    Must always move beside me, where are you, light?
        Indeed the heart's awake, but, wrathful,
           Always astonishing Night constricts me.

For then I'd look for herbs of the wood, and on
    The hillside hear soft game; and never in vain.
        And never once your birds deceived me,
           Never; but almost too promptly then you

Would come, when foal or garden contented you,
    Advising, for the heart's sake; where are you, light?
        The heart's awake once more, but, heartless,
           Always most powerful Night allures me.

That one was I, it seems. And of crocus, thyme
    And corn then Earth would pick the first bunch for me.
        And in the cool of stars I learned, but
           Only the nameable. Disenchanting

That wild, sad open meadow the demigod,
    Zeus' servant came, the straight man, to lodge with me;
        Now here I sit alone in silence
           Hour after hour, and my mind devises

Shapes for itself – since poison divides us now –
    Made up of love's new earth and the clouds of love;
        And far I strain my hearing lest a
           Kindly deliverer perhaps is coming.

Dann hör' ich oft den Wagen des Donnerers
  Am Mittag, wenn er naht, der bekannteste,
    Wenn ihm das Haus bebt und der Boden
      Reiniget sich, und die Quaal Echo wird.

Den Retter hör' ich dann in der Nacht, ich hör'
  Ihn tödtend, den Befreier, und drunten voll
    Von üpp'gem Kraut, als in Gesichten
      Schau ich die Erd', ein gewaltig Feuer;

Die Tage aber wechseln, wenn einer dann
  Zusiehet denen, lieblich und bös', ein Schmerz,
    Wenn einer zweigestalt ist, und es
      Kennet kein einziger nicht das Beste;

Das aber ist der Stachel des Gottes; nie
  Kann einer lieben göttliches Unrecht sonst.
    Einheimisch aber ist der Gott dann
      Angesichts da, und die Erd' ist anders.

Tag! Tag! Nun wieder athmet ihr recht; nun trinkt,
  Ihr meiner Bäche Weiden! ein Augenlicht,
    Und rechte Stapfen gehn, und als ein
      Herrscher, mit Sporen, und bei dir selber

Örtlich, Irrstern des Tages, erscheinest du,
  Du auch, o Erde, friedliche Wieg', und du,
    Haus meiner Väter, die unstädtisch
      Sind, in den Wolken des Wilds, gegangen.

Nimm nun ein Roß, und harnische dich und nimm
  Den leichten Speer, o Knabe! Die Wahrsagung
    Zerreißt nicht, und umsonst nicht wartet,
      Bis sie erscheinet, Herakles Rükkehr.

Then often I can hear the great Thunderer's voice
  At noon when he, the best-known of all, draws near,
    When his own house quakes, the foundations,
      Shaken, are cleansed and my torment echoes.

The Saviour then I hear in the night, I hear
  Him kill, the liberator, and down below,
    As if in visions, full of luscious
      Weeds I see Earth, a tremendous fire;

But days go by, both lovely and bad, when one
  Observes their changes, suffering pain because
    Of twofold nature, and when none can
      Ever be sure what is best and fittest;

But that's the very sting of the god; and else
  Divine injustice never could claim men's love.
    But native then, at home, the god is
      Visibly present, and Earth is different.

Day! Day! Once more you can breathe, now drink,
  You willows of my streams, an illumined sight,
    And sure, true footsteps go, and as a
      Ruler, with spurs, and located in your

Own orbit you, the planet of day, appear,
  And you, O Earth, our cradle of peace, and you,
    House of my forbears who unurban
      Travelled in clouds with the woodland creatures.

Now take a horse and armour and lastly, boy,
  Take up the slender spear! For the prophecy
    Will not be torn, and not for nothing
      Heracles' promised return awaits it.

Thränen

Himmlische Liebe! zärtliche! wenn ich dein
  Vergäße, wenn ich, o ihr geschiklichen,
    Ihr feur'gen, die voll Asche sind und
      Wüst und vereinsamet ohnediß schon,

Ihr lieben Inseln, Augen der Wunderwelt!
  Ihr nemlich geht nun einzig allein mich an,
    Ihr Ufer, wo die abgöttische
      Büßet, doch Himmlischen nur, die Liebe.

Denn allzudankbar haben die Heiligen
  Gedienet dort in Tagen der Schönheit und
    Die zorn'gen Helden; und viel Bäume
      Sind, und die Städte daselbst gestanden,

Sichtbar, gleich einem sinnigen Mann; izt sind
  Die Helden todt, die Inseln der Liebe sind
    Entstellt fast. So muß übervortheilt,
      Albern doch überall seyn die Liebe.

Ihr waichen Thränen, löschet das Augenlicht
  Mir aber nicht ganz aus; ein Gedächtniß doch,
    Damit ich edel sterbe, laßt ihr
      Trügrischen, Diebischen, mir nachleben.

Tears

O heavenly love, the tender, if you I should
    Forget, if you, the site that a fate has marked,
        The fiery that are full of ash and
            Even before that were wild, deserted,

Dear islands, you, the eyes of the wondrous world!
    Since only you concern me and matter now,
        You banks where the idolatrous, where
            Love, but to heaven alone, does penance.

For too devoutly almost, too gratefully
    In days of beauty there did the holy serve,
        And furious heroes; and no lack of
            Trees, and the cities at one time stood there,

Visible, like a pondering man; now dead
    Those heroes are, the islands of love defaced,
        Disfigured nearly. So for ever
            Love is outwitted, for ever silly.

And yet, soft tears, not utterly now put out
    For me the light of vision; a memory,
        To make my dying noble, still, you
            Thievish, deceitful ones, let outlast me.

An die Hofnung

O Hofnung! holde! gütiggeschäfftige!
    Die du das Haus der Trauernden nicht verschmähst,
        Und gerne dienend, Edle! zwischen
            Sterblichen waltest und Himmelsmächten,

Wo bist du? wenig lebt' ich; doch athmet kalt
    Mein Abend schon. Und stille, den Schatten gleich,
        Bin ich schon hier; und schon gesanglos
            Schlummert das schaudernde Herz im Busen.

Im grünen Thale, dort, wo der frische Quell
    Vom Berge täglich rauscht, und die liebliche
        Zeitlose mir am Herbsttag aufblüht,
            Dort, in der Stille, du Holde, will ich

Dich suchen, oder wenn in der Mitternacht
    Das unsichtbare Leben im Haine wallt,
        Und über mir die immerfrohen
            Blumen, die blühenden Sterne, glänzen,

O du des Aethers Tochter! erscheine dann
    Aus deines Vaters Gärten, und darfst du nicht
        Ein Geist der Erde, kommen, schrök', o
            Schröke mit anderem nur das Herz mir.

To Hope

O hope, benignly active one, dear to men,
    Who do not scorn the house of the sorrowing
        And, noble, love to serve, to fashion
            Links between mortals and heavenly powers,

Where are you? Little yet I have lived; but cold
    My evening breathes. And silent already, like
        The shades, I walk here while within me
            Songless my shuddering heart is drowsing.

That vale so green where down from the mountain purls
    The spring's cool water daily, and now for me
        The lovely autumn crocus opens,
            There in the stillness I'll wait and, dear one,

Look out for you, or when in the rustling grove
    At midnight wild, invisible creatures teem
        And when, above, the ever-joyful
            Blossoms, the flowering stars, are gleaming,

Then come, O Aether's daughter, appear to me
    Out of your father's gardens; and if you may
        Not wear the shape of earthly spirits,
            Frighten my heart with a different aspect.

Vulkan

Jezt komm und hülle, freundlicher Feuergeist,
  Den zarten Sinn der Frauen in Wolken ein,
    In goldne Träum' und schüze sie, die
      Blühende Ruhe der Immerguten.

Dem Manne laß sein Sinnen, und sein Geschäfft,
  Und seiner Kerze Schein, und den künftgen Tag
    Gefallen, laß des Unmuths ihm, der
      Häßlichen Sorge zu viel nicht werden,

Wenn jezt der immerzürnende Boreas,
  Mein Erbfeind, über Nacht mit dem Frost das Land
    Befällt, und spät, zur Schlummerstunde,
      Spottend der Menschen, sein schröklich Lied singt,

Und unsrer Städte Mauren und unsern Zaun,
  Den fleißig wir gesezt, und den stillen Hain
    Zerreißt, und selber im Gesang die
      Seele mir störet, der Allverderber,

Und rastlos tobend über den sanften Strom
  Sein schwarz Gewölk ausschüttet, daß weit umher
    Das Thal gährt, und, wie fallend Laub, vom
      Berstenden Hügel herab der Fels fällt.

Wohl frömmer ist, denn andre Lebendige,
  Der Mensch; doch zürnt es draußen, gehöret der
    Auch eigner sich, und sinnt und ruht in
      Sicherer Hütte, der Freigeborne.

Vulcan

You come now, friendly spirit of fire, and wrap
　　The women's delicate minds in a veil of clouds,
　　　　In golden dreams, and there keep safe the
　　　　　　Blossoming peace of the ever-kindly.

The man leave still content with his pondering,
　　His work, his candle's gleam and the day to come,
　　　　And not too many vexing tangles,
　　　　　　Ugly small cares let impose upon him

When now the ever-raging one, Boreas,
　　My enemy from birth, overnight assails
　　　　The land with frost, and late, past midnight,
　　　　　　Jeering at men, sings his dreadful war-song,

And blasts our city walls and tears down the fence
　　That in long toil we built, and the quiet grove,
　　　　And even interrupts my soul in
　　　　　　Making its music, for all provokes him,

And wild with fury over the gentle stream
　　Pours out his black cloud-bundles, till far and wide
　　　　The valley seethes, like falling foliage
　　　　　　Down come great rocks from the bursting hillside.

More godly, true, than all that shares life with him
　　Is Man. Yet, faced with fury outside, he too
　　　　Is more himself and rests and ponders
　　　　　　Safe in his cottage, the free-born mortal.

Und immer wohnt der freundlichen Genien
   Noch Einer gerne seegnend mit ihm, und wenn
      Sie zürnten all', die ungelehrgen
         Geniuskräfte, doch liebt die Liebe.

And one at least, one spirit friendly to Man,
    Still, blessing, gladly dwells with him there, and though
        All others, fierce untutored spirit
            Powers, were to rage, yet will Love be loving.

Dichtermuth

Erste Fassung

Sind denn dir nicht verwandt alle Lebendigen?
  Nährt zum Dienste denn nicht selber die Parze dich?
    Drum! so wandle nur wehrlos
      Fort durch's Leben und sorge nicht!

Was geschiehet, es sei alles geseegnet dir,
  Sei zur Freude gewandt! oder was könnte denn
    Dich belaidigen, Herz! was
      Da begegnen, wohin du sollst?

Denn, wie still am Gestad, oder in silberner
  Fernhintönender Fluth, oder auf schweigenden
    Wassertiefen der leichte
      Schwimmer wandelt, so sind auch wir,

Wir, die Dichter des Volks, gerne, wo Lebendes
  Um uns athmet und wallt, freudig, und jedem hold,
    Jedem trauend; wie sängen
      Sonst wir jedem den eignen Gott?

Wenn die Wooge denn auch einen der Muthigen,
  Wo er treulich getraut, schmeichlend hinunterzieht,
    Und die Stimme des Sängers
      Nun in blauender Halle schweigt;

Freudig starb er und noch klagen die Einsamen,
  Seine Haine, den Fall ihres Geliebtesten;
    Öfters tönet der Jungfrau
      Vom Gezweige sein freundlich Lied.

The Poet's Courage

First Version

Is not all that's alive close and akin to you,
    Does the Fate not herself keep you to serve her ends?
        Well, then, travel defenceless
            On through life, and fear nothing there!

All that happens there be welcome, be blessed to you,
    Be an adept in joy, or is there anything
        That could harm you there, heart, that
            Could offend you, where you must go?

For, as quiet near shores, or in the silvery
    Flood resounding afar, or over silent deep
        Water travels the flimsy
            Swimmer, likewise we love to be

Where around us there breathe, teem those alive, our kin,
    We, their poets; and glad, friendly to every man,
        Trusting all. And how else for
            Each of them could we sing his god?

Though the wave will at times, flattering, drag below
    One such brave man where, true, trusting he makes his way,
        And the voice of that singer
            Now falls mute as the hall turns blue;

Glad he died there, and still lonely his groves lament
    Him whom most they had loved, lost, though with joy he drowned;
        Often a virgin will bear his
            Kindly song in the distant boughs.

Wenn des Abends vorbei Einer der Unsern kömmt,
   Wo der Bruder ihm sank, denket er manches wohl
     An der warnenden Stelle,
       Schweigt und gehet gerüsteter.

When at nightfall a man like him, of our kind, comes
    Past the place where he sank, many a thought he'll give
        To the site and the warning,
            Then in silence, more armed, walk on.

Blödigkeit

Sind denn dir nicht bekannt viele Lebendigen?
    Geht auf Wahrem dein Fuß nicht, wie auf Teppichen?
        Drum, mein Genius! tritt nur
            Baar in's Leben, und sorge nicht!

Was geschiehet, es sei alles gelegen dir!
    Sei zur Freude gereimt, oder was könnte denn
        Dich belaidigen, Herz, was
            Da begegnen, wohin du sollst?

Denn, seit Himmlischen gleich Menschen, ein einsam Wild
    Und die Himmlischen selbst führet, der Einkehr zu,
        Der Gesang und der Fürsten
            Chor, nach Arten, so waren auch

Wir, die Zungen des Volks, gerne bei Lebenden,
    Wo sich vieles gesellt, freudig und jedem gleich,
        Jedem offen, so ist ja
            Unser Vater, des Himmels Gott,

Der den denkenden Tag Armen und Reichen gönnt,
    Der, zur Wende der Zeit, uns die Entschlafenden
        Aufgerichtet an goldnen
            Gängelbanden, wie Kinder, hält.

Gut auch sind und geschikt einem zu etwas wir,
    Wenn wir kommen, mit Kunst, und von den Himmlischen
        Einen bringen. Doch selber
            Bringen schikliche Hände wir.

Timidness

Of the living are not many well-known to you?
    On the truth don't your feet walk as they would on rugs?
        Boldly, therefore, my genius,
            Step right into the thick of life!

All that happens there be welcome, a boon to you!
    Be disposed to feel joy, or is there anything
        That could harm you there, heart, that
            Could affront you, where you must go?

For since gods grew like men, lonely as woodland beasts,
    And since, each in its way, song and the princely choir
        Brought the Heavenly in person
            Back to earth, so we too, the tongues

Of the people, have liked living men's company,
    Where all kinds are conjoined, equal and open to
        Everyone, full of joy – for
            So our Father is, Heaven's God,

Who to rich men and poor offers the thinking day,
    At the turning of Time holds us, the sleepy ones,
        Upright still with his golden
            Leading-strings, as one holds a child.

Someone, some way, we too serve, are of use, are sent
    When we come, with our art, and of the heavenly powers
        Bring one with us. But fitting,
            Skilful hands we ourselves provide.

Der gefesselte Strom

Was schläfst und träumst du, Jüngling, gehüllt in dich,
   Und säumst am kalten Ufer, Geduldiger,
      Und achtest nicht des Ursprungs, du, des
         Oceans Sohn, des Titanenfreundes!

Die Liebesboten, welche der Vater schikt,
   Kennst du die lebenathmenden Lüfte nicht?
      Und trift das Wort dich nicht, das hell von
         Oben der wachende Gott dir sendet?

Schon tönt, schon tönt es ihm in der Brust, es quillt,
   Wie, da er noch im Schoose der Felsen spielt',
      Ihm auf, und nun gedenkt er seiner
         Kraft, der Gewaltige, nun, nun eilt er,

Der Zauderer, er spottet der Fesseln nun,
   Und nimmt und bricht und wirft die Zerbrochenen
      Im Zorne, spielend, da und dort zum
         Schallenden Ufer und an der Stimme

Des Göttersohns erwachen die Berge rings,
   Es regen sich die Wälder, es hört die Kluft
      Den Herold fern und schaudernd regt im
         Busen der Erde sich Freude wieder.

Der Frühling kommt; es dämmert das neue Grün;
   Er aber wandelt hin zu Unsterblichen;
      Denn nirgend darf er bleiben, als wo
         Ihn in die Arme der Vater aufnimmt.

The Fettered River

Why do you sleep and dream, in yourself wrapped up,
　　And by the cold bank linger, too patient youth,
　　　　And do not heed your origin, you
　　　　　　Son of great Ocean, the friend of Titans!

Those messengers of love whom your father sends,
　　Do you not know those winds breathing life at you?
　　　　Does not that word strike home which, bright, the
　　　　　　Vigilant god from above dispatches?

Yet now, already now it resounds in him,
　　Wells up for him as when in the lap of rocks
　　　　He played, and he recalls his strength, the
　　　　　　Power of his youth now, and now he hurries,

The loiterer, and laughs at his fetters now
　　And takes and tears and throws the torn fetters down
　　　　In fury, playing, here and there on
　　　　　　Banks that re-echo, and at the voice of

That son of gods the mountains all round awake,
　　The woods begin to stir, the ravine can hear
　　　　The distant herald, roused within the
　　　　　　Bosom of Earth with a shudder joy stirs.

Spring comes; new verdure glistens, a dawn of leaves;
　　But he far off departs, to immortal kin;
　　　　For nowhere he may rest, but where the
　　　　　　Arms of his father once more receive him.

Ganymed

Was schläfst du, Bergsohn, liegest in Unmuth, schief,
  Und frierst am kahlen Ufer, Gedultiger!
    Denkst nicht der Gnade du, wenn's an den
      Tischen die Himmlischen sonst gedürstet?

Kennst drunten du vom Vater die Boten nicht,
  Nicht in der Kluft der Lüfte geschärfter Spiel?
    Trift nicht das Wort dich, das voll alten
      Geists ein gewanderter Mann dir sendet?

Schon tönet's aber ihm in der Brust. Tief quillt's,
  Wie damals, als hoch oben im Fels er schlief,
    Ihm auf. Im Zorne reinigt aber
      Sich der Gefesselte nun, nun eilt er

Der Linkische; der spottet der Schlaken nun,
  Und nimmt und bricht und wirft die Zerbrochenen
    Zorntrunken, spielend, dort und da zum
      Schauenden Ufer und bei des Fremdlings

Besondrer Stimme stehen die Heerden auf,
  Es regen sich die Wälder, es hört tief Land
    Den Stromgeist fern, und schaudernd regt im
      Nabel der Erde der Geist sich wieder.

Der Frühling kömmt. Und jedes, in seiner Art,
  Blüht. Der ist aber ferne; nicht mehr dabei.
    Irr gieng er nun; denn allzugut sind
      Genien; himmlisch Gespräch ist sein nun.

Ganymede

Why do you sleep, lie crooked, ill-humoured here,
    And freeze on banks all bare, you the mountains' son?
        Too patient, do not think of grace, when
            Once there was thirst at the heavenly tables?

Nor know your father's messengers now, down there,
    In the ravine the breezes' more whetted play?
        Does not that word strike home which now a
            Travelled man sends you, its ancient meaning?

But now it sounds in him, as deeply wells up
    As when before high up on the rock he slept.
        And in his anger now the fettered
            Cleanses himself, and now he hurries,

The clumsy one; he laughs at his fetters now,
    And takes and tears and throws the torn fetters down,
        Wrath-drunken, playing, here and there on
            Banks that observe him, and at the stranger's

Peculiar voice, the herds that were resting rise,
    The woods awake, far down all the land can hear
        The river-god, and roused within the
            Navel of Earth now the spirit shivers.

Spring comes. And everything, in its way and kind,
    Blossoms. But he's far off; is no longer there.
        Has gone astray; for all too good are
            Genii; heavenly talk is his now.

Hexameters and Elegies
(1800–1801)

Der Archipelagus

Kehren die Kraniche wieder zu dir, und suchen zu deinen
Ufern wieder die Schiffe den Lauf? umathmen erwünschte
Lüfte dir die beruhigte Fluth, und sonnet der Delphin,
Aus der Tiefe gelokt, am neuen Lichte den Rüken?
Blüht Ionien? ists die Zeit? denn immer im Frühling,
Wenn den Lebenden sich das Herz erneut und die erste
Liebe den Menschen erwacht und goldner Zeiten Erinnrung,
Komm' ich zu dir und grüß' in deiner Stille dich, Alter!

Immer, Gewaltiger! lebst du noch und ruhest im Schatten
Deiner Berge, wie sonst; mit Jünglingsarmen umfängst du
Noch dein liebliches Land, und deiner Töchter, o Vater!
Deiner Inseln ist noch, der blühenden, keine verloren.
Kreta steht und Salamis grünt, umdämmert von Lorbeern,
Rings von Stralen umblüht, erhebt zur Stunde des Aufgangs
Delos ihr begeistertes Haupt, und Tenos und Chios
Haben der purpurnen Früchte genug, von trunkenen Hügeln
Quillt der Cypriertrank, und von Kalauria fallen
Silberne Bäche, wie einst, in die alten Wasser des Vaters.
Alle leben sie noch, die Heroënmütter, die Inseln,
Blühend von Jahr zu Jahr, und wenn zu Zeiten, vom Abgrund
Losgelassen, die Flamme der Nacht, das untre Gewitter,
Eine der holden ergriff, und die Sterbende dir in den Schoos sank,
Göttlicher! du, du dauertest aus, denn über den dunkeln
Tiefen ist manches schon dir auf und untergegangen.

Auch die Himmlischen, sie, die Kräfte der Höhe, die stillen,
Die den heiteren Tag und süßen Schlummer und Ahnung
Fernher bringen über das Haupt der fühlenden Menschen
Aus der Fülle der Macht, auch sie, die alten Gespielen,

The Archipelago

Are the cranes returning to you, and the mercantile vessels
Making again for your shores? Do breezes longed for and prayed for
Blow for you round the quieter flood and, lured from beneath it,
Does the dolphin now warm his back in a new year's gathering radiance?
Is Ionia in flower? Is it the season? For always in springtime
When the hearts of the living renew themselves, the first love of
Human kind, reawakened, stirs and the golden age is remembered,
You, old Sea-God, I visit and you I greet in your stillness.

Even now you live on and, mighty as ever, untroubled
Rest in the shade of your mountains; with arms ever youthful
Still embrace your beautiful land, and still of your daughters, O Father,
Of your islands, the flowering, not one has been taken.
Crete remains, and Salamis lies in a dark-green twilight of laurels,
In a ring of blossoming beams even now at the hour of sunrise
Delos lifts her ecstatic head, and Tenos and Chios
Still have plenty of purple fruit, and the Cyprian liquor
Gushes from drunken hillsides while from Calauria the silver
Brooks cascade, as before, into the Father's old vastness.
Every one of them lives, those mothers of heroes, the islands,
Flowering year after year, and if at times the subterranean
Thunder, the flame of Night, let loose from the primal abysses,
Seized on one of the dear isles and, dying, she sank in your waters,
You, divine one, endured, for much already has risen,
Much gone down for you here above your deeper foundations.

And the heavenly, too, the powers up above us, the silent,
Who from afar bring the cloudless day, delicious sleep and forebodings
Down to the heads of sentient mortals, bestowing
Gifts in their fullness and might, they too, your playmates as ever,

Wohnen, wie einst, mit dir, und oft am dämmernden Abend,
Wenn von Asiens Bergen herein das heilige Mondlicht
Kömmt und die Sterne sich in deiner Wooge begegnen,
Leuchtest du von himmlischem Glanz, und so, wie sie wandeln,
Wechseln die Wasser dir, es tönt die Weise der Brüder
Droben, ihr Nachtgesang, im liebenden Busen dir wieder.
Wenn die allverklärende dann, die Sonne des Tages,
Sie, des Orients Kind, die Wunderthätige, da ist,
Dann die Lebenden all' im goldenen Traume beginnen,
Den die Dichtende stets des Morgens ihnen bereitet,
Dir, dem trauernden Gott, dir sendet sie froheren Zauber,
Und ihr eigen freundliches Licht ist selber so schön nicht
Denn das Liebeszeichen, der Kranz, den immer, wie vormals,
Deiner gedenk, doch sie um die graue Loke dir windet.
Und umfängt der Aether dich nicht, und kehren die Wolken,
Deine Boten, von ihm mit dem Göttergeschenke, dem Strale
Aus der Höhe dir nicht? dann sendest du über das Land sie,
Daß am heißen Gestad die gewittertrunkenen Wälder
Rauschen und woogen mit dir, daß bald, dem wandernden Sohn gleich,
Wenn der Vater ihn ruft, mit den tausend Bächen Mäander
Seinen Irren enteilt und aus der Ebne Kayster
Dir entgegenfrohlokt, und der Erstgeborne, der Alte,
Der zu lange sich barg, dein majestätischer Nil izt
Hochherschreitend aus fernem Gebirg, wie im Klange der Waffen,
Siegreich kömmt, und die offenen Arme der sehnende reichet.

Dennoch einsam dünkest du dir; in schweigender Nacht hört
Deine Weheklage der Fels, und öfters entflieht dir
Zürnend von Sterblichen weg die geflügelte Wooge zum Himmel.
Denn es leben mit dir die edlen Lieblinge nimmer,
Die dich geehrt, die einst mit den schönen Tempeln und Städten
Deine Gestade bekränzt, und immer suchen und missen,
Immer bedürfen ja, wie Heroën den Kranz, die geweihten
Elemente zum Ruhme das Herz der fühlenden Menschen.

Dwell with you as before, and often in evening's glimmer
When from Asia's mountains the holy moonlight comes drifting
In and the stars commingle and meet in your billows,
With a heavenly brightness you shine, and just as they circle
So do your waters turn, and the theme of your brothers, their night song
Vibrant up there, re-echoes lovingly here in your bosom.
When the all-transfiguring, then, she, the child of the Orient,
Miracle-worker, the sun of our day-time, is present,
All that's alive in a golden dream recommences,
Golden dream the poetic one grants us anew every morning,
Then to you, the sorrowing god, she will send a still gladder enchantment,
And her own beneficent light is not equal in beauty
To the token of love, the wreath, which even now and as ever
Mindful of you, she winds round your locks that are greying.
Does not Aether enfold you, too, and your heralds, the clouds, do
They not return to you with his gift, the divine, with the rays that
Come from above? And then you scatter them over the country
So that drunken with thunder-storms woods on the sweltering coastline
Heave and roar as you do, and soon like a boy playing truant,
Hearing his father call out, with his thousand sources Meander
Hurries back from his wanderings and from his lowlands Cayster
Cheering rushes towards you, and even the first-born, that old one
Who too long lay hidden, your Nile, the imperious, majestic,
Haughtily striding down from the distant peaks, as though armed with
Clanging weapons, victorious arrives, and longs to enfold you.

Yet you think yourself lonely; at night in the silence the rock hears
Your repeated lament, and often, winged in their anger,
Up to heaven away from mortals your waves will escape you.
For no longer they live beside you, these noble beloved ones
Who revered you, who once with beautiful temples and cities
Wreathed your shores; and always they seek it and miss it,
Always, as heroes need garlands, the hallowed elements likewise
Need the hearts of us men to feel and to mirror their glory.

Sage, wo ist Athen? ist über den Urnen der Meister
Deine Stadt, die geliebteste dir, an den heiligen Ufern,
Trauernder Gott! dir ganz in Asche zusammengesunken,
Oder ist noch ein Zeichen von ihr, daß etwa der Schiffer,
Wenn er vorüberkommt, sie nenn' und ihrer gedenke?
Stiegen dort die Säulen empor und leuchteten dort nicht
Sonst vom Dache der Burg herab die Göttergestalten?
Rauschte dort die Stimme des Volks, die stürmischbewegte,
Aus der Agora nicht her, und eilten aus freudigen Pforten
Dort die Gassen dir nicht zu geseegnetem Hafen herunter?
Siehe! da löste sein Schiff der fernhinsinnende Kaufmann,
Froh, denn es wehet' auch ihm die beflügelnde Luft und die Götter
Liebten so, wie den Dichter, auch ihn, dieweil er die guten
Gaahen der Erd' ausglich und Fernes Nahem vereinte.
Fern nach Cypros ziehet er hin und ferne nach Tyros,
Strebt nach Kolchis hinauf und hinab zum alten Aegyptos,
Daß er Purpur und Wein und Korn und Vließe gewinne
Für die eigene Stadt, und öfters über des kühnen
Herkules Säulen hinaus, zu neuen seeligen Inseln
Tragen die Hoffnungen ihn und des Schiffes Flügel, indessen
Anders bewegt, am Gestade der Stadt ein einsamer Jüngling
Weilt und die Wooge belauscht, und Großes ahndet der Ernste,
Wenn er zu Füßen so des erderschütternden Meisters
Lauschet und sizt, und nicht umsonst erzog ihn der Meergott.

Denn des Genius Feind, der vielgebietende Perse,
Jahrlang zählt' er sie schon, der Waffen Menge, der Knechte,
Spottend des griechischen Lands und seiner wenigen Inseln,
Und sie deuchten dem Herrscher ein Spiel, und noch, wie ein Traum, war
Ihm das innige Volk, vom Göttergeiste gerüstet.
Leicht aus spricht er das Wort und schnell, wie der flammende Bergquell,
Wenn er furchtbar umher vom gährenden Aetna gegossen,
Städte begräbt in der purpurnen Fluth und blühende Gärten,
Bis der brennende Strom im heiligen Meere sich kühlet,

Tell me, where now is Athens? Over the urns of the masters
Here, on your shores, on the holy, sorrowing god, has your city
Dearest of all to you perished, utterly crumbled to ashes,
Or does a token, a trace remain, just so much that a sailor
Passing by will mention her name, will notice the site and recall her?
There did not columns rise high, and there on the citadel roof-top
Did not shining figures of gods once gaze down at the people?
And the voice of the people, did it not roar like a wind-lashed
Forest from the Agora, and there, to a prosperous harbour
From the joyful gates did the streets not come hurrying down to meet you?
Look, the distantly scheming merchant unmoored his good ship there,
Glad, since the winged breeze blew for his sake no less and him also,
Like their poets, the gods could love for his service in sharing
Out the good gifts of Earth and linking far countries to near ones.
Far away to Cyprus he sails and still farther to Tyros,
Makes his way up to Colchis and down to the ancient Aegyptos,
Bringing the purple dye and the wine and the corn and the fleeces
Back to his native town and even at times well beyond the
Pillars of daring Hercules, to the new, to the fortunate islands
Widely ranging hope and his vessel's taut wings will convey him,
While, quite differently moved, a lonely young man on the shore will
Long sit listening, and much that's great from the waves he will gather
Sitting there at the feet of him, the world-battering master,
Listening to waves; and not in vain was he reared by the Sea-God.

For the foe of genius, the vastly, far-governing Persian,
Now for years has been counting the strength of his weapons and soldiers,
Laughing at Greece, full of scorn at her handful of minuscule islands,
Less than a trifle to him, and still like a dream to that ruler
Seemed the fervent people of Greece, the divinely defended.
Lightly he speaks the command and fast as the flames of the torrent
Horribly spurted and poured from Etna's ebullient crater
Buries towns in its purple flood, and blossoming gardens,
Till the glowing effusion cools in the holy sea's waters —

So mit dem Könige nun, versengend, städteverwüstend,
Stürzt von Ekbatana daher sein prächtig Getümmel;
Weh! und Athene, die herrliche, fällt; wohl schauen und ringen
Vom Gebirg, wo das Wild ihr Geschrei hört, fliehende Greise
Nach den Wohnungen dort zurük und den rauchenden Tempeln;
Aber es wekt der Söhne Gebet die heilige Asche
Nun nicht mehr, im Thal ist der Tod, und die Wolke des Brandes
Schwindet am Himmel dahin, und weiter im Lande zu erndten,
Zieht, vom Frevel erhizt, mit der Beute der Perse vorüber.

　　Aber an Salamis Ufern, o Tag an Salamis Ufern!
Harrend des Endes stehn die Athenerinnen, die Jungfraun,
Stehn die Mütter, wiegend im Arm das gerettete Söhnlein,
Aber den Horchenden schallt von Tiefen die Stimme des Meergotts
Heilweissagend herauf, es schauen die Götter des Himmels
Wägend und richtend herab, denn dort an den bebenden Ufern
Wankt seit Tagesbeginn, wie langsamwandelnd Gewitter,
Dort auf schäumenden Wassern die Schlacht, und es glühet der Mittag,
Unbemerket im Zorn, schon über dem Haupte den Kämpfern.
Aber die Männer des Volks, die Heroënenkel, sie walten
Helleren Auges jezt, die Götterlieblinge denken
Des beschiedenen Glüks, es zähmen die Kinder Athenes
Ihren Genius, ihn, den todverachtenden, jezt nicht.
Denn wie aus rauchendem Blut das Wild der Wüste noch einmal
Sich zulezt verwandelt erhebt, der edleren Kraft gleich,
Und den Jäger erschrökt; kehrt jezt im Glanze der Waffen,
Bei der Herrscher Gebot, furchtbargesammelt den Wilden,
Mitten im Untergang die ermattete Seele noch einmal.
Und entbrandter beginnts; wie Paare ringender Männer
Fassen die Schiffe sich an, in die Wooge taumelt das Steuer,
Unter den Streitern bricht der Boden, und Schiffer und Schiff sinkt.

　　Aber in schwindelnden Traum vom Liede des Tages gesungen,
Rollt der König den Blik; irrlächelnd über den Ausgang

So with that King now: a fire destroying, devouring the cities,
Down from Ekbatana his gaudily flashing wild hordes rush;
Oh, and glorious Athene falls; though high up in their mountain
Refuge where animals hear their outcry, old men do their utmost
Even now to press back to their dwellings and smouldering temples,
Yet no prayer of their sons will awaken those ashes, the holy,
Now that death is let loose in the valley, the cloud of destruction
Drifts away in the sky, and whetted by one crime the Persian
Passes by with his booty and on to more plentiful harvest.

But by the shores of Salamis – O day by the shores of Salamis! –
Waiting there for the end, the Athenian virgins and mothers
Stand and rock in their arms small daughters and sons who were rescued;
As they strain their ears, from the depths now the voice of the Sea-God
Rises, predicting salvation; weighing and judging, the eyes of
Heaven's gods now gaze down, for there by the shores which repeated
Tremors rock, on the waves all foaming, like slow-moving thunder
Ever since dawn a battle has hung in the balance, and noon now
Glows on the combatants' heads, unnoticed by them in their fury.
But the Grecian men, the grandsons of heroes, with brighter
Eyes give battle now; beloved of the gods, they grow mindful
Of the triumph allotted to them; and no longer Athene's
Children suppress their genius, the reckless and death-deprecating.
As, in the end, from its steaming blood the wild beast of the desert
Rises once more, transformed, restored to his prowess, his pride, and
Startling the huntsman, turns; so now, with their weapons aglitter,
At their rulers' command, to the terribly straining, ferocious,
In the midst of defeat their once flagging spirit returns now.
And the battle flares up, like pairs of interlocked wrestlers
Triremes engage and grapple, the rudder's ripped off and adrift the
Floating battlefield cracks, and down go both trireme and sailors.

Yet lulled off into dizzying dream by the song which that day crooned,
Now the King rolls his eyes; and, smiling askew at the outcome,

Droht er, und fleht, und frohlokt, und sendet, wie Blize, die Boten.
Doch er sendet umsonst, es kehret keiner ihm wieder.
Blutige Boten, Erschlagne des Heers, und berstende Schiffe,
Wirft die Rächerin ihm zahllos, die donnernde Wooge,
Vor den Thron, wo er sizt am bebenden Ufer, der Arme,
Schauend die Flucht, und fort in die fliehende Menge gerissen,
Eilt er, ihn treibt der Gott, es treibt sein irrend Geschwader
Über die Fluthen der Gott, der spottend sein eitel Geschmeid ihm
Endlich zerschlug und den Schwachen erreicht' in der drohenden Rüstung.

Aber liebend zurük zum einsamharrenden Strome
Kommt der Athener Volk und von den Bergen der Heimath
Woogen, freudig gemischt, die glänzenden Schaaren herunter
Ins verlassene Thal, ach! gleich der gealterten Mutter,
Wenn nach Jahren das Kind, das verlorengeachtete, wieder
Lebend ihr an die Brüste kehrt, ein erwachsener Jüngling,
Aber im Gram ist ihr die Seele gewelkt und die Freude
Kommt der hoffnungsmüden zu spät und mühsam vernimmt sie,
Was der liebende Sohn in seinem Danke geredet;
So erscheint den Kommenden dort der Boden der Heimath.
Denn es fragen umsonst nach ihren Hainen die Frommen,
Und die Sieger empfängt die freundliche Pforte nicht wieder,
Wie den Wanderer sonst sie empfieng, wenn er froh von den Inseln
Wiederkehrt' und die seelige Burg der Mutter Athene
Über sehnendem Haupt ihm fernherglänzend heraufgieng.
Aber wohl sind ihnen bekannt die verödeten Gassen
Und die trauernden Gärten umher und auf der Agora,
Wo des Portikus Säulen gestürzt und die göttlichen Bilder
Liegen, da reicht in der Seele bewegt, und der Treue sich freuend,
Jezt das liebende Volk zum Bunde die Hände sich wieder.
Bald auch suchet und sieht den Ort des eigenen Haußes
Unter dem Schutt der Mann; ihm weint am Halse, der trauten
Schlummerstäte gedenk, sein Weib, es fragen die Kindlein
Nach dem Tische, wo sonst in lieblicher Reihe sie saßen,

Threatens, beseeches, exults and sends away runners like lightning.
But he sends them in vain: not one will return with a message.
Runners all covered in blood, and corpses of soldiers and wrecks of
Ships that have split, the thundering wave, the avenger,
Hurls at the poor man's throne where quaking he sits on the shore and
Watches his hordes in retreat; till, himself swept up by the fleeing,
Off he hurries, spurred on by the god, his squadrons all scattered
Driven to sea by the god, who, laughing at last at the weakling,
Smashed his vain baubles and reached him under his threatening armour.

But now lovingly back to the river that, lonely, awaits them
Come the Athenians, and down from their homeland's neighbourly mountains,
Joyfully mingled, they surge, a colourful, shining procession
Into the desolate valley – but oh, like a time-ravaged mother
When the child long ago given up for lost after years comes
Back alive to her breast, no child but a fully grown youth now,
But with grieving her soul has withered, and joy comes too late for
Her, exhausted with hoping, and hardly she hears and can follow
What her loving son in gratitude hastens to tell her;
So to the people come back now seemed the old soil of their homeland.
For in vain after grove and garden the pious enquire now
And no friendly old door is waiting to welcome the victors
As it used to do once when, happy, a man voyaged homeward
From the islands and, blessed, the fortress of Mother Athene,
Distantly gleaming, appeared to eyes uplifted in longing.
Yet familiar enough, though stripped and deserted, the streets are,
All the gardens that mourn within and beyond the Agora,
Where the portico's pillars and limbs of the gods lie in pieces,
There, stirred up in their souls and rejoicing in faith, now the people
Lovingly link their hands in token of newly pledged union.
Soon the man, too, will seek and find the old site of his dwelling
Under the rubble; his wife, recalling the look of their bedroom,
Weeps and embraces him; the children excitedly ask him
For the table at which they'd sit in a circle at mealtimes

Von den Vätern gesehn, den lächelnden Göttern des Haußes.
Aber Gezelte bauet das Volk, es schließen die alten
Nachbarn wieder sich an, und nach des Herzens Gewohnheit
Ordnen die luftigen Wohnungen sich umher an den Hügeln.
So indessen wohnen sie nun, wie die Freien, die Alten,
Die, der Stärke gewiß und dem kommenden Tage vertrauend,
Wandernden Vögeln gleich, mit Gesange von Berge zu Berg' einst
Zogen, die Fürsten des Forsts und des weitumirrenden Stromes.
Doch umfängt noch, wie sonst, die Muttererde, die treue,
Wieder ihr edel Volk, und unter heiligem Himmel
Ruhen sie sanft, wenn milde, wie sonst, die Lüfte der Jugend
Um die Schlafenden wehn, und aus Platanen Ilissus
Ihnen herüberrauscht, und neue Tage verkündend,
Lokend zu neuen Thaten, bei Nacht die Wooge des Meergotts
Fernher tönt und fröhliche Träume den Lieblingen sendet.
Schon auch sprossen und blühn die Blumen mälig, die goldnen,
Auf zertretenem Feld, von frommen Händen gewartet,
Grünet der Ölbaum auf, und auf Kolonos Gefilden
Nähren friedlich, wie sonst, die Athenischen Rosse sich wieder.

Aber der Muttererd' und dem Gott der Wooge zu Ehren
Blühet die Stadt izt auf, ein herrlich Gebild, dem Gestirn gleich
Sichergegründet, des Genius Werk, denn Fesseln der Liebe
Schafft er gerne sich so, so hält in großen Gestalten,
Die er selbst sich erbaut, der immerrege sich bleibend.
Sieh! und dem Schaffenden dienet der Wald, ihm reicht mit den andern
Bergen nahe zur Hand der Pentele Marmor und Erze,
Aber lebend, wie er, und froh und herrlich entquillt es
Seinen Händen, und leicht, wie der Sonne, gedeiht das Geschäfft ihm.
Brunnen steigen empor und über die Hügel in reinen
Bahnen gelenkt, ereilt der Quell das glänzende Beken;
Und umher an ihnen erglänzt, gleich festlichen Helden
Am gemeinsamen Kelch, die Reihe der Wohnungen, hoch ragt
Der Prytanen Gemach, es stehn Gymnasien offen,

Watched by ancestors, by benevolent gods of the household.
But the people raise tents, and neighbours renew their old friendships,
Choosing familiar sites, and true to the heart and its habits
Airy new habitations fall into place on the hillsides.
Meanwhile, however, they live as did their forefathers, the free ones,
Who, assured of their strength and trusting the day and its morrow
As do migrant birds, from mountain to mountain once travelled
Singing, the princes of woods and of far-meandering rivers.
Yet their maternal earth, the faithful, as ever enfolds her
Noble people once more, and under a heaven still holy
Gently they sleep, while mild as ever the breezes of youth blow
Over each sleeping head, and out of the plane trees Ilissus,
Murmuring, makes himself known and nightly the wave of the Sea-God,
Which, predicting new days, to new deeds lures them on and inspires them,
Sounds from afar and grants enlivening dreams to his loved ones.
And already their crops, the golden, spring up and burst into flower
In the trampled fields, and piously, patiently tended,
Olive trees are in leaf, and once again at Colonus
In their old pasture, at peace, Athenian horses are grazing.

But to please the maternal earth and honour the god of the waters
Now the city revives, a glorious artifice, firmly
Founded as galaxies, wrought by genius that readily thus will
Make himself fetters of love, and thus in majestic constructions,
Raised for his restless self, maintains a durable dwelling.
Look, and the forest serves that creator; Pentele, like other
Mountains near by, provides rich ores and offers him marble,
But alive as he is, and glad and splendid it seems to
Leap from his hands, and his work seems easily done, like the sun's work.
Fountains rise from the ground, and over the hills in pure conduits
Quickly the spring is conveyed and rushes to fill the bright basin;
Round about them, bright, as heroes dressed up for a banquet
Gleam round the communal cup, a circle of houses; above it
Looms the Prytanean hall, and now the gymnasia are open.

Göttertempel entstehn, ein heiligkühner Gedanke
Steigt, Unsterblichen nah, das Olympion auf in den Aether
Aus dem seeligen Hain; noch manche der himmlischen Hallen!
Mutter Athene, dir auch, dir wuchs dein herrlicher Hügel
Stolzer aus der Trauer empor und blühte noch lange,
Gott der Woogen und dir, und deine Lieblinge sangen
Frohversammelt noch oft am Vorgebirge den Dank dir.

O die Kinder des Glüks, die frommen! wandeln sie fern nun
Bei den Vätern daheim, und der Schiksaalstage vergessen,
Drüben am Lethestrom, und bringt kein Sehnen sie wieder?
Sieht mein Auge sie nie? ach! findet über den tausend
Pfaden der grünenden Erd', ihr göttergleichen Gestalten!
Euch das Suchende nie, und vernahm ich darum die Sprache,
Darum die Sage von euch, daß immertrauernd die Seele
Vor der Zeit mir hinab zu euern Schatten entfliehe?
Aber näher zu euch, wo eure Haine noch wachsen,
Wo sein einsames Haupt in Wolken der heilige Berg hüllt,
Zum Parnassos will ich, und wenn im Dunkel der Eiche
Schimmernd, mir Irrenden dort Kastalias Quelle begegnet,
Will ich, mit Thränen gemischt, aus blüthenumdufteter Schaale
Dort, auf keimendes Grün, das Wasser gießen, damit doch,
O ihr Schlafenden all! ein Todtenopfer euch werde.
Dort im schweigenden Thal, an Tempes hangenden Felsen,
Will ich wohnen mit euch, dort oft, ihr herrlichen Nahmen!
Her euch rufen bei Nacht, und wenn ihr zürnend erscheinet,
Weil der Pflug die Gräber entweiht, mit der Stimme des Herzens
Will ich, mit frommem Gesang euch sühnen, heilige Schatten!
Bis zu leben mit euch, sich ganz die Seele gewöhnet.
Fragen wird der Geweihtere dann euch manches, ihr Todten!
Euch, ihr Lebenden auch, ihr hohen Kräfte des Himmels,
Wenn ihr über dem Schutt mit euren Jahren vorbeigeht,
Ihr in der sicheren Bahn! denn oft ergreiffet das Irrsaal
Unter den Sternen mir, wie schaurige Lüfte, den Busen,

Temples are built for the gods and, near to immortals, a thought as
Holy as it is bold, the Olympion rises to Aether
From the sacred grove; still many a heavenly hall rose,
Mother Athene, for you; and prouder your glorious hill rose
From its affliction, and long it flourished there, also for your sake,
God of the waters, yours too, and happily gathered your loved ones
Often yet would intone their paean to you on the foothills.

   O the children of bliss, the godly, far off are they walking
With their ancestors now, at home, on the far side of Lethe,
Fate's own days quite forgotten? And never will yearning recall them?
Shall my eyes never see them? Nor yet, though he tries all the thousand
Paths of the greening earth, the seeker his life long discover
You, most godlike of men? And was it for this that I heard your
Language, your legend, that now for ever saddened my soul should
Flee me before it is time, drawn down to your shadowy regions?
Yet more close to you rather, where still your orchards are growing,
Where the holy mountain's lone head lies cloud-veiled as ever,
To Parnassus I'll go, and when there in the darkness of oak trees,
Gleaming, Castalia's spring appears to me, aimlessly roving,
Then, mixed with tears, from the cup that blossoms make fragrant
Water I'll pour on a site all green again now and all budding,
One libation at least for you sleepers who will not awaken.
There in the valley now hushed, where Tempe's great rocks hang suspended,
I will live with you all and often invoke you, the glorious
Names of the dead, in the night, and if then you appear, but in anger
Since your graves are profaned by the plough, with the voice of the heart, with
Pious song I'll appease you all, holy shades, till my soul is
Wholly accustomed and fit to live with you, heroes and wise men.
Many a question, you dead, then the more hallowed will ask you,
You, the living, no less, exalted and heavenly powers,
When with your years you pass by above the Grecian rubble,
You of the certain course! For often, like shivery breezes
Wild confusion grips me till lost I wander in starlight,

Daß ich spähe nach Rath, und lang schon reden sie nimmer
Trost den Bedürftigen zu, die prophetischen Haine Dodonas,
Stumm ist der delphische Gott, und einsam liegen und öde
Längst die Pfade, wo einst, von Hoffnungen leise geleitet,
Fragend der Mann zur Stadt des redlichen Sehers heraufstieg.
Aber droben das Licht, es spricht noch heute zu Menschen,
Schöner Deutungen voll und des großen Donnerers Stimme
Ruft es: denket ihr mein? und die trauernde Wooge des Meergotts
Hallt es wieder: gedenkt ihr nimmer meiner, wie vormals?
Denn es ruhn die Himmlischen gern am fühlenden Herzen;
Immer, wie sonst, geleiten sie noch, die begeisternden Kräfte,
Gerne den strebenden Mann und über Bergen der Heimath
Ruht und waltet und lebt allgegenwärtig der Aether,
Daß ein liebendes Volk in des Vaters Armen gesammelt,
Menschlich freudig, wie sonst, und Ein Geist allen gemein sei.
Aber weh! es wandelt in Nacht, es wohnt, wie im Orkus,
Ohne Göttliches unser Geschlecht. Ans eigene Treiben
Sind sie geschmiedet allein, und sich in der tosenden Werkstatt
Höret jeglicher nur und viel arbeiten die Wilden
Mit gewaltigem Arm, rastlos, doch immer und immer
Unfruchtbar, wie die Furien, bleibt die Mühe der Armen.
Bis, erwacht vom ängstigen Traum, die Seele den Menschen
Aufgeht, jugendlich froh, und der Liebe seegnender Othem
Wieder, wie vormals oft, bei Hellas blühenden Kindern,
Wehet in neuer Zeit und über freierer Stirne
Uns der Geist der Natur, der fernherwandelnde, wieder
Stilleweilend der Gott in goldnen Wolken erscheinet.
Ach! und säumest du noch? und jene, die göttlichgebornen,
Wohnen immer, o Tag! noch als in Tiefen der Erde
Einsam unten, indeß ein immerlebender Frühling
Unbesungen über dem Haupt den Schlafenden dämmert?
Aber länger nicht mehr! schon hör' ich ferne des Festtags
Chorgesang auf grünem Gebirg' und das Echo der Haine,
Wo der Jünglinge Brust sich hebt, wo die Seele des Volks sich

Looking for guidance, advice, and long now they've ceased to speak words of
Comfort to men in such need, the prophetic groves of Dodona,
Mute is the Delphian god, and desolate, long now deserted
Lie the pathways where once, while hopes would gently escort him,
Up walked the questioning man to the town of the truth-loving seer.
But the light above speaks kindly to mortals as ever,
Full of promises, hints, and the great Thunderer's voice, it
Cries: do you think of me? and the sorrowing wave of the Sea-God
Echoes it back: do you never think of me now, as you once did?
For the Heavenly like to repose on a human heart that can feel them;
Still the enrapturing powers, as ever, are glad to escort a
Man who seeks and aspires, and still does ubiquitous Aether
Rest and govern and live above the old hills of their homeland,
So that a loving people conjoined in the arms of the Father
Shall be humanly glad, *one* spirit be common to all men.
Ah, but our kind walks in darkness, it dwells as in Orcus,
Severed from all that's divine. To his own industry only
Each man is forged, and can hear only himself in the workshop's
Deafening noise; and much the savages toil there, for ever
Moving their powerful arms, they labour, yet always and always
Vain, like the Furies, unfruitful the wretches' exertions remain there.
Till the nightmare ends, and the human spirit, awakened,
Burgeons, youthfully glad, and love like a gentle warm breath blows
Over this new age as often once it would blow over Hellas,
Blessing her children in flower, and over our brows less constricted
Nature's spirit that comes to men from far-distant places,
Calmly abiding, in clouds all golden the god reappears now.
What, and you hesitate still? And they, though their birth was divine, still
Live as they did before, O day, as though lonely, confined in
Gloomy depths of the earth, while a springtime eternally living
Glimmers away unsung above the heads of those sleepers?
Not a moment longer! Already I hear on far foothills
Choric song, the feast-day's, and hear the green groves all re-echo,
Where the young men more deeply breathe, where the soul of the people

Stillvereint im freieren Lied, zur Ehre des Gottes,
Dem die Höhe gebührt, doch auch die Thale sind heilig;
Denn, wo fröhlich der Strom in wachsender Jugend hinauseilt,
Unter Blumen des Lands, und wo auf sonnigen Ebnen
Edles Korn und der Obstwald reift, da kränzen am Feste
Gerne die Frommen sich auch, und auf dem Hügel der Stadt glänzt,
Menschlicher Wohnung gleich, die himmlische Halle der Freude.
Denn voll göttlichen Sinns ist alles Leben geworden,
Und vollendend, wie sonst, erscheinst du wieder den Kindern
Überall, o Natur! und, wie vom Quellengebirg, rinnt
Seegen von da und dort in die keimende Seele dem Volke.
Dann, dann, o ihr Freuden Athens! ihr Thaten in Sparta!
Köstliche Frühlingszeit im Griechenlande! wenn unser
Herbst kömmt, wenn ihr gereift, ihr Geister alle der Vorwelt!
Wiederkehret und siehe! des Jahrs Vollendung ist nahe!
Dann erhalte das Fest auch euch, vergangene Tage!
Hin nach Hellas schaue das Volk, und weinend und dankend
Sänftige sich in Erinnerungen der stolze Triumphtag!

Aber blühet indeß, bis unsre Früchte beginnen,
Blüht, ihr Gärten Ioniens! nur, und die an Athens Schutt
Grünen, ihr Holden! verbergt dem schauenden Tage die Trauer!
Kränzt mit ewigem Laub, ihr Lorbeerwälder! die Hügel
Eurer Todten umher, bei Marathon dort, wo die Knaben
Siegend starben, ach! dort auf Chäroneas Gefilden,
Wo mit den Waffen ins Blut die lezten Athener enteilten,
Fliehend vor dem Tage der Schmach, dort, dort von den Bergen
Klagt ins Schlachtthal täglich herab, dort singet von Oetas
Gipfeln das Schiksaalslied, ihr wandelnden Wasser, herunter!
Aber du, unsterblich, wenn auch der Griechengesang schon
Dich nicht feiert, wie sonst, aus deinen Woogen, o Meergott!
Töne mir in die Seele noch oft, daß über den Wassern
Furchtlosrege der Geist, dem Schwimmer gleich, in der Starken
Frischem Glüke sich üb', und die Göttersprache, das Wechseln

Quietly gathers in freer singing in praise of that god whose
Realm is the mountain heights, but the valleys also are holy;
For where youthful and growing the river lightheartedly hurries
Out amid flowers of the land, and where on sun-flooded plains the
Noble corn and the orchards mature, there too on the feast-day
Pious folk like to wear bright garlands, and up in the town gleams,
Not unlike human homes, the heavenly hall of pure gladness.
For the gods have restored to all life their spirit, their meaning,
And perfecting, as once you did, you appear to your children
Everywhere, Nature, once more, and as from the brook-threaded mountains
Blessings from this place and that transfuse the new soul of the people.
Then, O then, you joys of Athens, you deeds done at Sparta,
You delicious springtime in Grecian lands! When our autumn
Comes, when you all, grown mature, you genii known in the ancient
World return – and, look, the year's consummation approaches –
Then may the feast-day preserve you also, great era long ended,
May the people look towards Hellas and thanksgiving, weeping,
Make the proud day of their triumph gentle with solemn remembrance!

  Meanwhile, however, flower, till our fruition commences,
Flower, Ionian gardens, no less, and you others, you dear ones
Green behind Athens' rubble, hide her, lest day see her sadness!
And with evergreen leaves, you laurel woods, garland the gravemounds
Of your dead there at Marathon, where in the act of winning
Boys fell dead, and oh, there too, on the plains of Charonea
Where the last Athenians rushed into blood with their weapons,
Fleeing the day of disgrace, and there, over there, from the mountains
Daily down to the battlefield sound your lament, from Oeta's
Peaks give voice to your hymn of destiny, wandering waters!
You, however, immortal although the great hymns of the Grecians
Now do not praise you, may you, O God of the Sea, from your breakers
Often yet with your music infuse my soul, so that on your
Waters fearlessly nimble my mind like a swimmer may practise
Joy which the strong know, fresh joy, and master the language of gods, of

Und das Werden versteh', und wenn die reißende Zeit mir
Zu gewaltig das Haupt ergreifft und die Noth und das Irrsaal
Unter Sterblichen mir mein sterblich Leben erschüttert,
Laß der Stille mich dann in deiner Tiefe gedenken.

All that changes and grows; and if Time, as it rushes on ruthless
Seizes my head too firmly, and need, and this walking bewildered,
Lost, among mortals at last should shatter my mortal existence,
Then in your deeps the tranquillity let me remember.

Menons Klagen um Diotima

1

Täglich geh' ich heraus, und such' ein Anderes immer,
    Habe längst sie befragt alle die Pfade des Lands;
Droben die kühlenden Höhn, die Schatten alle besuch' ich,
    Und die Quellen; hinauf irret der Geist und hinab,
Ruh' erbittend; so flieht das getroffene Wild in die Wälder,
    Wo es um Mittag sonst sicher im Dunkel geruht;
Aber nimmer erquikt sein grünes Lager das Herz ihm,
    Jammernd und schlummerlos treibt es der Stachel umher.
Nicht die Wärme des Lichts, und nicht die Kühle der Nacht hilft,
    Und in Woogen des Stroms taucht es die Wunden umsonst.
Und wie ihm vergebens die Erd' ihr fröhliches Heilkraut
    Reicht, und das gährende Blut keiner der Zephyre stillt,
So, ihr Lieben! auch mir, so will es scheinen, und niemand
    Kann von der Stirne mir nehmen den traurigen Traum?

2

Ja! es frommet auch nicht, ihr Todesgötter! wenn einmal
    Ihr ihn haltet, und fest habt den bezwungenen Mann,
Wenn ihr Bösen hinab in die schaurige Nacht ihn genommen,
    Dann zu suchen, zu flehn, oder zu zürnen mit euch,
Oder geduldig auch wohl im furchtsamen Banne zu wohnen,
    Und mit Lächeln von euch hören das nüchterne Lied.
Soll es seyn, so vergiß dein Heil, und schlummere klanglos!
    Aber doch quillt ein Laut hoffend im Busen dir auf,
Immer kannst du noch nicht, o meine Seele! noch kannst du's
    Nicht gewohnen, und träumst mitten im eisernen Schlaf!
Festzeit hab' ich nicht, doch möcht' ich die Loke bekränzen;
    Bin ich allein denn nicht? aber ein Freundliches muß
Fernher nahe mir seyn, und lächeln muß ich und staunen,
    Wie so seelig doch auch mitten im Leide mir ist.

Menon's Lament for Diotima

1

Daily I search, now here, now there my wandering takes me
    Countless times I have probed every highway and path;
Coolness I seek on those hilltops, all the shades I revisit,
    Then the well-springs again; up my mind roves and down
Begging for rest; so a wounded deer will flee to the forests
    Where he used to lie low, safe in the dark towards noon;
Yet his green lair no longer now can refresh him or soothe him,
    Crying and sleepless he roams, cruelly pricked by the thorn,
Neither the warmth of the daylight nor the cool darkness of night helps,
    In the river's waves too vainly he washes his wounds.
And as vainly to him now Earth offers herbs that might heal them,
    Cheer him, and none of the winds quiets his feverish blood,
So, beloved ones, it seems, with me it is too, and can no one
    Lift this dead weight from my brow, break the all-saddening dream?

2

And indeed, gods of death, when once you have utterly caught him,
    Seized and fettered the man, so that he cringes, subdued,
When you evil ones down into horrible night have conveyed him
    Useless it is to implore, then to be angry with you,
Useless even to bear that grim coercion with patience,
    Smiling to hear you each day chant him the sobering song.
If you must, then forget your welfare and drowse away tuneless!
    Yet in your heart even now, hoping, a sound rises up,
Still, my soul, even now you cling to your habit of music,
    Will not give in yet, and dream deep in the lead of dull sleep!
Cause I have none to be festive, but long to put on a green garland;
    Am I not quite alone? Yet something kind now must be
Close to me from afar, so that I smile as I wonder
    How in the midst of my grief I can feel happy and blessed.

3

Licht der Liebe! scheinest du denn auch Todten, du goldnes!
  Bilder aus hellerer Zeit leuchtet ihr mir in die Nacht?
Liebliche Gärten seid, ihr abendröthlichen Berge,
  Seid willkommen und ihr, schweigende Pfade des Hains,
Zeugen himmlischen Glüks, und ihr, hochschauende Sterne,
  Die mir damals so oft seegnende Blike gegönnt!
Euch, ihr Liebenden auch, ihr schönen Kinder des Maitags,
  Stille Rosen und euch, Lilien, nenn' ich noch oft!
Wohl gehn Frühlinge fort, ein Jahr verdränget das andre,
  Wechselnd und streitend, so tost droben vorüber die Zeit
Über sterblichem Haupt, doch nicht vor seeligen Augen,
  Und den Liebenden ist anderes Leben geschenkt.
Denn sie alle die Tag' und Jahre der Sterne sie waren
  Diotima! um uns innig und ewig vereint;

4

Aber wir, zufrieden gesellt, wie die liebenden Schwäne,
  Wenn sie ruhen am See, oder, auf Wellen gewiegt,
Niedersehn in die Wasser, wo silberne Wolken sich spiegeln,
  Und ätherisches Blau unter den Schiffenden wallt,
So auf Erden wandelten wir. Und drohte der Nord auch,
  Er, der Liebenden Feind, klagenbereitend, und fiel
Von den Ästen das Laub, und flog im Winde der Reegen,
  Ruhig lächelten wir, fühlten den eigenen Gott
Unter trautem Gespräch; in Einem Seelengesange,
  Ganz in Frieden mit uns kindlich und freudig allein.
Aber das Haus ist öde mir nun, und sie haben mein Auge
  Mir genommen, auch mich hab' ich verloren mit ihr.
Darum irr' ich umher, und wohl, wie die Schatten, so muß ich
  Leben, und sinnlos dünkt lange das Übrige mir.

3

Golden light of love, for dead men, for shades, do you shine then?
  Radiant visions recalled, even this night, then, you pierce?
Pleasant gardens, and mountains tinged with crimson at sunset,
  Welcome I call you, and you, murmurless path of the grove,
Witness to heavenly joy, and stars more loftily gazing,
  Who so freely would grant looks that were blessings to me!
And you lovers, you too, the May-day's beautiful children,
  Quiet roses, and you, lilies, I often invoke!
Springs, it is true, go by, one year still supplanting the other,
  Changing and warring, so Time over us mortal men's heads
Rushes past up above, but not in the eyes of the blessed ones,
  Nor of lovers, to whom different life is vouchsafed.
For all these, all the days and years of the heavenly planets,
  Diotima, round us closely, for ever, conjoined;

4

Meanwhile we – like the mated swans in their summer contentment
  When by the lake they rest or on the waves, lightly rocked,
Down they look, at the water, and silvery clouds through that mirror
  Drift, and ethereal blue flows where the voyagers pass –
Moved and dwelled on this earth. And though the North Wind was threatening
  Hostile to lovers, he, gathering sorrows, and down
Came dead leaves from the boughs, and rain filled the spluttering storm-gusts
  Calmly we smiled, aware, sure of the tutelar god
Present in talk only ours, one song that our two souls were singing,
  Wholly at peace with ourselves, childishly, raptly alone.
Desolate now is my house, and not only her they have taken,
  No, but my own two eyes, myself I have lost, losing her.
That is why, astray, like wandering phantoms I live now,
  Must live, I fear, and the rest long has seemed senseless to me.

5

Feiern möcht' ich; aber wofür? und singen mit Andern,
  Aber so einsam fehlt jegliches Göttliche mir.
Diß ist's, diß mein Gebrechen, ich weiß, es lähmet ein Fluch mir
  Darum die Sehnen, und wirft, wo ich beginne, mich hin,
Daß ich fühllos size den Tag, und stumm wie die Kinder,
  Nur vom Auge mir kalt öfters die Thräne noch schleicht,
Und die Pflanze des Felds, und der Vögel Singen mich trüb macht,
  Weil mit Freuden auch sie Boten des Himmlischen sind,
Aber mir in schaudernder Brust die beseelende Sonne,
  Kühl und fruchtlos mir dämmert, wie Stralen der Nacht,
Ach! und nichtig und leer, wie Gefängnißwände, der Himmel
  Eine beugende Last über dem Haupte mir hängt!

6

Sonst mir anders bekannt! o Jugend, und bringen Gebete
  Dich nicht wieder, dich nie? führet kein Pfad mich zurük?
Soll es werden auch mir, wie den Götterlosen, die vormals
  Glänzenden Auges doch auch saßen an seeligem Tisch',
Aber übersättiget bald, die schwärmenden Gäste,
  Nun verstummet, und nun, unter der Lüfte Gesang,
Unter blühender Erd' entschlafen sind, bis dereinst sie
  Eines Wunders Gewalt sie, die Versunkenen, zwingt,
Wiederzukehren, und neu auf grünendem Boden zu wandeln. –
  Heiliger Othem durchströmt göttlich die lichte Gestalt,
Wenn das Fest sich beseelt, und Fluthen der Liebe sich regen,
  Und vom Himmel getränkt, rauscht der lebendige Strom,
Wenn es drunten ertönt, und ihre Schäze die Nacht zollt,
  Und aus Bächen herauf glänzt das begrabene Gold. –

5

Celebrate – yes, but what? And gladly with others I'd sing now,
  Yet alone as I am nothing that's godlike rings true,
This, I know, is it, my failing, a curse maims my sinews
  Only because of this, making me flag from the start,
So that numb all day long I sit like a child that is moping
  Dumb, though at times a tear coldly creeps out of my eyes,
And the flowers of the field, the singing of birds make me sad now,
  Being heralds of heaven, bearers of heavenly joy,
But to me, in my heart's dank vault, now the soul-giving sun dawns
  Cool, infertile, in vain, feeble as rays of the night,
Oh, and futile and empty, walls of a prison, the heavens
  Press, a smothering load heaped on my head from above!

6

Once, how different it was! O youth, will no prayer bring you back, then,
  Never again? And no path ever again lead me back?
Shall it be my fate, as once it was that of the godless,
  Bright-eyed to sit for a time feasting at heavenly boards
But to be cloyed with that food, all those fantastical guests now
  Fallen silent, and now, deaf to the music of winds,
Under the flowering earth asleep, till a miracle's power shall
  Force them one day to return, deep though they lie now, at rest,
Force them to walk anew the soil that is sprouting new verdure. –
  Holy breath, then, divine, through their bright bodies will flow
While the feast is inspired and love like great floodwaters gathers,
  Fed by the heavens themselves, on sweeps the river, alive,
When the deep places boom, Night pays her tribute of riches
  And from the beds of streams up glitters gold long submerged. –

7

Aber o du, die schon am Scheidewege mir damals,
  Da ich versank vor dir, tröstend ein Schöneres wies,
Du, die Großes zu sehn, und froher die Götter zu singen,
  Schweigend, wie sie, mich einst stille begeisternd gelehrt;
Götterkind! erscheinest du mir, und grüßest, wie einst, mich,
  Redest wieder, wie einst, höhere Dinge mir zu?
Siehe! weinen vor dir, und klagen muß ich, wenn schon noch,
  Denkend edlerer Zeit, dessen die Seele sich schämt.
Denn so lange, so lang auf matten Pfaden der Erde
  Hab' ich, deiner gewohnt, dich in der Irre gesucht,
Freudiger Schuzgeist! aber umsonst, und Jahre zerrannen,
  Seit wir ahnend um uns glänzen die Abende sahn.

8

Dich nur, dich erhält dein Licht, o Heldinn! im Lichte,
  Und dein Dulden erhält liebend, o Gütige, dich;
Und nicht einmal bist du allein; Gespielen genug sind,
  Wo du blühest und ruhst unter den Rosen des Jahrs;
Und der Vater, er selbst, durch sanftumathmende Musen
  Sendet die zärtlichen Wiegengesänge dir zu.
Ja! noch ist sie es ganz! noch schwebt vom Haupte zur Sohle,
  Stillherwandelnd, wie sonst, mir die Athenerinn vor.
Und wie, freundlicher Geist! von heitersinnender Stirne
  Seegnend und sicher dein Stral unter die Sterblichen fällt;
So bezeugest du mir's, und sagst mir's, daß ich es andern
  Wiedersage, denn auch Andere glauben es nicht,
Daß unsterblicher doch, denn Sorg' und Zürnen, die Freude
  Und ein goldener Tag täglich am Ende noch ist.

7

You, though, who even then, already then at the crossroads
　　When I fell at your feet, comforting showed me the way,
Taught me to see what is great, to sing with a beauty more mellow,
　　Joy more serene, the gods, silent as gods are yourself,
Child of the gods, will you appear to me, greet me once more now,
　　Quietly raising me up, speak to me now of those things?
Look, in your presence I weep, lament, though remembering always
　　Worthier times that are past, deep in my soul I feel shame.
For so very long on weary paths of the earth now,
　　Still accustomed to you, you I have sought in the wilds,
Tutelar spirit, but all in vain, and whole years have gone by since
　　Late in the evenings we walked, bathed in that ominous glow.

8

You, only you, your own light, O heroine, keeps in the light still,
　　And your patience still keeps you both loving and kind;
Nor indeed are you lonely; playmates enough are provided
　　Where amid roses you bloom, rest with the flowers of the year;
And the Father himself by means of the balm-breathing Muses
　　Sends you those cradle-songs warm as a southerly breeze.
Yes, she is quite the same! From her head to her heels the Athenian,
　　Quiet and poised as before hovers in front of my eyes.
And as blessing and sure your radiance falls upon mortals,
　　Tender soul, from your brow rapt in deep thought, yet serene,
So you prove it to me, and tell me, that also to others
　　Then I may pass it on, others who doubt as I doubt,
That more enduring than care and anger is holy rejoicing
　　And that golden the day daily still shines in the end.

9

So will ich, ihr Himmlischen! denn auch danken, und endlich
  Athmet aus leichter Brust wieder des Sängers Gebet.
Und wie, wenn ich mit ihr, auf sonniger Höhe mit ihr stand,
  Spricht belebend ein Gott innen vom Tempel mich an.
Leben will ich denn auch! schon grünt's! wie von heiliger Leier
  Ruft es von silbernen Bergen Apollons voran!
Komm! es war wie ein Traum! Die blutenden Fittige sind ja
  Schon genesen, verjüngt leben die Hoffnungen all.
Großes zu finden, ist viel, ist viel noch übrig, und wer so
  Liebte, gehet, er muß, gehet zu Göttern die Bahn.
Und geleitet ihr uns, ihr Weihestunden! ihr ernsten,
  Jugendlichen! o bleibt, heilige Ahnungen, ihr
Fromme Bitten! und ihr Begeisterungen und all ihr
  Guten Genien, die gerne bei Liebenden sind;
Bleibt so lange mit uns, bis wir auf gemeinsamem Boden
  Dort, wo die Seeligen all niederzukehren bereit,
Dort, wo die Adler sind, die Gestirne, die Boten des Vaters,
  Dort, wo die Musen, woher Helden und Liebende sind,
Dort uns, oder auch hier, auf thauender Insel begegnen,
  Wo die Unsrigen erst, blühend in Gärten gesellt,
Wo die Gesänge wahr, und länger die Frühlinge schön sind,
  Und von neuem ein Jahr unserer Seele beginnt.

9

Thanks, once more, then, I'll give to you up in heaven; once more now
  Freely at last can my prayer rise from a heart unoppressed.
And, as before, when with her I stood on a sun-gilded hilltop,
  Quickening, to me now a god speaks from the temple within.
I will live, then! New verdure! As though from a lyre that is hallowed
  Onward! from silvery peaks, Apollo's mountains ring out.
Come, it was all like a dream, the wounds in your wings have already
  Healed, and restored to youth all your old hopes leap alive.
Knowledge of greatness is much, yet much still remains to be done, and
  One who loved as you loved only to gods can move on.
You conduct us, then, you solemn ones, Hours of Communion,
  Youthful ones, stay with us, holy Presentiments also,
Pious prayers, and you, Inspirations, and all of you kindly
  Spirits who like to attend lovers, to be where they are.
Stay with us two until on communal ground, reunited
  Where, when their coming is due, all the blessed souls will return,
Where the eagles are, the planets, the Father's own heralds,
  Where the Muses are still, heroes and lovers began,
There we shall meet again, or here, on a dew-covered island
  Where what is ours for once, blooms that a garden conjoins,
All our poems are true and springs remain beautiful longer
  And another, a new year of our souls can begin.

Der Wanderer

Einsam stand ich und sah in die Afrikanischen dürren
    Ebnen hinaus; vom Olymp reegnete Feuer herab,
Reißendes! milder kaum, wie damals, da das Gebirg hier
    Spaltend mit Stralen der Gott Höhen und Tiefen gebaut.
Aber auf denen springt kein frischaufgrünender Wald nicht
    In die tönende Luft üppig und herrlich empor.
Unbekränzt ist die Stirne des Bergs und beredtsame Bäche
    Kennet er kaum, es erreicht selten die Quelle das Thal.
Keiner Heerde vergeht am plätschernden Brunnen der Mittag,
    Freundlich aus Bäumen hervor blikte kein gastliches Dach.
Unter dem Strauche saß ein ernster Vogel gesanglos,
    Aber die Wanderer flohn eilend, die Störche, vorbei.
Da bat ich um Wasser dich nicht, Natur! in der Wüste,
    Wasser bewahrte mir treulich das fromme Kameel.
Um der Haine Gesang, ach! um die Gärten des Vaters
    Bat ich vom wandernden Vogel der Heimath gemahnt.
Aber du sprachst zu mir; auch hier sind Götter und walten,
    Groß ist ihr Maas, doch es mißt gern mit der Spanne der Mensch.

Und es trieb die Rede mich an, noch Andres zu suchen,
    Fern zum nördlichen Pol kam ich in Schiffen herauf.
Still in der Hülse von Schnee schlief da das gefesselte Leben,
    Und der eiserne Schlaf harrte seit Jahren des Tags.
Denn zu lang nicht schlang um die Erde den Arm der Olymp hier,
    Wie Pygmalions Arm um die Geliebte sich schlang.
Hier bewegt' er ihr nicht mit dem Sonnenblike den Busen,
    Und in Reegen und Thau sprach er nicht freundlich zu ihr;
Und mich wunderte deß und thörig sprach ich: o Mutter
    Erde, verlierst du denn immer, als Wittwe, die Zeit?

The Traveller

Lonely I stood and looked out into African desert, unbroken
    Plains; and, standing there, saw fire from Olympus rain down,
Ravening fire scarcely more gentle than when in the same mountain ranges,
    Blasting their bulk with his rays, God made the heights and the depths.
Never on these, though, a forest with newly green leafage
    Into the resonant air, luscious and glorious, will rise.
All ungarlanded is the brow of this mountain, and eloquent torrents
    Hardly are known to it, brooks rarely complete their descent.
Noon by no murmuring well-spring goes by for the somnolent cattle,
    Not one hospitable roof amiably beckoned from trees.
Under dry bushes there sat a serious bird, never singing.
    But those migrants, the storks, hurriedly passed on their way.
Nature, not you did I ask for water there in the desert,
    But on the good camel's back only for drink could rely.
For the song of the groves, ah, and the gardens, my father's,
    Yes, I did ask – by the birds, migrants from homeland, recalled.
Then, though, you said to me: here also gods are, and they govern,
    Great is their measure, but men take as their measure the span.

And those words impelled me to look for other things also,
    Far off to the northern pole sailing I made my way.
Packed in its wrapping of snow a fettered life seemed to sleep there
    And for years iron sleep there had been waiting for day.
For not too long around Earth did Olympus wrap a fond arm here
    As Pygmalion's arm round his belovèd was wrapped.
Here with his sunny gaze he awakens no warmth in her bosom,
    Never with rain or with dew whispered those words that seduce;
And I marvelled at that, and I foolishly said to her: Mother
    Earth, will you always, then, waste, widowed, your time and your life?

Nichts zu erzeugen ist ja und nichts zu pflegen in Liebe,
  Alternd im Kinde sich nicht wieder zu sehn, wie der Tod.
Aber vieleicht erwarmst du dereinst am Strale des Himmels,
  Aus dem dürftigen Schlaf schmeichelt sein Othem dich auf;
Daß, wie ein Saamkorn, du die eherne Schaale zersprengest,
  Los sich reißt und das Licht grüßt die entbundene Welt,
All' die gesammelte Kraft aufflammt in üppigem Frühling,
  Rosen glühen und Wein sprudelt im kärglichen Nord.

Also sagt' ich und jezt kehr' ich an den Rhein, in die Heimath,
  Zärtlich, wie vormals, weh'n Lüfte der Jugend mich an;
Und das strebende Herz besänftigen mir die vertrauten
  Offnen Bäume, die einst mich in den Armen gewiegt,
Und das heilige Grün, der Zeuge des seeligen, tiefen
  Lebens der Welt, es erfrischt, wandelt zum Jüngling mich um.
Alt bin ich geworden indeß, mich blaichte der Eispol,
  Und im Feuer des Süds fielen die Loken mir aus.
Aber wenn einer auch am lezten der sterblichen Tage,
  Fernher kommend und müd bis in die Seele noch jezt
Wiedersähe diß Land, noch Einmal müßte die Wang' ihm
  Blüh'n, und erloschen fast glänzte sein Auge noch auf.
Seeliges Thal des Rheins! kein Hügel ist ohne den Weinstok,
  Und mit der Traube Laub Mauer und Garten bekränzt,
Und des heiligen Tranks sind voll im Strome die Schiffe,
  Städt' und Inseln sie sind trunken von Weinen und Obst.
Aber lächelnd und ernst ruht droben der Alte, der Taunus,
  Und mit Eichen bekränzt neiget der Freie das Haupt.

Und jezt kommt vom Walde der Hirsch, aus Wolken das Tagslicht,
  Hoch in heiterer Luft siehet der Falke sich um.
Aber unten im Thal, wo die Blume sich nähret von Quellen,
  Strekt das Dörfchen bequem über die Wiese sich aus.
Still ists hier. Fern rauscht die immer geschäfftige Mühle,
  Aber das Neigen des Tags künden die Gloken mir an.

When to give birth to nothing and nothing to lovingly care for,
    Never to see your own self imaged in children, is death.
Or in the heavenly beam after all still one day you'll be basking,
    Out of the dearth of your sleep raised by his breath after all;
And, like the living seed-grain, burst out of the husk that constricts you,
    So that the world, unbound, tears itself loose and greets light,
All the strength so long gathered flares up in a springtime luxuriance,
    Roses glow and rich wine gushes in northerly dearth.

So I addressed her, and now I return to the Rhine, to my homeland,
    Feel, as I used to do, childhood's mild breeze on my face;
And my heart, the far-roaming, is soothed again by familiar
    Welcoming trees that before cradled the child in their arms
And the holy verdure betokening blissful and deeper
    Life in this world makes it new, changes the man to a youth.
Old in the meantime I've grown, and was blanched by the ice of the Arctic,
    In the fire of the South lost many locks of my hair.
Yet if a man on his very last day as a mortal,
    Coming from far away, weary right down to his soul,
Were to revisit this country, once more to his cheeks must the colour
    Rise, and his eyes almost dimmed brightly would gleam once again.
Blessèd valley, the Rhine's! Not one hill but is covered with vineyards,
    And with leaves of the grape garden and wall are adorned,
And on the rivers the ships are full of the drink that is holy,
    Cities and islands are all drunken with wines and with fruit.
Smiling and serious above them the ancient one, Taunus, reposes
    And his head crowned with oaks proudly the free one inclines.

And from the wood comes the stag now, from clouds comes the daylight,
    Up in a sky that is clear now hangs the hawk and looks round.
But in the valley below where the flowers are nourished by well-springs,
    Look, the small village spreads out among meadows, relaxed.
Quiet it's here. Prom afar comes the noise of the mill-wheels revolving,
    But the day's decline church bells convey to my ear.

Lieblich tönt die gehämmerte Sens' und die Stimme des Landmanns,
　　Der heimkehrend dem Stier gerne die Schritte gebeut,
Lieblich der Mutter Gesang, die im Grase sizt mit dem Söhnlein;
　　Satt vom Sehen entschliefs; aber die Wolken sind roth,
Und am glänzenden See, wo der Hain das offene Hofthor
　　Übergrünt und das Licht golden die Fenster umspielt,
Dort empfängt mich das Haus und des Gartens heimliches Dunkel,
　　Wo mit den Pflanzen mich einst liebend der Vater erzog;
Wo ich frei, wie Geflügelte, spielt' auf luftigen Ästen,
　　Oder ins treue Blau blikte vom Gipfel des Hains.
Treu auch bist du von je, treu auch dem Flüchtlinge blieben,
　　Freundlich nimmst du, wie einst, Himmel der Heimath, mich auf.

Noch gedeihn die Pfirsiche mir, mich wundern die Blüthen,
　　Fast, wie die Bäume, steht herrlich mit Rosen der Strauch.
Schwer ist worden indeß von Früchten dunkel mein Kirschbaum,
　　Und der pflükenden Hand reichen die Zweige sich selbst.
Auch zum Walde zieht mich, wie sonst, in die freiere Laube
　　Aus dem Garten der Pfad oder hinab an den Bach,
Wo ich lag, und den Muth erfreut' am Ruhme der Männer
　　Ahnender Schiffer; und das konnten die Sagen von euch,
Daß in die Meer' ich fort, in die Wüsten mußt', ihr Gewalt'gen!
　　Ach! indeß mich umsonst Vater und Mutter gesucht.
Aber wo sind sie? du schweigst? du zögerst? Hüter des Haußes!
　　Hab' ich gezögert doch auch! habe die Schritte gezählt,
Da ich nahet', und bin, gleich Pilgern, stille gestanden.
　　Aber gehe hinein, melde den Fremden, den Sohn,
Daß sich öffnen die Arm' und mir ihr Seegen begegne,
　　Daß ich geweiht und gegönnt wieder die Schwelle mir sei!
Aber ich ahn' es schon, in heilige Fremde dahin sind
　　Nun auch sie mir, und nie kehret ihr Lieben zurük.

Vater und Mutter? und wenn noch Freunde leben, sie haben
　　Andres gewonnen, sie sind nimmer die Meinigen mehr.

Pleasantly clangs the hammered scythe and the voice of the farmer
    Who, going home with his bull, likes to command and to curb,
Pleasant the mother's song as she sits in the grass with her infant;
    Sated with seeing he sleeps; clouds, though, are tinged now with red,
And by the glistening lake where the orchard extends its full branches
    Over the open yard gate, window-panes glitter with gold,
There I'm received by the house and the garden's secretive half-light,
    Where together with plants fondly my father reared me;
Where as free as the winged ones I played in the boughs' airy greenness
    Or from the orchard's crest gazed into spaces all blue.
Loyal you were, and loyal remain to the fugitive even,
    Kindly as ever you were, heaven of home, take me back.

Still do the peaches grow ripe for me, still at the blossom I marvel,
    Almost as tall as the trees gloriously rose-bushes flower.
Heavy meanwhile with fruit and dark has my cherry tree grown now,
    And to the gathering hand branches now proffer themselves.
Still to the woods by the path, as before, to the free-lying bower
    Out of the garden I'm drawn, down to the stream, where before
I would lie, with my mind cheered by the fame of those men, the
    Prescient mariners; and such was the power of your love
That to the oceans, the deserts, your valour compelled me to follow,
    Ah, while in vain they looked, father and mother, for me.
But where are they? You're silent? You hesitate, you, my home's keeper?
    Hesitate? Well, so did I, counting my steps to the door,
As I drew near and, like pilgrims, awe-stricken slowed them, and halted.
    Go inside, nonetheless, say: there's a stranger, your son,
So that they open their arms and receive me once more with their blessing,
    So that they sanctify me, grant me the threshold once more.
Yet already I guess it: to holy remoteness they also
    Now have passed on and to me never again will return.

Father and mother? And if there are friends living still, they as well have
    Found new pursuits, other gains, are not the friends who were mine.

Kommen werd' ich, wie sonst, und die alten, die Nahmen der Liebe
    Nennen, beschwören das Herz, ob es noch schlage, wie sonst,
Aber stille werden sie seyn. So bindet und scheidet
    Manches die Zeit. Ich dünk' ihnen gestorben, sie mir.
Und so bin ich allein. Du aber, über den Wolken,
    Vater des Vaterlands! mächtiger Aether! und du
Erd' und Licht! ihr einigen drei, die walten und lieben,
    Ewige Götter! mit euch brechen die Bande mir nie.
Ausgegangen von euch, mit euch auch bin ich gewandert,
    Euch, ihr Freudigen, euch bring' ich erfahrner zurük.
Darum reiche mir nun, bis oben an von des Rheines
    Warmen Bergen mit Wein reiche den Becher gefüllt!
Daß ich den Göttern zuerst und das Angedenken der Helden
    Trinke, der Schiffer, und dann eures, ihr Trautesten! auch
Eltern und Freund'! und der Mühn und aller Leiden vergesse
    Heut' und morgen und schnell unter den Heimischen sei.

Though as before I come and address by love's names, by the old ones,
    All that I see, and adjure heart-beats that once would respond,
Utter silence will meet me. For so it is: much is bound by,
    Much is severed by time. I to them will seem dead, they to me;
And I'm left all alone. But with you, up there above clouds, my
    Fatherland's father, you, powerful Aether, and you
Earth and Light, unanimous three who love and who govern,
    Deathless gods, with you never my bonds I shall break.
Out of you originated, with you I have also travelled,
    You, the joyous ones, you, filled with more knowledge, bring back.
Therefore pass to me now the cup that is filled, overflowing
    With the wine from those grapes grown on warm hills of the Rhine,
That I may drink to the gods at first and then remember those others,
    Mariners, heroes, and then you, the still closer to me,
Parents and friends, and forget my whole load of afflictions and labours
    This and the next day, and soon be among those of my kind.

Stutgard

AN SIEGFRIED SCHMIDT

I

Wieder ein Glük ist erlebt. Die gefährliche Dürre geneset,
Und die Schärfe des Lichts senget die Blüthe nicht mehr.
Offen steht jezt wieder ein Saal, und gesund ist der Garten,
Und von Reegen erfrischt rauschet das glänzende Thal,
Hoch von Gewächsen, es schwellen die Bäch' und alle gebundnen
Fittige wagen sich wieder ins Reich des Gesangs.
Voll ist die Luft von Fröhlichen jezt und die Stadt und der Hain ist
Rings von zufriedenen Kindern des Himmels erfüllt.
Gerne begegnen sie sich, und irren untereinander,
Sorgenlos, und es scheint keines zu wenig, zu viel.
Denn so ordnet das Herz es an, und zu athmen die Anmuth,
Sie, die geschikliche, schenkt ihnen ein göttlicher Geist.
Aber die Wanderer auch sind wohlgeleitet und haben
Kränze genug und Gesang, haben den heiligen Stab
Vollgeschmükt mit Trauben und Laub bei sich und der Fichte
Schatten; von Dorfe zu Dorf jauchzt es, von Tage zu Tag,
Und wie Wagen, bespannt mit freiem Wilde, so ziehn die
Berge voran und so träget und eilet der Pfad.

2

Aber meinest du nun, es haben die Thore vergehens
Aufgethan und den Weg freudig die Götter gemacht?
Und es schenken umsonst zu des Gastmahls Fülle die Guten
Nebst dem Weine noch auch Beeren und Honig und Obst?
Schenken das purpurne Licht zu Festgesängen und kühl und
Ruhig zu tieferem Freundesgespräche die Nacht?
Hält ein Ernsteres dich, so spars dem Winter und willst du
Freien, habe Gedult, Freier beglüket der Mai.

Stuttgart

TO SIEGFRIED SCHMIDT

1

Once again a joy has been lived. The dangerous dryness recovers
    And the sharp edge of light singes no leaf and no flower.
Open once more stands the hall, and the garden also is healthy
    And the rill-rushing vale glistens, refreshed by the rain,
Lush with new growth, and the brooks swell up and the long-constricted
    Wings now venture again into the purlieus of song.
Full is the air of merry ones now and the city and woodland
    All around are filled, teem with those children of air.
Happy they are to meet and ramble one with another,
    Carefree, and nothing to them now seems too little, too much.
For it's so the heart would have it, to breathe in such beauty,
    Grace that is destined, a god's spirit now grants as a gift.
But the travellers too are well-directed, not lacking
    Garlands enough or song, carry the sanctified stave
Richly adorned with grapes and foliage and shade of the fir tree;
    As their cheer spills from village to village, from day to day,
And like chariots drawn by wild beasts, so the mountains
    Surge ahead and so leads and so hurries the path.

2

Could it be, you think, that for nothing the gods have thrown open
    Gates that were closed and in vain opened a pathway for joy?
That for nothing the kindly ones add to the plentiful banquet
    Not only wine but more, berries and honey and fruit?
Give us the crimson light for festive music and, cool and
    Calm for discourse more deep, friendship's, the blessing of night?
If you have graver cares on your mind, save them up for the winter,
    If it's a wife you want, wait, lovers do better in May.

Jezt ist Anderes Noth, jezt komm' und feire des Herbstes
    Alte Sitte, noch jezt blühet die Edle mit uns.
Eins nur gilt für den Tag, das Vaterland und des Opfers
    Festlicher Flamme wirft jeder sein Eigenes zu.
Darum kränzt der gemeinsame Gott umsäuselnd das Haar uns,
    Und den eigenen Sinn schmelzet, wie Perlen, der Wein.
Diß bedeutet der Tisch, der geehrte, wenn, wie die Bienen,
    Rund um den Eichbaum, wir sizen und singen um ihn,
Diß der Pokale Klang, und darum zwinget die wilden
    Seelen der streitenden Männer zusammen der Chor.

3

Aber damit uns nicht, gleich Allzuklugen, entfliehe
    Diese neigende Zeit, komm' ich entgegen sogleich,
Bis an die Grenze des Lands, wo mir den lieben Geburtsort
    Und die Insel des Stroms blaues Gewässer umfließt.
Heilig ist mir der Ort, an beiden Ufern, der Fels auch,
    Der mit Garten und Haus grün aus den Wellen sich hebt.
Dort begegnen wir uns; o gütiges Licht! wo zuerst mich
    Deiner gefühlteren Stralen mich einer betraf.
Dort begann und beginnt das liebe Leben von neuem;
    Aber des Vaters Grab seh' ich und weine dir schon?
Wein' und halt' und habe den Freund und höre das Wort, das
    Einst mir in himmlischer Kunst Leiden der Liebe geheilt.
Andres erwacht! ich muß die Landesheroën ihm nennen,
    Barbarossa! dich auch, gütiger Kristoph, und dich,
Konradin! wie du fielst, so fallen Starke, der Epheu
    Grünt am Fels und die Burg dekt das bacchantische Laub,
Doch Vergangenes ist, wie Künftiges heilig den Sängern,
    Und in Tagen des Herbsts sühnen die Schatten wir uns.

Now there is need for other things. Come and celebrate autumn's
    Ancient ritual, for still we and great Earth are in flower.
One thing only counts for this day, the fatherland; each of us offers
    Up to the festive flame that which is his to cast in.
Therefore the communal god is a wind in our hair, is a garland,
    And our selfhood, each one's, melts, as a pearl does, in wine.
This the table betokens, the honoured, whenever, as bees do,
    Round the oak tree we sit, singing and clustering there,
This the ringing of cups, and for this are the fierce souls of fighters
    Brought into unison, fused by a common compulsion, the choir's.

3

Not, though, like those all too clever, letting it slip and elude me,
    Now that the season declines, promptly to meet it I come,
Up to the bordering regions, our country's, where bluish water
    Laps the birthplace I love, laps the small river-girt isle.
Holy the place is to me, and on both of the banks, as the rock is
    Which with garden and house rises all green from the waves.
There, kindly light, we can meet, for there too for the first time
    One of your rays, the more felt, touching me, marked what it touched.
There began and begins anew now a life truly living;
    Yet my father's grave – one little look, and I burst into tears?
Weep and go to and cling to the friend and hear the same word that
    Once amid heavenly art healed all the anguish of love.
Other things waken. I name, I have to, my homeland's own heroes,
    Barbarossa, and you, kind-hearted Christoph, and you,
Conradin, how you fell, strong men fall so, and the ivy
    Green on the rock and the keep dark with bacchantical leaves,
But things past, like the things yet to come, are holy to singers,
    And on autumnal days shades we seek out and appease.

4

So der Gewaltgen gedenk und des herzerhebenden Schiksaals,
    Thatlos selber, und leicht, aber vom Aether doch auch
Angeschauet und fromm, wie die Alten, die göttlicherzognen
    Freudigen Dichter ziehn freudig das Land wir hinauf.
Groß ist das Werden umher. Dort von den äußersten Bergen
    Stammen der Jünglinge viel, steigen die Hügel herab.
Quellen rauschen von dort und hundert geschäfftige Bäche,
    Kommen bei Tag und Nacht nieder und bauen das Land.
Aber der Meister pflügt die Mitte des Landes, die Furchen
    Ziehet der Nekarstrom, ziehet den Seegen herab.
Und es kommen mit ihm Italiens Lüfte, die See schikt
    Ihre Wolken, sie schikt prächtige Sonnen mit ihm.
Darum wächset uns auch fast über das Haupt die gewaltge
    Fülle, denn hieher ward, hier in die Ebne das Gut
Reicher den Lieben gebracht, den Landesleuten, doch neidet
    Keiner an Bergen dort ihnen die Gärten, den Wein
Oder das üppige Gras und das Korn und die glühenden Bäume,
    Die am Wege gereiht über den Wanderern stehn.

5

Aber indeß wir schaun und die mächtige Freude durchwandeln,
    Fliehet der Weg und der Tag uns, wie den Trunkenen, hin.
Denn mit heiligem Laub umkränzt erhebet die Stadt schon
    Die gepriesene, dort leuchtend ihr priesterlich Haupt.
Herrlich steht sie und hält den Rebenstab und die Tanne
    Hoch in die seeligen purpurnen Wolken empor.
Sei uns hold! dem Gast und dem Sohn, o Fürstin der Heimath!
    Glükliches Stutgard, nimm freundlich den Fremdling mir auf!
Immer hast du Gesang mit Flöten und Saiten gebilligt,
    Wie ich glaub' und des Lieds kindlich Geschwäz und der Mühn

4

So recalling those powerful ones and the fate that raises our hearts up,
    Deedless ourselves, of small weight, but by Aether nevertheless
Not overlooked, devout as the ancients, those god-instructed
    Joy-breathing poets, we joyously roam through the land.
Great is the growth all around. Up there, from the bordering mountains,
    Many a youth descends, born there, the gentle-sloped hills,
Well-springs bubble from there and a hundred brooklets, as busy,
    Come both by day and by night into the lowlands, to till.
But the master it is who ploughs up the heartland and centre,
    Draws the furrows himself, Neckar, draws blessings down.
With him there come the Italian breezes, the sea sends
    Clouds for his way and sends sunshine, magnificent suns.
Hence it is that almost over our heads it may rise then,
    Superabundant, for here, down to the lowlands the wealth
Even more richly was brought to the favoured, the region's people,
    Yet not one of the mountain-folk ever begrudges them wine,
Gardens, luxuriant grass or their corn or their glowing
    Fruit trees that line the roads, shadow us wayfaring men.

5

While we look on, though, and move through profusion of gladness,
    Both our road and our day pass like a drunken man's, flee.
For already the city, the famed, with garlands of hallowing leafage,
    Luminous over there, raises her reverend head.
Glorious she stands with thyrsus held up and the fir tree
    High, as far as the clouds, crimsonly blessed by the light.
Now be gracious to us! To the guest and your son now returning,
    Fortunate Stuttgart, with grace welcome the stranger for me.
Anthems with flute or with strings you have always approved of,
    So I believe, and the song's childlike babble, and sweet

316 · *Hexameters and Elegies*

Süße Vergessenheit bei gegenwärtigem Geiste,
    Drum erfreuest du auch gerne den Sängern das Herz.
Aber ihr, ihr Größeren auch, ihr Frohen, die allzeit
    Leben und walten, erkannt, oder gewaltiger auch,
Wenn ihr wirket und schafft in heiliger Nacht und allein herrscht
    Und allmächtig empor ziehet ein ahnendes Volk,
Bis die Jünglinge sich der Väter droben erinnern,
    Mündig und hell vor euch steht der besonnene Mensch –

6

Engel des Vaterlands! o ihr, vor denen das Auge,
    Sei's auch stark und das Knie bricht dem vereinzelten Mann,
Daß er halten sich muß an die Freund' und bitten die Theuern,
    Daß sie tragen mit ihm all die beglükende Last,
Habt, o Gütige, Dank für den und alle die Andern,
    Die mein Leben, mein Gut unter den Sterblichen sind.
Aber die Nacht kommt! laß uns eilen, zu feiern das Herbstfest
    Heut noch! voll ist das Herz, aber das Leben ist kurz,
Und was uns der himmlische Tag zu sagen geboten,
    Das zu nennen, mein Schmidt! reichen wir beide nicht aus.
Trefliche bring' ich dir und das Freudenfeuer wird hoch auf
    Schlagen und heiliger soll sprechen das kühnere Wort.
Siehe! da ist es rein! und des Gottes freundliche Gaaben
    Die wir theilen, sie sind zwischen den Liebenden nur.
Anderes nicht – o kommt! o macht es wahr! denn allein ja
    Bin ich und niemand nimmt mir von der Stirne den Traum?
Kommt und reicht, ihr Lieben, die Hand! das möge genug seyn,
    Aber die größere Lust sparen dem Enkel wir auf.

Rest from labour, oblivion that's entered with minds that are wakeful,
    Always prepared to please singers and gladden their hearts.
Yet you still greater ones, you the serene who at all times
    Live and hold sway, whether known, named, or more mighty still
When in holy night you're at work and create and alone you
    Rule and almightily draw upward a people by signs,
Till the young remember their forefathers gathered above them,
    And before you, matured, stands a more thoughtful mankind –

6

Angels of home, our country's, O you in whose presence the vision,
    Strong though it be, and the knees break of a man on his own,
So that to friends he must look for support and the dear ones
    That they may help him to bear all the great load of his joy,
Kind ones, accept my thanks for him and for all the others
    Who are my life and my wealth here amid mortals, on earth.
Night is coming, though. Let us hurry to celebrate autumn
    This very day. Though the heart, full, may forget it, our lives are short
And those things that a heavenly day has commanded we speak of,
    Them to make known, dear friend, is too much both for you and for me.
Excellent men I bring you, the fire of rejoicing high up shall
    Leap and more sacredly then speak the more venturesome word.
Look, there it's pure. And the generous presents the god gives,
    When we share them, cohere only when love makes the bond.
Nothing else can. Oh, come, then, and make it true. For alone I
    Am, after all; and can none lift the bad dream from my brow?
Come, dear friends, and hold out your hands. Let that token suffice us,
    While for the grandson we save greater and deeper delight.

Brod und Wein

AN HEINZE

1

Rings um ruhet die Stadt; still wird die erleuchtete Gasse,
　　Und, mit Fakeln geschmükt, rauschen die Wagen hinweg.
Satt gehn heim von Freuden des Tags zu ruhen die Menschen,
　　Und Gewinn und Verlust wäget ein sinniges Haupt
Wohlzufrieden zu Haus; leer steht von Trauben und Blumen,
　　Und von Werken der Hand ruht der geschäfftige Markt.
Aber das Saitenspiel tönt fern aus Gärten; vieleicht, daß
　　Dort ein Liebendes spielt oder ein einsamer Mann
Ferner Freunde gedenkt und der Jugendzeit; und die Brunnen
　　Immerquillend und frisch rauschen an duftendem Beet.
Still in dämmriger Luft ertönen geläutete Gloken,
　　Und der Stunden gedenk rufet ein Wächter die Zahl.
Jezt auch kommet einWehn und regt die Gipfel des Hains auf,
　　Sieh! und das Schattenbild unserer Erde, der Mond
Kommet geheim nun auch; die Schwärmerische, die Nacht kommt,
　　Voll mit Sternen und wohl wenig bekümmert um uns,
Glänzt die Erstaunende dort, die Fremdlingin unter den Menschen
　　Über Gebirgeshöhn traurig und prächtig herauf.

2

Wunderbar ist die Gunst der Hocherhabnen und niemand
　　Weiß von wannen und was einem geschiebet von ihr.
So bewegt sie die Welt und die hoffende Seele der Menschen,
　　Selbst kein Weiser versteht, was sie bereitet, denn so
Will es der oberste Gott, der sehr dich liebet, und darum
　　Ist noch lieber, wie sie, dir der besonnene Tag.
Aber zuweilen liebt auch klares Auge den Schatten
　　Und versuchet zu Lust, eh' es die Noth ist, den Schlaf,

Bread and Wine

TO HEINSE

1

Round us the town is at rest; the street, in pale lamplight, falls quiet
  And, their torches ablaze, coaches rush through and away.
People go home to rest, replete with the day and its pleasures,
  There to weigh up in their heads, pensive, the gain and the loss,
Finding the balance good; stripped bare now of grapes and of flowers,
  As of their handmade goods, quiet the market stalls lie.
But faint music of strings comes drifting from gardens; it could be
  Someone in love who plays there, could be a man all alone
Thinking of distant friends, the days of his youth; and the fountains,
  Ever welling and new, plash amid balm-breathing beds.
Church bells ring; every stroke hangs still in the quivering half-light
  And the watchman calls out, mindful, no less, of the hour.
Now a breeze rises too and ruffles the crests of the coppice,
  Look, and in secret our globe's shadowy image, the moon,
Slowly is rising too; and Night, the fantastical, comes now
  Full of stars and, I think, little concerned about us,
Night, the astonishing, there, the stranger to all that is human,
  Over the mountain-tops mournful and gleaming draws on.

2

Marvellous is her favour, Night's, the exalted, and no one
  Knows what it is or whence comes all she does and bestows.
So she works on the world and works on our souls ever hoping,
  Not even wise men can tell what is her purpose, for so
God, the Highest, has willed, who very much loves you, and therefore
  Dearer even than Night reasoning Day is to you.
Nonetheless there are times when clear eyes too love the shadows,
  Tasting sleep uncompelled, trying the pleasure it gives,

Oder es blikt auch gern ein treuer Mann in die Nacht hin,
　　Ja, es ziemet sich ihr Kränze zu weihn und Gesang,
Weil den Irrenden sie geheiliget ist und den Todten,
　　Selber aber besteht, ewig, in freiestem Geist.
Aber sie muß uns auch, daß in der zaudernden Weile,
　　Daß im Finstern für uns einiges Haltbare sei,
Uns die Vergessenheit und das Heiligtrunkene gönnen,
　　Gönnen das strömende Wort, das, wie die Liebenden, sei,
Schlummerlos und vollern Pokal und kühneres Leben,
　　Heilig Gedächtniß auch, wachend zu bleiben bei Nacht.

3

Auch verbergen umsonst das Herz im Busen, umsonst nur
　　Halten den Muth noch wir, Meister und Knaben, denn wer
Möcht' es hindern und wer möcht' uns die Freude verbieten?
　　Göttliches Feuer auch treibet, bei Tag und bei Nacht
Aufzubrechen. So komm! daß wir das Offene schauen,
　　Daß ein Eigenes wir suchen, so weit es auch ist.
Fest bleibt Eins; es sei um Mittag oder es gehe
　　Bis in die Mitternacht, immer bestehet ein Maas,
Allen gemein, doch jeglichem auch ist eignes beschieden,
　　Dahin gehet und kommt jeder, wohin er es kann.
Drum! und spotten des Spotts mag gern frohlokkender Wahnsinn,
　　Wenn er in heiliger Nacht plözlich die Sänger ergreift.
Drum an den Isthmos komm! dorthin, wo das offene Meer rauscht
　　Am Parnaß und der Schnee delphische Felsen umglänzt,
Dort ins Land des Olymps, dort auf die Höhe Cithärons,
　　Unter die Fichten dort, unter die Trauben, von wo
Thebe drunten und Ismenos rauscht im Lande des Kadmos,
　　Dorther kommt und zurük deutet der kommende Gott.

Or a loyal man too will gaze into Night and enjoy it,
    Yes, and rightly to her garlands we dedicate, hymns,
Since to all those astray, the mad and the dead, she is sacred,
    Yet herself remains firm, always, her spirit most free.
But to us in her turn, so that in the wavering moment,
    Deep in the dark there shall be something at least that endures,
Holy drunkenness she must grant and frenzied oblivion,
    Grant the on-rushing word, sleepless as lovers are too,
And a wine-cup more full, a life more intense and more daring,
    Holy remembrance too, keeping us wakeful at night.

3

And in vain we conceal our hearts deep within us, in vain we,
    Master and novice alike, still keep our courage in check.
For who now would stop us, who would forbid us rejoicing?
    Day-long, night-long we're urged on by a fire that's divine.
Urged to be gone. Let us go, then! Off to see open spaces,
    Where we may seek what is ours, distant, remote though it be!
One thing is sure even now: at noon or just before midnight,
    Whether it's early or late, always a measure exists,
Common to all, though his own to each one is also allotted,
    Each of us makes for the place, reaches the place that he can.
Well, then, may jubilant madness laugh at those who deride it,
    When in hallowed Night poets are seized by its power;
Off to the Isthmus, then! To land where wide open the sea roars
    Near Parnassus and snow glistens on Delphian rocks;
Off to Olympian regions, up to the heights of Cithaeron,
    Up to the pine trees there, up to the grapes, from which rush
Thebe down there and Ismenos, loud in the country of Cadmus:
    Thence has come and back there points the god who's to come.

4

Seeliges Griechenland! du Haus der Himmlischen alle,
    Also ist wahr, was einst wir in der Jugend gehört?
Festlicher Saal! der Boden ist Meer! und Tische die Berge,
    Wahrlich zu einzigem Brauche vor Alters gebaut!
Aber die Thronen, wo? die Tempel, und wo die Gefäße,
    Wo mit Nectar gefüllt, Göttern zu Lust der Gesang?
Wo, wo leuchten sie denn, die fernhintreffenden Sprüche?
    Delphi schlummert und wo tönet das große Geschik?
Wo ist das schnelle? wo brichts, allgegenwärtigen Glüks voll
    Donnernd aus heiterer Luft über die Augen herein?
Vater Aether! so riefs und flog von Zunge zu Zunge
    Tausendfach, es ertrug keiner das Leben allein;
Ausgetheilet erfreut solch Gut und getauscht, mit Fremden,
    Wirds ein Jubel, es wächst schlafend des Wortes Gewalt
Vater! heiter! und hallt, so weit es gehet, das uralt
    Zeichen, von Eltern geerbt, treffend und schaffend hinab.
Denn so kehren die Himmlischen ein, tiefschütternd gelangt so
    Aus den Schatten herab unter die Menschen ihr Tag.

5

Unempfunden kommen sie erst, es streben entgegen
    Ihnen die Kinder, zu hell kommet, zu blendend das Glük,
Und es scheut sie der Mensch, kaum weiß zu sagen ein Halbgott,
    Wer mit Nahmen sie sind, die mit den Gaaben ihm nahn.
Aber der Muth von ihnen ist groß, es füllen das Herz ihm
    Ihre Freuden und kaum weiß er zu brauchen das Gut,
Schafft, verschwendet und fast ward ihm Unheiliges heilig,
    Das er mit seegnender Hand thörig und gütig berührt.
Möglichst dulden die Himmlischen diß; dann aber in Wahrheit
    Kommen sie selbst und gewohnt werden die Menschen des Glüks
Und des Tags und zu schaun die Offenbaren, das Antliz
    Derer, welche, schon längst Eines und Alles genannt,

4

Happy land of the Greeks, you house of them all, of the Heavenly,
    So it is true what we heard then, in the days of our youth?
Festive hall, whose floor is ocean, whose tables are mountains,
    Truly, in time out of mind built for a purpose unique!
But the thrones, where are they? Where are the temples, the vessels,
    Where, to delight the gods, brim-full with nectar, the songs?
Where, then, where do they shine, the oracles winged for far targets?
    Delphi's asleep, and where now is great fate to be heard?
Where is the swift? And full of joy omnipresent, where does it
    Flash upon dazzled eyes, thundering fall from clear skies?
Father Aether! one cried, and tongue after tongue took it up then,
    Thousands, no man could bear life so intense on his own;
Shared, such wealth gives delight and later, when bartered with strangers,
    Turns to rapture; the word gathers new strength when asleep:
Father! Clear light! and long resounding it travels, the ancient
    Sign handed down, and far, striking, creating, rings out.
So do the Heavenly enter, shaking the deepest foundations,
    Only so from the gloom down to mankind comes their Day.

5

Unperceived at first they come, and only the children
    Surge towards them, too bright, dazzling, this joy enters in,
So that men are afraid, a demigod hardly can tell yet
    Who they are, and name those who approach him with gifts.
Yet their courage is great, his heart soon is full of their gladness
    And he hardly knows what's to be done with such wealth,
Busily runs and wastes it, almost regarding as sacred
    Trash which his blessing hand foolishly, kindly has touched.
This, while they can, the Heavenly bear with; but then they appear in
    Truth, in person, and now men grow accustomed to joy,
And to Day, and the sight of godhead revealed, and their faces –
    One and All long ago, once and for all, they were named –

Tief die verschwiegene Brust mit freier Genüge gefüllet,
  Und zuerst und allein alles Verlangen beglükt;
So ist der Mensch; wenn da ist das Gut, und es sorget mit Gaaben
  Selber ein Gott für ihn, kennet und sieht er es nicht.
Tragen muß er, zuvor; nun aber nennt er sein Liebstes,
  Nun, nun müssen dafür Worte, wie Blumen, entstehn.

6

Und nun denkt er zu ehren in Ernst die seeligen Götter,
  Wirklich und wahrhaft muß alles verkünden ihr Lob.
Nichts darf schauen das Licht, was nicht den Hohen gefället,
  Vor den Aether gebührt müßigversuchendes nicht.
Drum in der Gegenwart der Himmlischen würdig zu stehen,
  Richten in herrlichen Ordnungen Völker sich auf
Untereinander und baun die schönen Tempel und Städte
  Vest und edel, sie gehn über Gestaden empor –
Aber wo sind sie? wo blühn die Bekannten, die Kronen des Festes?
  Thebe welkt und Athen; rauschen die Waffen nicht mehr
In Olympia, nicht die goldnen Wagen des Kampfspiels,
  Und bekränzen sich denn nimmer die Schiffe Korinths?
Warum schweigen auch sie, die alten heilgen Theater?
  Warum freuet sich denn nicht der geweihete Tanz?
Warum zeichnet, wie sonst, die Stirne des Mannes ein Gott nicht,
  Drükt den Stempel, wie sonst, nicht dem Getroffenen auf?
Oder er kam auch selbst und nahm des Menschen Gestalt an
  Und vollendet' und schloß tröstend das himmlische Fest.

7

Aber Freund! wir kommen zu spät. Zwar leben die Götter,
  Aber über dem Haupt droben in anderer Welt.
Endlos wirken sie da und scheinens wenig zu achten,
  Ob wir leben, so sehr schonen die Himmlischen uns.
Denn nicht immer vermag ein schwaches Gefäß sie zu fassen,
  Nur zu Zeiten erträgt göttliche Fülle der Mensch.

Who with free self-content had deeply suffused silent bosoms,
   From the first and alone satisfied every desire.
Such is man; when the wealth is there, and no less than a god in
   Person tends him with gifts, blind he remains, unaware.
First he must suffer; but now he names his most treasured possession,
   Now for it words like flowers leaping alive he must find.

6

Now in earnest he means to honour the gods who have blessed him,
   Now in truth and in deed all must re-echo their praise.
Nothing must see the light but what to those high ones is pleasing,
   Idle and bungled work never for Aether was fit.
So, to be worthy and stand unashamed in the heavenly presence,
   Nations rise up and soon, gloriously ordered, compete
One with the other in building beautiful temples and cities
   Noble and firm they tower high above river and sea –
Only, where are they? Where thrive those famed ones, the festival's garlands?
   Athens is withered, and Thebes; now do no weapons ring out
In Olympia, nor now those chariots, all golden, in games there,
   And no longer are wreaths hung on Corinthian ships?
Why are they silent too, the theatres, ancient and hallowed?
   Why not now does the dance celebrate, consecrate joy?
Why no more does a god imprint on the brow of a mortal
   Struck, as by lightning, the mark, brand him, as once he would do?
Else he would come himself, assuming a shape that was human,
   And, consoling the guests, crowned and concluded the feast.

7

But, my friend, we have come too late. Though the gods are living,
   Over our heads they live, up in a different world.
Endlessly there they act and, such is their kind wish to spare us,
   Little they seem to care whether we live or do not.
For not always a frail, a delicate vessel can hold them,
   Only at times can our kind bear the full impact of gods.

Traum von ihnen ist drauf das Leben. Aber das Irrsaal
   Hilft, wie Schlummer und stark machet die Noth und die Nacht,
Biß daß Helden genug in der ehernen Wiege gewachsen,
   Herzen an Kraft, wie sonst, ähnlich den Himmlischen sind.
Donnernd kommen sie drauf. Indessen dünket mir öfters
   Besser zu schlafen, wie so ohne Genossen zu seyn,
So zu harren und was zu thun indeß und zu sagen,
   Weiß ich nicht und wozu Dichter in dürftiger Zeit?
Aber sie sind, sagst du, wie des Weingotts heilige Priester,
   Welche von Lande zu Land zogen in heiliger Nacht.

8

Nemlich, als vor einiger Zeit, uns dünket sie lange,
   Aufwärts stiegen sie all, welche das Leben beglükt,
Als der Vater gewandt sein Angesicht von den Menschen,
   Und das Trauern mit Recht über der Erde begann,
Als erschienen zu lezt ein stiller Genius, himmlisch
   Tröstend, welcher des Tags Ende verkündet' und schwand,
Ließ zum Zeichen, daß einst er da gewesen und wieder
   Käme, der himmlische Chor einige Gaaben zurük,
Derer menschlich, wie sonst, wir uns zu freuen vermöchten,
   Denn zur Freude, mit Geist, wurde das Größre zu groß
Unter den Menschen und noch, noch fehlen die Starken zu höchsten
   Freuden, aber es lebt stille noch einiger Dank.
Brod ist der Erde Frucht, doch ists vom Lichte geseegnet,
   Und vom donnernden Gott kommet die Freude des Weins.
Darum denken wir auch dabei der Himmlischen, die sonst
   Da gewesen und die kehren in richtiger Zeit,
Darum singen sie auch mit Ernst die Sänger den Weingott
   Und nicht eitel erdacht tönet dem Alten das Lob.

Ever after our life is dream about them. But frenzy,
    Wandering, helps, like sleep; Night and distress make us strong
Till in that cradle of steel heroes enough have been fostered,
    Hearts in strength can match heavenly strength as before.
Thundering then they come. But meanwhile too often I think it's
    Better to sleep than to be friendless as we are, alone,
Always waiting, and what to do or to say in the meantime
    I don't know, and who wants poets at all in lean years?
But they are, you say, like those holy ones, priests of the wine-god
    Who in holy Night roamed from one place to the next.

8

For, when some time ago now – to us it seems ages –
    Up rose all those by whom life had been brightened, made glad,
When the Father had turned his face from the sight of us mortals
    And all over the earth, rightly, they started to mourn,
Lastly a Genius had come, dispensing heavenly comfort,
    He who proclaimed the Day's end, then himself went away,
Then, as a token that once they had been down here and once more would
    Come, the heavenly choir left a few presents behind,
Gifts in which now as ever humanly men might take pleasure,
    Since for spiritual joy great things had now grown too great
Here, among men, and even now there's a lack of those strong for
    Joy's extremity, but silent some thanks do live on.
Bread is a fruit of Earth, yet touched by the blessing of sunlight,
    From the thundering god issues the gladness of wine.
Therefore in tasting them we think of the Heavenly who once were
    Here and shall come again, come when their advent is due;
Therefore also the poets in serious hymns to the wine-god,
    Never idly devised, sound that most ancient one's praise.

9

Ja! sie sagen mit Recht, er söhne den Tag mit der Nacht aus,
    Führe des Himmels Gestirn ewig hinunter, hinauf,
Allzeit froh, wie das Laub der immergrünenden Fichte,
    Das er liebt, und der Kranz, den er von Epheu gewählt,
Weil er bleibet und selbst die Spur der entflohenen Götter
    Götterlosen hinab unter das Finstere bringt.
Was der Alten Gesang von Kindern Gottes geweissagt,
    Siehe! wir sind es, wir; Frucht von Hesperien ists!
Wunderbar und genau ists als an Menschen erfüllet,
    Glaube, wer es geprüft! aber so vieles geschieht,
Keines wirket, denn wir sind herzlos, Schatten, bis unser
    Vater Aether erkannt jeden und allen gehört.
Aber indessen kommt als Fakelschwinger des Höchsten
    Sohn, der Syrier, unter die Schatten herab.
Seelige Weise sehns; ein Lächeln aus der gefangnen
    Seele leuchtet, dem Licht thauet ihr Auge noch auf.
Sanfter träumet und schläft in Armen der Erde der Titan,
    Selbst der neidische, selbst Cerberus trinket und schläft.

9

Yes, and rightly they say he reconciles Day with our Night-time,
  Leads the stars of the sky upward and down without end,
Always glad, like the living boughs of the evergreen pine tree
  Which he loves, and the wreath wound out of ivy for choice
Since it lasts and conveys the trace of the gods now departed
  Down to the godless below, into the midst of their gloom.
What of the children of God was foretold in the songs of the ancients,
  Look, we are it, ourselves; fruit of Hesperia it is!
Strictly it has come true, fulfilled as in men by a marvel,
  Let those who have seen it believe! Much, however, occurs,
Nothing succeeds, because we are heartless, mere shadows until our
  Father Aether, made known, recognized, fathers us all.
Meanwhile, though, to us shadows comes the Son of the Highest,
  Comes the Syrian and down into our gloom bears his torch.
Blissful, the wise men see it; in souls that were captive there gleams a
  Smile, and their eyes shall yet thaw in response to the light.
Dreams more gentle and sleep in the arms of Earth lull the Titan,
  Even that envious one, Cerberus, drinks and lies down.

Heimkunft

AN DIE VERWANDTEN

1

Drinn in den Alpen ists noch helle Nacht und die Wolke,
    Freudiges dichtend, sie dekt drinnen das gähnende Thal.
Dahin, dorthin toset und stürzt die scherzende Bergluft,
    Schroff durch Tannen herab glänzet und schwindet ein Stral.
Langsam eilt und kämpft das freudigschauernde Chaos,
    Jung an Gestalt, doch stark, feiert es liebenden Streit
Unter den Felsen, es gährt und wankt in den ewigen Schranken,
    Denn bacchantischer zieht drinnen der Morgen herauf.
Denn es wächst unendlicher dort das Jahr und die heilgen
    Stunden, die Tage, sie sind kühner geordnet, gemischt.
Dennoch merket die Zeit der Gewittervogel und zwischen
    Bergen, hoch in der Luft weilt er und rufet den Tag.
Jezt auch wachet und schaut in der Tiefe drinnen das Dörflein
    Furchtlos, Hohem vertraut, unter den Gipfeln hinauf.
Wachstum ahnend, denn schon, wie Blize, fallen die alten
    Wasserquellen, der Grund unter den Stürzenden dampft,
Echo tönet umher, und die unermeßliche Werkstatt
    Reget hei Tag und Nacht, Gaaben versendend, den Arm.

2

Ruhig glänzen indeß die silbernen Höhen darüber,
    Voll mit Rosen ist schon droben der leuchtende Schnee.
Und noch höher hinauf wohnt über dem Lichte der reine
    Seelige Gott vom Spiel heiliger Stralen erfreut.
Stille wohnt er allein und hell erscheinet sein Antliz,
    Der ätherische scheint Leben zu geben geneigt,
Freude zu schaffen, mit uns, wie oft, wenn, kundig des Maases,
    Kundig der Athmenden auch zögernd und schonend der Gott

Homecoming

TO HIS RELATIVES

1

There in the Alps a gleaming night still delays and, composing
  Portents of gladness, the cloud covers a valley agape.
This way, that way roars and rushes the breeze of the mountains,
  Teasing, sheer through the firs falls a bright beam, and is lost.
Slowly it hurries and wars, this Chaos trembling with pleasure,
  Young in appearance, but strong, celebrates here amid rocks
Loving discord, and seethes, shakes in its bounds that are timeless,
  For more bacchantically now morning approaches within.
For more endlessly there the year expands, and the holy
  Hours and the days in there more boldly are ordered and mixed.
Yet the bird of thunder marks and observes the time, and
  High in the air, between peaks, hangs and calls out a new day.
Now, deep inside, the small village also awakens and fearless
  Looks at the summits around, long now familiar with height;
Growth it foreknows, for already ancient torrents like lightning
  Crash, and the ground below steams with the spray of their fall.
Echo sounds all around and, measureless, tireless the workshop,
  Sending out gifts, is astir, active by day and by night.

2

Quiet, meanwhile, above, the silvery peaks lie aglitter,
  Full of roses up there, flushed with dawn's rays, lies the snow.
Even higher, beyond the light, does the pure, never clouded
  God have his dwelling, whom beams, holy, make glad with their play.
Silent, alone he dwells, and bright his countenance shines now,
  He, the aethereal one, seems kindly, disposed to give life,
Generate joys, with us men, as often when, knowing the measure,
  Knowing those who draw breath, hesitant, sparing the God

Wohlgediegenes Glük den Städten und Häußern und milde
 Reegen, zu öffnen das Land, brütende Wolken, und euch,
Trauteste Lüfte dann, euch, sanfte Frühlinge, sendet,
 Und mit langsamer Hand Traurige wieder erfreut,
Wenn er die Zeiten erneut, der Schöpferische, die stillen
 Herzen der alternden Menschen erfrischt und ergreifft,
Und hinab in die Tiefe wirkt, und öffnet und aufhellt,
 Wie ers liebet, und jezt wieder ein Leben beginnt,
Anmuth blühet, wie einst, und gegenwärtiger Geist kömmt,
 Und ein freudiger Muth wieder die Fittige schwellt.

3

Vieles sprach ich zu ihm, denn, was auch Dichtende sinnen
 Oder singen, es gilt meistens den Engeln und ihm;
Vieles bat ich, zu lieb dem Vaterlande, damit nicht
 Ungebeten uns einst plözlich befiele der Geist;
Vieles für euch auch, die im Vaterlande besorgt sind,
 Denen der heilige Dank lächelnd die Flüchtlinge bringt,
Landesleute! für euch, indessen wiegte der See mich,
 Und der Ruderer saß ruhig und lobte die Fahrt.
Weit in des Sees Ebene wars Ein freudiges Wallen
 Unter den Seegeln und jezt blühet und hellet die Stadt
Dort in der Frühe sich auf, wohl her von schattigen Alpen
 Kommt geleitet und ruht nun in dem Hafen das Schiff.
Warm ist das Ufer hier und freundlich offene Thale,
 Schön von Pfaden erhellt grünen und schimmern mich an.
Gärten stehen gesellt und die glänzende Knospe beginnt schon,
 Und des Vogels Gesang ladet den Wanderer ein.
Alles scheinet vertraut, der vorübereilende Gruß auch
 Scheint von Freunden, es scheint jegliche Miene verwandt.

Sends well-allotted fortune both to the cities and houses,
    Showers to open the land, gentle, and you, brooding clouds,
You, then, most dearly loved breezes, followed by temperate springtime,
    And with a slow hand once more gladdens us mortals grown sad,
When he renews the seasons, he, the creative, and quickens,
    Moves once again those hearts weary and numb with old age,
Works on the lowest depths to open them up and to brighten
    All, as he loves to do; so now does life bud anew,
Beauty abounds, as before, and spirit is present, returned now,
    And a joyful zest urges furled wings to unfold.

3

Much I said to him; for whatever the poets may ponder,
    Sing, it mostly concerns either the angels or him.
Much I besought, on my country's behalf, lest unbidden one day the
    Spirit should suddenly come, take us by storm unprepared;
Much, too, for your sake to whom, though troubled now in our country,
    Holy gratitude brings fugitives back with a smile,
Fellow Germans, for your sake! Meanwhile the lake gently rocked me,
    Calmly the boatman sat, praising the weather, the breeze.
Out on the level lake one impulse of joy had enlivened
    All the sails, and at last, there in a new day's first hour
Brightening, the town unfurls, and safely conveyed from the shadows
    Cast by the Alps, now the boat glides to its mooring and rests.
Warm the shore is here, and valleys open in welcome,
    Pleasantly lit by paths, greenly allure me and gleam.
Gardens, forgathered, lie here and already the dew-laden bud breaks
    And a bird's early song welcomes the traveller home.
All seems familiar; even the word or the nod caught in passing
    Seems like a friend's, every face looks like a relative's face.

4

Freilich wohl! das Geburtsland ists, der Boden der Heimath,
　　Was du suchest, es ist nahe, begegnet dir schon.Und umsonst nicht
steht, wie ein Sohn, am wellenumrauschten
　　Thor' und siehet und sucht liebende Nahmen für dich,
Mit Gesang ein wandernder Mann, glükseeliges Lindau!
　　Eine der gastlichen Pforten des Landes ist diß,
Reizend hinauszugehn in die vielversprechende Ferne,
　　Dort, wo die Wunder sind, dort, wo das göttliche Wild
Hoch in die Ebnen herab der Rhein die verwegene Bahn bricht,
　　Und aus Felsen hervor ziehet das jauchzende Thal,
Dort hinein, durchs helle Gehirg, nach Komo zu wandern,
　　Oder hinab, wie der Tag wandelt, den offenen See;
Aber reizender mir bist du, geweihete Pforte!
　　Heimzugehn, wo bekannt blühende Wege mir sind,
Dort zu besuchen das Land und die schönen Thale des Nekars,
　　Und die Wälder, das Grün heiliger Bäume, wo gern
Sich die Eiche gesellt mit stillen Birken und Buchen,
　　Und in Bergen ein Ort freundlich gefangen mich nimmt.

5

Dort empfangen sie mich. O Stimme der Stadt, der Mutter!
　　O du triffest, du regst Langegelerntes mir auf!
Dennoch sind sie es noch! noch blühet die Sonn' und die Freud' euch,
　　O ihr Liebsten! und fast heller im Auge, wie sonst.
Ja! das Alte noch ists! Es gedeihet und reifet, doch keines
　　Was da lebt und liebt, lässet die Treue zurük.
Aber das Beste, der Fund, der unter des heiligen Friedens
　　Bogen lieget, er ist Jungen und Alten gespart.
Thörig red ich. Es ist die Freude. Doch morgen und künftig
　　Wenn wir gehen und schaun draußen das lebende Feld
Unter den Blüthen des Baums, in den Feiertagen des Frühlings
　　Red' und hoff ich mit euch vieles, ihr Liehen! davon.

4

And no wonder! Your native country and soil you are walking,
　　What you seek, it is near, now comes to meet you halfway.
Nor by mere chance like a son a wandering man now stands gazing
　　Here by the wavelet-loud gate, looking for names to convey
Love to you in his poem, Lindau, the favoured and happy!
　　Not the least of our land's many hospitable doors,
Urging men to go out allured by the promise of distance,
　　Go where the wonders are, go where that godlike wild beast,
High up the Rhine blasts his reckless way to the plains of the lowlands,
　　Where out of rocks at last bursts the lush valley's delight,
Wander in there, through the sunlit mountain range, making for Como,
　　Or, as the day drifts on, drift on the wide open lake;
Yet, you door that are hallowed, me much more strongly you urge to
　　Make for home where I know blossoming pathways and lanes,
There to visit the fields and the Neckar's beautiful valleys,
　　And the woods, green leaves holy to me, where the oak
Does not disdain to consort with quiet birches and beeches,
　　Where amid mountains one place holds me, a captive content.

5

There they too receive me. Voice of my town, of my mother!
　　How to your sound respond things that I learned long ago!
Yet they are still themselves! More radiantly, almost, than ever,
　　Dearest ones, in your eyes joy and the sun are alight.
Yes, it's all what it was. It thrives and grows ripe, but no creature
　　Living and loving there ever abandons its faith.
But the best thing of all, the find that's been saved up beneath the
　　Holy rainbow of peace, waits for the young and the old.
Like a fool I speak. In my joy. But tomorrow and later
　　When we go outside, look at the living green field
Under the trees in blossom, on holidays due in the springtime,
　　Much of those things with you, dear ones, I'll speak and I'll hope.

Vieles hab' ich gehört vom großen Vater und habe
    Lange geschwiegen von ihm, welcher die wandernde Zeit
Droben in Höhen erfrischt, und waltet über Gebirgen
    Der gewähret uns bald himmlische Gaaben und ruftHellern Gesang
Und schikt viel gute Geister. O säumt nicht,
    Kommt, Erhaltenden ihr! Engel des Jahres! und ihr,

6

Engel des Haußes, kommt! in die Adern alle des Lebens,
    Alle freuend zugleich, theile das Himmlische sich!
Adle! verjünge! damit nichts Menschlichgutes, damit nicht
    Eine Stunde des Tags ohne die Frohen und auch
Solche Freude, wie jezt, wenn Liebende wieder sich finden,
    Wie es gehört für sie, schiklich geheiliget sei.
Wenn wir seegnen das Mahl, wen darf ich nennen und wenn wir
    Ruhn vom Leben des Tags, saget, wie bring' ich den Dank?
Nenn' ich den Hohen dabei? Unschikliches liebet ein Gott nicht,
    Ihn zu fassen, ist fast unsere Freude zu klein.
Schweigen müssen wir oft; es fehlen heilige Nahmen,
    Herzen schlagen und doch bleibet die Rede zurük?
Aber ein Saitenspiel leiht jeder Stunde die Töne
    Und erfreuet vieleicht Himmlische, welche sich nahn.
Das bereitet und so ist auch beinahe die Sorge
    Schon befriediget, die unter das Freudige kam.
Sorgen, wie diese, muß, gern oder nicht, in der Seele
    Tragen ein Sänger und oft, aber die anderen nicht.

Much in the meantime I've heard of him, the great Father, and long now
    I have kept silent about him who on summits renews
Wandering Time up above and governs the high mountain ranges,
    Him who soon now will grant heavenly gifts and calls forth
Song more effulgent, and sends us many good spirits. No longer
    Wait now, preservers, the year's angels, O come now, and you,

6

Angels, too, of our house, re-enter the veins of all life now,
    Gladdening all at once, let what is heavenly be shared!
Make us noble and new! Till nothing that's humanly good, no
    Hour of the day without them, them the most joyful, or such
Joy as now too is known when lovers return to each other,
    Passes, as fitting for them, hallowed as angels demand.
When we bless the meal, whose name may I speak, and when late we
    Rest from the life of each day, tell me, to whom give my thanks?
Him, the most High, should I name then? A god does not love what's
                            [unseemly,
    Him to embrace and to hold our joy is too small.
Silence often hehoves us: deficient in names that are holy,
    Hearts may beat high, while the lips hesitate, wary of speech?
Yet a lyre to each hour lends the right mode, the right music,
    And, it may be, delights heavenly ones who draw near.
This make ready, and almost nothing remains of the care that
    Darkened our festive day, troubled the promise of joy.
Whether he like it or not, and often, a singer must harbour
    Cares like these in his soul; not, though, the wrong sort of cares.

Der Tod des Empedokles

ein Trauerspiel
in
fünf Acten

The Death of Empedocles

Fragments of a Tragedy
in
Five Acts

Zweite Fassung

PERSONEN

EMPEDOKLES
PAUSANIAS
PANTHEA
DELIA
HERMOKRATES
MEKADES
AMPHARES
DEMOKLES   Agrigentiner
HYLAS

Der Schauplaz ist theils in Agrigent, theils am Aetna.

Second Version

CHARACTERS

EMPEDOCLES
PAUSANIAS
PANTHEA
DELIA
HERMOCRATES
MECADES
AMPHARES
DEMOCLES   Citizens of Agrigentum
HYLAS

The action takes place partly at Agrigentum, partly at the foot of Etna.

Erster Act

Erster Auftritt

CHOR DER AGRIGENTINER in der Ferne
MEKADES. HERMOKRATES

MEKADES

Hörst du das trunkne Volk?

HERMOKRATES

Sie suchen ihn.

MEKADES

Der Geist des Manns
Ist mächtig unter ihnen.

HERMOKRATES

Ich weiß, wie dürres Gras
Entzünden sich die Menschen.

MEKADES

Daß Einer so die Menge bewegt, mir ists,
Als wie wenn Jovis Bliz den Wald
Ergreift, und furchtbarer.

HERMOKRATES

Drum binden wir den Menschen auch
Das Band ums Auge, daß sie nicht
Zu kräftig sich am Lichte nähren.
Nicht gegenwärtig werden
Darf Göttliches vor ihnen.

Act One

Scene One

CHORUS OF AGRIGENTINES in the distance
MECADES. HERMOCRATES

MECADES

Do you hear the frenzied crowd?

HERMOCRATES

They're looking for him.

MECADES

The spirit of that man
Persuades, pervades them.

HERMOCRATES

I know, like withered grass
The minds of men catch fire.

MECADES

That any man should have such power to move
The mob, to me is like Jove's lightning
Loose in a forest, and more terrible.

HERMOCRATES

And that is why we wrap that band
Around men's eyes, lest all too richly
They feed upon the light.
Never what is divine
Must be quite present to them,

Es darf ihr Herz
Lebendiges nicht finden.
Kennst du die Alten nicht,
Die Lieblinge des Himmels man nennt?
Sie nährten die Brust
An Kräften der Welt
Und den Hellaufblikenden war
Unsterbliches nahe,
Drum beugten die Stolzen
Das Haupt auch nicht
Und vor den Gewaltigen konnt'
Ein Anderes nicht bestehn,
Es ward verwandelt vor ihnen.

MEKADES

Und er?

HERMOKRATES

Das hat zu mächtig ihn
Gemacht, daß er vertraut
Mit Göttern worden ist.
Es tönt sein Wort dem Volk',
Als käm es vom Olymp;
Sie dankens ihm,
Daß er vom Himmel raubt
Die Lebensflamm' und sie
Verräth den Sterblichen.

MEKADES

Sie wissen nichts, denn ihn,
Er soll ihr Gott,
Er soll ihr König seyn.
Sie sagen, es hab' Apoll
Die Stadt gebaut den Trojern,

Nor may their hearts
Take hold of what's alive.
Think of those ancients
Known as the darlings, favourites of Heaven:
They nourished their minds
With the world's own powers
And to their bright, upgazing eyes
Things immortal were near.
That's why those proud ones
Never would bow their heads
And, wilful, could not leave
Intact what was other than they;
Their very looking transformed it.

MECADES

And he?

HERMOCRATES

What's made him overreach
Himself, is that he's grown
Familiar with the gods.
To them, to the people, his word
Rings out as from Olympus.
They give him thanks
For stealing from very Heaven
The fire of life, and so
Betraying it to mortals.

MECADES

They've ears for none but him.
In him they see
Their god, their king.
They say, Apollo built
The Trojans their great city,

Doch besser sei es helf'
Ein hoher Mann durchs Leben.
Noch sprechen sie viel Unverständiges
Von ihm und achten kein Gesez
Und keine Noth und keine Sitte.
Ein Irrgestirn ist unser Volk
Geworden und ich fürcht',
Es deute dieses Zeichen
Zukünft'ges noch, das er
Im stillen Sinne brütet.

HERMOKRATES

Sei ruhig, Mekades!
Er wird nicht.

MEKADES

Bist du denn mächtiger?

HERMOKRATES

Der sie versteht,
Ist stärker, denn die Starken.
Und wohlbekannt ist dieser Seltne mir.
Zu glüklich wuchs er auf;
Ihm ist von Anbeginn
Der eigne Sinn verwöhnt, daß ihn
Geringes irrt; er wird es büßen
Daß er zu sehr geliebt die Sterblichen.

MEKADES

Mir ahndet selbst,
Es wird mit ihm nicht lange dauern,
Doch ist es lang genug,
So er erst fällt, wenn ihms gelungen ist.

But better still to be helped
And led through life by a man exalted.
And other things as foolish
They say about him, and respect
No law, no custom, no necessity.
Our people has turned
Into a dizzy comet;
The sign, I fear, portends
Much more to come which now
In silence he is hatching.

HERMOCRATES

Never fear, Mecades.
He will not.

MECADES

Are you more powerful, then?

HERMOCRATES

Stronger than strong men
Are those who understand them,
And this egregious one is known to me.
Too happily he grew up;
From the beginning
His will was pampered, so
That little things confuse him; he will pay
For having loved mere mortal men too well.

MECADES

I too have felt
That he will not last long,
Yet it is long enough
If by the time he falls he's won his game.

HERMOKRATES

Und schon ist er gefallen.

MEKADES

Was sagst du?

HERMOKRATES

Siehst du denn nicht? es haben
Den hohen Geist die Geistesarmen
Geirrt, die Blinden den Verführer.
Die Seele warf er vor das Volk, verrieth
Der Götter Gunst gutmüthig den Gemeinen,
Doch rächend äffte leeren Wiederhalls
Genug denn auch aus todter Brust den Thoren.
Und eine Zeit ertrug ers, grämte sich
Geduldig, wußte nicht,
Wo es gebrach; indessen wuchs
Die Trunkenheit dem Volke; schaudernd
Vernahmen sie's, wenn ihm vom eignen Wort
Der Busen bebt', und sprachen:
So hören wir nicht die Götter!
Und Nahmen, so ich dir nicht nenne, gaben
Die Knechte dann dem stolzen Trauernden.
Und endlich nimmt der Durstige das Gift,
Der Arme, der mit seinem Sinne nicht
Zu bleiben weiß und Ähnliches nicht findet,
Er tröstet mit der rasenden
Anbetung sich, verblindet, wird, wie sie,
Die seelenlosen Aberglaubigen;
Die Kraft ist ihm entwichen,
Er geht in einer Nacht, und weiß sich nicht
Herauszuhelfen und wir helfen ihm.

HERMOCRATES

Already he has fallen.

MECADES

What are you saying?

HERMOCRATES

Oh, can't you see it? That noble mind
Has been confounded by the feeble-minded,
That one-eyed king misguided by the blind.
His very soul he cast before the people,
Good-naturedly betrayed to vulgar men
The grace of gods; but amply was repaid
With hollow echoes from their own dead hearts,
The fool. And bore it for a time, and grieved,
But patiently, not knowing
Where lay the fault; meanwhile
The people's frenzy grew; and shuddering
They listened when with his own word
His breast reverberated, saying:
It is not thus we listen to gods!
And, servile as they are, went on to call
The proudly sorrowing by names I will not repeat,
And in the end the thirsty man drinks the poison,
That wretch who neither can contain his mind
Nor yet find other minds, akin to it,
And with their raving adoration
Consoles himself, goes blind, becomes like them,
That superstitious rabble with no soul;
His power has ebbed away.
He walks in his own night and cannot find
His own way out – so we shall help him.

MEKADES

Deß bist du so gewiß?

HERMOKRATES

Ich kenn' ihn.

MEKADES

Ein übermüthiges Gerede fällt
Mir bei, das er gemacht, da er zulezt
Auf der Agora war. Ich weiß es nicht,
Was ihm das Volk zuvor gesagt; ich kam
Nur eben, stand von fern; ihr ehret mich,
Antwortet' er, und thuet recht daran;
Denn stum ist die Natur,
Es leben Sonn und Luft und Erd' und ihre Kinder
Fremd umeinander,
Die Einsamen, als gehörten sie sich nicht.
Wohl wandeln immerkräftig
Im Göttergeiste die freien
Unsterblichen Mächte der Welt
Rings um der andern
Vergänglich Leben,
Doch wilde Pflanzen
Auf wilden Grund
Sind in den Schoos der Götter
Die Sterblichen alle gesäet
Die Kärglichgenährten und todt
Erschiene der Boden wenn Einer nicht
Deß wartete, lebenerwekend,
Und mein ist das Feld. Mir tauschen
Die Kraft und Seele zu Einem,
Die Sterblichen und die Götter.
Und wärmer umfangen die ewigen Mächte

MECADES

Are you so sure of that?

HERMOCRATES

I know him.

MECADES

A piece of arrogant talk occurs to me
That issued from the babbler's lips when last
He came to the Agora. I did not catch
What spokesmen of the mob had said to him;
Newly arrived, and far from him, I heard
These words: You honour me, and rightly so,
For inarticulate is Nature,
For Sun and Air and Earth and all her children
Like strangers live together,
And lonely, as though no bond connected them.
True, ever strong, by virtue
Of spirit that is divine,
The free, immortal powers of the world
Revolve around those others'
Ephemeral lives,
But wild flowers growing
On soil as wild
We mortals on to the lap of the gods
Have all been sown,
But scantily nourished, and dead
That soil would appear, did not someone
Attend to it, raising up life,
And mine is that field. My strength and
My soul are fused into one,
By mortals and by the gods.
And more warmly immortal powers embrace

Das strebende Herz und kräftger gedeihn
Vom Geiste der Freien die fühlenden Menschen,
Und wach ists! Denn ich
Geselle das Fremde,
Das Unbekannte nennet mein Wort,
Und die Liebe der Lebenden trag'
Ich auf und nieder; was Einem gebricht,
Ich bring es vom andern, und binde
Beseelend, und wandle
Verjüngend die zögernde Welt
Und gleiche keinem und Allen.
So sprach der Übermüthige.

HERMOKRATES

Das ist noch wenig. Aergers schläft in ihm.
Ich kenn' ihn, kenne sie, die überglüklichen
Verwöhnten Söhne des Himmels,
Die anders nicht, denn ihre Seele, fühlen.
Stört einmal sie der Augenblik heraus –
Und leichtzerstörbar sind die Zärtlichen
Dann stillet nichts sie wieder, brennend
Treibt eine Wunde sie, unheilbar gährt
Die Brust. Auch er! so still er scheint,
So glüht ihm doch, seit ihm das Volk mißfällt,
Im Busen die tyrannische Begierde,
Er oder wir! Und Schaden ist es nicht,
So wir ihn opfern. Untergehen muß
Er doch!

MEKADES

O reiz ihn nicht! schaff ihr nicht Raum und laß
Sie sich erstiken, die verschloßne Flamme!
Laß ihn! gieb ihm nicht Anstoß! findet den
Zu frecher That der Übermüthge nicht,

The aspiring heart and, infused with
The freedom of their spirit, feeling mortals more richly thrive,
And all's awake! For I
Conjoin the estranged,
My word can name the unknown,
And the love of the living I carry
Now up, now down; what one of them lacks
I bring to him from another
And, soul-inspiring, connect,
Rejuvenating, transform
This hesitant world,
And resemble no one and all.
Those were his arrogant words.

HERMOCRATES

That's very little. Worse lies dormant in him.
I know him, know his kind, the all too happy,
Heaven's own spoilt and darling sons
Aware of nothing else than their own souls.
If once the moment shakes them out of themselves –
And those too tender ones are easily shaken –
Then nothing calms or comforts them, they're driven
This way and that way by a burning wound,
Their hearts incurably seething. And he too,
Calm though he seems; disgusted with the people,
Deep down he glows now with despotic lust.
His rule or ours! And we shall do no wrong
In sacrificing him. His ruin is sure
In any case.

MECADES

Do not provoke him, though. Do not let loose,
But let it starve and choke, the pent-up flame!
Leave him alone! Give him no cause to act!

Und kann er nur im Worte sündigen,
So stirbt er, als ein Thor, und schadet uns
Nicht viel. Ein kräftger Gegner macht ihn furchtbar.
Sieh nur, dann erst, dann fühlt er seine Macht.

HERMOKRATES

Du fürchtest ihn und alles, armer Mann!

MEKADES

Ich mag die Reue nur mir gerne sparen,
Mag gerne schonen, was zu schonen ist.
Das braucht der Priester nicht, der alles weiß,
Der Heilge der sich alles heiliget.

HERMOKRATES

Begreife mich, Unmündiger! eh du
Mich lästerst. Fallen muß der Mann; ich sag'
Es dir und glaube mir, wär' er zu schonen,
Ich würd' es mehr, wie du. Denn näher ist
Er mir, wie dir. Doch lerne diß:
Verderblicher denn Schwerd und Feuer ist
Der Menschengeist, der götterähnliche
Wenn er nicht schweigen kan, und sein Geheimniß
Unaufgedekt bewahren. Bleibt er still
In seiner Tiefe ruhn, und giebt, was noth ist,
Wohlthätig ist er dann, ein fressend Feuer,
Wenn er aus seiner Fessel bricht.
Hinweg mit ihm, der seine Seele blos
Und ihre Götter giebt, verwegen
Aussprechen will Unauszusprechendes
Und sein gefährlich Gut, als wär es Wasser,
Verschüttet und vergeudet, schlimmer ists
Wie Mord, und du, du redest für diesen?

If he, the arrogant, himself finds none
For insolent deeds, and only in words can sin,
He dies a fool and does us little harm.
Daydreaming let him walk on clouds, or fly!
A strong opponent makes him dangerous,
And only then, you see, he'll feel his power.

HERMOCRATES

You fear him, and fear all things, my poor friend.

MECADES

No, but I wish to spare myself remorse,
And like to spare whatever can be spared.
Different in that from the omniscient priest
Who, holy, hallows all his ends and means.

HERMOCRATES

First understand me, novice that you are,
Before insulting me. The man must fall,
I tell you. If he could be spared, be sure
I'd spare him more than you would, being closer
To him than you are. But take note of this:
More ruinous than sword or raging fire
Is human spirit, though akin to gods,
If it can not keep silent and contain
Its secret unexposed. If in its depth
It lies at rest and proffers what is needed,
Wholesome it is; a wild, devouring flame
As soon as from its fetters it breaks loose.
Away with that man who lays bare his soul
And, with it, his soul's gods, recklessly seeks
To utter the unutterable, wasting
His dangerous wealth like water lightly spilt.
That folly is worse than murder; and can you,

Bescheide dich! Sein Schiksaal ists. Er hat
Es sich gemacht und leben soll,
Wie er, und vergehn wie er, in Weh und Thorheit jeder,
Der Göttliches verräth, und allverkehrend
Verborgenherrschendes
In Menschenhände liefert!
Er muß hinab!

MEKADES

So theuer büßen muß er, der sein Bestes
Aus voller Seele Sterblichen vertraut?

HERMOKRATES

Er mag es, doch es bleibt die Nemesis nicht aus,
Mag große Worte sagen, mag
Entwürdigen das keuschverschwiegne Leben,
Ans Tageslicht das Gold der Tiefe ziehn.
Er mag es brauchen, was zum Brauche nicht
Den Sterblichen gegeben ist, ihn wirds
Zuerst zu Grunde richten – hat es ihm
Den Sinn nicht schon verwirrt, ist ihm
Bei seinem Volke denn die volle Seele
Die Zärtliche, wie ist sie nun verwildert?
Wie ist denn nun ein Eigenmächtiger
Geworden dieser Allmittheilende?
Der gütge Mann! wie ist er so verwandelt
Zum Frechen, der wie seiner Hände Spiel
Die Götter und die Menschen achtet.

MEKADES

Du redest schröklich, Priester, und es dünkt
Dein dunkel Wort mir wahr. Es sei!
Du hast zum Werke mich. Nur weiß ich nicht,

Can you, of all men, plead on his behalf?
Accept the inevitable! *His* fate it is,
He made it for himself, and like him
Shall all those live, all perish in pain and folly
Who have betrayed the divine and, all-perverting,
Delivered up into human hands
That which rules us in secret!
He shall not live!

MECADES

So dear, then, must he pay who of his soul's
Most treasured wealth entrusts the best to mortals?

HERMOCRATES

Let him, but Nemesis will surely come.
Let him mouth mighty words, and let him
Dishonour life that should be chastely veiled,
Drag into daylight the deeply hidden gold.
Let him make use of that which was not given
To mortals for their use, but he will be
The first to perish. Has it not confused
His mind already? Is his entire soul
Vested, as he pretends, in his dear people?
That tender soul, how it has run to waste!
And how self-willed, tyrannical he has grown
Whose one desire was to communicate all,
Kind as he is! How utterly he's turned
Into an insolent man who looks upon
Both gods and men as playthings for his hands.

MECADES

Of dreadful things you speak; and, Priest, it seems
To me that your dark words are true. So be it!
I'll serve your cause. My only doubt is how

Wo er zu fassen ist. Es sei der Mann
So groß er will, zu richten ist nicht schwer.
Doch mächtig seyn des Übermächtigen,
Der, wie ein Zauberer, die Menge leitet,
Es dünkt ein anders mir, Hermokrates.

HERMOKRATES

Gebrechlich ist sein Zauber, Kind, und leichter,
Denn nötig ist, hat er es uns bereitet.
Es wandte zur gelegnen Stunde sich
Sein Unmuth um, der stolze stillempörte Sinn
Befeindet izt sich selber, hätt' er auch
Die Macht, er achtets nicht, er trauert nur,
Und siehet seinen Fall, er sucht
Rükkehrend das verlorne Leben,
Den Gott, den er aus sich
Hinweggeschwäzt.
Versammle mir das Volk; ich klag' ihn an,
Ruf über ihn den Fluch, erschreken sollen sie
Vor ihrem Abgott, sollen ihn
Hinaus verstoßen in die Wildniß
Und nimmer wiederkehrend soll er dort
Mirs büßen, daß er mehr, wie sich gebührt,
Verkündiget den Sterblichen.

MEKADES

Doch weß beschuldigest du ihn?

HERMOKRATES

Die Worte, so du mir genannt,
Sie sind genug.

To lay our hands on him. However great
A man may be, to try him is not hard;
To overpower a man supremely powerful, though,
Who like a skilled magician rules the mob,
This is another thing, Hermocrates.

HERMOCRATES

Frail is his magic, child, and he has made
Our business easier than he need have done.
For at a moment opportune to us
His anger turned; his proud, indignant mood
Turns in upon itself, and though he had
The power, he would not heed it, only grieves
And broods upon his downfall,
Retracing, looks for his lost life,
The god whom by his prattling
He's driven out of himself.
The people now assemble; I will charge him,
Pronounce the curse on him, make them recoil
In horror from their idol
And cast him out into the wilderness,
And, never more returning, there he shall pay
For making manifest to mortals more
Than they are fit to hear.

MECADES

But of what crime will you accuse him?

HERMOCRATES

Those words of his you cited,
They'll do.

MEKADES

        Mit dieser schwachen Klage
Willst du das Volk ihm von der Seele ziehn?

HERMOKRATES

Zu rechter Zeit hat jede Klage Kraft
Und nicht gering ist diese.

MEKADES

Und klagtest du des Mords ihn an vor ihnen,
Es wirkte nichts.

HERMOKRATES

Diß eben ists! die offenbare That
Vergeben sie, die Aberglaubigen,
Unsichtbar Aergerniß für sie
Unheimlich muß es seyn! ins Auge muß es
Sie treffen, das bewegt die Blöden.

MEKADES

Es hängt ihr Herz an ihm, das bändigest,
Das lenkst du nicht so leicht! Sie lieben ihn!

HERMOKRATES

Sie liehen ihn? ja wohl! so lang er blüht'
Und glänzt'
                naschen sie.
Was sollen sie mit ihm, nun er
Verdüstert ist, verödet? Da ist nichts
Was nüzen könnt, und ihre lange Zeit
Verkürzen, abgeerndtet ist das Feld.
Verlassen liegts, und nach Gefallen gehn
Der Sturm und unsre Pfade drüber hin.

MECADES

        And with that feeble charge alone
You hope to wean them from their sustenance?

HERMOCRATES

At the right time, friend, any charge will work,
And this one is not slight.

MECADES

I say that if you charged that man with murder
In front of them, they would not flinch.

HERMOCRATES

Quite true! The flagrant act they will forgive,
That superstitious mob! Mysterious
The offence must be for them,
Occult, uncanny; hit them in the eye,
And blind them – then the timid herd will run.

MECADES

Their hearts are bound to him, and these you will
Not easily tame or guide; they love the man!

HERMOCRATES

They love him? Certainly, as long as he
Is glorious, prospers
                they will nibble.
Much good he'll do them, though,
Now that he's darkened, desolate! There's nothing
Here they could use with which to while away
The tedious hours; that field has been picked bare,
It lies forsaken now, and over it
The gales may freely run now – and our paths.

MEKADES

Empör' ihn nur! empör' ihn! siehe zu!

HERMOKRATES

Ich hoffe, Mekades! er ist geduldig.

MEKADES

So wird sie der geduldige gewinnen!

HERMOKRATES

Nichts weniger!

MEKADES

Du achtest nichts, wirst dich
Und mich und ihn und alles verderben.

HERMOKRATES

Das Träumen und das Schäumen
Der Sterblichen, ich acht' es wahrlich nicht!
Sie möchten Götter seyn, und huldigen
Wie Göttern sich, und eine Weile dauerts!
Sorgst du, es möchte sie der Leidende
Gewinnen, der Geduldige?
Empören wird er gegen sich die Thoren,
An seinem Laide werden sie den theuern
Betrug erkennen, werden unbarmherzig
Ihms danken, daß der Angebetete
Doch auch ein Schwacher ist, und ihm
Geschiehet recht, warum bemengt er sich
Mit ihnen.

MEKADES

Ich wollt', ich wär aus dieser Sache, Priester!

MECADES

Provoke him, then, provoke him! But take care!

HERMOCRATES

I hope, Mecades, that he's a patient man.

MECADES

The patient man, in that case, will persuade them.

HERMOCRATES

Never!

MECADES

You've no respect for anything, and so will
Ruin yourself and me and him and all things.

HERMOCRATES

The dreaming and the scheming
Of mortals – no, I never will respect it.
Gods they would like to be, and as to gods
Do homage to each other – for a while!
Are you afraid the suffering man will sway them,
The patient win them over?
Not so! To fury he will rouse the fools,
And by his suffering they'll recognize
The dearly paid imposture, brutally
Exacting retribution from their idol
For being weak as they are; and it serves
Him right, I say. He should have had no truck
With them.

MECADES

I wish I were well out of this business, Priest.

HERMOKRATES

Vertraue mir und scheue nicht, was noth ist.

MEKADES

Dort kömt er. Suche nur dich selbst,
Du irrer Geist! indeß verlierst du alles.

HERMOKRATES

Laß ihn! hinweg!

HERMOCRATES

Rely on me, and do not shirk what must be.

MECADES

Look, there he comes. Go on, then, seek yourself,
You poor crazed mind! And meanwhile you lose all.

HERMOCRATES

Leave him! Away!

Zweiter Auftritt

EMPEDOKLES
(*allein*)

In meine Stille kamst du leise wandelnd,
Fandst drinnen in der Halle Dunkel mich aus,
Du Freundlicher! du kamst nicht unverhoft
Und fernher, wirkend über der Erde vernahm
Ich wohl dein Wiederkehren, schöner Tag
Und meine Vertrauten euch, ihr schnellgeschäftgen
Kräfte der Höh! – und nahe seid auch ihr
Mir wieder, seid wie sonst ihr Glüklichen
Ihr irrelosen Bäume meines Hains!
Ihr ruhetet und wuchs't und täglich tränkte
Des Himmels Quelle die Bescheidenen
Mit Licht und Lebensfunken säte
Befruchtend auf die Blühenden der Aether. –
O innige Natur! ich habe dich
Vor Augen, kennest du den Freund noch
Den Hochgeliebten kennest du mich nimmer?
Den Priester, der lebendigen Gesang,
Wie frohvergoßnes Opferblut, dir brachte?

O bei den heilgen Brunnen,
Wo Wasser aus Adern der Erde
Sich sammeln und
Am heißen Tag
Die Dürstenden erquiken! in mir
In mir, ihr Quellen des Lebens, strömtet
Aus Tiefen der Welt ihr einst
Zusammen und es kamen
Die Dürstenden zu mir wie ists denn nun?

Scene Two

EMPEDOCLES

(*alone*)

Your movement hushed, you came into my stillness,
Deep in the gloomy hall you sought me out,
You kindly light; and not unhoped for came,
But from afar, at work above the earth,
Well I could hear you come again, bright Day!
And my familiars, you, the quick and busy
Powers of the heights – now you are close to me
Once more, as once you were, the joyous,
Trees of my grove that neither stray nor falter!
You rested there and grew there well-contented
Since daily Heaven's own well-springs watered you
With light, and Aether on the flowering scattered
Sparks of pure life that fertilized their bloom.
O intimate Nature, close again to my eyes,
Do you still know your friend, the fondly loved,
Or never again will you acknowledge me,
The priest who brought you gifts of living song,
Offered it up like life-blood gladly shed?

O by the holy wells
Where waters from veins of Earth
Collect, and on
A summer day
Refresh the thirsty man! In me,
In me, you well-springs of life, you flowed
Together once from depths of the world, and
The thirsty came to me – how is it now?

Vertrauert? bin ich ganz allein?
Und ist es Nacht hier außen auch am Tage?
Der höhers, denn ein sterblich Auge, sah
Der Blindgeschlagene tastet nun umher –
Wo seid ihr, meine Götter?
Weh! laßt ihr nun
Wie einen Bettler mich
Und diese Brust
Die liebend euch geahndet,
Was stoßt ihr sie hinab
Und schließt sie mir in schmählichenge Bande
Die Freigeborene, die aus sich
Und keines andern ist? und wandeln soll
Er nun so fort, der Langverwöhnte,
Der seelig oft mit allen Lebenden
Ihr Leben, ach, in heiligschöner Zeit
Sie, wie das Herz gefühlt von einer Welt,
Und ihren königlichen Götterkräften,
Verdammt in seiner Seele soll er so
Da hingehn, ausgestoßen? freundlos er,
Der Götterfreund? an seinem Nichts
Und seiner Nacht sich waiden immerdar
Unduldbares duldend gleich den Schwächlingen, die
Ans Tagewerk im scheuen Tartarus
Geschmiedet sind. Was daherab
Gekommen? um nichts? ha! Eines
Eins mußtet ihr mir lassen! Thor! bist du
Derselbe doch und träumst, als wärest du
Ein Schwacher. Einmal noch! noch Einmal
Soll mirs lebendig werden, und ich wills!
Fluch oder Seegen! täusche nun die Kraft
Demüthiger! dir nimmer aus dem Busen!
Weit will ichs um mich machen, tagen solls
Von eigner Flamme mir! Du sollst

All saddened? Am I quite alone?
And is it night out here in daytime too?
He who saw higher things than ever did mortal eye,
Now struck with blindness faltering picks his way —
Where are you now, my gods?
O will you now
Leave me a beggar,
And why do you cast off
This heart that once
By loving you divined you,
And into shamefully narrow bonds confine it,
A heart born free, that to itself
And no one else belonged? And is he now
To drag his days out thus who long was pampered,
Who often, one with all the living, felt
Their life, in holy, lovely times was blessed
To feel them as the heart of a whole world
And of that world's divinely regal powers?
Damned in his very soul, shall he now perish
An outcast? And without a single friend,
Who was the friend of gods? For ever feed
Upon his nothingness, upon his night,
Bear the unbearable like those weaklings who
Are welded to their daily drudgery
In cringing Tartarus? Reduced to that?
For no good reason? Ah, but one thing,
One thing you had to leave me. Fool, for still
You are the man you were, and only dream
That you are feeble. Once again, once more
All shall become alive for me; I will it!
Blessing or curse, no longer, humble man,
Disarm the strength in you by self-deception!
I will have space around me! My own flame
Shall make a new day dawn! Poor mind immured,

Zufrieden werden, armer Geist,
Gefangener! sollst frei und groß und reich
In eigner Welt dich fühlen –
Und wieder einsam, weh! und wieder einsam?

Weh! einsam! einsam! einsam!
Und nimmer find ich
Euch, meine Götter,
Und nimmer kehr ich
Zu deinem Leben, Natur!
Dein Geächteter! – weh! hab ich doch auch
Dein nicht geachtet, dein
Mich überhoben, hast du
Umfangend doch mit den warmen Fittigen einst
Du Zärtliche! mich vom Schlafe gerettet?
Den Thörigen ihn, den Nahrungsscheuen,
Mitleidig schmeichelnd zu deinem Nectar
Gelokt, damit er trank und wuchs
Und blüht', und mächtig geworden und trunken,
Dir ins Angesicht höhnt' – o Geist,
Geist, der mich groß genährt, du hast
Dir deinen Herrn, hast, alter Saturn,
Dir einen neuen Jupiter
Gezogen, einen schwächern nur und frechern.
Denn schmähen kann die böse Zunge dich nur,
Ist nirgend ein Rächer, und muß ich denn allein
Den Hohn und Fluch in meine Seele sagen?
Muß einsam seyn auch so?

You shall be satisfied again,
Shall feel in your own world –
And yet be lonely now, for ever lonely?

Ah, lonely, lonely, lonely!
And nevermore
I shall find you,
My gods, and nevermore,
Nature, return to your life!
Your outcast! And, oh, it's true, I paid
No heed to you then, but thought
Myself superior to you, although,
Enfolding me tenderly once with your warm wings,
You saved me from sleep,
And in your compassion, flattering, lured
The fool to your nectar,
So that, drinking of it, he would grow
And thrive, and then, grown mighty and drunken,
Would mock you to your face – O spirit,
Spirit that raised me to manhood,
You've raised your master, old Saturn,
A second Jupiter you've raised
For yourself, only weaker, more insolent,
For this malicious tongue can only revile you.
With no avenger anywhere, must I myself
Heap all the scorn and curses on my soul?
Even in that be lonely?

Dritter Auftritt

PAUSANIAS. EMPEDOKLES

EMPEDOKLES

Ich fühle nur des Tages Neige, Freund!
Und dunkel will es werden mir und kalt!
Es gehet rükwärts, lieber! nicht zur Ruh,
Wie wenn der beutefrohe Vogel sich
Das Haupt verhüllt zu frischer erwachendem
Zufriednem Schlummer, anders ists mit mir!
Erspare mir die Klage! laß es mir!

PAUSANIAS

Sehr fremde bist du mir geworden,
Mein Empedokles! kennest du mich nicht?
Und kenn' ich nimmer dich, du Herrlicher? –
Du konntst dich so verwandeln, konntest so
Zum Räthsel werden, edel Angesicht,
Und so zur Erde beugen darf der Gram
Die Lieblinge des Himmels? bist du denn
Es nicht? und sieh! wie danken dir es all',
Und so in goldner Freude mächtig war
Kein anderer, wie du, in seinem Volke.

EMPEDOKLES

Sie ehren mich? o sag es ihnen doch,
Sie sollens lassen – Übel steht

Scene Three

PAUSANIAS. EMPEDOCLES

EMPEDOCLES

I feel the day declining now, my friend,
And all is growing dark for me, and cold.
Backward I go, dear friend, but not to rest
As when provided, satisfied with booty
A bird will swathe his head for pleasant sleep
And fresher wakening – different it is with me.
But spare me the complaint. Ask no more questions.

PAUSANIAS

How very strange to me you have become,
Empedocles. Do you not know me now?
Nor I know you, the glorious, as I did?
Can you be so transformed, your noble face
Now an enigma to me, and remote?
And so to earth may suffering bow down
Heaven's own favourite? Are you not he?
And yet we thank you for it, all of us,
And never, amid golden joy, a man
Wielded such power as yours upon his people.

EMPEDOCLES

They honour me? Go quickly, then, and tell them
They are to cease. That ornament

Der Schmuk mir an und welkt
Das grüne Laub doch auch
Dem ausgerißnen Stamme!

PAUSANIAS

Noch stehst du ja, und frisch Gewässer spielt
Um deine Wurzel dir, es athmet mild
Die Luft um deine Gipfel, nicht von Vergänglichem
Gedeiht dein Herz; es walten über dir
Unsterblichere Kräfte.

EMPEDOKLES

Du mahnest mich der Jugendtage, lieber!

PAUSANIAS

Noch schöner dünkt des Lebens Mitte mir.

EMPEDOKLES

Und gerne sehen, wenn es nun
Hinab sich neigen will, die Augen
Der Schnellhinschwindenden noch Einmal
Zurük, der Dankenden. O jene Zeit!
Ihr Liebeswonnen, da die Seele mir
Von Göttern, wie Endymion, gewekt,
Die kindlich schlummernde, sich öffnete,
Lebendig sie, die Immerjugendlichen,
Des Lebens große Genien
Erkannte – schöne S o n n e ! Menschen hatten mich
Es nicht gelehrt, mich trieb mein eigen Herz
Unsterblich liebend zu Unsterblichen,
Zu dir, zu dir, ich konnte Göttlichers
Nicht finden, stilles Licht! und so wie du
Das Leben nicht an deinem Tage sparst
Und sorgenfrei der goldnen Fülle dich

Not well befits me now.
And does not the green foliage
Wilt, too, on trunks uprooted?

PAUSANIAS

But you still stand, and the cool brooklets play
About your roots, and mildly round your crest
The sweet air wafts, and that which is not transient
Sustains your core; the more immortal powers
Shape and watch over you.

EMPEDOCLES

It is my youth you call to mind, dear friend.

PAUSANIAS

The noon of life seems lovelier still to me.

EMPEDOCLES

And gladly, now that noon declines,
Once more the eyes of those look back
Who still more swiftly, and for ever, fade,
Look back, but to give thanks. O time of youth!
Delights of love, you ecstasies when my soul,
Awakened like Endymion by the gods,
Out of its childish drowsiness opened wide,
And, thrilled alive, it knew the ever-youthful
Spirits of life in their magnificence,
The genii – great *Sun!* No man had taught me
To name, to know them; it was my own heart,
Immortally loving, drove me to immortals,
To you, to you, for nothing more divine
Than you, still light, I found here; and as you
Never stint life in your day's daily fulness
And lavishly, taking no care, expend

Entledigest, so gönnt' auch ich, der Deine,
Den Sterblichen die beste Seele gern
Und furchtlosoffen gab
Mein Herz, wie du, der ernsten E r d e sich,
Der schiksaalvollen; ihr in Jünglingsfreude
Das Leben so zu eignen bis zulezt,
Ich sagt' ihrs oft in trauter Stunde zu,
Band so den theuern Todeshund mit ihr.
Da rauscht' es anders, denn zuvor, im Hain,
Und zärtlich tönten ihrer Berge Quellen –
All deine Freuden, E r d e ! wahr, wie sie,
Und warm und voll, aus Müh' und Liebe reifen,
Sie alle gabst du mir. Und wenn ich oft
Auf stiller Bergeshöhe saß und staunend
Der Menschen wechselnd Irrsaal übersann,
Zu tief von deinen Wandlungen ergriffen,
Und nah mein eignes Welken ahndete,
Dann athmete der A e t h e r, so wie dir,
Mir heilend um die liebeswunde Brust,
Und, wie Gewölk der Flamme, löseten
Im hohen Blau die Sorgen mir sich auf.

PAUSANIAS

O Sohn des Himmels!

EMPEDOKLES

Ich war es! ja! und möcht es nun erzählen,
Ich Armer! möcht es Einmal noch
Mir in die Seele rufen,
Das Wirken deiner Geniuskräfte
Der Herrlichen deren Genoß ich war, o Natur,
Daß mir die stumme todesöde Brust
Von deinen Tönen allen wiederklänge,
Bin ich es noch? o Leben! und rauschten sie mir

Your golden wealth, so I, being yours, was glad
To give away to mortals my best soul
And, fearlessly candid, so
My heart to serious *Earth* I dedicated,
The many-destined; to her in youthful joy
As now, so lifelong, to devote my life
I promised her at many a solemn hour,
Pledging a firm, dear pact with her till death.
Then through the grove a different rustle ran,
And tenderly her mountains' well-springs murmured –
Yes, all your pleasures, *Earth*, which true as she,
And warm and full, with love and labour ripen,
All these you gave me. Often, when I sat
High up, on some calm peak, and marvelling
Pondered the tangled, mutable ways of men,
Too deeply gripped by your vicissitudes,
And felt the nearness of my own decline,
Suddenly *Aether*, as on you, would waft
On me his breath, balm to the wounds of love,
And like the clouds of fire, my care and grief
Up in the cerulean heights were lost.

PAUSANIAS

You son of Heaven!

EMPEDOCLES

Yes, that I was, and now will tell the story,
Wretch that I am, once more, and only once
Recall to my own soul
The working of those spirit powers,
Nature, your glorious powers whose companion I was,
So that my silent, desolate heart once more
With all your various music may resound.
Am I myself, O life, and did they once

All deine geflügelten Melodien und hört
Ich deinen alten Einklang, große Natur?
Ach! ich der Einsame, lebt ich nicht
Mit dieser heilgen Erd und diesem Licht
Und dir, von dem die Seele nimmer läßt,
O Vater Aether, und mit allen Lebenden
Der Götter Freund im gegenwärtigen
Olymp? ich bin heraus geworfen, bin
Ganz einsam, und das Weh ist nun
Mein Tagsgefährt' und Schlafgenosse mir.
Bei mir ist nicht der Seegen, geh!
Geh! frage nicht! denkst du, ich träum'?
O sieh mich an! und wundre deß dich nicht,
Du Guter, daß ich daherab
Gekommen bin; des Himmels Söhnen ist,
Wenn überglüklich sie geworden sind,
Ein eigner Fluch beschieden.

PAUSANIAS

Ich duld' es nicht,
Weh! solche Reden! du? ich duld es nicht.
Du solltest so die Seele dir und mir
Nicht ängstigen. Ein böses Zeichen dünkt
Es mir, wenn so der Geist, der immerfrohe, sich
Der Mächtigen umwölket.

EMPEDOKLES

Fühlst dus? Es deutet, daß er bald
Zur Erd' hinab im Ungewitter muß.

PAUSANIAS

O laß den Unmuth, lieber!
O dieser, was that er euch, dieser Reine,
Daß ihm die Seele so verfinstert ist,

Ring out to me, all your winged melodies, and did
I hear your ancient harmony, great Nature?
Oh, did I not, the lonely, live with her
This holy Earth, and live with you, this light,
And you from whom no soul can bear to part,
You, Father Aether, and with all that lives,
The friend of gods at home on real Olympus?
And now they've cast me out, and now they've left me
Utterly lonely, and now anguish is
My work-mate, playmate, bedfellow, all in one.
No, do not come to me for blessings, friend!
Ask me no questions. Do you think I'm dreaming?
Just look at me! Nor is there any need,
Kind as you are, to wonder how it can be
That I have come to this; for sons of Heaven,
When too much joy, good fortune has been theirs,
A downfall like no other is reserved.

PAUSANIAS

I'll not allow it!
Such words from you! From you? I'll not allow it.
You should not frighten your own soul and mine
With blasphemous talk. It seems an evil omen
To see the ever clear and radiant minds
Of mighty men beclouded.

EMPEDOCLES

You sense it, then? It means that soon
They must come down to earth in a thunderstorm.

PAUSANIAS

Enough of this ill-humour, friend.
What has he done to you, you gods of death,
This pure one, to deserve the darkness fallen

Ihr Todesgötter! haben die Sterblichen denn
Kein Eigenes nirgendswo, und reicht
Das Furchtbare denn ihnen bis ans Herz,
Und herrscht es in der Brust den Stärkeren noch
Das ewige Schiksaal? Bändige den Gram
Und übe deine Macht, bist du es doch
Der mehr vermag, denn andere, o sieh
An meiner Liebe, wer du bist,
Und denke dein, und lebe!

EMPEDOKLES

Du kennest mich und dich und Tod und Leben nicht.

PAUSANIAS

Den Tod, ich kenn' ihn wenig nur,
Denn wenig dacht' ich seiner.

EMPEDOKLES

Allein zu seyn,
Und ohne Götter, ist der Tod.

PAUSANIAS

Laß ihn, ich kenne d i c h , an deinen Thaten
Erkannt' ich dich, in seiner Macht
Erfuhr ich deinen Geist, und seine Welt,
Wenn oft ein Wort von dir
Im heilgen Augenblik
Das Leben vieler Jahre mir erschuff,
Daß eine neue große Zeit von da
Dem Jünglinge begann. Wie zahmen Hirschen,
Wenn ferne rauscht der Wald und sie
Der Heimath denken, schlug das Herz mir oft,
Wenn du vom Glük der alten Urwelt sprachst,
Der reinen Tage kundig und dir lag

Upon his soul? Is it that mortals have
Nothing that is their own, not anywhere,
But the dark powers reach to their very hearts,
And even in the stronger men's bosoms is it
Eternal Fate that governs? Tame your grief
And use your strength, for still you are the one
Who can do more than others. Let my love
Remind you of the man you were and are,
Think of yourself, and live!

EMPEDOCLES

You do not know me, nor yourself, nor life, nor death.

PAUSANIAS

Death I know little, true,
For I have given it little thought.

EMPEDOCLES

To be alone
And without gods is death.

PAUSANIAS

Forget it, I know *you*, and by your deeds
I came to know you, when death held me
First felt your spirit's force in a dead world,
Within one holy moment often
A single word from you
Made real for me the life of many years,
So that at once a whole great age began
For your disciple; and like tame stags' hearts
When far away the forest roars, recalling
Their natural home to them, my heart would beat
When you evoked primeval worlds of bliss,
Versed in those pure days' lore, and all Fate's ways

Das ganze Schiksaal offen, zeichnetest
Du nicht der Zukunft große Linien
Mir vor das Auge, sichern Bliks, wie Künstler
Ein fehlend Glied zum ganzen Bilde reihn?
Und kennst du nicht die Kräfte der Natur,
Daß du vertraulich wie kein Sterblicher
Sie, wie du willst, in stiller Herrschaft lenkest?

EMPEDOKLES

Recht! alles weiß ich, alles kann ich meistern.
Wie meiner Hände Werk, erkenn ich es
Durchaus, und lenke, wie ich will
Ein Herr der Geister, das Lebendige.
Mein ist die Welt, und unterthan und dienstbar
Sind alle Kräfte mir,

                    zur Magd ist mir
Die herrnbedürftige Natur geworden.
Und hat sie Ehre noch, so ists von mir.
Was wäre denn der Himmel und das Meer
Und Inseln und Gestirn, und was vor Augen
Den Menschen alles liegt, was wär es,
Diß todte Saitenspiel, gäb' ich ihm Ton
Und Sprach' und Seele nicht? was sind
Die Götter und ihr Geist, wenn ich sie nicht
Verkündige? nun! sage, wer bin ich?

PAUSANIAS

Verhöhne nur im Unmuth dich und alles
Was Menschen herrlich macht,
Ihr Wirken und ihr Wort, verlaide mir
Den Muth im Busen, schröke mich zum Kinde
Zurük. O sprich es nur heraus! du hassest dich
Und was dich liebt und was dir gleichen möcht';

Lay open to you. Did you not trace for me,
With mighty strokes, the very future's lines,
Your hand, your eye as sure as any painter's
Who adds the missing detail to the whole?
Are you not intimate with the powers of Nature,
And like no other mortal easily
Do you not rule them as you please in silence?

EMPEDOCLES

Quite true, I know all things, can master all.
Like my own handiwork thoroughly I control it
And as I please, a lord of spirits, rule,
Manipulate, make use of all that lives.
Mine is the world, submissive and subservient
To me are all its powers,

                    Nature herself,
Unfit, as well you know, to have her way,
Is now my servant girl; such honour
As men accord her still, she owes to me.
And what indeed would Heaven be and Ocean
And islands and the stars, and all that meets
The eyes of men, what would it mean or be,
This dead stringed instrument, did I not lend it
A resonance, a language and a soul?
What are the gods, and what their spirit, if I
Do not proclaim them? Tell me now, who am I?

PAUSANIAS

Out of mere bitterness mock yourself and all
That makes men glorious,
Their workings and their word; make me ashamed
Of my own courage, cow me and drive me back
Into my childhood. Freely admit: You hate

Ein anders willst du, denn du bist, genügst dir
In deiner Ehre nicht und opferst dich an Fremdes.
Du willst nicht bleiben, willst
Zu Grunde gehen. Ach! in deiner Brust
Ist minder Ruhe, denn in mir.

EMPEDOKLES

Unschuldiger!

PAUSANIAS

Und dich verklagst du?
Was ist es denn? o mache mir dein Leiden
Zum Räthsel länger nicht! mich peinigets!

EMPEDOKLES

Mit Ruhe wirken soll der Mensch,
Der sinnende, soll entfaltend
Das Leben um ihn fördern und heitern
denn hoher Bedeutung voll,
Voll schweigender Kraft umfängt
Den ahnenden, daß er bilde die Welt,
Die große Natur,
Daß ihren Geist hervor er rufe, strebt
Tief wurzelnd
Das gewaltige Sehnen ihm auf.
Und viel vermag er und herrlich ist
Sein Wort, es wandelt die Welt
Und unter den Händen

Yourself and those who love and follow you;
Your will is bent on what you are not, your fame,
Grown strange to you, to strangers will betray you.
Not to remain on earth
Is your desire, you long to perish. Oh,
Your heart at last is less serene than mine.

EMPEDOCLES

You innocent!

PAUSANIAS

        And you accuse yourself?
What is it, then? O cease to make a riddle
Of your affliction. You are tormenting me.

EMPEDOCLES

Serenely, true, should men,
The pondering, act upon
The life around them, to further and make bright
        for full of lofty purpose,
Of power contained, unexpressed,
Great Nature surrounds their
Foreknowing minds, to bid them fashion a world,
Deep-rooted
Within them a mighty longing leaps up
So that her spirit will come to light.
And much he can do, and glorious is
Man's word, it transforms the world
And where his hands have

Der Schluss des zweiten Aktes

PANTHEA

Hast du doch, menschlich Irrsaal!
Ihm nicht das Herz verwöhnt,
Du Unbedeutendes! was gabst
Du Armes ihm? nun da der Mann
Zu seinen Göttern fort sich sehnt,
Wundern sie sich, als hätten sie
Die Thörigen ihm, die hohe Seele, geschaffen.
Umsonst nicht sind, o, die du alles ihm
Gegeben, Natur!
Vergänglicher deine Liebsten, denn andre!
Ich weiß es wohl!
Sie kommen und werden groß, und keiner sagt,
Wie sie's geworden, so entschwinden sie auch,
Die Glüklichen! wieder, ach! laßt sie doch.

DELIA

Ists denn nicht schön,
Bei Menschen wohnen; es weiß
Mein Herz von andrem nicht, es ruht
In diesem Einen, aber traurig dunkel droht
Vor meinem Auge das Ende
Des Unbegreiflichen, und du heißest ihn auch
Hinweggehn, Panthea?

Act Two (Conclusion)

PANTHEA

Surely not you it was,
The human labyrinth,
The insignificant, that spoiled
His heart? What could you give him,
Poor as you are? Now that the man
Longs to be gone and join his gods
They wonder at it, as if it were they, the foolish,
Who had endowed him with a lofty soul.
Nature, who gave him all, not without reason
Those you love best more briefly linger here!
Too well I know it.
They come and grow, and none of us can say
How they grew great, and so again they vanish,
Those happy ones. O leave them, let them go!

DELIA

Is it not good
To live among mortals? My heart
Knows of no other joy, it rests
Upon this *one* man, but sadly, darkly before
My eyes now threatens the end
Of him, the inscrutable, yet even you,
Panthea, bid him go?

PANTHEA

Ich muß. Wer will ihn binden?
Ihm sagen, mein bist du,
Ist doch sein eigen der Lebendige,
Und nur sein Geist ihm Gesez,
Und soll er die Ehre der Sterblichen
Zu retten, die ihn geschmäht,
Verweilen, wenn ihm
Der Vater die Arme
Der Aether öffnet?

DELIA

Sieh! herrlich auch
Und freundlich ist die Erde.

PANTHEA

Ja herrlich, und herrlicher izt.
Es darf nicht unbeschenkt
Von ihr ein Kühner scheiden.
Noch weilt er wohl
Auf deiner grünen Höhen einer, o Erde
Du Wechselnde!
Und siehet über die woogenden Hügel
Hinab ins freie Meer! und nimmt
Die lezte Freude sich. Vieleicht sehn wir
Ihn nimmer. Gutes Kind!
Mich trift es freilich auch und gerne möcht'
Ichs anders, doch ich schäme dessen mich.
Thut er es ja! Ists so nicht heilig?

PANTHEA

I must. For who could bind him,
Say to him, you are mine,
When to himself that living one belongs,
For him no law but his own mind is valid?
And should he stay here to save
The honour of mortals
Who have reviled him, when now
The Father himself,
When Aether opens
His arms to him?

DELIA

Look! Glorious too
And kindly our Earth is.

PANTHEA

Glorious, true, and more glorious now.
Not without presents may
A bold man part from her.
Still he must be delaying
On one of your verdant summits, O Earth,
The for ever changing,
And gazes now across the billowing hills
Down to the open sea, and snatches
A joy from you, the last. Perhaps we shall
Not see him again. Dear child,
Me too, believe me, it hurts, and gladly I
Would have it otherwise, but feel ashamed of the wish.
His choice it is! That, surely, hallows the deed?

DELIA

Wer ist der Jüngling, der
Vom Berge dort herabkömt?

PANTHEA

Pausanias. Ach! müssen wir so
Uns wiederfinden, Vaterloser?

DELIA

What young man is that
Coming down from the mountain there?

PANTHEA

Pausanias; poor fatherless boy!
Like this we must meet again?

Letzter Auftritt des zweiten Aktes

PAUSANIAS. PANTHEA. DELIA

PAUSANIAS

Wo ist er? o Panthea!
Du ehrst ihn, suchest ihn auch,
Willst Einmal noch ihn sehn,
Den furchtbarn Wanderer, ihn, dem allein
Beschieden ist, den Pfad zu gehen mit Ruhm,
Den ohne Fluch betritt kein anderer.

PANTHEA

Ists from von ihm und groß
Das Allgefürchtete?
Wo ist er?

PAUSANIAS

Er sandte mich hinweg, indessen sah
Ich ihn nicht wieder. Droben rief
Ich im Gebürg' ihn, doch ich fand ihn nicht.
Er kehrt gewiß. Bis in die Nacht
Versprach er freundlich mir zu bleiben.
O käm er! Es flieht, geschwinder, wie Pfeile
Die liebste Stunde vorüber.
Denn freuen werden wir uns noch mit ihm,
Du wirst es, Panthea, und sie,
Die edle Fremdlingin, die ihn
Nur Einmal sieht, ein herrlich Meteor.
Von seinem Tode, ihr Weinenden
Habt ihr gehört?
Ihr Trauernden! o sehet ihn

Last Scene of Act Two

PAUSANIAS. PANTHEA. DELIA

PAUSANIAS

Where is he? O Panthea,
You respect him, look for him too,
And long to see him once more,
That frightening wanderer who alone is fated
With glory to walk that path
Which to all other men a curse forbids.

PANTHEA

Is it godly for him, and great,
This way that all men fear?
Where is he?

PAUSANIAS

He sent me away, and I have not seen
Him since. Up in the mountains
I called his name, but did not find him.
He will surely return, having kindly promised me
That until nightfall he would stay.
If only he'd come! More swiftly
Than arrows the loveliest hour goes by.
For we shall yet enjoy his presence,
You, Panthea, and she as well,
The noble stranger who only once
Will see him, bright and brief, a meteor.
But you are weeping. Of his death
You've heard, then?
You grieve for him. O in his prime

In seiner Blüthe, den Hohen,
Ob trauriges nicht
Und was den Sterblichen schröklich dünkt,
Sich sänftige vor seeligem Auge.

DELIA

Wie liebst du ihn! und batest umsonst
Den Ernsten? mächtger ist, denn er
Die Bitte, Jüngling! und ein schöner Sieg
Wärs dir gewesen!

PAUSANIAS

Wie konnt' ich? trift
Er doch die Seele mir, wenn er
Antwortet, was sein Will ist.
Denn Freude nur giebt sein Versagen.
Diß ists und es tönt, je mehr auf seinem
Der Wunderbare besteht,
Nur tiefer das Herz ihm wieder. Es ist
Nicht eitel Überredung, glaub es mir,
Wenn er des Lebens sich
Bemächtiget.
Oft wenn er stille war
In seiner Welt,
Der Hochgenügsame, sah' ich ihn
Nur dunkel ahnend, rege war,
Und voll die Seele mir, doch konnt' ich nicht
Sie fühlen, und es ängstigte mich fast
Die Gegenwart des Unberührbaren.
Doch kam entscheidend von seiner Lippe das Wort,
Dann tönt' ein Freudenhimmel nach in ihm
Und mir und ohne Widerred
Ergriff es mich, doch fühlt' ich nur mich freier.
Ach, könnt' er irren, inniger

Envisage that exalted man.
And that which grieves you,
That which to mortals seems most terrible,
May well look milder to eyes that are blessed.

DELIA

How you love him! And yet in vain
Implored the earnest man? The plea
Is mightier than himself, and you deserved
To win him over.

PAUSANIAS

How could I, when
In answering he speaks his will
And overwhelms my soul?
For his refusal even gladdens us.
What could I do? The more that marvellous man
Insists on his own way,
The deeper is the resonance in our hearts.
Nor is it mere persuasiveness, believe me,
When over life itself
He gains such power.
When he was quiet
In his own world,
Uniquely self-sufficient,
Often I watched him in his vague divining,
My own soul active, full of vigour, yet
I could not feel it, and almost I was awed
By his impalpable presence.
Yet when the decisive word came from his lips
A heaven of joy re-echoed both in him
And me, and without contradiction
I yielded to it, relieved and liberated.
If he could err, why, all the more deeply

Erkennt' ich daran den unerschöpflich Wahren
Und stirbt er, so flammt aus seiner Asche nur heller
Der Genius mir empor.

DELIA

Dich entzündet, große Seele! der Tod
Des Großen, aber es sonnen
Die Herzen der Sterblichen auch
An mildem Lichte sich gern, und heften
Die Augen an Bleibendes. O sage, was soll
Noch leben und dauern? Die Stillsten reißt
Das Schiksaal doch hinaus und haben
Sie ahnend sich gewagt, verstößt
Es bald die Trauten wieder, und es stirbt
An ihren Hofnungen die Jugend.
In seiner Blüthe bleibt
Kein Lebendes – ach! und die Besten,
Noch treten zur Seite der tilgenden,
Der Todesgötter, auch sie und gehen dahin
Mit Lust und machen zur Schmach es uns
Bei Sterblichen zu weilen!

PAUSANIAS

Verdammest du

DELIA

O warum lässest du
Zu sterben deinen Helden

By that I should know the inexhaustible truth of him.
And if he died, all the more brightly his genius
From his ashes would rise for me.

DELIA

Being great, your soul is kindled
By a great man's death, but the hearts
Of mortals too like to bask
In milder light, and attach
Their eyes to that which is lasting. O tell us,
What now shall live and last? The most quiet
Fate uproots and sweeps away,
And if, prophetic, they ventured out,
Soon it repels those brave ones; the young
Die of the hopes that sustained them.
Nothing that lives remains
In its flower and prime – and the best,
Even they seek out their destroyers,
The gods of death, and with pleasure
They perish, and make it our shame
To linger, to dwell among mortals.

PAUSANIAS

Do you condemn

DELIA

O Nature, why do you
Make it so easy

So leicht es werden, Natur?
Zu gern nur, Empedokles,
Zu gerne opferst du dich,
Die Schwachen wirft das Schiksaal um, und die andern
Die Starken achten es gleich, zu fallen, zu stehn,
Und werden, wie die Gebrechlichen.
Du Herrlicher! was du littest
Das leidet kein Knecht
Und ärmer denn die andern Bettler
Durchwandertest du das Land,
Ja! freilich wahr ists,
Nicht die Verworfensten
Sind elend, wie eure Lieben, wenn einmal
Schmähliches sie berührt, ihr Götter.
Schön hat ers genommen.

PANTHEA

O nicht wahr?
Wie sollt er auch nicht?
Muß immer und immer doch
Was übermächtig ist
Der Genius überleben – gedachtet ihr,
Es halte der Stachel ihn auf? es beschleunigen ihm
Die Schmerzen den Flug und wie der Wagenlenker,
Wenn ihm das Rad in der Bahn
Zu rauchen beginnt, eilt
Der Gefährdete nur schneller zum Kranze!

DELIA

So freudig bist du, Panthea?

PANTHEA

Nicht in der Blüth' und Purpurtraub'
Ist heilge Kraft allein, es nährt

For your hero to die?
Empedocles, all too eagerly
You sacrifice yourself.
The weak by Fate are hurled down, and those others,
The strong, care little whether they fall or stand
And so become like the frail.
You glorious man, what you suffered
No slave could suffer,
And poorer than the poorest beggar
You roam across the land.
Yes, indeed it's true,
Not the utterly damned and rejected
Are wretched as are your loved ones, you gods,
Once disgrace has touched them.
And well he took it.

PANTHEA

Yes, well he took it
And how could he not?
When always and always the genius
Must outlive
That which is stronger than he – did you think
The goad would check him? The pain makes faster
His flight, and like the charioteer
When wheels begin to smoke on the track,
All the more swiftly
He, the endangered, rushes towards his garland.

DELIA

It's joy you feel, then, Panthea?

PANTHEA

Not in the blossom and purple grape
Alone is holy energy, but life

Das Leben vom Laide sich, Schwester!
Und trinkt, wie mein Held, doch auch
Am Todeskelche sich glüklich!

DELIA

Weh! must du so
Dich trösten, Kind?

PANTHEA

O nicht! es freuet mich nur,
Daß heilig, wenn es geschehn muß,
Das Gefürchtete, daß es herrlich geschieht.
Sind nicht, wie er, auch
Der Heroen einige zu den Göttern gegangen?
Erschroken kam, lautweinend
Vom Berge, das Volk, ich sah
Nicht einen, ders ihm hätte gelästert,
Denn nicht, wie die Verzweifelnden
Entfliehet er heimlich, sie hörten es all,
Und ihnen glänzt' im Laide das Angesicht
Vom Worte, das er gesprochen –

PAUSANIAS

So gehet festlich hinab
Das Gestirn und trunken
Von seinem Lichte glänzen die Thäler?

PANTHEA

Wohl geht er festlich hinab –
Der Ernste, dein Liebster, Natur!
Dein treuer, dein Opfer!
O die Todesfürchtigen lieben dich nicht,
Täuschend fesselt ihnen die Sorge
Das Aug', an deinem Herzen

By suffering too is nourished, sister;
And, like my hero, even from
The deadly cup draws gladness.

DELIA

Dear child, is that
Your only comfort?

PANTHEA

By no means! And yet it cheers me
That when it must be, must come about,
The dreaded thing, with glory it comes about.
Like him, in the past
Did not more than one of the heroes go to the gods?
Though startled, weeping aloud,
The people came from the mountain,
Not one I saw who reproached him,
For not like despairing men
In secret he flees, but all of them heard it,
And in their sorrow their faces shone
With the word that he had spoken.

PAUSANIAS

Festively, then, the planet
Goes down, and drunken
With its effulgence the valleys gleam?

PANTHEA

Festively, yes, he goes down –
The grave man, your favourite, Nature,
Your loyal one, sacrificed.
O they who fear death do not love you,
But care, the deluding, obstructs
Their eyes, and against your heart

Schlägt dann nicht mehr ihr Herz, sie verdorren
Geschieden von dir – o heilig All!
Lebendiges! inniges! dir zum Dank
Und daß er zeuge von dir, du Todesloses!
Wirft lächelnd seine Perlen ins Meer,
Aus dem sie kamen, der Kühne.
So mußt es geschehn.
So will es der Geist
Und die reifende Zeit,
Denn Einmal bedurften
Wir Blinden des Wunders.

No longer do their hearts beat, and they wither,
Divided from you – from the holy All.
And to bear witness to you, that are deathless,
Smiling into the sea, whence they came,
He throws his pearls now, the bold.
So it had to be.
So the spirit would have it
And ripening Time;
For we who are blind
Needed a miracle once.

Dritte Fassung

PERSONEN

EMPEDOKLES
PAUSANIAS, sein Freund
MANES, ein Aegyptier
STRATO, Herr von Agrigent, Bruder des Empedokles
PANTHEA, seine Schwester
GEFOLGE
    CHOR der Agrigentiner

Third Version

CHARACTERS

EMPEDOCLES
PAUSANIAS, his friend
MANES, an Egyptian
STRATO, Ruler of Agrigentum, brother of Empedocles
PANTHEA, his sister
ATTENDANTS
   CHORUS of Agrigentines

Erster Act

Erster Auftritt

EMPEDOKLES

(*vom Schlaf erwachend*)

Euch ruf ich über das Gefild herein
Vom langsamen Gewölk, ihr heißen Stralen
Des Mittags, ihr Gereiftesten, daß ich
An euch den neuen Lebenstag erkenne.
Denn anders ists wie sonst! vorbei, vorbei
Das menschliche Bekümmerniß! als wüchsen
Mir Schwingen an, so ist mir wohl und leicht
Hier oben, hier, und reich genug und froh
Und herrlich wohn' ich, wo den Feuerkelch
Mit Geist gefüllt bis an den Rand, bekränzt
Mit Blumen, die er selber sich erzog,
Gastfreundlich mir der Vater Aetna beut.
Und wenn das unterirrdische Gewitter
Izt festlich auferwacht zum Wolkensiz
Des nahverwandten Donnerers hinauf
Zur Freude fliegt, da wächst das Herz mir auch.
Mit Adlern sing ich hier Naturgesang.
Das dacht er nicht, daß in der Fremde mir
Ein anders Leben blühte, da er mich
Mit Schmach hinweg aus unsrer Stadt verwies,
Mein königlicher Bruder. Ach! er wußt es nicht,
Der kluge, welchen Seegen er bereitete,
Da er vom Menschenbande los, da er mich frei
Erklärte, frei, wie Fittige des Himmels.
Drum galt es auch! drum ward es auch erfüllt!
Mit Hohn und Fluch drum waffnete das Volk,

Act One

Scene One

EMPEDOCLES

(*awakening from sleep*)

You now I call upon across the fields,
Call down and in from the slow clouds, hot sunrays
Of noontide, you the most matured, so that
In you I'll recognize my new life's day.
For all is different now; and gone, dispelled,
My human grief! as though grown birdlike, graced
With pinions overnight, I feel so light
Up here, so well, and rich enough and glad
And glorious here I dwell where Father Etna
Tenders hospitably the fiery chalice
Filled to the brim with spirit, garlanded
With flowers that for himself he has reared up.
Whenever, too, the subterranean thunder
Festively roused now to the cloudy seat
Of his close relative, the Thunderer,
To joy flies up, then my heart also grows.
Here with the eagles I sing natural songs.
Of that he never thought, my royal brother,
When ignominiously he made me leave
Our city, that in exile, in the wilds
A different life would blossom out for me.
He never knew, that clever one, what blessing
He was bestowing on me when he severed
My human bonds, when he declared me free,
Free as the birds are, winged for heavenly flight.
And that was why! for that it was fulfilled!

Das mein war, gegen meine Seele sich
Und stieß mich aus und nicht vergebens gellt
Im Ohre mir das hundertstimmige,
Das nüchterne Gelächter, da der Träumer,
Der närrische, des Weges weinend gieng.
Beim Todtenrichter! wohl hab ichs verdient!
Und heilsam wars; die Kranken heilt das Gift
Und eine Sünde straft die andere.
Denn viel gesündiget hab ich von Jugend auf,
Die Menschen menschlich nie geliebt, gedient,
Wie Wasser nur und Feuer blinder dient,
Darum begegneten auch menschlich mir
Sie nicht, o darum schändeten sie mir
Mein Angesicht, und hielten mich, wie dich
Allduldende Natur! du hast mich auch,
Du hast mich, und es dämmert zwischen dir
Und mir die alte Liebe wieder auf,
Du rufst, du ziehst mich nah und näher an.
Vergessenheit – o wie ein glüklich Seegel
Bin ich vom Ufer los, des Lebens Welle
                    mich von selbst
Und wenn die Wooge wächst, und ihren Arm
Die Mutter um mich breitet, o was möcht'
Ich auch, was möcht' ich fürchten. Andre mag
Es freilich schröken. Denn es ist ihr Tod.
O du mir wohlbekant, du zauberische
Furchtbare Flamme! wie so stille wohnst
Du da und dort, wie scheuest du dich selbst
Und fliehest dich, du Seele des Lebendigen!
Lebendig wirst du mir und offenbar,
Mir birgst du dich, gebundner Geist, nicht länger,
Mir wirst du helle, denn ich fürcht es nicht.
Denn sterben will ja ich. Mein Recht ist diß.
Ha! Götter, schon, wie Morgenroth, ringsum

And they, the people once my own, could arm
Themselves with curses, taunts against my soul
And drive me out, and not for nothing still
My ears reverberate with the hundred-voiced,
Their hard, cold laughter when the fantast turned,
The silly dreamer, and weeping went his way.
By Hades! amply I deserved it all.
And it was good for me; poison heals the sick,
And we are purged of one sin by another.
For sinned I have, and greatly, from my youth,
Never have loved men humanly, but served
Only as fire or water blindly serves them.
And therefore too not humanly towards me
They acted, but defiled my face and used me
Like you, all-suffering Nature! And it is you
That hold me now, I'm yours, and between you
And me once more the old love rises up,
You call, you draw me close and ever closer.
Oblivion – O like a happy sail
I've left the shore behind, the wave of life
                              with its own force
And when the breaker swells and when the Mother
With her own arms enfolds me, O what could I,
What could I fear? Though other men, it's true,
Might well be frightened. For it is their death.
O you well-known to me, enchanting one,
Terrible flame! How quietly you dwell
Now here, now there, how you avoid yourself,
Flee from yourself, you soul of all that lives!
You grow alive to me, and manifest,
No longer hide, bound spirit, from my sight,
For me grow bright, because I do not fear it.
For death is what I seek. It is my right.
Already, gods, like sunrise all around me

Und drunten tost der alte Zorn vorüber!
Hinab hinab ihr klagenden Gedanken!
Sorgfältig Herz! ich brauche nun dich nimmer.
Und hier ist kein Bedenken mehr. Es ruft
Der Gott –
    (*da er den Pausanias gewahr wird*)
              und diesen Allzutreuen muß
Ich auch befrein, mein Pfad ist seiner nicht.

And underneath, the ancient wrath roars by.
Down with you, down, my poor complaining thoughts!
Painstaking heart, my need for you is over.
And no more scruples, wavering now. The god
It is who calls –
    (*becoming aware of Pausanias*)
                and this too loyal one
Shall have his freedom; my way is not his.

Zweiter Auftritt

PAUSANIAS. EMPEDOKLES

PAUSANIAS

Du scheinest freudig auferwacht, mein Wanderer.

EMPEDOKLES

Schon hab ich, lieber, und vergebens nicht
Mich in der neuen Heimath umgesehn.
Die Wildniß ist mir hold, auch dir gefällt,
                    die edle Burg,
                              unser Aetna.

PAUSANIAS

Sie haben uns verbannt, sie haben dich,
Du Gütiger! geschmäht und glaub' es mir,
Unleidlich warst du ihnen längst und innig
In ihre Trümmer schien, in ihre Nacht
Zu helle den Verzweifelten das Licht.
Nun mögen sie vollenden, ungestört
Im uferlosen Sturm, indeß den Stern
Die Wolke birgt, ihr Schiff im Kreise treiben.
Das wußt ich wohl, du Göttlicher, an dir
Entweicht der Pfeil, der andre trift und wirft.
Und ohne Schaden, wie am Zauberstab
Die zahme Schlange, spielt' um dich von je
Die ungetreue Menge, die du zogst,
Die du am Herzen hegtest, liebender!

Scene Two

PAUSANIAS. EMPEDOCLES

PAUSANIAS

It seems you had a glad awakening,
My exiled master.

EMPEDOCLES

                For some time, dear friend,
And not in vain, I have been up, surveying
The prospect and the site of this new home.
The wilderness delights me, and you also
Take pleasure in
                  this noble fortress
                        our Etna.

PAUSANIAS

They've banished us, reviled you, kindly man,
And, friend, believe me, long before that time
Found you insufferable; tenderly
Into their rubble and their night it shone,
Too bright for those despairing ones, your light.
Now let them end the business, undisturbed
Through shoreless squalls, while clouds conceal the star,
In circles let them now propel their ship.
This I knew well, divine one, that from you
That dart rebounds which wounds and fells another.
And harmlessly, as on a magic wand
Tame serpents will, around you ever played
The faithless mob that you yourself reared up,
Lovingly tended, warmed against your heart.

Nun! laß sie nur! sie mögen ungestalt
Lichtscheu am Boden taumeln der sie trägt,
Und allbegehrend, allgeängstiget
Sich müde rennen, brennen mag der Brand,
Bis er erlischt – wir wohnen ruhig hier!

EMPEDOKLES

Ja! ruhig wohnen wir; es öffnen groß
Sich hier vor uns die heilgen Elemente.
Die Mühelosen regen immergleich
In ihrer Kraft sich freudig hier um uns.
An seinen vesten Ufern wallt und ruht
Das alte Meer, und das Gebirge steigt
Mit seiner Ströme Klang, es woogt und rauscht
Sein grüner Wald von Thal zu Thal hinunter.
Und oben weilt das Licht, der Aether stillt
Den Geist und das geheimere Verlangen.
Hier wohnen ruhig wir!

PAUSANIAS

            So bleibst du wohl
Auf diesen Höhn, und lebst in deiner Welt,
Ich diene dir und sehe, was uns noth ist.

EMPEDOKLES

Nur weniges ist noth, und selber mag
Ich gerne diß von jezt an mir besorgen.

PAUSANIAS

Doch lieber! hab ich schon für einiges,
Was du zuerst bedarfst, zuvorgesorgt.

EMPEDOKLES

Weist du, was ich bedarf?

Well, let them be. Misshapen let them reel
Close to the soil that bears them, shunning light,
And all-desiring, all-intimidated,
Run themselves weary; let their slow fire burn
Till it goes out – peacefully we live here.

EMPEDOCLES

Yes, we live peacefully; and vastly here
The holy elements reveal themselves.
Ever the same, the untoiling joyously,
Surely and powerfully stir around us.
On its firm shores advances and reposes
The ancient sea, and the great mountains rise
With music of their springs, the green woods flow
And roar and rustle down from vale to vale.
And at the top light lingers, Aether stills
Our minds and the more secret of our longings.
Here we live peacefully.

PAUSANIAS

              So you will stay
Here on these heights, and live in your own world,
And I shall serve you, see to what we need.

EMPEDOCLES

Little is needed, and that willingly
From now on I will see to and provide.

PAUSANIAS

Nevertheless, already, my dear teacher,
I've made provision for your urgent needs.

EMPEDOCLES

And do you know them?

PAUSANIAS

                    Als wüßt ich nicht,
Womit genügt dem Hochgenügsamen.
Und wie das Leben, das zu lieber Noth
Der innigen Natur geworden ist,
Das kleinste dem Vertrauten viel bedeutet.
Indeß du gut auf kahler Erde hier
In heißer Sonne schliefst, gedacht' ich doch,
Ein waicher Boden, und die kühle Nacht
In einer sichern Halle wäre besser.
Auch sind wir hier, die Allverdächtigen,
Den Wohnungen der andern fast zu nah.
Nicht lange wollt ich ferne seyn von dir
Und eilt hinauf und glüklich fand ich bald,
Für dich und mich gebaut, ein ruhig Haus.
Ein tiefer Fels, von Eichen dicht umschirmt,
Dort in der dunkeln Mitte des Gebirgs,
Und nah entspringt ein Quell, es grünt umher
Die Fülle guter Pflanzen, und zum Bett
Ist Überfluß von Laub und Gras bereitet.
Da lassen sie dich ungeschmäht, und tief und still
Ists wenn du sinnst, und wenn du schläfst, um dich,
Ein Heiligtum ist mir mit dir die Grotte.
Komm, siehe selbst, und sage nicht, ich tauge
Dir künftig nicht, wem taugt' ich anders denn?

EMPEDOKLES

Du taugst zu gut.

PAUSANIAS

                    Wie könt ich diß?

PAUSANIAS

How could I not know
What would suffice the highly self-sufficient;
How in that life which now is the dear care
Of tender Nature, even smallest things
Mean much to one long grown familiar to me.
While you slept well here on the bare, hard ground
In blazing sunshine, yet it seemed to me,
A softer bed to lie on and cool night
Within firm walls, in safety, would be better.
Besides, all-suspect even in these wilds
Almost we are too near to other men's homes.
Not wishing to be far from you for long,
I hurried to these parts and quickly found
A quiet house, fitting for you and me.
Dense oak trees there surround a sheer great rock
Up in the mountain range's gloomy midst,
A spring wells up nearby, and all around
There's plenty of good plants, and more than plenty
Of leaves and grass for bedding. There they'll leave
You unmolested, and when you meditate,
And when you sleep, all's deep and still for you,
A holy place that grotto, shared with you.
See for yourself now, come, and never say
You've no more use for me – who else should use me?

EMPEDOCLES

You are too useful.

PAUSANIAS

Could I be?

EMPEDOKLES

                                    Auch du
Bist allzutreu, du bist ein thöricht Kind.

PAUSANIAS

Das sagst du wohl, doch klügers weiß ich nicht,
Wie deß zu seyn, dem ich geboren bin.

EMPEDOKLES

Wie bist du sicher?

PAUSANIAS

                     Warum denn nicht?
Wofür denn hättest du auch einst, da ich,
Der Waise gleich, am heldenarmen Ufer
Mir einen Schuzgott sucht und traurig irrte,
Du Gütiger, die Hände mir gereicht?
Wofür mit irrelosem Auge wärst du
Auf deiner stillen Bahn, du edles Licht
In meiner Dämmerung mir aufgegangen?
Seitdem bin ich ein anderer, und dein
Und näher dir und einsamer mit dir,
Wächst froher nur die Seele mir und freier.

EMPEDOKLES

O still davon!

PAUSANIAS

                  Warum? Was ists? wie kan
Ein freundlich Wort dich irren, theurer Mann?

EMPEDOCLES

                              You too
Are all too loyal; you're a foolish child.

PAUSANIAS

Well you may say so, but I can be no wiser
Than to belong to him whose child I am.

EMPEDOCLES

Are you so sure of that?

PAUSANIAS

                        How can I help it?
Why else, when like an orphan on a shore
That breeds few heroes, sadly I strayed about
Seeking a tutelary god, did you,
Most kind one, offer me your band? Why else
With your unstraying eyes, in your sure orbit,
Did you, most noble light, rise in my dawn?
Since then I have been different, and am yours,
And closer to you, lonelier with you,
My soul grows all the gladder and more free.

EMPEDOCLES

No, please – not that.

PAUSANIAS

                    Why not? What is it? Can
A friendly word distress you, then, my teacher?

EMPEDOKLES

Geh! folge mir, und schweig und schone mich
Und rege du nicht auch das Herz mir auf. –
Habt ihr zum Dolche die Erinnerung
Nicht mir gemacht? nun wundern sie sich noch
Und treten vor das Auge mir und fragen.
Nein! du bist ohne Schuld – nur kann ich, Sohn!
Was mir zu nahe kömmt, nicht wohl ertragen.

PAUSANIAS

Und mich, mich stößest du von dir? o denk an dich,
Sei, der du bist, und siehe mich, und gieb,
Was ich nun weniger entbehren kann,
Ein gutes Wort aus reicher Brust mir wieder.

EMPEDOKLES

Erzähle, was dir wohlgefällt, dir selbst,
Für mich ist, was vorüber ist, nicht mehr.

PAUSANIAS

Ich weiß es wohl, was dir vorüber ist,
Doch du und ich, wir sind uns ja geblieben.

EMPEDOKLES

Sprich lieber mir von anderem, mein Sohn!

PAUSANIAS

Was hab ich sonst?

EMPEDOKLES

                Verstehest du mich auch?
Hinweg! ich hab es dir gesagt und sag
Es dir, es ist nicht schön, daß du dich

EMPEDOCLES

Come, follow me, keep silent, friend, and spare me,
Unlike those others, do not stir my heart.
Did they not turn my memories into daggers?
And after that they wonder at it all,
And seek me out, and ask me this and that.
No, you are not to blame – only, my son,
I cannot bear too deep, too close a probing.

PAUSANIAS

And so you cast me off! Think of yourself,
Be what you are and look at me and give me
What now less easily I can do without,
A token of your former self and friendship.

EMPEDOCLES

Tell any tales you please – but to yourself;
For me what's past is done with once for all.

PAUSANIAS

O, I know well enough what's past for you,
But you and I, must our good bonds be broken?

EMPEDOCLES

I beg you, speak of other things, my son.

PAUSANIAS

What else is there?

EMPEDOCLES

               But do you understand me?
Away! I've told you once and say again,
It is not right that uninvited here

So ungefragt mir an die Seele dringest,
An meine Seite stets, als wüßtest du
Nichts anders mehr, mit armer Angst dich hängst.
Du must es wissen, dir gehör ich nicht
Und du nicht mir, und deine Pfade sind
Die meinen nicht; mir blüht es anderswo.
Und was ich mein', es ist von heute nicht,
Da ich geboren wurde, wars beschlossen.
Sieh auf und wags! was Eines ist, zerbricht,
Die Liebe stirbt in ihrer Knospe nicht
Und überall in freier Freude theilt
Des Lebens luftger Baum sich auseinander.
Kein zeitlich Bündniß bleibet, wie es ist,
Wir müssen scheiden, Kind! und halte nur
Mein Schiksaal mir nicht auf und zaudre nicht.

O sieh! es glänzt der Erde trunknes Bild,
Das göttliche, dir gegenwärtig, Jüngling,
Es rauscht und regt durch alle Lande sich
Und wechselt, jung und leicht, mit frommem Ernst
Der geschäfftge Reigentanz, womit den Geist
Die Sterblichen, den alten Vater, feiern.
Da gehe du und wandle taumellos
Und menschlich mit und denk am Abend mein.
Mir aber ziemt die stille Halle, mir
Die hochgelegene, geräumige,
Denn Ruhe brauch' ich wohl, zu träge sind,
Zum schnellgeschäftigen Spiel der Sterblichen,
Die Glieder mir und hab ich sonst dabei
Ein feiernd Lied in Jugendlust gesungen,
Zerschlagen ist das zarte Saitenspiel.
O Melodien über mir! es war ein Scherz!
Und kindisch wagt' ich sonst euch nachzuahmen,
Ein fühllos leichtes Echo tönt' in mir,

You prod my soul, as though incapable
Of other movement now, in pitiable fear
Always you cling to me. But you must know,
I am not yours, no more than you are mine,
Where you walk, I do not; my blossoming
Elsewhere awaits me. And that of which I speak
Not now has come about, not on this day,
But at my birth already was decided.
Look up and dare to know it: what is one
Breaks up, yet in its bud love does not die,
And everywhere in bold, untrammelled joy,
Unforced, the airy tree of life divides.
No temporal tie remains what it has been;
Child, we must part; and, please, do not obstruct
My destiny, and do not hesitate.

But, look! Earth's drunken image gleams,
Holy, divine, and present to you, friend;
Through every land it roars, it teems and rushes,
And youthful, light, yet serious too and pious,
It changes, that perpetual round dance
Wherewith we mortals celebrate the Spirit,
The ancient Father. There now go, join in,
There move ungiddied, humanly, and think
Of me at evening. But as for me,
It is the quiet hall that's fitting, one
More spacious, higher up, remote, aloof,
For rest is what I need, too heavy now
My limbs have grown for the quick, busy dance
Of mortals, and if in it once I sang
A canticle of praise with youthful zest,
The delicate instrument, my lyre, is shattered.
O melodies above me! It was all a jest!
And childlike then I dared to imitate you,

Und unverständlich nach –
Nun hör ich ernster euch, ihr Götterstimmen.

PAUSANIAS

Ich kenne nimmer dich, nur traurig ist
Mir, was du sagst, doch alles ist ein Räthsel.
Was hab ich auch, was hab ich dir gethan,
Daß du mich so, wie dirs gefällt, bekümmerst
Und nahmenlos dein Herz, des Einen noch,
Des Lezten los zu seyn, sich freut und müht.
Das hofft' ich nicht, da wir Geächtete
Den Wohnungen der Menschen scheu vorüber
Zusammen wandelten in wilder Nacht,
Und darum, lieber! war ich nicht dabei,
Wenn mit den Thränen dir des Himmels Reegen
Vom Angesichte trof, und sah es an,
Wenn lächelnd du das rauhe Sclavenkleid
Mittags an heißer Sonne troknetest
Auf schattenlosem Sand, wenn du die Spuren
Wohl manche Stunde wie ein wundes Wild
Mit deinem Blute zeichnetest, das auf
Den Felsenpfad von nakter Sohle rann.
Ach! darum lies ich nicht mein Haus und lud
Des Volkes und des Vaters Fluch mir auf,
Daß du mich, wo du wohnen willst und ruhn,
Wie ein verbraucht Gefäß, bei Seite werfest.
Und willst du weit hinweg? wohin? wohin?
Ich wandre mit, zwar steh ich nicht wie du
Mit Kräften der Natur in trautem Bunde,
Mir steht wie dir Zukünftiges nicht offen,
Doch freudig in der Götter Nacht hinaus
Schwingt seine Fittige mein Sinn, und fürchtet
Noch immer nicht die mächtigeren Blike.
Ja! wär ich auch ein Schwacher, dennoch wär

A light unfeeling echo rang in me,
Incomprehensibly reverberated –
More gravely now I hear you, voices of the gods.

PAUSANIAS

I do not recognize you, only sad
To me is what you say, but all a riddle.
What have I done, what have I done to you
That now, as the mood takes you, you offend me
And namelessly your heart strives and rejoices
To rid itself of this one friend, the last.
I never dreamed of that when after exile,
Shyly avoiding human habitations,
Together through the desolate night we trudged,
And not for that I was beside you, dear one,
When mixed with tears the rain of heaven poured
Down from your face, nor yet for that looked on
When smiling in the noonday sun you dried
Your rough slave's tunic on the shadowless sand,
When like a wounded animal's, hour after hour
The trail you left was one of blood that trickled
From your bare heels on to the rocky path.
Oh, not for that I left my house and bore
The curse both of my father and my people,
That now, because you wish to rest and settle,
You'd cast me off like a discarded vessel.
And is it far you're going? Where? O where?
I'll stay with you, for though no secret pact,
Such as you formed, binds me to powers of Nature,
The future things you see are closed to me,
Yet bravely out into the night of gods
My mind directs its flight, and even now
Goes in no fear of those more mighty glances.
Indeed, if I were feeble in myself,

Ich, weil ich so dich liebe, stark, wie du.
Beim göttlichen Herakles! stiegst du auch,
Um die Gewaltigen, die drunten sind,
Versöhnend die Titanen heimzusuchen,
Ins bodenlose Thal, vom Gipfel dort,
Und wagtest dich ins Heiligtum des Abgrunds,
Wo duldend vor dem Tage sich das Herz
Der Erde birgt und ihre Schmerzen dir
Die dunkle Mutter sagt, o du der Nacht
Des Aethers Sohn! ich folgte dir hinunter.

EMPEDOKLES

So bleib!

PAUSANIAS

     Wie meinst du diß?

EMPEDOKLES

              Du gabst
Dich mir, bist mein; so frage nicht!

PAUSANIAS

             Es sei!

EMPEDOKLES

Und sagst du mirs noch einmal, Sohn, und giebst
Dein Blut und deine Seele mir für immer?

PAUSANIAS

Als hätt ich so ein loses Wort gesagt
Und zwischen Schlaf und Wachen dirs versprochen?
Unglaubiger! ich sags und wiederhohl' es:
Auch diß, auch diß, es ist von heute nicht,
Da ich geboren wurde, wars beschlossen.

My love for you would make me strong as you are.
By Hercules, the divine! though you resolved
To visit and appease those violent ones
Who dwell below, the Titans, and climbed down
Into the bottomless valley from that summit there,
Daring to tread the sanctum of the abyss
Where, patient, Earth conceals her heart from day
And the dark Mother will confide to you
Her sufferings, her griefs, O son of Night,
Of Aether, even then I'd follow you down.

EMPEDOCLES

Then stay!

PAUSANIAS

        How do you mean that?

EMPEDOCLES

                         You have given
Yourself to me, are mine; now ask no questions!

PAUSANIAS

So be it!

EMPEDOCLES

        Will you say that once again,
And pledge your blood and soul to me for ever?

PAUSANIAS

As though I'd only blabbed an idle word
And made a promise between sleep and waking?
You doubting man! I say it and repeat it:
This too, this too was not determined now,
But at my birth already was decided.

EMPEDOKLES

Ich bin nicht, der ich bin, Pausanias,
Und meines Bleibens ist auf Jahre nicht,
Ein Schimmer nur, der bald vorüber muß,
Im Saitenspiel ein Ton –

PAUSANIAS

        So tönen sie,
So schwinden sie zusammen in die Luft!
Und freundlich spricht der Wiederhall davon.
Versuche nun mich länger nicht und laß
Und gönne du die Ehre mir, die mein ist!
Hab ich nicht Laid genug, wie du, in mir?
Wie möchtest du mich noch belaidigen!

EMPEDOKLES

O allesopfernd Herz! und dieser giebt
Schon mir zu lieb die goldne Jugend weg!
Und ich! o Erd und Himmel! siehe! noch,
Noch bist du nah, indeß die Stunde flieht,
Und blühest mir, du Freude meiner Augen.
Noch ists, wie sonst, ich halt im Arme,
Als wärst du mein, wie meine Beute dich,
Und mich bethört der holde Traum noch einmal.
Ja! herrlich wärs, wenn in die Grabesflamme
So Arm in Arm statt Eines Einsamen
Ein festlich Paar am Tagesende gieng',
Und gerne nähm' ich, was ich hier geliebt,
Wie seine Quellen all ein edler Strom,
Der heilgen Nacht zum Opfertrank, hinunter.
Doch besser ists, wir gehen unsern Pfad
Ein jeder, wie der Gott es ihm beschied.
Unschuldiger ist diß, und schadet nicht.

EMPEDOCLES

I am not what I am, Pausanias,
And not for years may sojourn here, become
Only a gleam, a glint that soon must pass,
One note the lyre-strings hold –

PAUSANIAS

                      Then let them sound,
Together let them vanish in the air!
And kindly will the echo of them speak.
No longer tempt me, try me now, but grant me
Such honour as deservedly is mine.
Am I not filled with grief enough, as you are?
How can you add the sting of your disdain!

EMPEDOCLES

All-sacrificing heart! So this one gives
His golden youth away, all for my sake!
And I! O Earth and Heaven, look, even now,
Still you are near, though now the hour runs out,
And blossom for me, and delight my eyes.
Still, as before, I hold you in my arms
As though you were mine, as though you were my booty,
And the dear dream beclouds me once again.
Yes, glorious it would be if to the pyre
Instead of one, a lonely man, arm in arm
Like this a festive pair towards nightfall went,
And gladly I would take what here I loved,
As might a noble river all its sources,
Down for libation into holy Night.
Yet it is better that each go his own way
And walk the path that God ordained for him.
More innocent it is, and does no harm;

Und billig ists und recht, daß überall
Des Menschen Sinn sich eigen angehört.
Und dann – es trägt auch leichter seine Bürde
Und sicherer der Mann, wenn er allein ist.
So wachsen ja des Waldes Eichen auch
Und keines kennt, so alt sie sind, das andre.

PAUSANIAS

Wie du es willst! Ich widerstrebe nicht.
Du sagst es mir und wahr ists wohl und lieb
Ist billig mir diß lezte Wort von dir.
So geh ich denn! und störe deine Ruhe
Dir künftig nicht, auch meinest du es gut,
Daß meinem Sinne nicht die Stille tauge.

EMPEDOKLES

Doch, lieber, zürnst du nicht?

PAUSANIAS

                              Mit dir? Mit dir?

EMPEDOKLES

Was ist es denn? ja! weist du nun, wohin?

PAUSANIAS

Gebiet es mir.

EMPEDOKLES

                    Es war mein lezt Gebot,
Pausanias! die Herrschaft ist am Ende.

PAUSANIAS

Mein Vater! rathe mir!

And it is meet and right that everywhere
Men's minds should be self-governed and self-owned.
Besides – more safely and more easily
A man will bear his burden when alone.
So too the oak trees of the forest grow
And, ancient though it be, none knows the other.

PAUSANIAS

Have your own will! I'll not oppose my own.
You say so, and no doubt it's true, and precious
To me, and apt, this parting word from you.
I'll go, then, and in future shall not trouble
Your peace of mind; and for my own good surely
You hint that stillness ill becomes my kind.

EMPEDOCLES

But you're not angry, friend?

PAUSANIAS

                                   With you? With you?

EMPEDOCLES

What is it, then? Your way, it is not clear now?

PAUSANIAS

Tell me, direct me!

EMPEDOCLES

                        That was my last command,
Pausanias. My government is ended.

PAUSANIAS

My father, counsel me!

EMPEDOKLES
                    Wohl manches sollt
Ich sagen, doch verschweig ich dirs,
Es will zum sterblichen Gespräche fast
Und eitlem Wort die Zunge nimmer dienen.
Sieh! liebster! anders ists und leichter bald
Und freier athm' ich auf, und wie der Schnee
Des hohen Aetna dort am Sonnenlichte
Erwarmt und schimmert und zerrinnt, und los
Vom Berge woogt und Iris froher Bogen sich
Der blühende beim Fall der Woogen schwingt,
So rinnt und woogt vom Herzen mir es los,
So hallt es weg, was mir die Zeit gehäuft,
Die Schwere fällt, und fällt, und helle blüht
Das Leben das ätherische, darüber.
Nun wandre muthig, Sohn, ich geb und küsse
Verheißungen auf deine Stirne dir,
Es dämmert dort Italiens Gebirg,
Das Römerland, das thatenreiche, winkt,
Dort wirst du wohlgedeihn, dort, wo sich froh
Die Männer in der Kämpferbahn begegnen,
O Heldenstädte dort! und du, Tarent!
Ihr brüderlichen Hallen, wo ich oft
Lichttrunken einst mit meinem Plato gieng
Und immerneu uns Jünglingen das Jahr
Und jeder Tag erschien in heilger Schule.
Besuch ihn auch, o Sohn, und grüß ihn mir,
Den alten Freund an seiner Heimath Strom,
Am blumigen Ilissus, wo er wohnt.
Und will die Seele dir nicht ruhn, so geh
Und frage sie, die Brüder in Aegyptos.
Dort hörest du das ernste Saitenspiel

EMPEDOCLES

                    No doubt there's much
That I should say, yet I withhold it from you,
For almost now for mortal conversation
And idle words my tongue will serve no more.
Look, dearest one, it's different now, and soon
More lightly and more freely I shall breathe,
And as that snow up there on Etna's peak
Grows warm in sunlight, gleams and melts away,
And loosened from the mountain billows down
And the glad bow of Iris, the bright-blossoming,
Flexed, rises up where those quick billows fall,
So from my heart it billows and pours down,
And dies away, what time heaped up for me,
The heaviness falls and falls, and brightly blooms
That other life, aetherial life, above me.
Now bravely travel, son; upon your brow
With heart and soul and lips I lay good wishes,
There in the distance glimmer Italy's hills,
The Roman land, the rich in deeds, is beckoning,
There you will prosper, there, where gladly bold
In the arena men compete with men,
Cities of heroes there! And you, Tarentum,
You brotherly mansions where so often once
Drunken with light I walked at Plato's side
And to us youths for ever new the year,
And every day seemed, in our holy school.
Visit him too, my son, and take my greetings
To my old friend by his own homeland's river,
By flowery Ilissus where he dwells.
And if your spirit will not rest, then go
And question them, my brothers in Aegyptos.
There you will hear the lilt of serious lyres,

Uraniens und seiner Töne Wandel.
Dort öffnen sie das Buch des Schiksaals dir.
Geh! fürchte nichts! es kehret alles wieder.
Und was geschehen soll, ist schon vollendet.

(*Pausanias geht ab*)

Urania's, and modulated music.
There they will open destiny's book for you.
Go, and fear nothing. Everything recurs.
And what's to come already is completed.

(*Exit Pausanias*)

Dritter Auftritt

MANES. EMPEDOKLES

MANES

Nun! säume nicht! bedenke dich nicht länger.
Vergeh! vergeh! damit es ruhig bald
Und helle werde, Trugbild!

EMPEDOKLES

                    Was? woher?
Wer bist du, Mann!

MANES

          Der Armen Einer auch
Von diesem Stamm, ein Sterblicher, wie du.
Zu rechter Zeit gesandt, dir, der du dich
Des Himmels Liebling dünkst, des Himmels Zorn,
Des Gottes, der nicht müßig ist, zu nennen.

EMPEDOKLES

Ha! kennst du den?

MANES

              Ich habe manches dir
Am fernen Nil gesagt.

EMPEDOKLES

            Und du? du hier?
Kein Wunder ists! Seit ich den Lebenden
Gestorben bin, erstehen mir die Todten.

Scene Three

MANES. EMPEDOCLES

MANES

Well, long enough you've pondered and delayed.
Now perish, perish! so that soon it will
Grow bright and quiet, phantom!

EMPEDOCLES

                    What? Where from?
Who are you, man!

MANES

              One of the wretched, too,
And of this race, a mortal, as you are.
Sent at the right time, sent to you who think
Yourself the favourite of Heaven, to name
The wrath of Heaven, that God's who never rests.

EMPEDOCLES

Ha, so you know him?

MANES

              This and that I told you
Once by the distant Nile.

EMPEDOCLES

            And you? You here?
No wonder. Now that to the living I
Have died, it is the dead who rise for me.

MANES

Die Todten reden nicht, wo du sie fragst.
Doch wenn du eines Worts bedarfst, vernimm.

EMPEDOKLES

Die Stimme, die mich ruft, vernehm ich schon.

MANES

So redet es mit dir?

EMPEDOKLES

                  Was soll die Rede, Fremder!

MANES

Ja! fremde bin ich hier und unter Kindern.
Das seid ihr Griechen all. Ich hab es oft
Vormals gesagt. Doch wolltest du mir nicht,
Wie dirs ergieng bei deinem Volke, sagen?

EMPEDOKLES

Was mahnst du mich? Was rufst du mir noch einmal?
Mir gieng es, wie es soll.

MANES

                 Ich wußt es auch
Schon längst voraus, ich hab es dir geweissagt.

EMPEDOKLES

Nun denn! was hältst du es noch auf? was drohst
Du mit der Flamme mir des Gottes, den
Ich kenne, dem ich gern zum Spiele dien',
Und richtest mir mein heilig Recht, du Blinder!

MANES

The dead refuse to speak, where you consult them.
Yet if you need a word from me, then hear.

EMPEDOCLES

The voice that calls to me I hear already.

MANES

And that is how it talks?

EMPEDOCLES

What does your talk mean, stranger?

MANES

Yes, I'm a stranger here, and among children.
For all you Greeks are that — as before now
I've often said. But was it not your will
To tell me how you fared among your people?

EMPEDOCLES

Why do you raise the past? And call to me again?
I fared as fare I must.

MANES

And I foreknew it
All long ago, and prophesied it to you.

EMPEDOCLES

Well, then, why do you now detain it? Threaten
Me with the flame of that God whom I know,
Whom as a plaything willingly I serve,
And make to judge my sacred right, you blind man!

MANES

Was dir begegnen muß, ich ändr' es nicht.

EMPEDOKLES

So kamst du her, zu sehen, wie es wird?

MANES

O scherze nicht, und ehre doch dein Fest,
Umkränze dir dein Haupt, und schmük es aus,
Das Opferthier, das nicht vergebens fällt.
Der Tod, der jähe, er ist ja von Anbeginn,
Das weist du wohl, den Unverständigen
Die deinesgleichen sind, zuvorbeschieden.
Du willst es und so seis! Doch sollst du mir
Nicht unbesonnen, wie du bist, hinab,
Ich hab ein Wort, und diß bedenke, Trunkner!
Nur Einem ist es Recht, in dieser Zeit,
Nur Einen adelt deine schwarze Sünde.
Ein größrer ists, denn ich! denn wie die Rebe
Von Erd und Himmel zeugt, wenn sie getränkt
Von hoher Sonn aus dunklem Boden steigt,
So wächst er auf, aus Licht und Nacht geboren.
Es gährt um ihn die Welt, was irgend nur
Beweglich und verderbend ist im Busen
Der Sterblichen, ist aufgeregt von Grund aus.
Der Herr der Zeit, um seine Herrschaft bang,
Thront finster blikend über der Empörung.
Sein Tag erlischt, und seine Blize leuchten,
Doch was von oben flammt, entzündet nur,
Und was von unten strebt, die wilde Zwietracht.
Der Eine doch, der neue Retter faßt
Des Himmels Stralen ruhig auf, und liebend
Nimmt er, was sterblich ist, an seinen Busen,

MANES

That which awaits you now I shall not alter.

EMPEDOCLES

So you came here to see how it turns out?

MANES

O do not jest, but honour your festive day,
Garland your head, and solemnly array it,
The votive beast that not in vain will fall.
Death, sudden death, as well you know, for those
Who do not comprehend, for such as you,
From the beginning has been preordained.
You wish it, and so be it! Yet not unthinking
As now you are, would I have you go down,
I have a word, and, drunken man, that consider:
One only has the privilege, at this time,
One only your black sin serves to ennoble.
Greater he is than I. For as the vine
To Earth and Heaven bears witness, when transfused
By the high sun it rises from dark soil,
So he grows up, born of both light and darkness.
Round him the world ferments, whatever is
Movable and pernicious in the hearts
Of mortals, from its depth and centre is stirred up.
The Lord of Time, afraid for his dominion,
Glowering on his throne surveys revolt.
His day extinguishes, his lightning shines,
Yet that which flames above, and that which presses
Up from below, further ignite contention.
The One, however, the new saviour calmly
Seizes the rays of Heaven, and lovingly
Takes to his bosom those of mortal mould,

Und milde wird in ihm der Streit der Welt.
Die Menschen und die Götter söhnt er aus
Und nahe wieder leben sie, wie vormals.
Und daß, wenn er erschienen ist, der Sohn
Nicht größer, denn die Eltern sei, und nicht
Der heilge Lebensgeist gefesselt bleibe
Vergessen über ihm, dem Einzigen,
So lenkt er aus, der Abgott seiner Zeit,
Zerbricht, er selbst, damit durch reine Hand
Dem Reinen das Nothwendige geschehe,
Sein eigen Glük, das ihm zu glüklich ist,
Und giebt, was er besaß, dem Element,
Das ihn verherrlichte, geläutert wieder.
Bist du der Mann? derselbe? bist du diß?

EMPEDOKLES

Ich kenne dich im finstern Wort, und du,
Du Alleswissender, erkennst mich auch.

MANES

O sage, wer du bist! und wer bin ich?

EMPEDOKLES

Versuchst du noch, noch immer mich, und kömst,
Mein böser Geist, zu mir in solcher Stunde?
Was lässest du mich nicht stille gehen, Mann?
Und wagst dich hier an mich und reizest mich,
Daß ich im Zorn die heilgen Pfade wandle?
Ein Knabe war ich, wußte nicht, was mir
Ums Auge fremd am Tage sich bewegt',
Und wunderbar umfiengen mir die großen
Gestalten dieser Welt, die freudigen,
Mein unerfahren schlummernd Herz im Busen.
Und staunend hört ich oft die Wasser gehn

And in him the world's conflict is allayed.
Between the gods and men he mediates,
The gods live near again, as in the past,
And so that, having once appeared, the Son
Shall not be greater than his parents, nor
The holy Spirit of life remain in bondage,
Forgotten because of him, the Only One,
He turns aside, the idol of his time.
And, that a pure hand for the Pure may do
What must be done, by his own choice he breaks
His own good fortune, grown too great for him,
And to the element that gave him glory
Gives back all his possessions, purified.
Are you that man? The same? That very man?

EMPEDOCLES

I know you in the darkening word, and you,
Omniscient one, me too have recognized.

MANES

O tell me who you are! And who am I?

EMPEDOCLES

Still do you tempt me, even now, and come,
My evil spirit, to me at this hour?
And will not let me go in peace now. Why?
And dare accost me here and bait and rouse me
So that in anger I walk the holy paths?
I was a boy and did not know what things
They were that stirred about my eyes in daylight,
And marvellously the world's powers and shapes,
The great and joyous, wrapped themselves around
My slumbering, my inexperienced heart.
And wondering often I heard the waters flow

Und sah die Sonne blühn, und sich an ihr
Den Jugendtag der stillen Erd entzünden.
Da ward in mir Gesang und helle ward
Mein dämmernd Herz im dichtenden Gebete,
Wenn ich die Fremdlinge, die gegenwärt'gen,
Die Götter der Natur mit Nahmen nannt'
Und mir der Geist im Wort, im Bilde sich,
Im seeligen, des Lebens Räthsel löste.
So wuchs ich still herauf, und anderes
War schon bereitet. Denn gewaltsamer,
Wie Wasser, schlug die wilde Menschenwelle
Mir an die Brust, und aus dem Irrsaal kam
Des armen Volkes Stimme mir zum Ohre.
Und wenn, indeß ich in der Halle schwieg,
Um Mitternacht der Aufruhr weheklagt,
Und durchs Gefilde stürzt, und lebensmüd
Mit eigner Hand sein eignes Haus zerbrach,
Und die verlaideten verlaßnen Tempel,
Wenn sich die Brüder flohn, und sich die Liebsten
Vorübereilten, und der Vater nicht
Den Sohn erkannt, und Menschenwort nicht mehr
Verständlich war, und menschliches Gesez,
Da faßte mich die Deutung schaudernd an:
Es war der scheidende Gott meines Volks!
Den hört ich, und zum schweigenden Gestirn
Sah ich hinauf, wo er herabgekommen.
Und ihn zu sühnen, gieng ich hin. Noch wurden uns
Der schönen Tage viel. Noch schien es sich
Am Ende zu verjüngen; und es wich,
Der goldnen Zeit, der allvertrauenden,
Des hellen kräftgen Morgens eingedenk,
Der Unmuth mir, der furchtbare vom Volk,
Und freie veste Bande knüpften wir,
Und riefen die lebendgen Götter an.

And saw the sun in flower, and by that flame
Kindled the youthful day of quiet Earth.
Then song arose in me, my darkling heart,
Illumined, warmed by poetry that was prayer,
When by their names I called those alien ones,
Those closely present ones, the gods of Nature,
And spirit in the word, life's mystery
In the found image blissfully was resolved.
So quietly I grew up, and other things
Already were prepared. More forcefully yet,
Like water, did the savage human wave
Beat on my breast, and the poor people's voice,
Humming in blind confusion, reach my ear.
And when, while silent in my room I sat,
At midnight tumult and revolt cry out,
And through the fields they rush, and weary of life
With their own hands break up their own good houses
And temples, long made odious, and forsaken,
When brothers fled each other, men hurried past
Those they loved most, and fathers no longer knew
Their sons, and human language had become
Incomprehensible, and human law,
The meaning of it, shivering me, struck home:
It was the departure of my people's god!
Him I could hear, and up to the silent planet
Whence he had come to us, I turned my gaze.
And to propitiate him I set out.
Still many a happy day was granted us.
Still, in the end, renewal seemed at hand;
And, my mind fixed upon the golden age,
When trust was general, that bright, strong morning,
My gloom, the people's terrible gloom, dispersed
And we made pacts as firm as they were free,
And once again invoked the living gods.

Doch oft, wenn mich des Volkes Dank bekränzte,
Wenn näher immer mir, und mir allein,
Des Volkes Seele kam, befiel es mich,
Denn wo ein Land ersterben soll, da wählt
Der Geist noch Einen sich zulezt, durch den
Sein Schwanensang, das lezte Leben tönet.
Wohl ahndet ichs, doch dient' ich willig ihm.
Es ist geschehn. Den Sterblichen gehör ich
Nun nimmer an. O Ende meiner Zeit!
O Geist, der uns erzog, der du geheim
Am hellen Tag und in der Wolke waltest,
Und du o Licht! und du, du Mutter Erde!
Hier bin ich, ruhig, denn es wartet mein
Die längstbereitete, die neue Stunde.
Nun nicht im Bilde mehr, und nicht, wie sonst,
Bei Sterblichen, im kurzen Glük, ich find'
Im Tode find ich den Lebendigen
Und heute noch begegn' ich ihm, denn heute
Bereitet er, der Herr der Zeit, zur Feier
Zum Zeichen ein Gewitter mir und sich.
Kennst du die Stille rings? kennst du das Schweigen
Des schlummerlosen Gotts? erwart' ihn hier!
Um Mitternacht wird er es uns vollenden.
Und wenn du, wie du sagst, des Donnerers
Vertrauter bist, und Eines Sinns mit ihm
Dein Geist mit ihm, der Pfade kundig, wandelt,
So komm mit mir, wenn izt, zu einsam sich,
Das Herz der Erde klagt, und eingedenk
Der alten Einigkeit die dunkle Mutter
Zum Aether aus die Feuerarme breitet
Und izt der Herrscher kömt in seinem Stral,
Dann folgen wir, zum Zeichen, daß wir ihm

Yet often, when the people's gratitude
Crowned me with wreaths, and ever closer to me,
To me alone, the people's soul drew, quickly
It dawned on me: that where a land must die
The Spirit at the last elects one more
Through whom the swansong, the last life, shall sound.
Well I divined it, yet I served him gladly.
Now it is done. And nevermore shall I
Belong to mortals. O my evening time!
O Spirit, you that reared us, secretly
Both in the cloud and in the bright noon govern,
And you, O light, and you, O Mother Earth,
See, I am here, and calm, for now awaits me
The hour long since matured, the turning-point.
No longer in the image now, nor yet
As formerly, with mortals, in brief joy,
No, but in death I find the Living One
And this day shall confront him, for this day
It is that he, the Lord of Time, in token,
In celebration of it, ushers in
A thunder-storm prepared for him and me.
Is it intelligible, known to you,
The stillness all around us here, the silence
Of the unslumbering god? Await him here!
At midnight he will consummate it for us.
If, as you say, you are the Thunderer's
Familiar, and unanimous with him,
Acquainted with the paths, your spirit journeys,
Then come with me when now, too much alone,
The heart of Earth laments, and mindful of
The ancient unity, now the dark Mother
Up towards Aether extends her fiery arms,
And now the Ruler comes within his beam,
And thereupon, to prove ourselves his kin,

Verwandte sind, hinab in heil'ge Flammen.
Doch wenn du lieber ferne bleibst, für dich,
Was gönnst du mir es nicht? wenn dir es nicht
Beschieden ist zum Eigentum, was nimmst
Und störst du mirs! O euch, ihr Genien,
Die ihr, da ich begann, mir nahe waret,
Ihr Fernentwerfenden! euch dank ich, daß ihr mirs
Gegeben habt, die lange Zahl der Leiden
Zu enden hier, befreit von andrer Pflicht
In freiem Tod, nach göttlichem Geseze!
Dir ists verbotne Frucht! drum laß und geh,
Und kannst du mir nicht nach, so richte nicht!

MANES

Dir hat der Schmerz den Geist entzündet, Armer.

EMPEDOKLES

Was heilst du denn, Unmächtiger, ihn nicht?

MANES

Wie ists mit uns? siehst du es so gewiß?

EMPEDOKLES

Das sage du mir, der du alles siehst!

MANES

Laß still uns seyn, o Sohn! und immer lernen.

EMPEDOKLES

Du lehrtest mich, heut lerne du von mir.

MANES

Hast du nicht alles mir gesagt?

We follow him down amid the holy flames.
But if you'd rather stand aside, aloof,
Why grudge it, then, to me? If as your own
To you it was not granted, why deprive
And trouble me? You rather, heavenly spirits,
Who when I started out were near to me,
You far-designing ones, to you I owe it
That here I may cut off and put an end
To the long chain of suffering, liberated
From other duties, in self-chosen death
And in accordance with god-given laws!
Forbidden fruit for you, man! Therefore leave me,
And if you cannot follow me, do not judge!

MANES

Pain has inflamed your mind. I pity you.

EMPEDOCLES

Sage that you are, then why do *you* not heal it?

MANES

How is it with us? Do you see so clearly?

EMPEDOCLES

You ask me that? You that can see all things?

MANES

Let us be silent, son, and always learn.

EMPEDOCLES

You taught me once; now this day learn from me.

MANES

Have you not told me everything?

EMPEDOKLES

                        O nein!

MANES

So gehst du nun?

EMPEDOKLES

                  Noch geh ich nicht, o Alter!
Von dieser grünen guten Erde soll
Mein Auge mir nicht ohne Freude gehen.
Und denken möcht' ich noch vergangner Zeit,
Der Freunde meiner Jugend noch, der Theuern,
Die fern in Hellas frohen Städten sind,
Des Bruders auch, der mir geflucht, so mußt'
Es werden; laß mich izt, wenn dort der Tag
Hinunter ist, so siehest du mich wieder.

EMPEDOCLES

                  Far from it!

MANES

And now you're going?

EMPEDOCLES

                  No, not yet, old seer!
No, from this good green earth my eye shall not
Depart without a tribute of late gladness.
And still I wish to dwell upon things past,
Recall once more the dear friends of my youth
Remote now in the happy towns of Hellas,
My brother too, who cursed me – so it had
To be. Now leave me. When over there the light
Of day goes down, you'll see me once again.

Schlusschor des ersten Aktes (Entwurf)

Neue Welt

       und es hängt, ein ehern Gewölbe
der Himmel über uns, es lähmt Fluch
die Glieder den Menschen, und die stärkenden, die erfreuenden
Gaaben der Erde sind, wie Spreu, es
spottet unser, mit ihren Geschenken, die Mutter
und alles ist Schein –
O wann wann
    schon öffnet sie sich
    die Fluth über die Dürre.

Aber wo ist er?

    Daß er beschwöre den lebendigen Geist

Draft for the Concluding Chorus of Act One

New world

        and a brazen vault
Heaven hangs over us, a curse
freezes the limbs of mortals, and the strengthening,
joy-giving presents of Earth are like chaff, the
Mother mocks us with her gifts
and all is mere semblance –
O when, when
      will it break at last,
      the flood, over the parched land.

But where is he?

    That he might adjure the living spirit

Plan for the Subsequent Acts

† Chorus   Future

SECOND ACT
Scene I.
Pausanias   Panthea

Scene II.
Strato.   Attendants.

Scene III.
Strato alone.

Chorus?

THIRD ACT
Empedocles. Pausanias. Panthea. Strato.
Manes.
Attendants of Strato.
Agrigentines.
Chorus?

FOURTH ACT
Scene I.

lyric or   Empedocles. Pausanias. Panthea.
epic?
                      Scene II.
Elegiac heroic   Empedocles.
Heroic eleg.   Scene III.

Lyric heroic   Manes, Empedocles.
                   Scene IV.
Heroic lyric   Empedocles.

FIFTH ACT
Manes. Pausanias. Panthea. Strato
† Agrigentines, Attendants of Strato.

† Manes, the all-experienced, the seer, astonished by Empedocles' speeches, and by his mind, says that he is the one who was called, who kills and gives life, in whom and through whom a world was being at once destroyed and renewed. And that man who felt his country's decline with such deadly force could have a presentiment of such a new life. The following day, the day of the Saturnalia, he will proclaim to them what was the last will of Empedocles.

The Hymns
(1799–1803)

Lebensalter

Ihr Städte des Euphrats!
Ihr Gassen von Palmyra!
Ihr Säulenwälder in der Eb'ne der Wüste,
Was seid ihr?
Euch hat die Kronen,
Dieweil ihr über die Gränze
Der Othmenden seid gegangen,
Von Himmlischen der Rauchdampf und
Hinweg das Feuer genommen;
Jezt aber siz' ich unter Wolken, darin
Ein jedes eine Ruh' hat eigen, unter
Wohleingerichteten Eichen, auf
Der Heide des Rehs, und fremd
Erscheinen und gestorben mir
Der Seeligen Geister.

The Ages of Life

You cities of Euphrates,
You streets at Palmyra,
You forests of pillars in the desert plain,
What are you?
Your crests, as you passed beyond
The bounds of those who breathe,
By smoke of heavenly powers and
By fire were taken away;
But now I sit beneath clouds, in which
Peculiar quiet comes to each one, beneath
A pleasing order of oak trees, on
The heath where the roe-deer feed, and strange
To me, remote and dead seem
The souls of the blessèd.

Der Winkel von Hahrdt

Hinunter sinket der Wald,
Und Knospen ähnlich, hängen
Einwärts die Blätter, denen
Blüht unten auf ein Grund,
Nicht gar unmündig.
Da nemlich ist Ulrich
Gegangen; oft sinnt, über den Fußtritt,
Ein groß Schiksaal
Bereit, an übrigem Orte.

The Nook at Hardt

Down slopes the forest
And, bud-like, inward
Hang the leaves, for which
Down below a ground blossoms forth,
Quite able to speak for itself.
For there Ulrich
Once walked; and often, over the footprint,
A great destiny ponders,
Made ready, on the residual site.

Hälfte des Lebens

Mit gelben Birnen hänget
Und voll mit wilden Rosen
Das Land in den See,
Ihr holden Schwäne,
Und trunken von Küssen
Tunkt ihr das Haupt
Ins heilignüchterne Wasser.

Weh mir, wo nehm' ich, wenn
Es Winter ist, die Blumen, und wo
Den Sonnenschein,
Und Schatten der Erde?
Die Mauern stehn
Sprachlos und kalt, im Winde
Klirren die Fahnen.

Half of Life ·

With yellow pears hangs down
And full of wild roses
The land into the lake,
You loving swans,
And drunk with kisses
You dip your heads
Into water, the holy-and-sober.

But oh, where shall I find
When winter comes, the flowers, and where
The sunshine
And shade of the earth?
The walls loom
Speechless and cold, in the wind
Weathercocks clatter.

Wie wenn am Feiertage . . .

Wie wenn am Feiertage, das Feld zu sehn
Ein Landmann geht, des Morgens, wenn
Aus heißer Nacht die kühlenden Blize fielen
Die ganze Zeit und fern noch tönet der Donner,
In sein Gestade wieder tritt der Strom,
Und frisch der Boden grünt
Und von des Himmels erfreuendem Reegen
Der Weinstok trauft und glänzend
In stiller Sonne stehn die Bäume des Haines:

So stehn sie unter günstiger Witterung
Sie die kein Meister allein, die wunderbar
Allgegenwärtig erzieht in leichtem Umfangen
Die mächtige, die göttlichschöne Natur.
Drum wenn zu schlafen sie scheint zu Zeiten des Jahrs
Am Himmel oder unter den Pflanzen oder den Völkern
So trauert der Dichter Angesicht auch,
Sie scheinen allein zu seyn, doch ahnen sie immer.
Denn ahnend ruhet sie selbst auch.

Jezt aber tagts! Ich harrt und sah es kommen,
Und was ich sah, das Heilige sei mein Wort.
Denn sie, sie selbst, die älter denn die Zeiten
Und über die Götter des Abends und Orients ist,
Die Natur ist jezt mit Waffenklang erwacht,
Und hoch vom Aether bis zum Abgrund nieder
Nach vestem Geseze, wie einst, aus heiligem Chaos gezeugt,
Fühlt neu die Begeisterung sich,
Die Allerschaffende wieder.

As on a holiday . . .

As on a holiday, to see the field
A countryman goes out, at morning, when
Out of hot night the cooling flashes had fallen
For hours on end, and thunder still rumbles afar,
The river enters its banks once more,
New verdure sprouts from the soil,
And with the gladdening rain of heaven
The grapevine drips, and gleaming
In tranquil sunlight stand the trees of the grove:

So now in favourable weather they stand
Whom no mere master teaches, but in
A light embrace, miraculously omnipresent,
God-like in power and beauty, Nature brings up.
So when she seems to be sleeping at times of the year
Up in the sky or among plants or the peoples,
The poets' faces likewise are sad,
They seem to be alone, but are always divining,
For divining too she herself is at rest.

But now day breaks! I waited and saw it come,
And what I saw, the hallowed, my word shall convey,
For she, she herself, who is older than the ages
And higher than the gods of Orient and Occident,
Nature has now awoken amid the clang of arms,
And from high Aether down to the low abyss,
According to fixed law, begotten, as in the past, on holy Chaos,
Delight, the all-creative,
Delights in self-renewal.

Und wie im Aug' ein Feuer dem Manne glänzt,
Wenn hohes er entwarf; so ist
Von neuem an den Zeichen, den Thaten der Welt jezt
Ein Feuer angezündet in Seelen der Dichter.
Und was zuvor geschah, doch kaum gefühlt,
Ist offenbar erst jezt,
Und die uns lächelnd den Aker gebauet,
In Knechtsgestalt, sie sind erkannt,
Die Alllebendigen, die Kräfte der Götter.

Erfrägst du sie? im Liede wehet ihr Geist
Wenn es der Sonne des Tags und warmer Erd
Entwächst, und Wettern, die in der Luft, und andern
Die vorbereiteter in Tiefen der Zeit,
Und deutungsvoller, und vernehmlicher uns
Hinwandeln zwischen Himmel und Erd und unter den Völkern.
Des gemeinsamen Geistes Gedanken sind,
Still endend in der Seele des Dichters,

Daß schnellbetroffen sie, Unendlichem
Bekannt seit langer Zeit, von Erinnerung
Erhebt, und ihr, von heilgem Stral entzündet,
Die Frucht in Liebe geboren, der Götter und Menschen Werk
Der Gesang, damit er beiden zeuge, glükt.
So fiel, wie Dichter sagen, da sie sichtbar
Den Gott zu sehen begehrte, sein Bliz auf Semeles Haus
Und die göttlichgetroffne gebahr,
Die Frucht des Gewitters, den heiligen Bacchus.

Und daher trinken himmlisches Feuer jezt
Die Erdensöhne ohne Gefahr.
Doch uns gebührt es, unter Gottes Gewittern,
Ihr Dichter! mit entblößtem Haupte zu stehen
Des Vaters Stral, ihn selbst, mit eigner Hand

And as a fire gleams in the eye of that man
Who has conceived a lofty design,
Once more by the tokens, the deeds of the world now
A fire has been lit in the souls of the poets.
And that which happened before, but hardly was felt,
Only now is manifest,
And they who smiling worked our fields for us,
Assuming the shape of labourers, now are known,
The all-alive, all-animating powers of the gods.

Do you ask where they are? In song their spirit wafts
When from the sun of day and from warm soil
It grows, and storms that are in the air, and others
That, more prepared in the depths of time,
More full of meaning and more audible to us,
Drift on between Heaven and Earth and amid the peoples.
The thoughts of the communal spirit they are,
And quietly come to rest in the poet's soul,

So that quickly struck and long familiar
To infinite powers, it shakes
With recollection and kindled by
The holy ray, that fruit conceived in love, the work of gods and men,
To bear witness to both, the song succeeds.
So once, the poets tell, when she desired to see
The god in person, visible, did his lightning fall
On Semele's house, and the divinely struck gave birth to
The thunder-storm's fruit, to holy Bacchus.

And hence it is that without danger now
The sons of Earth drink heavenly fire.
Yet, fellow poets, us it behoves to stand
Bareheaded beneath God's thunder-storms,
To grasp the Father's ray, no less, with our own two hands

Zu fassen und dem Volk ins Lied
Gehüllt die himmlische Gaabe zu reichen.
Denn sind nur reinen Herzens,
Wie Kinder, wir, sind schuldlos unsere Hände,

Des Vaters Stral, der reine versengt es nicht
Und tieferschüttert, die Leiden des Stärkeren
Mitleidend, bleibt in den hochherstürzenden Stürmen
Des Gottes, wenn er nahet, das Herz doch fest.
Doch weh mir! wenn von

Weh mir!

Und sag ich gleich,

Ich sei genaht, die Himmlischen zu schauen,
Sie selbst, sie werfen mich tief unter die Lebenden
Den falschen Priester, ins Dunkel, daß ich
Das warnende Lied den Gelehrigen singe.
Dort

And, wrapping in song the heavenly gift,
To offer it to the people.
For if only we are pure in heart,
Like children, and our hands are guiltless,

   The Father's ray, the pure, will not sear our hearts
And, deeply convulsed, and sharing his sufferings
Who is stronger than we are, yet in the far-flung down-rushing
                                    [storms of
The God, when he draws near, will the heart stand fast.
But, oh, my shame! when of

My shame!

   And let me say at once

That I approached to see the Heavenly,
And they themselves cast me down, deep down
Below the living, into the dark cast down
The false priest that I am, to sing,
For those who have ears to hear, the warning song.
There

Der Mutter Erde

GESANG DER BRÜDER
OTTMAR HOM TELLO

OTTMAR

Statt offner Gemeine sing' ich Gesang.
So spielt von erfreulichen Händen
Wie zum Versuche berühret, eine Saite
Von Anfang. Aber freudig ernster neigt
Bald über die Harfe
Der Meister das Haupt und die Töne
Bereiten sich ihm, und werden geflügelt
So viele sie sind und zusammen tönt es unter dem Schlage
Des Wekenden und voll, wie aus Meeren schwingt
Unendlich sich in die Lüfte die Wolke des Wohllauts.

Doch wird ein anderes noch
Wie der Harfe Klang
Der Gesang seyn
Der Chor des Volks.
Denn wenn er schon der Zeichen genug
Und Fluthen in seiner Macht und Wetterflammen
Wie Gedanken hat der heilige Vater,
       unaussprechlich wär er wohl
Und nirgend fänd er wahr sich unter den Lebenden wieder
Wenn zum Gesange nicht hätt ein Herz die Gemeinde.

Noch aber

Doch wie der Fels erst ward,

For Mother Earth

SONG OF THE BROTHERS
OTTMAR HOM TELLO

OTTMAR

Instead of open community, song I sing.
So, touched by pleasing hands
As though to try it out only, a string
Plays from the start. But more happily serious
Soon the master bows
His head over the harp, and the tones
Respond to him, and grow winged
However many of them, and they sound in unison, plucked
By him who awakened them, full, as though out of oceans
Infinite up into winds the cloud of euphony soars.

Yet other even than
The sound of the harp
Will the song be,
The people's choir.
For though he has tokens enough
And floods in his power and thunder-flames
Like thoughts, the holy Father,
yet, it seems, he would be unutterable
And nowhere he would find himself truly again among the living
If the community had no heart for singing.

But as yet

But as the rock was first shaped

Und geschmiedet wurden in schattiger Werkstatt,
    die ehernen Vesten der Erde,
Noch ehe Bäche rauschten von den Bergen
Und Hain' und Städte blüheten an den Strömen,
So hat er donnernd schon
Geschaffen ein reines Gesez,
Und reine Laute gegründet.

HOM

    Indessen schon', o Mächtiger deß
Der einsam singt, und gieb uns Lieder genug,
Bis ausgesprochen ist, wie wir
Es meinen unserer Seele Geheimniß.
Denn öfters hört' ich
Des alten Priesters Gesänge

        und so
Zu danken bereite die Seele mir auch.

    Doch wandeln im Waffensaale
Mit gebundener Hand in müßigen Zeiten
Die Männer und schauen die Rüstungen an,
Voll Ernstes stehen sie und einer erzählt,
Wie die Väter sonst den Bogen gespannet
Fernhin des Zieles gewiß,
Und alle glauben es ihm
Doch keiner darf es versuchen
Wie ein Gott   sinken die Arme
Der Menschen,
Auch ziemt ein Feiergewand an jedem Tage sich nicht.

    Die Tempelsäulen stehn
Verlassen in Tagen der Noth,

And in the shadowy workshop were forged
       the brazen fortresses of Earth,
Even before any stream roared down from the mountains
Or groves and cities flowered by the rivers,
So already thundering He
Has created a law that is pure
And established pure sounds.

HOM

   Meanwhile, O mighty one, spare
Him who lonely sings, and give us tunes enough
Until uttered as we intend it
Is the mystery of our souls.
For at times I have heard
The hymns of the ancient priest

         and now
Likewise to offer thanks prepare my soul also.

   Yet with tied hands in the armoury
Men wander about in idle ages,
Gazing up at the coats of mail,
Full of gravity stand, and one of them tells
How the forefathers once had flexed the bow,
Sure of their aim from afar,
And all believe what he says
Yet none may try it
Like a god   the arms of men
Hang loose,
Nor is a festive garment fitting for every day.

   The temple columns stand
Forsaken in days of need,

Wohl tönet des Nordsturms Echo
        tief in den Hallen,
Und der Reegen machet sie rein,
Und Moos wächst und es kehren die Schwalben,
In Tagen des Frühlings, nahmlos aber ist
In ihnen der Gott, und die Schaale des Danks
Und Opfergefäß und alle Heiligtümer
Begraben dem Feind in verschwiegener Erde.

TELLO

    Wer will auch danken, eh' er empfängt,
Und Antwort geben, eh' er gehört hat?
Ni   indeß ein Höherer spricht,
Zu fallen in die tönende Rede.
Viel hat er zu sagen und anders Recht,
Und Einer ist, der endet in Stunden nicht,
Und die Zeiten des Schaffenden sind,
Wie Gebirg,
Das hochaufwoogend von Meer zu Meer
Hinziehet über die Erde,

    Es sagen der Wanderer viele davon,
Und das Wild irrt in den Klüften,
Und die Horde schweifet über die Höhen,
In heiligem Schatten aber,
Am grünen Abhang wohnet
Der Hirt und schauet die Gipfel.
So

And though the northern gale's echo
Resounds   deep in the halls
And rain washes them clean
And moss grows, and the swallows return
In the spring season, yet nameless in them
Is the God, and the cup of thanks
And the vessel of sacrifice and all the holy things
Buried against the foe in a place kept secret.

TELLO

    And who would give thanks before he receives
And give an answer before he has heard?
Not   while a higher one speaks
To interrupt the resounding speech.
He has much to say and a different law,
And One there is who does not end within hours
And the ages of him who creates
Are like a mountain range
Which billowing high from sea to sea
Stretches over the Earth,

    Many travellers tell of it,
And the wild animals roam in ravines,
And the horde sweeps on over the high passes,
But in holy shade
On the green slope dwells
The shepherd and looks up at the peaks.
So

Am Quell der Donau

Denn, wie wenn hoch von der herrlichgestimmten, der Orgel
Im heiligen Saal,
Reinquillend aus den unerschöpflichen Röhren,
Das Vorspiel, wekend, des Morgens beginnt
Und weitumher, von Halle zu Halle,
Der erfrischende nun, der melodische Strom rinnt,
Bis in den kalten Schatten das Haus
Von Begeisterungen erfüllt,
Nun aber erwacht ist, nun, aufsteigend ihr,
Der Sonne des Fests, antwortet
Der Chor der Gemeinde; so kam
Das Wort aus Osten zu uns,
Und an Parnassos Felsen und am Kithäron hör' ich
O Asia, das Echo von dir und es bricht sich
Am Kapitol und jählings herab von den Alpen

Kommt eine Fremdlingin sie
Zu uns, die Erwekerin,
Die menschenbildende Stimme.
Da faßt' ein Staunen die Seele

At the Source of the Danube

For as when high from the gloriously voiced, the organ
Within a holy hall
Untainted welling from inexhaustible pipes,
The prelude, awakening men, rings out in the morning
And far and wide, from mansion to mansion,
Now pours the refreshing, the melodious current,
Down to the chilly shadows even filling
The house with inspirations,
But now awake and rising to it, to
The sun of celebration, responds the
Community's choir – so the word
Came down to us from the East,
And by the rocks of Parnassus and by Cithaeron,
O Asia, I hear the echo of you, and it breaks
Upon the Capitol and sudden down from the Alps

A stranger it comes
To us, that quickening word,
The voice that moulds and makes human.
Amazement then took hold of

Der Getroffenen all und Nacht
War über den Augen der Besten.
Denn vieles vermag
Und die Fluth und den Fels und Feuersgewalt auch
Bezwinget mit Kunst der Mensch
Und achtet, der Hochgesinnte, das Schwerdt
Nicht, aber es steht
Vor Göttlichem der Starke niedergeschlagen,

   Und gleichet dem Wild fast; das,
Von süßer Jugend getrieben,
Schweift rastlos über die Berg'
Und fühlet die eigene Kraft
In der Mittagshizze. Wenn aber
Herabgeführt, in spielenden Lüften,
Das heilige Licht, und mit dem kühleren Stral
Der freudige Geist kommt zu
Der seeligen Erde, dann erliegt es, ungewohnt
Des Schönsten und schlummert wachenden Schlaf,
Noch ehe Gestirn naht. So auch wir. Denn manchen erlosch
Das Augenlicht schon vor den göttlichgesendeten Gaben,

   Den freundlichen, die aus Ionien uns,
Auch aus Arabia kamen, und froh ward
Der theuern Lehr' und auch der holden Gesänge
Die Seele jener Entschlafenen nie,
Doch einige wachten. Und sie wandelten oft
Zufrieden unter euch, ihr Bürger schöner Städte,
Beim Kampfspiel, wo sonst unsichtbar der Heros
Geheim bei Dichtern saß, die Ringer schaut und lächelnd
Pries, der gepriesene, die müßigernsten Kinder.
Ein unaufhörlich Lieben wars und ists.
Und wohlgeschieden, aber darum denken
Wir aneinander doch, ihr Fröhlichen am Isthmos,

The souls of all who were struck, and night
Obscured the eyes of the best men.
For much can our kind
Accomplish, and flood and rock and even the might of fire
With art can subdue,
Nor, noble in mind, recoils from
The sword-blade, but faced with powers divine
The strong will stand abashed,

    And almost are like the beast of the wilds; which
Impelled by sweet youth
Roams restless over the hills
And feels its own strength in
The noonday heat. But when,
Led down, in frolicking breezes,
The holy light, and with its cool beam
The joyful spirit descend
To blessèd Earth, it succumbs, unfamiliar
With utmost beauty, and drowses in waking sleep,
Though stars are not rising yet. So it is with us. For many's
The man whose vision went out in face of those god-sent gifts,

    The kindly, that from Ionia came
To us, from Arabia too, and never
The souls of these now gone to their rest were glad
Of precious doctrine nor yet of the lovely songs,
Yet some kept awake. And often, you citizens
Of beautiful towns, they walked among you contented,
At Games, where once in secret the hero
Invisible sat with poets, watched the wrestlers and smiling
Praised – he, the recipient of praise – those idly serious children.
An endless loving it was, and is.
And rightly severed; yet nonetheless we think
Of one another still, you happy ones at the Isthmus,

Und am Cephyß und am Taygetos,
Auch eurer denken wir, ihr Thale des Kaukasos,
So alt ihr seid, ihr Paradiese dort
Und deiner Patriarchen und deiner Propheten,

    O Asia, deiner Starken, o Mutter!
Die furchtlos vor den Zeichen der Welt,
Und den Himmel auf Schultern und alles Schiksaal,
Taglang auf Bergen gewurzelt,
Zuerst es verstanden,
Allein zu reden
Zu Gott. Die ruhn nun. Aber wenn ihr
Und diß ist zu sagen,
Ihr Alten all, nicht sagtet, woher?
Wir nennen dich, heiliggenöthiget, nennen,
Natur! dich wir, und neu, wie dem Bad entsteigt
Dir alles Göttlichgeborne.

    Zwar gehn wir fast, wie die Waisen;
Wohl ists, wie sonst, nur jene Pflege nicht wieder;
Doch Jünglinge, der Kindheit gedenk,
Im Hauße sind auch diese nicht fremde.
Sie leben dreifach, eben wie auch
Die ersten Söhne des Himmels.
Und nicht umsonst ward uns
In die Seele die Treue gegeben.
Nicht uns, auch Eures bewahrt sie,
Und bei den Heiligtümern, den Waffen des Worts
Die scheidend ihr den Ungeschikteren uns
Ihr Schiksaalssöhne, zurükgelassen

    Ihr guten Geister, da seid ihr auch,
Oftmals, wenn einen dann die heilige Wolk umschwebt,

And by Cephissus and by Taygetus,
And you we think of, vales of the Caucasus,
However ancient, you paradises there,
And of your patriarchs and of your prophets,

    O Asia, of all your mighty ones, Mother,
Who fearless in face of the signs of the world,
The heavens heaped upon shoulders and all manner of fate,
For days were rooted on mountains
And were the first who knew
How to speak alone
To God. These now are at rest. But if,
And this must be said, you ancients
Would never tell us whence it is that
We name you, under a holy compulsion we
Now name you Nature, and new, as from a bath
From you emerges all that's divinely born.

    True, like orphans almost we walk;
Though much is what it was, that tutelage now is lacking;
But youths who are mindful of childhood,
These are not strangers now in the house.
Threefold they live, as did
The very first-born of Heaven.
And not for nothing in
Our souls was loyalty fixed.
Not us alone, but that which is yours it preserves
And in those holy relics, the weapons of the word
Which, parting, you sons of Fate,
You left behind for us the less fated,
The less endowed with rightness,

    You kindly spirits, in them you are present too,
And often, when the holy cloud is hovering round a man,

Da staunen wir und wissens nicht zu deuten.
Ihr aber würzt mit Nectar uns den Othem
Und dann frohloken wir oft oder es befällt uns
Ein Sinnen, wenn ihr aber einen zu sehr liebt
Er ruht nicht, bis er euer einer geworden.
Darum, ihr Gütigen! umgehet mich leicht,
Damit ich bleiben möge, denn noch ist manches zu singen,
Jezt aber endiget, seeligweinend,
Wie eine Sage der Liebe,
Mir der Gesang, und so auch ist er
Mir, mit Erröthen, Erblassen,
Von Anfang her gegangen. Doch Alles geht so.

We are amazed and do not know the meaning.
But you with nectar spice our breath, and then
We may exult or else a pondering befalls us,
But when too greatly you love a man
He finds no rest till he is one of you.
Therefore, benign ones, surround me lightly,
And let me stay a while, for much remains to be sung;
But now, like a legend of love,
 Blissfully weeping, my song
Comes to its end, and so too,
Amid blushing and blanching, it's gone
With me from the start. But that is how all things go.

Die Wanderung

Glükseelig Suevien, meine Mutter,
Auch du, der glänzenderen, der Schwester
Lombarda drüben gleich,
Von hundert Bächen durchflossen!
Und Bäume genug, weißblühend und röthlich,
Und dunklere, wild, tiefgrünenden Laubs voll
Und Alpengebirg der Schweiz auch überschattet
Benachbartes dich; denn nah dem Heerde des Haußes
Wohnst du, und hörst, wie drinnen
Aus silbernen Opferschaalen
Der Quell rauscht, ausgeschüttet
Von reinen Händen, wenn berührt

Von warmen Stralen
Krystallenes Eis und umgestürzt
Vom leichtanregenden Lichte
Der schneeige Gipfel übergießt die Erde
Mit reinestem Wasser. Darum ist
Dir angeboren die Treue. Schwer verläßt,
Was nahe dem Ursprung wohnet, den Ort.
Und deine Kinder, die Städte,
Am weithindämmernden See,
An Nekars Weiden, am Rheine,
Sie alle meinen, es wäre
Sonst nirgend besser zu wohnen.

Ich aber will dem Kaukasos zu!
Denn sagen hört' ich
Noch heut in den Lüften:

The Journey

    Most happy Swabia, my mother,
Whom like the more shining, your sister
Lombarda over there
A hundred rivulets thread!
And trees enough, white-flowering and reddish
And darker ones, wild, full of deeply greening foliage,
And alpine ranges of Switzerland cast their shade
On you, the neighbouring, too; for close to the hearth of
The house you dwell, and hear how within
From silver votive vessels
The well-spring purls, poured out
By hands that are pure, when touched

    By warming beams
The crystalline ice and, tumbled
By gently quickening light
The snowy summit drenches the earth
With purest water. Therefore
Innate in you is loyalty. For whatever dwells
Close to its origin is loath to leave the place.
And so your children, the towns by
The distantly glimmering lake,
By Neckar's willows and by the Rhine,
All these affirm that
No dwelling-place could be better.

    But I am bound for the Caucasus!
For only today
I heard it said in the breezes

Frei sei'n, wie Schwalben, die Dichter.
Auch hat mir ohnediß
In jüngeren Tagen Eines vertraut,
Es seien vor alter Zeit
Die Eltern einst, das deutsche Geschlecht,
Still fortgezogen von Wellen der Donau
Am Sommertage, da diese
Sich Schatten suchten, zusammen
Mit Kindern der Sonn'
Am schwarzen Meere gekommen;
Und nicht umsonst sei diß
Das gastfreundliche genennet.

    Denn, als sie erst sich angesehen,
Da nahten die Anderen erst; dann sazten auch
Die Unseren sich neugierig unter den Ölbaum.
Doch als sich ihre Gewande berührt,
Und keiner vernehmen konnte
Die eigene Rede des andern, wäre wohl
Entstanden ein Zwist, wenn nicht aus Zweigen herunter
Gekommen wäre die Kühlung,
Die Lächeln über das Angesicht
Der Streitenden öfters breitet, und eine Weile
Sahn still sie auf, dann reichten sie sich
Die Hände liebend einander. Und bald

    Vertauschten sie Waffen und all
Die lieben Güter des Haußes,
Vertauschten das Wort auch und es wünschten
Die freundlichen Väter umsonst nichts
Beim Hochzeitjubel den Kindern.
Denn aus den heiligvermählten
Wuchs schöner, denn Alles,
Was vor und nach

That free as swallows the poets are.
Besides, when I was younger
Someone confided to me
That time out of mind our parents,
The German people, had quietly
Departed from the waves of the Danube
One summer day, and when those
Were looking for shade, had met
With children of the Sun
Not far from the Black Sea's beaches;
And not for nothing that sea
Was called the hospitable.

   For when they first exchanged glances
It was the others who first approached; only then did
Our people too, inquisitive, seat themselves under the olive tree.
But when their garments had touched
And none could comprehend
The other's peculiar speech, a quarrel
Might well have begun, if coolness had not fallen
Upon them from the boughs,
Eliciting a smile, as it often does,
From faces that frowned with anger; and for a while
They raised their eyes in silence, then
They lovingly held out their hands. And soon

   They bartered weapons and all
The precious goods of the house,
And bartered the word, and not in vain
Did kindly fathers bless there with any wish
Their children's jubilant nuptials.
For from the sacredly married
There sprang a people more beautiful
Than all who before or since

Von Menschen sich nannt', ein Geschlecht auf. Wo,
Wo aber wohnt ihr, liebe Verwandten,
Daß wir das Bündniß wiederbegehn
Und der theuern Ahnen gedenken?

   Dort an den Ufern, unter den Bäumen
Ionias, in Ebenen des Kaisters,
Wo Kraniche, des Aethers froh,
Umschlossen sind von fernhindämmernden Bergen;
Dort wart auch ihr, ihr Schönsten! oder pflegtet
Der Inseln, die mit Wein bekränzt,
Voll tönten von Gesang; noch andere wohnten
Am Tayget, am vielgepriesnen Himettos,
Die blühten zulezt; doch von
Parnassos Quell bis zu des Tmolos
Goldglänzenden Bächen erklang
Ein ewiges Lied; so rauschten
Damals die Wälder und all
Die Saitenspiele zusamt
Von himmlischer Milde gerühret.

   O Land des Homer!
Am purpurnen Kirschbaum oder wenn
Von dir gesandt im Weinberg mir
Die jungen Pfirsiche grünen,
Und die Schwalbe fernher kommt und vieles erzählend
An meinen Wänden ihr Haus baut, in
Den Tagen des Mais, auch unter den Sternen
Gedenk' ich, o Ionia, dein! doch Menschen
Ist Gegenwärtiges lieb. Drum bin ich
Gekommen, euch, ihr Inseln, zu sehn, und euch,
Ihr Mündungen der Ströme, o ihr Hallen der Thetis,
Ihr Wälder, euch, und euch, ihr Wolken des Ida!

Have called themselves human. But where,
O where do you dwell, dear kin,
So that we may renew the pact
And remember those worthy forbears?

There on the shores, beneath the trees of
Ionia, on plains of the Cayster
Where, gladdened by Aether, cranes
Are surrounded by mountains distantly glimmering,
There you were also, loveliest ones, or haunted
The islands garlanded with vines
And filled with resonant song; or others dwelled
Beside Taygetus, by widely praised Hymettus,
These were the last to thrive; but from
Parnassus' well-spring down to the brooks,
Gold-glittering, of Tmolus rang
An everlasting melody; so then did all
The holy woods and all
The lyres in unison resound
When heavenly gentleness touched them.

O land of Homer!
Beside the crimson cherry tree, or when,
Your emissaries, in the vineyard for me
The young green peaches cling
And the swallow comes from afar and, telling many a tale,
Builds on my walls her house,
In May-time days, and also under the stars,
Ionia, I think of you! And that is why
I've come to see you, you islands, and you,
The river estuaries, halls of Thetis,
You woods, and you, the clouds over Ida!

Doch nicht zu bleiben gedenk ich.
Unfreundlich ist und schwer zu gewinnen
Die Verschlossene, der ich entkommen, die Mutter.
Von ihren Söhnen einer, der Rhein,
Mit Gewalt wollt' er ans Herz ihr stürzen und schwand
Der Zurükgestoßene, niemand weiß, wohin, in die Ferne.
Doch so nicht wünscht' ich gegangen zu seyn,
Von ihr und nur, euch einzuladen,
Bin ich zu euch, ihr Gratien Griechenlands,
Ihr Himmelstöchter, gegangen,
Daß, wenn die Reise zu weit nicht ist,
Zu uns ihr kommet, ihr Holden!

Wenn milder athmen die Lüfte,
Und liebende Pfeile der Morgen
Uns Allzugedultigen schikt,
Und leichte Gewölke blühn
Uns über den schüchternen Augen,
Dann werden wir sagen, wie kommt
Ihr, Charitinnen, zu Wilden?
Die Dienerinnen des Himmels
Sind aber wunderbar,
Wie alles Göttlichgeborne.
Zum Traume wirds ihm, will es Einer
Beschleichen und straft den, der
Ihm gleichen will mit Gewalt;
Oft überraschet es einen,
Der eben kaum es gedacht hat.

    Yet not to stay I am minded,
Ungracious and intractable is
The taciturn whom I fled from, my mother.
One of her sons, the Rhine,
By force once tried to rush to her heart and vanished,
Repulsed, no one knows where, in the distance;
Not so, however, would I depart
From her and only to invite you here,
You Graces of Hellas, you daughters
Of Heaven, I went to you,
So that, if the journey is not too far,
You may come to us, beloved ones.

    When milder the breezes blow
And morning sends loving arrows
To us the all too patient,
And downy clouds like blossom
Drift over our diffident eyes,
Then we shall say, how did
You Charities come to barbarians?
But like all that's divinely born,
The servant girls of Heaven
Are strange, miraculous.
If someone tries to grasp it by stealth, he holds
A dream in his hand, and him who uses force
To make himself its peer, it punishes.
Yet often it takes by surprise
A man whose mind it has hardly entered.

Germanien

Nicht sie, die Seeligen, die erschienen sind,
Die Götterbilder in dem alten Lande,
Sie darf ich ja nicht rufen mehr, wenn aber
Ihr heimatlichen Wasser! jezt mit euch
Des Herzens Liebe klagt, was will es anders,
Das Heiligtrauernde? Denn voll Erwartung liegt
Das Land und als in heißen Tagen
Herabgesenkt, umschattet heut
Ihr Sehnenden! uns ahnungsvoll ein Himmel.
Voll ist er von Verheißungen und scheint
Mir drohend auch, doch will ich bei ihm bleiben,
Und rükwärts soll die Seele mir nicht fliehn
Zu euch, Vergangene! die zu lieb mir sind.
Denn euer schönes Angesicht zu sehn,
Als wärs, wie sonst, ich fürcht' es, tödtlich ists,
Und kaum erlaubt, Gestorbene zu weken.

Entflohene Götter! auch ihr, ihr gegenwärtigen, damals
Wahrhaftiger, ihr hattet eure Zeiten!
Nichts läugnen will ich hier und nichts erbitten.
Denn wenn es aus ist, und der Tag erloschen
Wohl trifts den Priester erst, doch liebend folgt
Der Tempel und das Bild ihm auch und seine Sitte
Zum dunkeln Land und keines mag noch scheinen.
Nur als von Grabesflammen, ziehet dann
Ein goldner Rauch, die Sage drob hinüber,
Und dämmert jezt uns Zweifelnden um das Haupt,
Und keiner weiß, wie ihm geschieht. Er fühlt
Die Schatten derer, so gewesen sind,
Die Alten, so die Erde neubesuchen.

Germania

Not them, the blessed, who once appeared,
Those images of gods in the ancient land,
Them, it is true, I may not now invoke, but if,
You waters of my homeland, now with you
The love of my heart laments, what else does it want, in
Its hallowed sadness? For full of expectation lies
The country, and as though it had been lowered
In sultry dogdays, on us a heaven today,
You yearning rivers, casts prophetic shade.
With promises it is fraught, and to me
Seems threatening too, yet I will stay with it,
And backward now my soul shall not escape
To you, the vanished, whom I love too much.
To look upon your beautiful brows, as though
They were unchanged, I am afraid, for deadly
And scarcely permitted it is to awaken the dead.

Gods who are fled! And you also, present still,
But once more real, you had your time, your ages!
No, nothing here I'll deny and ask no favours.
For when it's over, and Day's light gone out,
The priest is the first to be struck, but lovingly
The temple and the image and the cult
Follow him down into darkness, and none of them now may shine.
Only as from a funeral pyre henceforth
A golden smoke, the legend of it, drifts
And glimmers on around our doubting heads
And no one knows what's happening to him. He feels
The shadowy shapes of those who once were here,
The ancients, newly visiting the earth.

Denn die da kommen sollen, drängen uns,
Und länger säumt von Göttermenschen
Die heilige Schaar nicht mehr im blauen Himmel.

    Schon grünet ja, im Vorspiel rauherer Zeit
Für sie erzogen das Feld, bereitet ist die Gaabe
Zum Opfermahl und Thal und Ströme sind
Weitoffen um prophetische Berge,
Daß schauen mag bis in den Orient
Der Mann und ihn von dort der Wandlungen viele bewegen.
Vom Aether aber fällt
Das treue Bild und Göttersprüche reegnen
Unzählbare von ihm, und es tönt im innersten Haine.
Und der Adler, der vom Indus kömmt,
Und über des Parnassos
Beschneite Gipfel fliegt, hoch über den Opferhügeln
Italias, und frohe Beute sucht
Dem Vater, nicht wie sonst, geübter im Fluge
Der Alte, jauchzend überschwingt er
Zulezt die Alpen und sieht die vielgearteten Länder.

    Die Priesterin, die stillste Tochter Gottes,
Sie, die zu gern in tiefer Einfalt schweigt,
Sie suchet er, die offnen Auges schaute,
Als wüßte sie es nicht, jüngst, da ein Sturm
Todtdrohend über ihrem Haupt ertönte;
Es ahnete das Kind ein Besseres,
Und endlich ward ein Staunen weit im Himmel
Weil Eines groß an Glauben, wie sie selbst,
Die seegnende, die Macht der Höhe sei;
Drum sandten sie den Boten, der, sie schnell erkennend,
Denkt lächelnd so: Dich, unzerbrechliche, muß
Ein ander Wort erprüfen und ruft es laut,
Der Jugendliche, nach Germania schauend:

For those who are to come now jostle us,
Nor longer will that holy host of beings
Divinely human linger in azure Heaven.

  Already, in the prelude of a rougher age
Raised up for them, the field grows green, prepared
Are offerings for the votive feast and valley
And rivers lie wide open round prophetic mountains,
So that into the very Orient
A man may look and thence be moved by many transformations.
But down from Aether falls
The faithful image, and words of gods rain down
Innumerable from it, and the innermost grove resounds.
And the eagle that comes from the Indus
And flies over the snow-covered peaks of
Parnassus, high above the votive hills
Of Italy, and seeks glad booty for
The Father, not as he used to, more practised in flight,
That ancient one, exultant, over the Alps
Wings on at last and sees the diverse countries.

  The priestess, her, the quietest daughter of God,
Too fond of keeping silent in deep ingenuousness,
Her now he seeks, who open-eyed looked up
As though she did not know it, lately when a storm,
Threatening death, rang out above her head;
A better destiny the child divined,
And in the end amazement spread in heaven
Because one being was as great in faith
As they themselves, the blessing powers on high;
Therefore they sent the messenger, who, quick to recognize her,
Smilingly thus reflects: you the unbreakable
A different word must try, and then proclaims,
The youthful, looking towards Germania:

»Du bist es, auserwählt,
»Allliebend und ein schweres Glük
»Bist du zu tragen stark geworden,

    Seit damals, da im Walde verstekt und blühendem Mohn
Voll süßen Schlummers, trunkene, meiner du
Nicht achtetest, lang, ehe noch auch geringere fühlten
Der Jungfrau Stolz und staunten weß du wärst und woher,
Doch du es selbst nicht wußtest. Ich miskannte dich nicht,
Und heimlich, da du träumtest, ließ ich
Am Mittag scheidend dir ein Freundeszeichen,
Die Blume des Mundes zurük und du redetest einsam.
Doch Fülle der goldenen Worte sandtest du auch
Glükseelige! mit den Strömen und sie quillen unerschöpflich
In die Gegenden all. Denn fast, wie der heiligen,
Die Mutter ist von allem
Die Verborgene sonst genannt von Menschen,
So ist von Lieben und Leiden
Und voll von Ahnungen dir
Und voll von Frieden der Busen.

    O trinke Morgenlüfte,
Biß daß du offen bist,
Und nenne, was vor Augen dir ist,
Nicht länger darf Geheimniß mehr
Das Ungesprochene bleiben,
Nachdem es lange verhüllt ist;
Denn Sterblichen geziemet die Schaam,
Und so zu reden die meiste Zeit,
Ist weise auch von Göttern.
Wo aber überflüssiger, denn lautere Quellen
Das Gold und ernst geworden ist der Zorn an dem Himmel,
Muß zwischen Tag und Nacht
Einsmals ein Wahres erscheinen.

'Yes, it is you, elected
All-loving and to bear
A burdensome good fortune have grown strong,

   'Since, hidden in the woods and flowering poppies
Filled with sweet drowsiness, you, drunken, did not heed
Me for a long time, before lesser ones even felt
The virgin's pride, and marvelled whose you are and where from,
But you yourself did not know. Yet I did not misjudge you
And secretly, while you dreamed, at noon,
Departing I left a token of friendship,
The flower of the mouth behind, and lonely you spoke.
Yet you, the greatly blessed, with the rivers too
Dispatched a wealth of golden words, and they well unceasing
Into all regions now. For almost as is the holy
The Mother of all things, upholder of the abyss,
Whom men at other times call the Concealed,
Now full of loves and sorrows
And full of presentiments
And full of peace is your bosom.

   'O drink the morning breezes
Until you are opened up
And name what you see before you;
No longer now the unspoken
May remain a mystery
Though long it has been veiled;
For shame behoves us mortals
And most of the time to speak thus
Of gods indeed is wise.
But where more superabundant than purest well-springs
The gold has become and the anger in Heaven earnest,
For once between Day and Night must
A truth be made manifest.

Dreifach umschreibe du es,
Doch ungesprochen auch, wie es da ist,
Unschuldige, muß es bleiben.

    O nenne Tochter du der heiligen Erd'
Einmal die Mutter. Es rauschen die Wasser am Fels
Und Wetter im Wald und bei dem Nahmen derselben
Tönt auf aus alter Zeit Vergangengöttliches wieder.
Wie anders ists! und rechthin glänzt und spricht
Zukünftiges auch erfreulich aus den Fernen.
Doch in der Mitte der Zeit
Lebt ruhig mit geweihter
Jungfräulicher Erde der Aether
Und gerne, zur Erinnerung, sind
Die unbedürftigen sie
Gastfreundlich bei den unbedürftgen
Bei deinen Feiertagen
Germania, wo du Priesterin bist
Und wehrlos Rath giebst rings
Den Königen und den Völkern.

Now threefold circumscribe it,
Yet unuttered also, just as you found it,
Innocent virgin, let it remain.

  'Once only, daughter of holy Earth,
Pronounce your Mother's name. The waters roar on the rock
And thunderstorms in the wood, and at their name
Divine things past ring out from time immemorial.
How all is changed! And to the right there gleam
And speak things yet to come, joy-giving, from the distance.
Yet at the centre of Time
In peace with hallowed,
With virginal Earth lives Aether
And gladly, for remembrance, they
The never-needy dwell
Hospitably amid the never-needy,
Amid your holidays,
Germania, where you are priestess and
Defenceless proffer all round
Advice to the kings and the peoples.'

Der Rhein

AN ISAAK VON SINCLAIR

Im dunkeln Epheu saß ich, an der Pforte
Des Waldes, eben, da der goldene Mittag,
Den Quell besuchend, herunterkam
Von Treppen des Alpengebirgs,
Das mir die göttlichgebaute,
Die Burg der Himmlischen heißt
Nach alter Meinung, wo aber
Geheim noch manches entschieden
Zu Menschen gelanget; von da
Vernahm ich ohne Vermuthen
Ein Schiksaal, denn noch kaum
War mir im warmen Schatten
Sich manches beredend, die Seele
Italia zu geschweift
Und fernhin an die Küsten Moreas.

Jezt aber, drinn im Gebirg,
Tief unter den silbernen Gipfeln
Und unter fröhlichem Grün,
Wo die Wälder schauernd zu ihm,
Und der Felsen Häupter übereinander
Hinabschaun, taglang, dort
Im kältesten Abgrund hört'
Ich um Erlösung jammern
Den Jüngling, es hörten ihn, wie er tobt',
Und die Mutter Erd' anklagt',
Und den Donnerer, der ihn gezeuget,
Erbarmend die Eltern, doch
Die Sterblichen flohn von dem Ort,

The Rhine

TO ISAAK VON SINCLAIR

Amid dark ivy I was sitting, at
The forest's gate, just as a golden noon,
To visit the well-spring there, came down
From steps of the Alpine ranges
Which, following ancient lore,
I call the divinely built,
The fortress of the Heavenly,
But where, determined in secret
Much even now reaches men; from there
Without surmise I heard
A destiny, for, debating
Now this, now that in the warm shade,
My soul had hardly begun
To make for Italy
And far away for the shores of Morea.

But now, within the mountains,
Deep down below the silvery summits
And in the midst of gay verdure,
Where shuddering the forests
And the heads of rocks overlapping
Look down at him, all day
There in the coldest chasm
I heard the youth implore
Release; and full of pity his parents heard
Him rage there and accuse
His Mother Earth and the Thunderer
Who fathered him, but mortals
Fled from the place, for dreadful,

Denn furchtbar war, da lichtlos er
In den Fesseln sich wälzte,
Das Rasen des Halbgotts.

    Die Stimme wars des edelsten der Ströme,
Des freigeborenen Rheins,
Und anderes hoffte der, als droben von den Brüdern,
Dem Tessin und dem Rhodanus,
Er schied und wandern wollt', und ungeduldig ihn
Nach Asia trieb die königliche Seele.
Doch unverständig ist
Das Wünschen vor dem Schiksaal.
Die Blindesten aber
Sind Göttersöhne. Denn es kennet der Mensch
Sein Haus und dem Thier ward, wo
Es bauen solle, doch jenen ist
Der Fehl, daß sie nicht wissen wohin?
In die unerfahrne Seele gegeben.

    Ein Räthsel ist Reinentsprungenes. Auch
Der Gesang kaum darf es enthüllen. Denn
Wie du anfiengst, wirst du bleiben,
So viel auch wirket die Noth,
Und die Zucht, das meiste nemlich
Vermag die Geburt,
Und der Lichtstral, der
Dem Neugebornen begegnet.
Wo aber ist einer,
Um frei zu bleiben
Sein Leben lang, und des Herzens Wunsch
Allein zu erfüllen, so
Aus günstigen Höhn, wie der Rhein,
Und so aus heiligem Schoose
Glüklich geboren, wie jener?

As without light he writhed
Within his fetters, was
The demigod's raving.

    The voice it was of the noblest of rivers,
Of freeborn Rhine,
And different were his hopes when up there from his brothers
Ticino and Rhodanus
He parted and longed to roam, and impatiently
His regal soul drove him on towards Asia.
Yet in the face of fate
Imprudent it is to wish.
The sons of gods, though,
Are blindest of all. For human beings know
Their house, and the animals
Where they must build, but in
Their inexperienced souls the defect
Of not knowing where was implanted.

    A mystery are those of pure origin.
Even song may hardly unveil it.
For as you began, so you will remain,
And much as need can effect,
And breeding, still greater power
Adheres to your birth
And the ray of light
That meets the newborn infant.
But where is anyone
So happily born as the Rhine
From such propitious heights
And from so holy a womb,
To remain free
His whole life long and alone fulfil
His heart's desire, like him?

Drum ist ein Jauchzen sein Wort.
Nicht liebt er, wie andere Kinder,
In Wikelbanden zu weinen;
Denn wo die Ufer zuerst
An die Seit ihm schleichen, die krummen,
Und durstig umwindend ihn,
Den Unbedachten, zu ziehn
Und wohl zu behüten begehren
Im eigenen Zahne, lachend
Zerreißt er die Schlangen und stürzt
Mit der Beut und wenn in der Eil'
Ein Größerer ihn nicht zähmt,
Ihn wachsen läßt, wie der Bliz, muß er
Die Erde spalten, und wie Bezauberte fliehn
Die Wälder ihm nach und zusammensinkend die Berge.

Ein Gott will aber sparen den Söhnen
Das eilende Leben und lächelt,
Wenn unenthattsam, aber gehemmt
Von heiligen Alpen, ihm
In der Tiefe, wie jener, zürnen die Ströme.
In solcher Esse wird dann
Auch alles Lautre geschmiedet,
Und schön ists, wie er drauf,
Nachdem er die Berge verlassen,
Stillwandelnd sich im deutschen Lande
Begnüget und das Sehnen stillt
Im guten Geschäffte, wenn er das Land baut
Der Vater Rhein und liebe Kinder nährt
In Städten, die er gegründet.

Doch nimmer, nimmer vergißt ers.
Denn eher muß die Wohnung vergehn,
Und die Sazung und zum Unbild werden

And that is why his word is a jubilant roar,
Nor is he fond, like other children,
Of weeping in swaddling bands;
For where the banks at first
Slink to his side, the crooked,
And greedily entwining him,
Desire to educate
And carefully tend the feckless
Within their teeth, he laughs,
Tears up the serpents and rushes
Off with his prey, and if in haste
A greater one does not tame him,
But lets him grow, like lightning he
Must rend the earth and like things enchanted
The forests join his flight and, collapsing, the mountains.

A god, however, wishes to spare his sons
A life so fleeting and smiles
When, thus intemperate but restrained
By holy Alps, the rivers
Like this one rage at him in the depth.
In such a forge, then, all
That's pure is given shape
And it is good to see
How then, after leaving the mountains,
Content with German lands he calmly
Moves on and stills his longing
In useful industry, when he tills the land,
Now Father Rhine, and supports dear children
In cities which he has founded.

Yet never, never does he forget.
For sooner the dwelling shall be destroyed,
And all the laws, and the day of men

Der Tag der Menschen, ehe vergessen
Ein solcher dürfte den Ursprung
Und die reine Stimme der Jugend.
Wer war es, der zuerst
Die Liebesbande verderbt
Und Strike von ihnen gemacht hat?
Dann haben des eigenen Rechts
Und gewiß des himmlischen Feuers
Gespottet die Trozigen, dann erst
Die sterblichen Pfade verachtend
Verwegnes erwählt
Und den Göttern gleich zu werden getrachtet.

    Es haben aber an eigner
Unsterblichkeit die Götter genug, und bedürfen
Die Himmlischen eines Dings,
So sinds Heroën und Menschen
Und Sterbliche sonst. Denn weil
Die Seeligsten nichts fühlen von selbst,
Muß wohl, wenn solches zu sagen
Erlaubt ist, in der Götter Nahmen
Theilnehmend fühlen ein Andrer,
Den brauchen sie; jedoch ihr Gericht
Ist, daß sein eigenes Haus
Zerbreche der und das Liebste
Wie den Feind schelt' und sich Vater und Kind
Begrabe unter den Trümmern,
Wenn einer, wie sie, seyn will und nicht
Ungleiches dulden, der Schwärmer.

    Drum wohl ihm, welcher fand
Ein wohlbeschiedenes Schiksaal,
Wo noch der Wanderungen
Und süß der Leiden Erinnerung

Become iniquitous, than such as he
Forget his origin
And the pure voice of his youth.
Who was the first to coarsen,
Corrupt the bonds of love
And turn them into ropes?
Then, sure of their own rights
And of the heavenly fire
Defiant rebels mocked, not till then
Despising mortal ways,
Chose foolhardy arrogance
And strove to become the equals of gods.

   But their own immortality
Suffices the gods, and if
The Heavenly have need of one thing,
It is of heroes and human beings
And other mortals. For since
The most Blessed in themselves feel nothing
Another, if to say such a thing is
Permitted, must, I suppose,
Vicariously feel in the name of the gods,
And him they need; but their rule is that
He shall demolish his
Own house and curse like an enemy
Those dearest to him and under the rubble
Shall bury his father and child,
When one aspires to be like them, refusing
To bear with inequality, the fantast.

   So happy he who has found
A well-allotted fate
Where still of his wanderings
And sweetly of his afflictions

Aufrauscht am sichern Gestade,
Daß da und dorthin gern
Er sehn mag bis an die Grenzen
Die bei der Geburt ihm Gott
Zum Aufenthalte gezeichnet.
Dann ruht er, seeligbescheiden,
Denn alles, was er gewollt,
Das Himmlische, von selber umfängt
Es unbezwungen, lächelnd
Jezt, da er ruhet, den Kühnen.

    Halbgötter denk' ich jezt
Und kennen muß ich die Theuern,
Weil oft ihr Leben so
Die sehnende Brust mir beweget.
Wem aber, wie, Rousseau, dir,
Unüberwindlich die Seele
Die starkausdauernde ward,
Und sicherer Sinn
Und süße Gaabe zu hören,
Zu reden so, daß er aus heiliger Fülle
Wie der Weingott, thörig göttlich
Und gesezlos sie die Sprache der Reinesten giebt
Verständlich den Guten, aber mit Recht
Die Achtungslosen mit Blindheit schlägt
Die entweihenden Knechte, wie nenn ich den Fremden?

    Die Söhne der Erde sind, wie die Mutter,
Allliebend, so empfangen sie auch
Mühlos, die Glüklichen, Alles.
Drum überraschet es auch
Und schrökt den sterblichen Mann,
Wenn er den Himmel, den
Er mit den liebenden Armen

The memory murmurs on banks that are sure,
So that this way, that way with pleasure
He looks as far as the bounds
Which God at birth assigned
To him for his term and site.
Then, blissfully humble, he rests,
For all that he has wanted,
Though heavenly, of itself surrounds
Him uncompelled, and smiles
Upon the bold one now that he's quiet.

Of demigods now I think
And I must know these dear ones
Because so often their lives
Move me and fill me with longing.
But he whose soul, like yours,
Rousseau, ever strong and patient,
Became invincible,
Endowed with steadfast purpose
And a sweet gift of hearing,
Of speaking, so that from holy profusion
Like the wine-god foolishly, divinely
And lawlessly he gives it away,
The language of the purest, comprehensible to the good,
But rightly strikes with blindness the irreverent,
The profaning rabble, what shall I call that stranger?

The sons of Earth, like their mother are
All-loving, so without effort too
All things those blessèd ones receive.
And therefore it surprises
And startles the mortal man
When he considers the heaven
Which with loving arms he himself

Sich auf die Schultern gehäufft,
Und die Last der Freude bedenket;
Dann scheint ihm oft das Beste,
Fast ganz vergessen da,
Wo der Stral nicht brennt
Im Schatten des Walds
Am Bielersee in frischer Grüne zu seyn,
Und sorglosarm an Tönen,
Anfängern gleich, bei Nachtigallen zu lernen.

    Und herrlich ists, aus heiligem Schlafe dann
Erstehen und aus Waldes Kühle
Erwachend, Abends nun
Dem milderen Licht entgegenzugehn,
Wenn, der die Berge gebaut
Und den Pfad der Ströme gezeichnet,
Nachdem er lächelnd auch
Der Menschen geschäfftiges Leben
Das othemarme, wie Seegel
Mit seinen Lüften gelenkt hat,
Auch ruht und zu der Schülerin jezt,
Der Bildner, Gutes mehr
Denn Böses findend,
Zur heutigen Erde der Tag sich neiget. –

    Dann feiern das Brautfest Menschen und Götter,
Es feiern die Lebenden all,
Und ausgeglichen
Ist eine Weile das Schiksaal.
Und die Flüchtlinge suchen die Heerberg,
Und süßen Schlummer die Tapfern,
Die Liebenden aber
Sind, was sie waren, sie sind
Zu Haußße, wo die Blume sich freuet

Has heaped upon his shoulders,
And feels the burden of joy;
Then often to him it seems best
Almost wholly forgotten to be
Where the beam does not sear,
In the forest's shade
By Lake Bienne amid foliage newly green,
And blithely poor in tones,
Like beginners, to learn from nightingales.

    And glorious then it is to arise once more
From holy sleep and awakening
From coolness of the woods, at evening
Walk now toward the softer light
When he who built the mountains
And drafted the paths of the rivers,
Having also smiling directed
The busy lives of men,
So short of breath, like sails,
And filled them with his breezes,
Reposes also, and down to his pupil
The master craftsmen, finding
More good than evil,
Day now inclines to the present Earth.

    Then gods and mortals celebrate their nuptials,
All the living celebrate,
And Fate for a while
Is levelled out, suspended.
And fugitives look for asylum,
For sweet slumber the brave,
But lovers are
What always they were, at home
Wherever flowers are glad

Unschädlicher Gluth und die finsteren Bäume
Der Geist umsäuselt, aber die Unversöhnten
Sind umgewandelt und eilen
Die Hände sich ehe zu reichen,
Bevor das freundliche Licht
Hinuntergeht und die Nacht kommt.

    Doch einigen eilt
Diß schnell vorüber, andere
Behalten es länger.
Die ewigen Götter sind
Voll Lebens allzeit; bis in den Tod
Kann aber ein Mensch auch
Im Gedächtniß doch das Beste behalten,
Und dann erlebt er das Höchste.
Nur hat ein jeder sein Maas.
Denn schwer ist zu tragen
Das Unglük, aber schwerer das Glük.
Ein Weiser aber vermocht es
Vom Mittag bis in die Mitternacht,
Und bis der Morgen erglänzte,
Beim Gastmahl helle zu bleiben.

    Dir mag auf heißem Pfade unter Tannen oder
Im Dunkel des Eichwalds gehüllt
In Stahl, mein Sinklair! Gott erscheinen oder
In Wolken, du kennst ihn, da du kennest, jugendlich,
Des Guten Kraft, und nimmer ist dir
Verborgen das Lächeln des Herrschers
Bei Tage, wenn
Es fieberhaft und angekettet das
Lebendige scheinet oder auch
Bei Nacht, wenn alles gemischt
Ist ordnungslos und wiederkehrt
Uralte Verwirrung.

Of harmless fervour and the spirit wafts
Around the darkling trees, but those unreconciled
Are changed and hurry now
To hold out their hands to the other
Before the benevolent light
Goes down, and night comes.

    For some, however,
This quickly passes, others
Retain it longer.
The eternal gods are full
Of life at all times; but until death
A mortal too can retain
And bear in mind what is best
And then is supremely favoured.
Yet each of us has his measure.
For hard to bear
Is misfortune, but good fortune harder.
A wise man, though, was able
From noon to midnight, and on
Till morning lit up the sky
To keep wide awake at the banquet.

    To you in the heat of a path under fir trees or
Within the oak forest's half-light, wrapped
In steel, my Sinclair, God may appear, or
In clouds, you'll know him, since, youthfully, you know
The good God's power, and never from you
The smile of the Ruler is hidden
By day, when all
That lives seems febrile
And fettered, or also
By night, when all is mingled
Chaotically and back again comes
Primaeval confusion.

Versöhnender der du Nimmergeglaubt ...

Vorstufen zur 'Friedensfeier'

Versöhnender der du nimmergeglaubt
Nun da bist,   Freundesgestalt mir
Annimmst Unsterblicher, aber wohl
Erkenn ich   das Hohe
Das mir die Knie beugt,
Und fast wie ein Blinder muß ich
Dich, himmlischer fragen wozu du mir,
Woher du seiest, seeliger Friede!
Diß Eine weiß ich, sterbliches bist du nichts,
Denn manches mag ein Weiser oder
Der treuanblikenden Freunde einer erhellen, wenn aber
Ein Gott erscheint, auf Himmel und Erd und Meer
Kömt allerneuende Klarheit.

(Einst freueten wir uns auch,
Zur Morgenstunde wo stille die Werkstatt war
Am Feiertag, und die Blumen in der Stille,
Wohl blühten schöner auch sie und helle quillten lebendige Brunnen.
Fern rauschte der Gemeinde schauerlicher Gesang,
Wo heiligem Wein gleich, die geheimeren Sprüche
Gealtert aber gewaltiger einst, aus Gottes
Gewittern im Sommer gewachsen,
Die Sorgen doch mir stillten
Und die Zweifel, aber nimmer wußt ich, wie mir geschah,
Denn kaum geboren, warum breitetet
Ihr mir schon über die Augen eine Nacht,
Daß ich die Erde nicht sah und mühsam
Euch athmen mußt, ihr himmlischen Lüfte.

Conciliator, you that no longer believed in . . .

Preliminary drafts for 'Celebration of Peace'

Conciliator, you that no longer believed in
Are here now,   assuming the shape of
A friend, immortal, yet indeed
I recognize   what exalted power
It is that bends my knees,
And almost like a blind man I
Must ask you, the heavenly, for what
And whence you have come to me, blessèd Peace!
This one thing I do know, a mortal you are not,
For much a wise man or one of
The loyally gazing friends may elucidate, but when
A god appears, on heaven and earth and ocean
An all-renewing clarity shines.

(Once, it is true, we rejoiced, at
The morning hour when the workshop was quiet on
A holiday, and indeed in that stillness the flowers
More beautifully blossomed and brightly the living fountains welled.
Far off, but awe-inspiring, droned the community's singing
Where like a holy wine, the more mysterious responses,
Aged now but once more mighty, grown up
In summer from the thunder-storms of God,
Could yet allay my cares
And doubts, but never I knew what was happening to me,
For why, when I had hardly been born,
Already did you cover my eyes with a night,
So that I could not see the earth and with
An effort must inhale you, heavenly breezes.

Zuvorbestimmt wars. Und es lächelt Gott,
Wenn unaufhaltsam aber von seinen Bergen gehemmt
Ihm zürnend in den ehernen Ufern brausen die Ströme,
Tief wo kein Tag die begrabenen nennt.
Und o, daß immer allerhaltender, du auch mich
So haltest, und leichtentfliehende Seele mir sparest,)
Drum hab ich heute das Fest, und abendlich in der Stille
Blüht rings der Geist und wär auch silbergrau mir die Loke,
Doch würd ich rathen, daß wir sorgten ihr Freunde
Für Gastmahl und Gesang, und Kränze genug und Töne
Bei solcher Zeit unsterblichen Jünglingen gleich.

Und manchen möcht' ich laden, aber o du,
Der freundlich ernst den Menschen zugethan
Dort unter syrischer Palme
Wo nahe lag die Stadt am Brunnen gerne weiltest,
Das Kornfeld rauschte rings   still athmete die Kühlung
Vom Dunkel des geweiheten Gebirgs,
Und die lieben Freunde, das treue Gewölk
Umschatteten dich auch, damit der reine, kühne
Durch Wildniß mild der Stral von oben kam o Jüngling!
Ach! aber dunkler umschattete, mitten im Wort dich
Furchtbar entscheidend ein tödtlich Verhängniß. So ist schnell
Vergänglich alles Himmlische; aber umsonst nicht.

Denn schonend rührt, des Maases allzeit kundig
Nur einen Augenblik die Wohnungen der Menschen
Ein Gott an, unversehn, und keiner weiß es, wer?
Und drüber hin darf alles Freche gehn,
Und kommen muß zum heilgen Ort das Wilde
Von Enden fern, und blindbetastend übt den Wahn
Am Göttlichen, und trift ein Schiksaal darin. Dank
Folgt niemals auf dem Fuße solchem Geschenke.

Preordained it was. And God smiles
When not to be stopped but restrained by his mountains
The rivers, raging, roar at him in their brazen banks,
Deep down where no day calls the buried by their names.
And O that ever, Upholder of All, me too you shall
Hold thus and spare my soul that all too readily flees,)
Today I celebrate, and vespertine now in the stillness
All round the spirit blossoms and though my hair
Were silver-grey, yet, my friends, I'd advise that
We see to banquet and song and garlands enough and music
At such a time like men immortally young.

    And there are many I would invite, but you,
O you that benignly, gravely disposed to men
Down there beneath the Syrian palm tree, where
The town lay near, by the well were fond of lingering,
Round you the cornfield rustled, quietly coolness breathed
From darkness of the hallowed mountain-sides
And your dear friends, the faithful cloud
Cast shade upon you too, so that the pure, the bold,
The beam through wilderness gently should fall from above, O youth.
But, oh, more darkly, even as you spoke
And dreadfully determining, a deadly doom overshadowed you there.
                                [So all
That's heavenly fleets on; but not for nothing.

    For sparingly, at all times knowing the measure,
A god for a moment only will touch the dwellings
Of men, by none foreseen, and no one knows who it was,
And over it all insolence may pass,
And to the holy place must come the savage
From ends remote, and blindly fingering, works out his
Delusion upon the divine, and fulfils a fate. But thanks
Will never follow at once upon such a gift.

Zu schwer ist jenes zu fassen,
Denn wäre der es giebt, nicht sparsam
Längst wäre vom Seegen des Heerds
Uns Gipfel und Boden entzündet.

    Des Göttlichen aber empfiengen wir
Doch viel. Es ward die Flamm uns
In die Hände gegeben, und Boden und Meersfluth.
Denn nur auf menschliche Weise, nimmermehr
Sind jene mit uns, die fremden Kräfte vertraut
Und es lehret das Gestirn dich, das
Vor Augen dir ist, denn nimmer kannst du ihm gleichen
Dem Alllebendigen von dem
Viel Freuden sind und Gesänge,

    Ist einer ein Sohn, ein Ruhigmächtiger ist er,
Denn nun erkennen wir ihn,
Jezt da wir kennen den Vater,
Und Feiertage zu halten
Der Hohe sich der Geist
Sich froh zu Menschen geneigt hat.

    Zur Herrschaft war der immer zu groß
Und geringer denn er, so weit es auch gereichet sein Feld.
Es mag ein Gott auch, Sterblichen gleich
Erwählen ein Tagewerk und theilen alles Schiksaal
Daß alle sich einander erfahren, und wenn
Die Stille wiederkehret, eine Sprache unter Lebenden
Sei. Wie der Meister tritt er dann, aus der
Werkstatt, und andres Gewand nicht denn ein festliches ziehet er an.
Die Geseze aber, die unter Liebenden gelten
Die schönausgleichenden sie sind dann allgeltend
Von der Erde bis hoch in den Himmel.

Too hard this is to grasp, for
If he who gives it were not sparing,
The wealth of our hearth long ago would
Have fired both the roof and the floor.

    Yet much that's divine nonetheless we
Received. The flame was entrusted
To us, and the ground we walk on and ocean flood,
Much more than humanly only, never again
Are these, the alien powers, familiar with us,
And you are taught by the stars
In front of your eyes, but never you can be like them.
Yet to the All-Living from whom
Many joys and songs have sprung

    There's one who is a son, and quietly powerful is he,
For now we recognize him
Now that we know the Father,
And to keep holidays
The Exalted, the Spirit
Has gladly inclined towards men.

    For dominion he has always been too great
And smaller than he, far though it stretches, his field.
A god, like mortals, too may choose
Mere daily tasks and share all manner of fate,
That all might have knowledge of all, and when
The silence returns, there might be a language among
The living. Like the master then he steps out of
His workshop, and none but a festive garment he puts on.
The laws, however, that count for lovers
And gently resolve their discords, then are all-prevailing
From Earth to high up in Heaven.

Denn siehe es ist der Abend der Zeit
Und der Vater thront nun nimmer oben allein.
Und andere sind noch bei ihm.
Viel hat erfahren der Mensch. Der Himmlischen viele genannt,
Seit ein Gespräch wir sind
Und hören können voneinander.

    Sei gegenwärtig Jüngling, jezt erst, denn noch ehe du ausgeredet
Rief es herab, und schnell verhüllt war jenes Freudige, das
Du reichtest, und weit umschattend breitete sich über dir
Und furchtbar ein Verhängniß,
So ist schnellvergänglich alles Himmlische, aber umsonst nicht.
Des Maases allzeit kundig rührt mit schonender Hand
Die Wohnungen der Menschen
Ein Gott an, einen Augenblik nur
Und sie wissen es nicht, doch lange
Gedenken sie deß, und fragen, wer es gewesen
Wenn aber eine Zeit vorbei ist, kennen sie es.

    Und menschlicher Wohlthat folget der Dank,
Auf göttliche Gaabe aber jahrlang
Die Mühn erst und das Irrsaal,
Daß milder auf die folgende Zeit
Der hohe Stral
Durch heilige Wildniß scheine.
Darum, o Göttlicher! sei gegenwärtig,
Und schöner, wie sonst, o sei
Versöhnender nun versöhnt daß wir des Abends
Mit den Freunden dich nennen, und singen
Von den Hohen, und neben dir noch andere sein.

    Denn versiegt fast, all in Opferflammen
War ausgeathmet das heilige Feuer

For, look, it is the Evening of Time, and
No longer alone the Father sits enthroned above.
And others now are with him.
Much men have learnt. Have called by their names many of those
                                    [in Heaven
Since we have been a discourse
And able to hear from each other.

    Be present, youth, only now, for before you had finished speaking
The voice cried, away, and quickly that joy was obscured which
You proffered, and widely overshadowing and terrible
A doom descended upon you;
So all that's heavenly fleets on, but not for nothing.
At all times knowing the measure, with a sparing hand
A god will touch the dwellings
Of men, for a moment only
And they do not know it, yet long they
Remember it and ask who it was.
Yet when a certain time has gone by, they know it.

    And human beneficence is followed by thanks,
But godsent gifts for years at first
By suffering and confusion
So that more mildly in the years that follow
The lofty beam
Through holy wilderness shall shine.
Therefore, divine one, be present now
And O more beautifully than before,
Conciliator, now be reconciled, so that at Evening
Together with your friends we may name you, and sing
Of them, the celestial, and there shall be others beside you.

    For almost exhausted, all breathed out
In sacrificial flames was the holy fire

Da schikte schnellentzündend der Vater
Das liebendste, was er hatte, herab
Damit entbrennend,
Und wenn fortzehrend von Geschlecht zu Geschlecht,
Die Menschen wären des Seegens zu voll,
Daß jeder sich genügt und übermüthig vergäße des Himmels,
Dann sprach er soll ein neues beginnen,
Und siehe! was du verschwiegest,
Der Zeiten Vollendung hat es gebracht.
Wohl wußtest du es, aber nicht zu leben, zu sterben warst du gesandt,
Und immer größer, denn sein Feld, wie der Götter Gott
Er selbst, muß einer der anderen auch seyn.

    Wenn aber die Stunde schlägt
Wie der Meister tritt er, aus der Werkstatt,
Und ander Gewand nicht, denn
Ein festliches ziehet er an
Zum Zeichen, daß noch anderes auch
Im Werk ihm übrig gewesen.
Geringer und größer erscheint er.
Und so auch du
Und gönnest uns, den Söhnen der liebenden Erde,
Daß wir, so viel herangewachsen
Der Feste sind, sie alle feiern und nicht
Die Götter zählen, Einer ist immer für alle.
Mir gleich dem Sonnenlichte! göttlicher sei
Am Abend deiner Tage gegrüßet.
Und mögen bleiben wir nun.

When swiftly kindling, the Father sent down the
Most loving of all that are his
To start a stronger blaze;
And if, consuming it generation after generation,
Mankind should be too full of blessings,
Each man becoming self-sufficient and arrogantly oblivious of Heaven
Then, so he said, a new age shall begin
And, look, what you kept unspoken
The end of the ages has brought to light.
And well you knew it, but not to live, to die you were sent,
And always greater than his field, like the God of gods
Himself, must one of the others be also.

   But when the hour strikes
Like the master he steps from his workshop
And none but a festive garment
He now puts on, as a sign
That he remained aware
Of things left undone in his work.
Both smaller and greater he seems now.
And likewise you,
Who grant us, the sons of this loving Earth,
That, many as are the holidays that have
Grown up, we may celebrate them all, and need
Not count the gods; one always stands for them all.
To me like the sunlight! divine one, let
Us greet you at the Evening of your days.
And may we now abide.

Friedensfeier

Ich bitte dieses Blatt nur gutmüthig zu lesen. So wird es sicher nicht unfaßlich, noch weniger anstößig seyn. Sollten aber dennoch einige eine solche Sprache zu wenig konventionell finden, so muß ich ihnen gestehen: ich kann nicht anders. An einem schönen Tage läßt sich ja fast jede Sangart hören, und die Natur, wovon es her ist, nimmts auch wieder.

Der Verfasser gedenkt dem Publikum eine ganze Sammlung von dergleichen Blättern vorzulegen, und dieses soll irgend eine Probe seyn davon.

Der himmlischen, still wiederklingenden,
Der ruhigwandelnden Töne voll,
Und gelüftet ist der altgebaute,
Seeliggewohnte Saal; um grüne Teppiche duftet
Die Freudenwolk' und weithinglänzend stehn,
Gereiftester Früchte voll und goldbekränzter Kelche,
Wohlangeordnet, eine prächtige Reihe,
Zur Seite da und dort aufsteigend über dem
Geebneten Boden die Tische.
Denn ferne kommend haben
Hieher, zur Abendstunde,
Sich liebende Gäste beschieden.

Und dämmernden Auges denk' ich schon,
Vom ernsten Tagwerk lächelnd,
Ihn selbst zu sehn, den Fürsten des Fests.
Doch wenn du schon dein Ausland gern verläugnest,
Und als vom langen Heldenzuge müd,
Dein Auge senkst, vergessen, leichtbeschattet,
Und Freundesgestalt annimmst, du Allbekannter, doch

Celebration of Peace

All I ask is that the reader be kindly disposed towards these pages. In that case he will certainly not find them incomprehensible, far less objectionable. But if, nonetheless, some should think such a language too unconventional, I must confess to them: I cannot help it. On a fine day – they should consider – almost every mode of song makes itself heard; and Nature, whence it originates, also receives it again.

The author intends to offer the public an entire collection of such pieces, and this one should be regarded as a kind of sample.

    With heavenly, quietly echoing,
With calmly modulating music filled,
And aired is the anciently built,
The sweetly familiar hall; upon green carpets wafts
The fragrant cloud of joy and, casting their brightness far,
Full of most mellow fruit and chalices wreathed with gold,
Arranged in seemly order, a splendid row,
Erected here and there on either side above
The levelled floor, stand the tables.
For, come from distant places,
Here, at the evening hour,
Loving guests have forgathered.

    And already with eyes dusk-dim,
With solemn day-labour smiling,
I think that I see him in person, the prince of the feast-day.
But though you like to disavow your foreign land,
And weary, it seems, with long heroic war,
Cast down your eyes, oblivious, lightly shaded,
Assuming the shape of a friend, you known to all men, yet

Beugt fast die Knie das Hohe. Nichts vor dir,
Nur Eines weiß ich, Sterbliches bist du nicht.
Ein Weiser mag mir manches erhellen; wo aber
Ein Gott noch auch erscheint,
Da ist doch andere Klarheit.

Von heute aber nicht, nicht unverkündet ist er;
Und einer, der nicht Fluth noch Flamme gescheuet,
Erstaunet, da es stille worden, umsonst nicht, jezt,
Da Herrschaft nirgend ist zu sehn bei Geistern und Menschen.
Das ist, sie hören das Werk,
Längst vorbereitend, von Morgen nach Abend, jezt erst,
Denn unermeßlich braußt, in der Tiefe verhallend,
Des Donnerers Echo, das tausendjährige Wetter,
Zu schlafen, übertönt von Friedenslauten, hinunter.
Ihr aber, theuergewordne, o ihr Tage der Unschuld,
Ihr bringt auch heute das Fest, ihr Lieben! und es blüht
Rings abendlich der Geist in dieser Stille;
Und rathen muß ich, und wäre silbergrau
Die Loke, o ihr Freunde!
Für Kränze zu sorgen und Mahl, jezt ewigen Jünglingen ähnlich.

Und manchen möcht' ich laden, aber o du,
Der freundlichernst den Menschen zugethan,
Dort unter syrischer Palme,
Wo nahe lag die Stadt, am Brunnen gerne war;
Das Kornfeld rauschte rings, still athmete die Kühlung
Vom Schatten des geweiheten Gebirges,
Und die lieben Freunde, das treue Gewölk,
Umschatteten dich auch, damit der heiligkühne
Durch Wildniß mild dein Stral zu Menschen kam, o Jüngling!
Ach! aber dunkler umschattete, mitten im Wort, dich

Almost it bends our knees, such loftiness. Nothing in
Your presence I know; but one thing: mortal you are not.
A wise man could elucidate much for me; but where
A God as well appears,
A different clarity shines.

    Yet not sprung up today, nor unproclaimed he comes
And one who did not balk at either flood or flame
Not without reason astonishes us, now that all is quiet,
Dominion nowhere to be seen among spirits or mortals.
That is, only now do they hear
The work that long has prepared them, from Orient to Occident,
For now immeasurably, fading away in the deeps,
The Thunderer's echo, the millennial storm
Rolls down to sleep, intermingled with peaceful music.
But you, grown dear to us, O days of innocence,
It's you, belovèd, that bring this feast-day too, and round us
The spirit flowers, vespertine in this quiet;
And, friends, I must advise you, though
Our hair had turned silver-grey,
To see to garlands and banquet, now like men immortally young.

    And many there are I would invite, but you,
O you that benignly, gravely disposed to men
Down there beneath the Syrian palm tree, where
The town lay near, by the well were glad to be;
Round you the cornfield rustled, quietly coolness breathed
From shadows of the hallowed mountainsides,
And your dear friends, the faithful clouds
Cast shade upon you too, so that the holy, the bold,
The beam through wilderness gently should fall on men, O youth.
But oh, more darkly, even as you spoke,

Furchtbarentscheidend ein tödtlich Verhängniß. So ist schnell
Vergänglich alles Himmlische; aber umsonst nicht;

    Denn schonend rührt des Maases allzeit kundig
Nur einen Augenblik die Wohnungen der Menschen
Ein Gott an, unversehn, und keiner weiß es, wenn?
Auch darf alsdann das Freche drüber gehn,
Und kommen muß zum heilgen Ort das Wilde
Von Enden fern, übt rauhbetastend den Wahn,
Und trift daran ein Schiksaal, aber Dank,
Nie folgt der gleich hernach dem gottgegebnen Geschenke;
Tiefprüfend ist es zu fassen.
Auch wär' uns, sparte der Gebende nicht
Schon längst vom Seegen des Heerds
Uns Gipfel und Boden entzündet.

    Des Göttlichen aber empfiengen wir
Doch viel. Es ward die Flamm' uns
In die Hände gegeben, und Ufer und Meersfluth.
Viel mehr, denn menschlicher Weise
Sind jene mit uns, die fremden Kräfte, vertrauet.
Und es lehret Gestirn dich, das
Vor Augen dir ist, doch nimmer kannst du ihm gleichen.
Vom Alllebendigen aber, von dem
Viel Freuden sind und Gesänge,
Ist einer ein Sohn, ein Ruhigmächtiger ist er,
Und nun erkennen wir ihn,
Nun, da wir kennen den Vater
Und Feiertage zu halten
Der hohe, der Geist
Der Welt sich zu Menschen geneigt hat.

And dreadfully determining a deadly doom overshadowed you there.
                                            [So all
That's heavenly fleets on; but not for nothing;

    For sparingly, at all times knowing the measure,
A God for a moment only will touch the dwellings
Of men, by none foreseen, and no one knows when.
And over it then all insolence may pass,
And to the holy place must come the savage
From ends remote, and roughly fingering works out his
Delusion, so fulfilling a fate, but thanks
Will never follow at once upon the godsent gift;
Probed deeply, this can be grasped.
And were not the giver sparing
The wealth of our hearth long ago would
Have fired both the roof and the floor.

    Yet much that's divine nonetheless we
Received. The flame was entrusted
To us, and shore and ocean flood.
Much more than humanly only
Are these, the alien powers, familiar with us.
And you are taught by the stars
In front of your eyes, but never you can be like them.
Yet to the All-Living from whom
Many joys and songs have sprung
There's one who is a son, and quietly powerful is he,
And now we recognize him,
Now that we know the Father
And to keep holidays
The exalted, the Spirit of
The World has inclined towards men.

Denn längst war der zum Herrn der Zeit zu groß
Und weit aus reichte sein Feld, wann hats ihn aber erschöpfet?
Einmal mag aber ein Gott auch Tagewerk erwählen,
Gleich Sterblichen und theilen alles Schiksaal.
Schiksaalgesez ist diß, daß Alle sich erfahren,
Daß, wenn die Stille kehrt, auch eine Sprache sei.
Wo aber wirkt der Geist, sind wir auch mit, und streiten,
Was wohl das Beste sei. So dünkt mir jezt das Beste,
Wenn nun vollendet sein Bild und fertig ist der Meister,
Und selbst verklärt davon aus seiner Werkstatt tritt,
Der stille Gott der Zeit und nur der Liebe Gesez,
Das schönausgleichende gilt von hier an bis zum Himmel.

    Viel hat von Morgen an,
Seit ein Gespräch wir sind und hören voneinander,
Erfahren der Mensch; bald sind wir aber Gesang.
Und das Zeitbild, das der große Geist entfaltet,
Ein Zeichen liegts vor uns, daß zwischen ihm und andern
Ein Bündniß zwischen ihm und andern Mächten ist.
Nicht er allein, die Unerzeugten, Ew'gen
Sind kennbar alle daran, gleichwie auch an den Pflanzen
Die Mutter Erde sich und Licht und Luft sich kennet.
Zulezt ist aber doch, ihr heiligen Mächte, für euch
Das Liebeszeichen, das Zeugniß
Daß ihrs noch seiet, der Festtag,

    Der Allversammelnde, wo Himmlische nicht
Im Wunder offenbar, noch ungesehn im Wetter,
Wo aber bei Gesang gastfreundlich untereinander
In Chören gegenwärtig, eine heilige Zahl
Die Seeligen in jeglicher Weise
Beisammen sind, und ihr Geliebtestes auch,
An dem sie hängen, nicht fehlt; denn darum rief ich

For long now he had been too great to rule
As Lord of Time, and wide his field extended, but when did it exhaust
[him?
For once, however, even a God may choose
Mere daily tasks, like mortals, and share all manner of fate.
This is a law of fate, that each shall know all others,
That when the silence returns there shall be a language too.
Yet where the Spirit is active, we too will stir and debate
What course might be the best. So now it seems best to me
If now the Master completes his image and, finished,
Himself transfigured by it, steps out of his workshop,
The quiet God of Time, and only the law of love,
That gently resolves all difference, prevails from here up to Heaven.

   Much, from the morning onwards,
Since we have been a discourse and have heard from one another,
Has human kind learnt; but soon we shall be song.
That temporal image too, which the great Spirit reveals,
As a token lies before us that between him and others,
Himself and other powers, there is a pact of peace.
Not he alone, the Unconceived, Eternal
Can all be known by this, as likewise by the plants
Our Mother Earth and light and air are known.
Yet ultimately, you holy powers, our token
Of love for you, and the proof
That still you are holy to us, is the feast-day,

   The all-assembling, where heavenly beings are
Not manifest in miracles, nor unseen in thunderstorms,
But where in hymns hospitably conjoined
And present in choirs, a holy number,
The blessèd in every way
Meet and forgather, and their best-beloved,
To whom they are attached, is not missing; for that is why

Zum Gastmahl, das bereitet ist,
Dich, Unvergeßlicher, dich, zum Abend der Zeit,
O Jüngling, dich zum Fürsten des Festes; und eher legt
Sich schlafen unser Geschlecht nicht,
Bis ihr Verheißenen all,
All ihr Unsterblichen, uns
Von eurem Himmel zu sagen,
Da seid in unserem Haußhe.

Leichtathmende Lüfte
Verkünden euch schon,
Euch kündet das rauchende Thal
Und der Boden, der vom Wetter noch dröhnet,
Doch Hoffnung röthet die Wangen,
Und vor der Thüre des Haußhes
Sizt Mutter und Kind,
Und schauet den Frieden
Und wenige scheinen zu sterben
Es hält ein Ahnen die Seele,
Vom goldnen Lichte gesendet,
Hält ein Versprechen die Ältesten auf.

Wohl sind die Würze des Lebens,
Von oben bereitet und auch
Hinausgeführet, die Mühen.
Denn Alles gefällt jezt,
Einfältiges aber
Am meisten, denn die langgesuchte,
Die goldne Frucht,
Uraltem Stamm
In schütternden Stürmen entfallen,
Dann aber, als liebstes Gut, vom heiligen Schiksaal selbst,
Mit zärtlichen Waffen umschüzt,
Die Gestalt der Himmlischen ist es.

You to the banquet now prepared I called,
The unforgettable, you, at the Evening of Time,
O youth, called you to the prince of the feast-day; nor shall
Our nation ever lie down to sleep until
All you that were prophesied,
Every one of you Immortals,
To tell us about your Heaven
Are here with us in our house.

Winds lightly breathing
Already announce you,
The vapour that drifts from the valley
And the ground still resounding with thunder,
But hope now flushes our cheeks,
In front of the door of their house
Sit mother and child,
And look upon peace,
And few now seem to be dying;
The souls of the oldest even
Held back by a hint, a promise
Conveyed by the golden light.

Indeed it is travails, designed from
Above and there carried out,
That are the spice of life.
For now all things are pleasing
But most of all the
Ingenuous, because the long-sought,
The golden fruit,
In shattering gales fallen down from
An age-old bough
But then, as the dearest possession, by Fate herself
Protected with tender weapons,
The shape of the Heavenly it is.

Wie die Löwin, hast du geklagt,
O Mutter, da du sie,
Natur, die Kinder verloren.
Denn es stahl sie, Allzuliebende, dir
Dein Feind, da du ihn fast
Wie die eigenen Söhne genommen,
Und Satyren die Götter gesellt hast.
So hast du manches gebaut,
Und manches begraben,
Denn es haßt dich, was
Du, vor der Zeit
Allkräftige, zum Lichte gezogen.
Nun kennest, nun lässest du diß;
Denn gerne fühllos ruht,
Bis daß es reift, furchtsamgeschäfftiges drunten.

Like the lioness you lamented,
O Mother, when you lost
Your children, Nature,
For they were stolen from you, the all too loving, by
Your enemy, when almost
Like your own sons you had nursed him
And with satyrs made gods consort.
So there is much you built
And much you buried,
For you are hated by
That which too soon
All-powerful, you raised to the light.
Now you know the fault, and desist,
For, till grown ripe, unfeeling
What's timidly busy likes to rest down below.

Der Einzige

Erste Fassung

Was ist es, das
An die alten seeligen Küsten
Mich fesselt, daß ich mehr noch
Sie liebe, als mein Vaterland?
Denn wie in himmlische
Gefangenschaft verkaufft
Dort bin ich, wo Apollo gieng
In Königsgestalt,
Und zu unschuldigen Jünglingen sich
Herablies Zevs und Söhn' in heiliger Art
Und Töchter zeugte
Der Hohe unter den Menschen?

Der hohen Gedanken
Sind nemlich viel
Entsprungen des Vaters Haupt
Und große Seelen
Von ihm zu Menschen gekommen.
Gehöret hab' ich
Von Elis und Olympia, bin
Gestanden oben auf dem Parnaß,
Und über Bergen des Isthmus,
Und drüben auch
Bei Smyrna und hinab
Bei Ephesos bin ich gegangen;

Viel hab' ich schönes gesehn,
Und gesungen Gottes Bild,
Hab' ich, das lebet unter

The Only One

First Version

What is it that
To the ancient, the happy shores
Binds me, so that I love them
Still more than my own homeland?
For as though into heavenly
Captivity sold,
I am where Apollo walked
In the guise of a king,
And Zeus condescended
To innocent youths, and sons in a holy fashion
Begot, and daughters,
The exalted, amid mankind.

For many a thought
Sublime and great
Has sprung from the Father's head
And lofty souls
Come down from him to mortals.
Of Elis and
Olympia I have heard, and stood
High up on the top of Parnassus
And up above hills of the Isthmus
And over there
By Smyrna too, and down
By Ephesus I have walked;

Have looked upon much that is lovely
And sung the image of God
As here among human kind

Den Menschen, aber dennoch
Ihr alten Götter und all
Ihr tapfern Söhne der Götter
Noch Einen such ich, den
Ich liebe unter euch,
Wo ihr den lezten eures Geschlechts
Des Haußes Kleinod mir
Dem fremden Gaste verberget.

    Mein Meister und Herr!
O du, mein Lehrer!
Was bist du ferne
Geblieben? und da
Ich fragte unter den Alten,
Die Helden und
Die Götter, warum bliebest
Du aus? Und jezt ist voll
Von Trauern meine Seele
Als eifertet, ihr Himmlischen, selbst
Daß, dien' ich einem mir
Das andere fehlet.

    Ich weiß es aber, eigene Schuld
Ists! Denn zu sehr,
O Christus! häng' ich an dir,
Wiewohl Herakles Bruder
Und kühn bekenn' ich, du
Bist Bruder auch des Eviers, der
An den Wagen spannte
Die Tyger und hinab
Bis an den Indus
Gebietend freudigen Dienst
Den Weinberg stiftet und
Den Grimm bezähmte der Völker.

It lives, and yet, and yet,
You ancient gods and all
You valiant sons of the gods,
One other I look for whom
Within your ranks I love,
Where hidden from the alien guest, from me,
You keep the last of your kind,
The treasured gem of the house.

   My Master and Lord!
O you, my teacher!
Why did you keep
Away? And when
I asked among the ancients
The heroes and
The gods, then why were you
Not there? And now my soul
is full of sadness as though
You Heavenly yourselves excitedly cried
That if I serve one I
Must lack the other.

   And yet I know, it is my
Own fault! For too greatly,
O Christ, I'm attached to you,
Although Heracles' brother.
And boldly I confess,
You are the brother also of Evius
Who to his chariot harnessed
The tigers and right down
As far as the Indus
Commanding joyful service,
First planted the vineyard and tamed
The fierceness and rage of the peoples.

Es hindert aber eine Schaam
Mich dir zu vergleichen
Die weltlichen Männer. Und freilich weiß
Ich, der dich zeugte, dein Vater,
Derselbe der,

Denn nimmer herrscht er allein.

Es hänget aber an Einem
Die Liebe. Diesesmal
Ist nemlich vom eigenen Herzen
Zu sehr gegangen der Gesang,
Gut machen will ich den Fehl
Wenn ich noch andere singe.
Nie treff ich, wie ich wünsche,
Das Maas. Ein Gott weiß aber
Wenn kommet, was ich wünsche das Beste.

And yet a shame forbids me
To associate with you
The worldly men. And indeed I know
That he who begot you, your Father,
The same who

For never he reigns alone.

To One alone, however,
Love clings. For this time too much
From my own heart the song
Has come; if other songs follow
I'll make amends for the fault.
Much though I wish to, never
I strike the right measure. But
A god knows when it comes, what I wish for, the best.

Denn wie der Meister
Gewandelt auf Erden
Ein gefangener Aar,

   Und viele, die
Ihn sahen, fürchteten sich,
Dieweil sein Äußerstes that
Der Vater und sein Bestes unter
Den Menschen wirkete wirklich,
Und sehr betrübt war auch
Der Sohn so lange, bis er
Gen Himmel fuhr in den Lüften,
Dem gleich ist gefangen die Seele der Helden.
Die Dichter müssen auch
Die geistigen weltlich seyn.

For as the Master
Once moved on earth,
A captive eagle,

    And many who
Looked on him were afraid,
While the Father did
His utmost, effectively bringing
The best to hear upon men,
And sorely troubled in mind
The Son was also until
To Heaven he rose in the winds,
So too, the souls of the heroes are captive.
The poets, and those no less who
Are spiritual, must be worldly.

Der Einzige

Zweite Fassung

Was ist es, das
An die alten seeligen Küsten
Mich fesselt, daß ich mehr noch
Sie liebe, als mein Vaterland?
Denn wie in himmlischer
Gefangenschaft gebükt, in flammender Luft
Dort bin ich, wo, wie Steine sagen Apollo gieng
In Königsgestalt,
Und zu unschuldigen Jünglingen sich
Herablies Zevs und Söhn in heiliger Art
Und Töchter zeugte
Der Hohe unter den Menschen?

Der hohen Gedanken
Sind nemlich viel
Entsprungen des Vaters Haupt
Und große Seelen
Von ihm zu Menschen gekommen.
Gehöret hab' ich.
Von Elis und Olympia, bin
Gestanden oben auf dem Parnaß,
Und über Bergen des Isthmus,
Und drüben auch
Bei Smyrna und hinab
Bei Ephesos bin ich gegangen;

Viel hab' ich schönes gesehn,
Und gesungen Gottes Bild
Hab' ich, das lebet unter

The Only One

Second Version

    What is it that
To the ancient, the happy shores
Binds me, so that I love them
Still more than my own homeland?
For as though in heavenly
Captivity cowering, in flaming air
I am where the stones tell Apollo walked
In the guise of a king
And Zeus condescended
To innocent youths, and sons in a holy fashion
Begot, and daughters,
The exalted, amid mankind.

    For many a thought
Sublime and great
Has sprung from the Father's head
And lofty souls
Come down from him to mortals.
Of Elis and
Olympia I have heard, and stood
High up on the top of Parnassus
And up above hills of the Isthmus
And over there
By Smyrna too, and down
By Ephesus I have walked;

    Have looked upon much that is lovely
And sung the image of God
As here among human kind

Den Menschen, denn sehr dem Raum gleich ist
Das Himmlische reichlich in
Der Jugend zählbar, aber dennoch
O du der Sterne Leben und all
Ihr tapfern Söhne des Lebens
Noch Einen such ich, den
Ich liebe unter euch,
Wo ihr den lezten eures Geschlechts
Des Haußes Kleinod mir
Dem fremden Gaste verberget.

    Mein Meister und Herr!
O du, mein Lehrer!
Was bist du ferne
Geblieben? und da
Ich fragte unter den Alten,
Die Helden und
Die Götter, warum bliebest
Du aus? Und jezt ist voll
Von Trauern meine Seele
Als eifertet, ihr Himmlischen, selbst
Daß, dien' ich einem, mir
Das andere fehlet.

    Ich weiß es aber, eigene Schuld ists! Denn zu sehr
O Christus! häng' ich an dir, wiewohl Herakles Bruder
Und kühn bekenn' ich, du bist Bruder auch des Eviers, der
Die Todeslust der Völker aufhält und zerreißet den Fallstrik,
Fein sehen die Menschen, daß sie
Nicht gehn den Weg des Todes und hüten das Maas, daß einer
Etwas für sich ist, den Augenblik
Das Geschik der großen Zeit auch
Ihr Feuer fürchtend, treffen sie, und wo
Des Wegs ein anderes geht, da sehen sie

It lives, for very much like space
In youth the Heavenly in plenty
Is numerable, and yet, and yet
O you the life of the stars and all
You valiant sons of life,
One other I look for whom
Within your ranks I love,
Where hidden from the alien guest, from me
You keep the last of your kind,
The treasured gem of the house.

    My Master and Lord!
O you, my teacher,
Why did you keep
Away? And when
I asked among the ancients
The heroes and
The gods, why were you
Not there? And now my soul
Is full of sadness as though
You Heavenly yourselves excitedly cried
That if I serve one I
Must lack the other.

    And yet I know, it is my own fault. For too greatly
O Christ, I'm attached to you, although Heracles' brother,
And boldly I confess, you are the brother also of Evius, who
Restrains the deathwish of the peoples and breaks up the snare,
Well men can see now, so that
They do not go the way of death and keep the measure, so that
A man shall be something in himself and fear
The moment, the destiny of great eras and
Their fires no less, they strike, and where
Another goes that way, they also see

Auch, wo ein Geschik sei, machen aber
Das sicher, Menschen gleichend oder Gesezen.

Es entbrennet aber sein Zorn; daß nemlich
Das Zeichen die Erde berührt, allmälich
Aus Augen gekommen, als an einer Leiter.
Dißmal. Eigenwillig sonst, unmäßig
Gränzlos, daß der Menschen Hand
Anficht das Lebende, mehr auch, als sich schiket
Für einen Halbgott, heiliggeseztes übergeht
Der Entwurf. Seit nemlich böser Geist sich
Bemächtiget des glüklichen Altertums, unendlich,
Langher währt Eines, gesangsfeind, klanglos, das
In Maasen vergeht, des Sinnes gewaltsames. Ungebundenes aber
Hasset Gott. Fürbittend aber

Hält ihn der Tag von dieser Zeit, stillschaffend,
Des Weges gehend, die Blüthe der Jahre.
Und Kriegsgetön, und Geschichte der Helden unterhält hartnäkig
[Geschik,
Die Sonne Christi, Gärten der Büßenden, und
Der Pilgrime Wandern und der Völker ihn, und des Wächters
Gesang und die Schrift
Des Barden oder Afrikaners. Ruhmloser auch
Geschik hält ihn, die an den Tag
Jezt erst recht kommen, das sind väterliche Fürsten. Denn
viel ist der Stand
Gottgleicher, denn sonst. Denn Männern mehr
Gehöret das Licht. Nicht Jünglingen.
Das Vaterland auch. Nemlich frisch

Where there's a destiny, but make
It safe, resembling human beings or laws.

    His fury flares up, however; that is, so that
The sign shall touch the earth, gradually
Released from eyes, as though by a ladder.
This time. Wilful at other times, immoderately
Boundless, so that the hands of men
Impugn whatever is living, more than is fitting for
A demigod, the design transgresses beyond
What's divinely ordained. For since evil spirit
Has taken possession of happy antiquity, unendingly
Long now one power has prevailed, hostile to song, without
                                [resonance,
That within measures transgresses the violence of the mind. But God
                                  [hates
The unbound. Yet interceding

    The day of this age holds him back, creating in silence,
Proceeding on its way, the blossom of the years.
And uproar of war and history of heroes holds him,
                        stiff-necked destiny,
The sun of Christ, gardens of the penitent, and
The wandering of pilgrims and of the peoples, and the song
Of the watchman and the writings
Of the bard or the African. And the destiny
Of those unfamous holds him, who only now
Are really having their day, paternal princes, that is. For
                       now that rank
Is much more godlike than before. For more to men
Now light belongs, not to youths.
Our homeland also. For fresh

Noch unerschöpfet und voll mit Loken.
Der Vater der Erde freuet nemlich sich deß
Auch, daß Kinder sind, so bleibet eine Gewißheit
Des Guten. So auch freuet
Das ihn, daß eines bleibet.
Auch einige sind, gerettet, als
Auf schönen Inseln. Gelehrt sind die.
Versuchungen sind nemlich
Gränzlos an die gegangen.
Zahllose gefallen. Also gieng es, als
Der Erde Vater bereitet ständiges
In Stürmen der Zeit. Ist aber geendet.

Still unexhausted and full of curls.
For the Father of Earth is glad of this too,
That there are children, so that a certainty
Of goodness remains. So too
He is glad that one remains.
And some there are, saved, as though
On beautiful islands. Learnèd are these,
For they have been subject to
Temptations without end.
Countless fallen. So it went when
The Father of Earth prepared what is constant
In storms of the age. But that is ended.

Patmos

DEM LANDGRAFEN VON HOMBURG

    Nah ist
Und schwer zu fassen der Gott.
Wo aber Gefahr ist, wächst
Das Rettende auch.
Im Finstern wohnen
Die Adler und furchtlos gehn
Die Söhne der Alpen über den Abgrund weg
Auf leichtgebaueten Brüken.
Drum, da gehäuft sind rings
Die Gipfel der Zeit, und die Liebsten
Nah wohnen, ermattend auf
Getrenntesten Bergen,
So gieb unschuldig Wasser,
O Fittige gieb uns, treuesten Sinns
Hinüberzugehn und wiederzukehren.

    So sprach ich, da entführte
Mich schneller, denn ich vermuthet
Und weit, wohin ich nimmer
Zu kommen gedacht, ein Genius mich
Vom eigenen Hauß'. Es dämmerten
Im Zwielicht, da ich gieng
Der schattige Wald
Und die sehnsüchtigen Bäche
Der Heimath; nimmer kannt' ich die Länder;
Doch bald, in frischem Glanze,
Geheimnißvoll
Im goldenen Rauche, blühte
Schnellaufgewachsen,

Patmos

FOR THE LANDGRAVE OF HOMBURG

    Near is
And difficult to grasp, the God.
But where danger threatens
That which saves from it also grows.
In gloomy places dwell
The eagles, and fearless over
The chasm walk the sons of the Alps
On bridges lightly built.
Therefore, since round about
Are heaped the summits of Time
And the most loved live near, growing faint
On mountains most separate,
Give us innocent water,
O pinions give us, with minds most faithful
To cross over and to return.

    So I spoke, when more swiftly
Than ever I had expected,
And far as I never thought
I should come, a Genius carried me
From my own house. There glimmered
In twilight, as I went,
The shadowy wood
And the yearning streams of
My homeland; no longer I knew those regions;
But soon, in a radiance fresh,
Mysteriously,
In the golden haze,
Quickly grown up,

Mit Schritten der Sonne,
Mit tausend Gipfeln duftend,

    Mir Asia auf, und geblendet sucht'
Ich eines, das ich kennete, denn ungewohnt
War ich der breiten Gassen, wo herab
Vom Tmolus fährt
Der goldgeschmükte Pactol
Und Taurus stehet und Messogis,
Und voll von Blumen der Garten,
Ein stilles Feuer; aber im Lichte
Blüht hoch der silberne Schnee;
Und Zeug unsterblichen Lebens
An unzugangbaren Wänden
Uralt der Epheu wächst und getragen sind
Von lebenden Säulen, Cedern und Lorbeern
Die feierlichen,
Die göttlichgebauten Palläste.

    Es rauschen aber um Asias Thore
Hinziehend da und dort
In ungewisser Meeresebene
Der schattenlosen Straßen genug,
Doch kennt die Inseln der Schiffer.
Und da ich hörte
Der nahegelegenen eine
Sei Patmos,
Verlangte mich sehr,
Dort einzukehren und dort
Der dunkeln Grotte zu nahn.
Denn nicht, wie Cypros,
Die quellenreiche, oder
Der anderen eine
Wohnt herrlich Patmos,

With strides of the sun,
And fragrant with a thousand peaks,

    Now Asia burst into flower for me, and dazzled
I looked for one thing there I might know, being unaccustomed
To those wide streets where down
From Tmolus drives
The golden-bedded Pactolus,
And Taurus stands, and Messogis,
And full of flowers the garden,
A quiet fire; but in the light, high up
There blossoms the silver snow
And, witness to life immortal,
On inaccessible walls
Pristine the ivy grows, and supported
On living pillars, cedars and laurels,
There stand the festive,
The palaces built by gods.

    But around Asia's gates there murmur,
Extending this way and that
In the uncertain plain of the sea,
Shadowless roads enough;
Yet the boatman knows the islands.
And when I heard
That of the near islands one
Was Patmos,
I greatly desired
There to be lodged, and there
To approach the dark grotto.
For not like Cyprus,
The rich in well-springs,
Nor any of the others
Magnificently does Patmos dwell,

Gastfreundlich aber ist
Im ärmeren Hauße
Sie dennoch
Und wenn vom Schiffbruch oder klagend
Um die Heimath oder
Den abgeschiedenen Freund
Ihr nahet einer
Der Fremden, hört sie es gern, und ihre Kinder
Die Stimmen des heißen Hains,
Und wo der Sand fällt, und sich spaltet
Des Feldes Fläche, die Laute
Sie hören ihn und liebend tönt
Es wieder von den Klagen des Manns. So pflegte
Sie einst des gottgeliebten,
Des Sehers, der in seeliger Jugend war

    Gegangen mit
Dem Sohne des Höchsten, unzertrennlich, denn
Es liebte der Gewittertragende die Einfalt
Des Jüngers und es sahe der achtsame Mann
Das Angesicht des Gottes genau,
Da, beim Geheimnisse des Weinstoks, sie
Zusammensaßen, zu der Stunde des Gastmals,
Und in der großen Seele, ruhigahnend den Tod
Aussprach der Herr und die lezte Liebe, denn nie genug
Hatt' er von Güte zu sagen
Der Worte, damals, und zu erheitern, da
Ers sahe, das Zürnen der Welt.
Denn alles ist gut. Drauf starb er. Vieles wäre
Zu sagen davon. Und es sahn ihn, wie er siegend blikte
Den Freudigsten die Freunde noch zulezt,

    Doch trauerten sie, da nun
Es Abend worden, erstaunt,

    Hospitable nonetheless
In her poorer house
She is,
And when, after shipwreck or lamenting for
His homeland or else for
The friend departed from him,
A stranger draws near
To her, she is glad to hear it, and her children,
The voices of the hot noonday copse,
And where the sand falls, and the field's
Flat surface cracks, the sounds –
These hear him, and lovingly all is loud
With the man's re-echoed lament. So once
She tended the God-beloved,
The seer who in blessèd youth

    Had walked with
The son of the Highest, inseparable, for
The bearer of thunder loved the disciple's
Ingenuousness, and the attentive man
Saw the face of the God exactly
When over the mystery of the vine
They sat together at the hour of the communal meal
And in his great soul, calmly foreknowing,
The Lord pronounced death and the ultimate love, for never
He could find words enough
To say about kindness, then, and to soothe, when
He saw it, the wrath of the world.
For all things are good. After that he died. Much could
Be said of it. And the friends at the very last
Saw him, the gladdest, looking up triumphant,

    Yet they were sad, now that
The evening had come, amazed,

Denn Großentschiedenes hatten in der Seele
Die Männer, aber sie liebten unter der Sonne
Das Leben und lassen wollten sie nicht
Vom Angesichte des Herrn
Und der Heimath. Eingetrieben war,
Wie Feuer im Eisen, das, und ihnen gieng
Zur Seite der Schatte des Lieben.
Drum sandt' er ihnen
Den Geist, und freilich bebte
Das Haus und die Wetter Gottes rollten
Ferndonnernd über
Die ahnenden Häupter, da, schwersinnend
Versammelt waren die Todeshelden,

 Izt, da er scheidend
Noch einmal ihnen erschien.
Denn izt erlosch der Sonne Tag
Der Königliche und zerbrach
Den geradestralenden,
Den Zepter, göttlichleidend, von selbst,
Denn wiederkommen sollt es
Zu rechter Zeit. Nicht wär es gut
Gewesen, später, und schroffabbrechend, untreu,
Der Menschen Werk, und Freude war es
Von nun an,
Zu wohnen in liebender Nacht, und bewahren
In einfältigen Augen, unverwandt
Abgründe der Weisheit. Und es grünen
Tief an den Bergen auch lebendige Bilder,

 Doch furchtbar ist, wie da und dort
Unendlich hin zerstreut das Lebende Gott.
Denn schon das Angesicht
Der theuern Freunde zu lassen

For the souls of these men contained
Things greatly predetermined, but under the sun they loved
This life and were loath to part from
The visible face of the Lord
And their homeland. Driven in,
Like fire into iron, was this, and beside them
The loved one's shadow walked.
Therefore he sent them
The Spirit, and mightily trembled
The house, and God's thunder-storms rolled
Distantly rumbling above
Their heads foreknowledge bowed, when deep in thought
Assembled were the heroes of death,

    Now that, departing,
Once more he appeared to them.
For now the kingly one extinguished
The day of the sun and broke
The straightly beaming, the sceptre,
Divinely suffering, yet of his own free will,
For it was to come back when
The time was due. To have done so later
Would not have been good, and the work of men
Abruptly broken off, disloyally, and from now on
A joy it was
To dwell in loving Night and in fixed,
Ingenuous eyes to preserve
Abysses of wisdom. And low down at
The foot of mountains, too, will living images thrive,

    Yet dreadful it is how here and there
Unendingly God disperses whatever lives.
For only to part from the sight
Of their dear friends

Und fernhin über die Berge zu gehn
Allein, wo zweifach
Erkannt, einstimmig
War himmlischer Geist; und nicht geweissagt war es, sondern
Die Loken ergriff es, gegenwärtig,
Wenn ihnen plözlich
Ferneilend zurük blikte
Der Gott und schwörend,
Damit er halte, wie an Seilen golden
Gebunden hinfort
Das Böse nennend, sie die Hände sich reichten –

    Wenn aber stirbt alsdenn
An dem am meisten
Die Schönheit hieng, daß an der Gestalt
Ein Wunder war und die Himmlischen gedeutet
Auf ihn, und wenn, ein Räthsel ewig füreinander
Sie sich nicht fassen können
Einander, die zusammenlebten
Im Gedächtniß, und nicht den Sand nur oder
Die Weiden es hinwegnimmt und die Tempel
Ergreifft, wenn die Ehre
Des Halbgotts und der Seinen
Verweht und selber sein Angesicht
Der Höchste wendet
Darob, daß nirgend ein
Unsterbliches mehr am Himmel zu sehn ist oder
Auf grüner Erde, was ist diß?

    Es ist der Wurf des Säemanns, wenn er faßt
Mit der Schaufel den Waizen,
Und wirft, dem Klaren zu, ihn schwingend über dieTenne.
Ihm fällt die Schaale vor den Füßen, aber
Ans Ende kommet das Korn,

And far across the mountains to go
Alone, when doubly
Perceived, heavenly spirit before had been
Unanimous; and not predicted was this,
But seized them by the hair, on the instant,
When suddenly the God
Far off in haste looked back
At them, and vowing,
So that he would stay, from now on goldenly
Bound fast as to ropes,
Calling the evil by name, they linked hands —

    But when thereupon he dies
To whom beauty most adhered, so that
A miracle was wrought in his person and
The Heavenly had pointed at him,
And when, an enigma to one another
For ever, they cannot understand
One another who lived together
Conjoined by remembrance, and not only
The sand or the willows it takes away,
And seizes the temples, when even
The demigod's honour and that of his friends
Is blown away by the wind, and the Highest
Himself averts his face
Because nowhere now
An immortal is to be seen in the skies or
On our green earth, what is this?

    It is the sower's cast when he scoops up
The wheat in his shovel
And throws it, towards clear space, swinging it over the threshing-floor.
The husk falls at his feet, but
The grain reaches its end,

Und nicht ein Übel ists, wenn einiges
Verloren gehet und von der Rede
Verhallet der lebendige Laut,
Denn göttliches Werk auch gleichet dem unsern,
Nicht alles will der Höchste zumal.
Zwar Eisen träget der Schacht,
Und glühende Harze der Aetna,
So hätt' ich Reichtum,
Ein Bild zu bilden, und ähnlich
Zu schaun, wie er gewesen, den Christ,

    Wenn aber einer spornte sich selbst,
Und traurig redend, unterweges, da ich wehrlos wäre
Mich überfiele, daß ich staunt' und von dem Gotte
Das Bild nachahmen möcht' ein Knecht –
Im Zorne sichtbar sah' ich einmal
Des Himmels Herrn, nicht, daß ich seyn sollt etwas, sondern
Zu lernen. Gütig sind sie, ihr Verhaßtestes aber ist,
So lange sie herrschen, das Falsche, und es gilt
Dann Menschliches unter Menschen nicht mehr.
Denn sie nicht walten, es waltet aber
Unsterblicher Schiksaal und es wandelt ihr Werk
Von selbst, und eilend geht es zu Ende.
Wenn nemlich höher gehet himmlischer
Triumphgang, wird genennet, der Sonne gleich
Von Starken der frohlokende Sohn des Höchsten,

    Ein Loosungszeichen, und hier ist der Stab
Des Gesanges, niederwinkend,
Denn nichts ist gemein. Die Todten weket
Er auf, die noch gefangen nicht
Vom Rohen sind. Es warten aber
Der scheuen Augen viele
Zu schauen das Licht. Nicht wollen

And there's no harm if some of it
Is lost, and of the speech
The living sound dies away,
For the work of gods, too, is like our own,
Not all things at once does the Highest intend.
The pit bears iron, though,
And glowing resins Etna,
And so I should have wealth
With which to form an image and see
The Christ as he truly was,

But if someone spurred himself on
And, talking sadly, on the road, when I was
Defenceless, attacked me, so that amazed I tried
To copy the God's own image, I, a servant —
In anger visible once I saw
The Lord of Heaven, not that I should be something, but
To learn. Benign they are, but what they most abhor,
While their reign lasts, is falsehood, and then
What's human no longer counts among human kind.
For they do not govern, the fate
It is of immortals that governs, and their work
Proceeds by its own force and hurrying seeks its end.
For when heavenly triumph goes higher
The jubilant son of the Highest
Is called like the sun by the strong,

A secret token, and here is the wand
Of song, signalling downward,
For nothing is common. The dead
He reawakens whom coarseness has not
Made captive yet. But many timid eyes
Are waiting to see the light.
They are reluctant to flower

Am scharfen Strale sie blühn,
Wiewohl den Muth der goldene Zaum hält.
Wenn aber, als
Von schwellenden Augenbrauen
Der Welt vergessen
Stillleuchtende Kraft aus heiliger Schrift fällt, mögen
Der Gnade sich freuend, sie
Am stillen Blike sich üben.

    Und wenn die Himmlischen jezt
So, wie ich glaube, mich lieben
Wie viel mehr Dich,
Denn Eines weiß ich,
Daß nemlich der Wille
Des ewigen Vaters viel
Dir gilt. Still ist sein Zeichen
Am donnernden Himmel. Und Einer stehet darunter
Sein Leben lang. Denn noch lebt Christus.
Es sind aber die Helden, seine Söhne
Gekommen all und heilige Schriften
Von ihm und den Bliz erklären
Die Thaten der Erde bis izt,
Ein Wettlauf unaufhaltsam. Er ist aber dabei. Denn seine Werke sind
Ihm alle bewußt von jeher.

    Zu lang, zu lang schon ist
Die Ebre der Himmlischen unsichtbar.
Denn fast die Finger müssen sie
Uns führen und schmählich
Entreißt das Herz uns eine Gewalt.
Denn Opfer will der Himmlischen jedes,
Wenn aber eines versäumt ward,
Nie hat es Gutes gebracht.

Beneath the searing beam, though it is
The golden bridle that curbs their courage.
But when, as if
By swelling eyebrows made
Oblivious of the world
A quietly shining strength falls from holy scripture,
Rejoicing in grace, they
May practise upon the quiet gaze.

    And if the Heavenly now
Love me as I believe,
How much more you
They surely love,
For one thing I know:
The eternal Father's will
Means much to you. Now silent is
His sign on thundering heaven. And there is one who stands
Beneath it his whole life long. For Christ lives yet.
But all the heroes, his sons,
Have come, and holy scriptures
About him, and lightning is explained by
The deeds of the world until now,
A race that cannot be stopped. But he is present in it. For known
To him are all his works from the beginning.

    Too long, too long now
The honour of the Heavenly has been invisible.
For almost they must guide
Our fingers, and shamefully
A power is wresting our hearts from us.
For every one of the Heavenly wants sacrifices, and
When one of these was omitted
No good ever came of it.

Wir haben gedienet der Mutter Erd'
Und haben jüngst dem Sonnenlichte gedient,
Unwissend, der Vater aber liebt,
Der über allen waltet,
Am meisten, daß gepfleget werde
Der veste Buchstab, und bestehendes gut
Gedeutet. Dem folgt deutscher Gesang.

We have served Mother Earth
And lately have served the sunlight,
Unwittingly, but what the Father
Who reigns over all loves most
Is that the solid letter
Be given scrupulous care, and the existing
Be well interpreted. This German song observes.

Patmos

DEM LANDGRAFEN VON HOMBURG

Bruchstücke der späteren Fassung

Voll Güt' ist; keiner aber fasset
Allein Gott.
Wo aber Gefahr ist, wächst
Das Rettende auch.
Im Finstern wohnen
Die Adler, und furchtlos gehn
Die Söhne der Alpen über den Abgrund weg
Auf leichtgebaueten Brüken.
Drum, da gehäuft sind rings, um Klarheit,
Die Gipfel der Zeit,
Und die Liebsten nahe wohnen, ermattend auf
Getrenntesten Bergen,
So gieb unschuldig Wasser,
O Fittige gieb uns, treuesten Sinns
Hinüberzugehn und wiederzukehren.

So sprach ich, da entführte
Mich künstlicher, denn ich vermuthet
Und weit, wohin ich nimmer
Zu kommen gedacht, ein Genius mich
Vom eigenen Hauß'. Es kleideten sich
Im Zwielicht, Menschen ähnlich, da ich gieng
Der schattige Wald
Und die sehnsüchtigen Bäche
Der Heimath; nimmer kannt' ich die Länder.
Viel aber mitgelitten haben wir, viel Maale. So
In frischem Glanze, geheimnißvoll,

Patmos

FOR THE LANDGRAVE OF HOMBURG

Fragments of the Later Version

   Most kind is; but no one by himself
Can grasp God.
But where danger threatens
That which saves from it also grows.
In gloomy places dwell
The eagles, and fearless over
The chasm walk the sons of the Alps
On bridges lightly built.
Therefore, since round about are heaped, around clearness,
The summits of Time,
And the most loved live near, growing faint
On mountains most separate,
Give us innocent water,
O pinions give us, with minds most faithful
To cross over and to return.

   So I spoke when more ingeniously
Than ever I had expected
And far as I never thought
I should come, a Genius carried me
From my own house. There clothed themselves,
Like men, in the twilight, as I went,
The shadowy wood
And the yearning streams of
My homeland; no longer I knew those regions.
Yet much we have suffered with them, many times.
So, in a radiance fresh, mysteriously,

In goldenem Rauche blühte
Schnellaufgewachsen,
Mit Schritten der Sonne,
Von tausend Tischen duftend, jezt,

    Mir Asia auf und geblendet ganz
Sucht' eins ich, das ich kennete, denn ungewohnt
War ich der breiten Gassen, wo herab
Vom Tmolus fährt
Der goldgeschmükte Pactol
Und Taurus stehet und Messogis,
Und schläfrig fast von Blumen der Garten,

    O Insel des Lichts!
Denn wenn erloschen ist der Ruhm die Augenlust und gehalten
                                 [nicht mehr
Von Menschen, schattenlos, die Pfade zweifeln und die Bäume,
Und Reiche, das Jugendland der Augen sind vergangen
Athletischer,
Im Ruin,   und Unschuld angeborne
Zerrissen ist. Von Gott aus nemlich kommt gediegen
Und gehet das Gewissen, Offenbarung, die Hand des Herrn
Reich winkt aus richtendem Himmel, dann und eine Zeit ist
Untheilbar Gesez, und Amt, und die Hände
Zu erheben, das, und das Niederfallen
Böser Gedanken, los, zu ordnen. Grausam nemlich hasset
Allwissende Stirnen Gott. Rein aber bestand

In the golden haze
Quickly grown up,
With strides of the sun,
And fragrant with a thousand tables,

   Now, Asia burst into flower for me, and wholly dazzled
I looked for one thing there I might know, being unaccustomed
To those wide streets where down
From Tmolus drives
The golden-bedded Pactolus,
And Taurus stands, and Messogis,
And drowsy almost with flowers the garden,

   O island of light!
For when extinguished is fame, the delight in seeing, and no longer
                                    [maintained
By human kind, shadowless, the paths succumb to doubt, and the trees,
And kingdoms, the youthful land of eyes, are perished,
More athletic
In ruin,   and inborn innocence
Is torn to shreds. For from God unalloyed
Does conscience come and go, revelation, the hand of the Lord
Richly beckons from judging Heaven, then and for a time there
Is indivisible law, and office, and hands to
Be raised, both this and to control
The falling of evil thoughts, loose. For cruelly
God hates omniscient brows. But pure

Auf ungebundnem Boden Johannes. Wenn einer
Für irrdisches prophetisches Wort erklärt

Vom Jordan und von Nazareth
Und fern vom See, an Capernaum,
Und Galiläa die Lüfte, und von Cana.
Eine Weile bleib ich, sprach er. Also mit Tropfen
Stillt er das Seufzen des Lichts, das durstigem Wild
War ähnlich in den Tagen, als um Syrien
Jammert der getödteten Kindlein heimatliche
Anmuth im Sterben, und das Haupt
Des Täuffers gepflükt, war unverwelklicher Schrift gleich
Sichtbar auf weilender Schüssel. Wie Feuer
Sind Stimmen Gottes. Schwer ists aber
Im Großen zu behalten das Große.
Nicht eine Waide. Daß einer
Bleibet im Anfang. Jezt aber
Geht dieses wieder, wie sonst.

Johannes. Christus. Diesen möcht'
Ich singen, gleich dem Herkules, oder
Der Insel, welche vestgehalten und gerettet, erfrischend
Die benachbarte mit kühlen Meereswassern aus der Wüste
Der Fluth, der weiten, Peleus. Das geht aber
Nicht. Anders ists ein Schiksaal. Wundervoller.
Reicher, zu singen. Unabsehlich
Seit jenem die Fabel. Und jezt

On a site unbound did John remain. When someone
Declares that a prophetic word is earthly

From Jordan and from Nazareth
And far from the lake, at Capernaum,
And Galilee the breezes, and from Canaan.
A little while I shall stay, he said. So with drops
He quenched the sighing of the light that was
Like thirsty wild beasts in those days, when for Syria
Lamented the native grace in dying of
Small children killed, and the Baptist's head,
Just picked, was visible like an unwithering script
On the abiding platter. Like fire
Are voices of God. Yet it is hard
In great events to preserve what is great.
Not a pasture. So that one shall
Abide in the beginning. But now
This goes on again, as before.

John. Christ. This latter now I wish
To sing, like Hercules or the island which
Was held and saved, refreshing
The neighbouring one with cool sea waters drawn
From ocean's desert, the vast, Peleus. But that's
Impossible. Differently it is a fate. More marvellous.
More rich to sing. Immeasurable
The fable ever since. And now

Möcht' ich die Fahrt der Edelleute nach
Jerusalem, und das Leiden irrend in Canossa,
Und den Heinrich singen. Daß aber
Der Muth nicht selber mich aussezze. Begreiffen müssen
Diß wir zuvor. Wie Morgenluft sind nemlich die Nahmen
Seit Christus. Werden Träume. Fallen, wie Irrtum
Auf das Herz und tödtend, wenn nicht einer

    Erwäget, was sie sind und begreift.
Es sah aber der achtsame Mann
Das Angesicht des Gottes,
Damals, da, beim Geheimnisse des Weinstoks sie
Zusammensaßen, zu der Stunde des Gastmals,
Und in der großen Seele, wohlauswählend, den Tod
Aussprach der Herr, und die lezte Liebe, denn nie genug
Hatt er, von Güte, zu sagen
Der Worte, damals, und zu bejahn bejahendes. Aber sein Licht war
Tod. Denn karg ist das Zürnen der Welt.
Das aber erkannt' er. Alles ist gut. Drauf starb er.
Es sahen aber, gebükt, deß ungeachtet, vor Gott die Gestalt
Des Verläugnenden, wie wenn
Ein Jahrhundert sich biegt, nachdenklich, in der Freude der Wahrheit
Noch zulezt die Freunde,

    Doch trauerten sie, da nun
Es Abend worden. Nemlich rein
Zu seyn, ist Geschik, ein Leben, das ein Herz hat,
Vor solchem Angesicht', und dauert über die Hälfte.
Zu meiden aber ist viel. Zu viel aber
Der Liebe, wo Anbetung ist,
Ist gefahrreich, triffet am meisten. Jene wollten aber
Vom Angesichte des Herrn
Nicht lassen und der Heimath. Eingeboren

I wish to sing the journey of the nobles to
Jerusalem, and anguish wandering at Canossa,
And Heinrich himself. If only
My very courage does not expose me. This first we
Must understand. For like morning air are the names
Since Christ. Become dreams. Fall on the heart
Like error, and killing, if one does not

    Consider what they are and understand.
But the attentive man saw
The face of God,
At that time, when over the mystery of the vine
They sat together, at the hour of the communal meal,
And in his great soul, carefully choosing, the Lord
Pronounced death, and the ultimate love, for never
He could find words enough
To say about kindness, then, and to affirm the affirmative. But his
                                      [light was
Death. For niggardly is the wrath of the world.
Yet this he recognized. All is good. Thereupon he died.
But nevertheless, bowed down, the friends at the very last
Before God saw the denier's presence, as when
A century bends, thoughtfully, in
The joy of truth,

    Yet they were sad, now that
The evening had come. For to
Be pure is a skill, a life that has a heart, in
The presence of such a face, and outlasts the middle.
But much is to be avoided. Too much
Of love, though, where there is idolatry,
Is dangerous, strikes home most. But those men were loath
To part from the face of the Lord
And from their homeland. Inborn

Wie Feuer war in dem Eisen das, und ihnen
Zur Seite gieng, wie eine Seuche, der Schatte des Lieben.
Drum sandt er ihnen
Den Geist, und freilich bebte
Das Haus und die Wetter Gottes rollten
Ferndonnernd, Männer schaffend, wie wenn Drachenzähne,
                                  prächtigen Schiksaals,

Like fire in iron was this, and beside them
Walked, like a plague, the loved one's shadow.
Therefore he sent them
The Spirit, and mightily trembled
The house and God's thunder-storms rolled
Distantly rumbling, creating men, as when dragons' teeth,
                                        of glorious fate,

Andenken

Der Nordost wehet,
Der liebste unter den Winden
Mir, weil er feurigen Geist
Und gute Fahrt verheißet den Schiffern.
Geh aber nun und grüße
Die schöne Garonne,
Und die Gärten von Bourdeaux
Dort, wo am scharfen Ufer
Hingehet der Steg und in den Strom
Tief fällt der Bach, darüber aber
Hinschauet ein edel Paar
Von Eichen und Silberpappeln;

Noch denket das mir wohl und wie
Die breiten Gipfel neiget
Der Ulmwald, über die Mühl',
Im Hofe aber wächset ein Feigenbaum.
An Feiertagen gehn
Die braunen Frauen daselbst
Auf seidnen Boden,
Zur Märzenzeit,
Wenn gleich ist Nacht und Tag,
Und über langsamen Stegen,
Von goldenen Träumen schwer,
Einwiegende Lüfte ziehen.

Es reiche aber,
Des dunkeln Lichtes voll,
Mir einer den duftenden Becher,
Damit ich ruhen möge; denn süß

Remembrance

The north-easterly blows,
Of winds the dearest to me
Because a fiery spirit
And happy voyage it promises mariners.
But go now, go and greet
The beautiful Garonne
And the gardens of Bordeaux
To where on the rugged bank
The path runs and into the river
Deep falls the brook, but above them
A noble pair of oaks
And white poplars looks out;

Still well I remember this, and how
The elm wood with its great leafy tops
Inclines, towards the mill,
But in the courtyard a fig tree grows.
On holidays there too
The brown women walk
On silken ground,
In the month of March,
When night and day are equal
And over slow footpaths,
Heavy with golden dreams,
Lulling breezes drift.

But someone pass me
The fragrant cup
Full of the dark light,
So that I may rest now; for sweet

Wär' unter Schatten der Schlummer.
Nicht ist es gut,
Seellos von sterblichen
Gedanken zu seyn. Doch gut
Ist ein Gespräch und zu sagen
Des Herzens Meinung, zu hören viel
Von Tagen der Lieb',
Und Thaten, welche geschehen.

    Wo aber sind die Freunde? Bellarmin
Mit dem Gefährten? Mancher
Trägt Scheue, an die Quelle zu gehn;
Es beginnet nemlich der Reichtum
Im Meere. Sie,
Wie Mahler, bringen zusammen
Das Schöne der Erd' und verschmähn
Den geflügelten Krieg nicht, und
Zu wohnen einsam, jahrlang, unter
Dem entlaubten Mast, wo nicht die Nacht durchglänzen
Die Feiertage der Stadt,
Und Saitenspiel und eingeborener Tanz nicht.

    Nun aber sind zu Indiern
Die Männer gegangen,
Dort an der luftigen Spiz'
An Traubenbergen, wo herab
Die Dordogne kommt,
Und zusammen mit der prächt'gen
Garonne meerbreit
Ausgehet der Strom. Es nehmet aber
Und giebt Gedächtniß die See,
Und die Lieb' auch heftet fleißig die Augen,
Was bleibet aber, stiften die Dichter.

It would be to drowse amid shadows.
It is not good
To be soulless
With mortal thoughts. But good
Is converse, and to speak
The heart's opinion, to hear many tales
About the days of love
And deeds that have occurred.

But where are the friends? Where Bellarmine
And his companion? Many a man
Is shy of going to the source;
For wealth begins in
The sea. And they,
Like painters, bring together
The beautiful things of the earth
And do not disdain winged war, and
To live in solitude for years, beneath die
Defoliate mast, where through the night do not gleam
The city's holidays
Nor music of strings, nor indigenous dancing.

But now to Indians
Those men have gone,
There on the airy peak
On grape-covered hills, where down
The Dordogne comes
And together with the glorious
Garonne as wide as the sea
The current sweeps out. But it is the sea
That takes and gives remembrance,
And love no less keeps eyes attentively fixed,
But what is lasting the poets provide.

Der Ister

Jezt komme, Feuer!
Begierig sind wir
Zu schauen den Tag,
Und wenn die Prüfung
Ist durch die Knie gegangen,
Mag einer spüren das Waldgeschrei.
Wir singen aber vom Indus her
Fernangekommen und
Vom Alpheus, lange haben
Das Schikliche wir gesucht,
Nicht ohne Schwingen mag
Zum Nächsten einer greifen
Geradezu
Und kommen auf die andere Seite.
Hier aber wollen wir bauen.
Denn Ströme machen urbar
Das Land. Wenn nemlich Kräuter wachsen
Und an denselben gehn
Im Sommer zu trinken die Thiere,
So gehn auch Menschen daran.

Man nennet aber diesen den Ister.
Schön wohnt er. Es brennet der Säulen Laub,
Und reget sich. Wild stehn
Sie aufgerichtet, untereinander; darob
Ein zweites Maas, springt vor
Von Felsen das Dach. So wundert
Mich nicht, daß er
Den Herkules zu Gaste geladen,

The Ister

Now come, fire!
We are impatient
To look upon Day,
And when the trial
Has passed through the knees
One may perceive the cries in the wood.
But, as for us, we sing from the Indus,
Arrived from afar, and
From the Alpheus, long we
Have sought what is fitting,
Not without wings may one
Reach out for that which is nearest
Directly
And get to the other side.
But here we wish to build.
For rivers make arable
The land. For when herbs are growing
And to the same in summer
The animals go to drink,
There too will human kind go.

This one, however, is called the Ister.
Beautifully he dwells. The pillars' foliage burns,
And stirs. Wildly they stand
Supporting one another; above,
A second measure, juts out
The roof of rocks. No wonder, therefore,
I say, this river
Invited Hercules,

Fernglänzend, am Olympos drunten,
Da der, sich Schatten zu suchen
Vom heißen Isthmos kam
Denn voll des Muthes waren
Daselbst sie, es bedarf aber, der Geister wegen,
Der Kühlung auch. Darum zog jener lieber
An die Wasserquellen hieher und gelben Ufer,
Hoch duftend oben, und schwarz
Vom Fichtenwald, wo in den Tiefen
Ein Jäger gern lustwandelt
Mittags, und Wachstum hörbar ist
An harzigen Bäumen des Isters,

   Der scheinet aber fast
Rükwärts zu gehen und
Ich mein, er müsse kommen
Von Osten.
Vieles wäre
Zu sagen davon. Und warum hängt er
An den Bergen gerad? Der andre
Der Rhein ist seitwärts
Hinweggegangen. Umsonst nicht gehn
Im Troknen die Ströme. Aber wie? Ein Zeichen braucht es
Nichts anderes, schlecht und recht, damit es Sonn
Und Mond trag' im Gemüth', untrennbar,
Und fortgeh, Tag und Nacht auch, und
Die Himmlischen warm sich fühlen aneinander.
Darum sind jene auch
Die Freude des Höchsten. Denn wie käm er
Herunter? Und wie Hertha grün,
Sind sie die Kinder des Himmels. Aber allzugedultig
Scheint der mir, nicht
Freier, und fast zu spotten. Nemlich wenn

Distantly gleaming, down by Olympus,
When he, to look for shadows,
Came up from the sultry isthmus,
For full of courage they were
In that place, but, because of the spirits,
There's need of coolness too. That is why that hero
Preferred to come here to the well-springs and yellow banks,
Highly fragrant on top, and black
With fir woods, in whose depths
A huntsman loves to amble
At noon, and growth is audible
In resinous trees of the Ister,

   Yet almost this river seems
To travel backwards and
I think it must come from
The East.
Much could
Be said about this. And why does
It cling to the mountains, straight? The other,
The Rhine, has gone away
Sideways. Not for nothing rivers flow
Through dry land. But how? A sign is needed,
Nothing else, plain and honest, so that
Sun and moon it may bear in mind, inseparable,
And go away, day and night no less, and
The Heavenly feel warm one beside the other.
That also is why these are
The joy of the Highest. For how
Would he get down? And like Hertha green
They are the children of Heaven. But all too patient
He seems to me, not
More free, and nearly derisive. For when

Angehen soll der Tag
In der Jugend, wo er zu wachsen
Anfängt, es treibet ein anderer da
Hoch schon die Pracht, und Füllen gleich
In den Zaum knirscht er, und weithin hören
Das Treiben die Lüfte,
Ist der zufrieden;
Es brauchet aber Stiche der Fels
Und Furchen die Erd',
Unwirthbar wär es, ohne Weile;
Was aber jener thuet der Strom,
Weis niemand.

Day is due to begin
In youth, where it starts
To grow, another already there
Drives high the splendour, and like foals
He grinds the bit, and far off the breezes
Can hear the commotion,
If he is contented;
But the rock needs incisions
And the earth needs furrows,
Would be desolate else, unabiding;
Yet what that one does, the river,
Nobody knows.

Mnemosyne

Dritte Fassung

Reif sind, in Feuer getaucht, gekochet
Die Frücht und auf der Erde geprüfet und ein Gesez ist
Daß alles hineingeht, Schlangen gleich,
Prophetisch, träumend auf
Den Hügeln des Himmels. Und vieles
Wie auf den Schultern eine
Last von Scheitern ist
Zu behalten. Aber bös sind
Die Pfade. Nemlich unrecht,
Wie Rosse, gehn die gefangenen
Element' und alten
Geseze der Erd. Und immer
Ins Ungebundene gehet eine Sehnsucht. Vieles aber ist
Zu behalten. Und Noth die Treue.
Vorwärts aber und rükwärts wollen wir
Nicht sehn. Uns wiegen lassen, wie
Auf schwankem Kahne der See.

Wie aber liebes? Sonnenschein
Am Boden sehen wir und trokenen Staub
Und heimatlich die Schatten der Wälder und es blühet
An Dächern der Rauch, bei alter Krone
Der Thürme, friedsam; gut sind nemlich
Hat gegenredend die Seele
Ein Himmlisches verwundet, die Tageszeichen.
Denn Schnee, wie Majenblumen
Das Edelmüthige, wo
Es seie, bedeutend, glänzet auf

Mnemosyne

Third Version

Ripe are, dipped in fire, cooked
The fruits and tried on the earth, and it is law,
Prophetic, that all must enter in
Like serpents, dreaming on
The mounds of heaven. And much
As on the shoulders a
Load of logs must be
Retained. But evil are
The paths, for crookedly
Like horses go the imprisoned
Elements and ancient laws
Of the earth. And always
There is a yearning that seeks the unbound. But much
Must be retained. And loyalty is needed.
Forward, however, and back we will
Not look. Be lulled and rocked as
On a swaying skiff of the sea.

But how, my dear one? On the ground
Sunshine we see and the dry dust
And, a native sight, the shadows of forests, and on roof-tops
There blossoms smoke, near ancient crests
Of the turrets, peaceable; for good indeed
When, contradicting, the soul
Has wounded one of the Heavenly, are the signs of day.
For snow, like lilies of the valley
By indicating where
The noble-minded is, shines brightly

Der grünen Wiese
Der Alpen, hälftig, da, vom Kreuze redend, das
Gesezt ist unterwegs einmal
Gestorbenen, auf hoher Straß
Ein Wandersmann geht zornig,
Fern ahnend mit
Dem andern, aber was ist diß?

    Am Feigenbaum ist mein
Achilles mir gestorben,
Und Ajax liegt
An den Grotten der See,
An Bächen, benachbart dem Skamandros.
An Schläfen Sausen einst, nach
Der unbewegten Salamis steter
Gewohnheit, in der Fremd', ist groß
Ajax gestorben
Patroklos aber in des Königes Harnisch. Und es starben
Noch andere viel. Am Kithäron aber lag
Elevtherä, der Mnemosyne Stadt. Der auch als
Ablegte den Mantel Gott, das abendliche nachher löste
Die Loken. Himmlische nemlich sind
Unwillig, wenn einer nicht die Seele schonend sich
Zusammengenommen, aber er muß doch; dem
Gleich fehlet die Trauer.

On the green meadow
Of the Alps, half melted, where
Discoursing of the cross which once was placed
There on the wayside for the dead,
High up, in anger, distantly divining
A traveller walks
With the other, but what is this?

   Beside the fig tree
My Achilles has died and is lost to me,
And Ajax lies
Beside the grottoes of the sea,
Beside brooks that neighbour Scamandros.
Of a rushing noise in his temples once,
According to the changeless custom of
Unmoved Salamis, in foreign parts
Great Ajax died,
Not so Patroclus, dead in the King's own armour.
And many others died. But by Cithaeron there stood
Eleutherae, Mnemosyne's town. From her also
When God laid down his festive cloak, soon after did
The powers of Evening sever a lock of hair. For the Heavenly, when
Someone has failed to collect his soul, to spare it,
Are angry, for still he must; like him
Here mourning is at fault.

Die Nymphe

Reif sind, in Feuer getaucht, gekochet
Die Frücht und auf der Erde geprüfet
Und ein Gesez, daß alles hineingeht,
Schlangen gleich ist
Prophetisch, träumend auf
Den Hügeln des Himmels. Und viel wie auf den Schultern eine
Last von Scheitern, ist
Zu behalten. Aber bös sind
Die Pfade. Nemlich
Wie Rosse, gehn unrecht die gefangenen
Element' und alten
Geseze der Erd. Und immer ins
Ungebundene gehet eine Sehnsucht.
Vieles aber ist
Zu behalten. Und Noth
Die Treue. Vorwärts aber und rükwärts wollen wir
Nicht sehn. Uns wiegen lassen, wie auf
Schwankem Kahne, auf der See.

Doch allzuscheu nicht, lieber sei
Unschiklich und gehe, mit der Erinnys, fort
Mein Leben. Denn alles fassen muß
Ein Halbgott oder ein Mensch, dem Leiden nach,
Indem er höret, allein, oder selber
Verwandelt wird, fernahnend die Rosse des Herrn, und
Das Horn des Wächters bei Tag
Und schenket das Liebste
Den Unfruchtbaren
Denn nimmer, von nun an

The Nymph

Ripe are, dipped in fire, cooked
The fruit and tried on the earth
And a law that all goes in
Like serpents is
Prophetic, dreaming on
The mounds of Heaven. And much as on the shoulders a
Load of logs is
To be retained. But evil are
The paths. For crookedly
Like horses, wrongly go the imprisoned
Elements and ancient
Laws of the earth. And always into
The unbound a yearning goes.
But much must
Be retained. And loyalty
Is needed. Forward, however, and back
We will not look. Abandon ourselves to be rocked as
In a swaying skiff, on the sea.

But not all too timid, rather be
Unseemly and, with the Erinnyes, rush off,
My life. For all things a demigod
Or a human being must grasp, in the way of affliction,
By hearing, alone, or by being
Transformed in person, foreknowing from afar the horses of the
                                                  [Lord, and
The watchman's bugle by day
And gives away the most loved,
To the fruitless,
For never from now on

Taugt zum Gebrauche das Heilge.
Ein Zeichen sind wir, deutungslos
Schmerzlos sind wir und haben fast
Die Sprache in der Fremde verloren.
Wenn nemlich ein Streit ist über Menschen
Am Himmel, und gewaltigen Schritt
Gestirne gehn, blind ist die Treue dann. Zweifellos
Ist aber Einer. Der

Kann täglich es ändern. Kaum bedarf er
Gesez, wie nemlich es
Bei Menschen bleiben soll und die Schrift tönt und
Es tönet das Blatt. Viel Männer möchten da
Seyn wahrer Sache.
Eichbäume wehn dann neben
Den Birnen. Denn nicht vermögen
Die Himmlischen alles. Nemlich es reichen
Die Sterblichen eh' an den Abgrund.
Also wendet es sich,
Das Echo
Mit diesen. Schön ist
Der Brauttag, bange sind wir aber
Der Ehre wegen. Furchtbar gehet
Es ungestalt, wenn Eines uns
Zu gierig genommen. Lang ist
Die Zeit, es ereignet sich aber
Das Wahre.

Immer, Liebes! gehet
Die Erd', und der Himmel hält. Sonnenschein
Am Boden sehen wir und trokenen Staub
Und tief mit Schatten die Wälder und es blühet
An Dächern der Rauch, bei alter Krone
Der Thürme, friedsam, und es girren

The sacred is good for use.
A cipher we are, no key decodes it,
Painless we are and almost
Have lost our speech in the alien lands.
For when there is a dispute about mortals
Up in Heaven, and planets move
With mighty strides, then loyalty goes blind. But One
Is beyond doubt. He

Daily can change it. Hardly he needs
Laws, that is, how
With mortals it is to remain; and the writ resounds and
The leaf resounds. Many men wish
To be there in the true cause.
Then oaks flutter beside
The pear trees. For the heavenly
Cannot achieve all things. For mortals too
Attain the abyss.
So then it turns,
The echo,
With these. Beautiful is
The wedding day, but we are anxious
On the score of honour. Terribly it goes,
Misshapenly, when One has been
Taken from us too greedily. Long is
Time, but the true thing
Occurs.

Always, dear one, the earth
Moves and the sky holds. Sunshine
We see on the ground and dry dust
And the woods deep with shade and on roofs
There blossoms smoke, by the ancient tops
Of towers, peaceable, and lost

Verloren in der Luft die Lerchen und unter dem Tage waiden
Wohlangeführt die Schaafe des Himmels.
Und Schnee, wie Majenblumen
Das Edelmüthige, wo
Es seie, bedeutend, glänzet mit
Der grünen Wiese
Der Alpen, dort
Vom Kreuze redend, das
Gesezt ist unterwegs einmal
Gestorbenen, geht auf der schroffen Straß'
Ein Wandersmann zornig, mit
Dem andern, aber was ist diß?

Am Feigenbaum ist mein
Achilles mir gestorben,
Und Ajax liegt
An Grotten der See,
An Bächen, benachbart dem Skamandros.
Bei Windessausen, nach
Der heimatlichen Salamis steter
Gewohnheit, in der Fremd', ist groß
Ajax gestorben.
Patroklos aber in des Königes Harnisch, und es starben
Noch andere viel. Mit eigener Hand
Viel traurige, wilden Muths, doch göttlich
Gezwungen, zulezt, die anderen aber
Im Geschike stehend, im Feld. Unwillig nemlich
Sind Himmlische, wenn einer nicht
Die Seele schonend sich
Zusammengenommen, aber er muß doch; dem gleich
Fehlet die Trauer.

In the air skylarks trill and under day
Well led on the sheep of heaven crop.
And snow, like lilies of the valley marking
The noble-minded, where
It is, glistens with
The green meadow
Of the alps; there,
Speaking of the cross that once was set
On his way, for those who died,
On the steep path walks
A travelling man, angry with
The other, but what is this?

Beside the fig tree
My Achilles died and is lost to me,
And Ajax lies
Beside the grottoes of the sea,
Beside brooks that neighbour Skamandros.
In the blast of winds, according
To his native Salamis's constant
Custom, in foreign parts
Great Ajax died,
Not so Patroclos dead in the King's own armour, and
Many others also died. By their own hands
Many sad ones, their courage driven wild, but divinely
Compelled, in the end, but the others
Standing fast in fate, on the field. For the heavenly
Are angry when someone, not sparing
His soul, has failed to collect
Himself, but he must, nonetheless; like him
Here mourning is at fault.

Fragments of Other Hymns
(1800–1805)

Deutscher Gesang

Wenn der Morgen trunken begeisternd heraufgeht
Und der Vogel sein Lied beginnt,
Und Stralen der Strom wirft, und rascher hinab
Die rauhe Bahn geht über den Fels,
Weil ihn die Sonne gewärmet.

Und der
Verlangend in anders Land
Die Jünglinge

Und das Thor erwacht und der Marktplaz,
Und von heiligen Flammen des Heerds
Der röthliche Duft steigt, dann schweigt er allein,
Dann hält er still im Busen das Herz,
Und sinnt in einsamer Halle.

Doch wenn

        dann sizt im tiefen Schatten,
Wenn über dem Haupt die Ulme säuselt,
Am kühlathmenden Bache der deutsche Dichter
Und singt, wenn er des heiligen nüchternen Wassers
Genug getrunken, fernhin lauschend in die Stille,
Den Seelengesang.
Und noch, noch ist er des Geistes zu voll,
Und die reine Seele

Bis zürnend er
Und es glühet ihm die Wange vor Schaam,
Unheilig jeder Laut des Gesangs.

German Song

When drunkenly inspiring the morning rises
And the bird begins his tune,
And the river flashes beams and more quickly takes
Its rough course over the rock,
Because the sun has warmed it.

And the
Longing to go to another land
The youths

And the gate awakens and the market-place,
And from holy flames of the hearth
The reddish odour rises, then he alone is silent,
Then quiet in his bosom he keeps his heart
And ponders in the solitary hall.

But when

then in the deep shade, when
Above his head the elm tree rustles,
By the stream that breathes out coolness the German poet sits
And sings, when of the hallowed sober water
Enough he has drunk, listening far out into silence,
The song of the soul.
And still, still his mind is too full of thought,
And his pure soul

Until in anger he
And his cheeks are flushed with shame,
Unholy every note of his song.

Doch lächeln über des Mannes Einfalt
Die Gestirne, wenn vom Orient her
Weissagend über den Bergen unseres Volks
Sie verweilen
Und wie des Vaters Hand ihm über den Loken geruht,
In Tagen der Kindheit,
So krönet, daß er schaudernd es fühlt
Ein Seegen das Haupt des Sängers,
Wenn dich, der du
Um deiner Schöne willen, bis heute,
Nahmlos geblieben o göttlichster!
O guter Geist des Vaterlands
Sein Wort im Liede dich nennet.

    Yet the planets smile at the man's
Simplicity when, come from the East,
They linger prophesying above
Our people's mountains
And as his father's hand had rested upon his locks
In childhood days,
A blessing, so that he feels a shiver,
Now crowns the singer's head,
When you that for
Your beauty's sake, till today, have been
Kept nameless, O most divine,
Good spirit of our homeland,
When you his word names in song.

Wie Vögel langsam ziehn . . .

Wie Vögel langsam ziehn
Es bliket voraus
Der Fürst und kühl wehn
An die Brust ihm die Begegnisse wenn
Es um ihn schweiget, hoch
In der Luft, reich glänzend aber hinab
Das Gut ihm liegt der Länder, und mit ihm sind
Das erstemal siegforschend die Jungen.
Er aber mäßiget mit
Der Fittige Schlag.

As slowly birds migrate . . .

As slowly birds migrate
He looks ahead,
The prince, and coolly blows
Against his breast all that he meets with when
There's silence round about him, high
Up in the air, but richly shining below him
Lies his estate of regions, and with him, for
The first time seeking victory, are the young.
But with his wingbeats
He moderates.

Wie Meeresküsten . . .

Wie Meeresküsten, wenn zu baun
Anfangen die Himmlischen und herein
Schifft unaufhaltsam, eine Pracht, das Werk
Der Woogen, eins ums andere, und die Erde
Sich rüstet aus, darauf vom Freudigsten eines
Mit guter Stimmung, zu recht es legend also schlägt es
Dem Gesang, mit dem Weingott, vielverheißend dem bedeutenden
Und der Lieblingin
Des Griechenlandes
Der meergeborenen, schiklich blikenden
Das gewaltige Gut ans Ufer.

As on to sea coasts . . .

As on to sea coasts, when to build
The heavenly begin and towards them surges
Quite irresistibly, a splendour, the work
Of the waves, one after another, and Earth
Prepares there one of the utmost joys
In a good mood, lays it out, so into song,
Together with the wine-god, promising much
To him, the significant,
And to the darling
Of Grecian lands,
The sea-born, whose fateful glances are fitting,
Great bounty sweeps to the shore.

Heimath

Und niemand weiß

Indessen laß mich wandeln
Und wilde Beeren pflüken
Zu löschen die Liebe zu dir
An deinen Pfaden, o Erd'

Hier wo – – –
              und Rosendornen
Und süße Linden duften neben
Den Buchen, des Mittags, wenn im falben Kornfeld
Das Wachstum rauscht, an geradem Halm,
Und den Naken die Ähre seitwärts beugt
Dem Herbste gleich, jezt aber unter hohem
Gewölbe der Eichen, da ich sinn
Und aufwärts frage, der Glokenschlag
Mir wohlbekannt
Fernher tönt, goldenklingend, um die Stunde, wenn
Der Vogel wieder wacht. So gehet es wohl.

Home

And no one knows

But meanwhile let me walk
And pick wild berries
To quench my love for you
Upon your paths, O Earth

Here where
          and thorns of roses
And sweet lime trees give out their fragrance
Beside the beeches, at noon, when in the yellowish cornfield
There is a whisper of growth, by the straight stalk,
And the ear inclines its neck to one side
Like autumn, but now beneath
The oaks' high vault, where I ponder
And question heavenward, the stroke of the bell,
Familiar to me,
Rings out from afar, with a golden ring, at the hour when
The bird's awake once more. Then all is well.

Wenn nemlich der Rebe Saft . . .

Wenn nemlich der Rebe Saft,
Das milde Gewächs suchet Schatten
Und die Traube wächset unter dem kühlen
Gewölbe der Blätter,
Den Männern eine Stärke,
Wohl aber duftend den Jungfraun,
Und Bienen,
Wenn sie, vom Wohlgeruche
Des Frühlings trunken, der Geist
Der Sonne rühret, irren ihr nach
Die Getriebenen, wenn aber
Ein Stral brennt, kehren sie
Mit Gesumm, vielahnend
        darob
          die Eiche rauschet,

For when the grape-vine's sap . . .

For when the grape-vine's sap,
That gentle plant, looks for shade
And the grape grows beneath the cool
Involutions of the leaves,
To men a source of strength,
But to young women pleasantly fragrant,
And bees
When, drunken with the fragrance
Of Spring, they are stirred
By the spirit of the sun,
Driven on, they fumble for it,
But when a ray burns,
Buzzing, they turn back,
Divining much
            above it
        the oak tree rustles,

Auf falbem Laube . . .

Auf falbem Laube ruhet
Die Traube, des Weines Hoffnung, also ruhet auf der Wange
Der Schatten von dem goldenen Schmuk, der hängt
Am Ohre der Jungfrau.

Und ledig soll ich bleiben
Leicht fanget aber sich
In der Kette, die
Es abgerissen, das Kälblein.

Fleißig

Es liebet aber der Sämann
Zu sehen eine,
Des Tages schlafend über
Dem Strikstrumpf.

Nicht will wohllauten
Der deutsche Mund
Aber lieblich
Am stechenden Bart rauschen
Die Küsse.

On fallow foliage . . .

On fallow foliage rests
The grape, the hope of wine, and so on the cheek rests
The shadow of the gold ornament that hangs
On the young woman's ear.

And I must not get married
Yet easily in the chain
It has torn off, the little
Calf entangles itself.

Busy

But the sower
Loves to see a woman
Fallen asleep in the daytime
Over a half-knitted stocking.

The German mouth
Will yield no euphony
But brushing the prickly beard
Charmingly patter
The kisses.

Was ist der Menschen Leben . . .

Was ist der Menschen Leben   ein Bild der Gottheit.
Wie unter dem Himmel wandeln die Irrdischen alle, sehen
Sie diesen. Lesend aber gleichsam, wie
In einer Schrift, die Unendlichkeit nachahmen und den Reichtum
Menschen. Ist der einfältige Himmel
Denn reich? Wie Blüthen sind ja
Silberne Wolken. Es regnet aber von daher
Der Thau und das Feuchte. Wenn aber
Das Blau ist ausgelöschet, das Einfältige, scheint
Das Matte, das dem Marmelstein gleichet, wie Erz,
Anzeige des Reichtums.

What is the life of men . . .

What is the life of men   an image of the godhead.
As all the earthly move under heaven they see
This heaven. But reading, so to speak,
As though in a script, men imitate
Infinity and riches. Is simple heaven
Rich, then? Surely like blossoms are
Silvery clouds. Yet from there it is that dew and
Moisture rain down. But when
The blueness is extinguished, the simpleness,
Then shines the pale hue that resembles marble, like ore,
An indication of riches.

Was ist Gott? . . .

Was ist Gott? unbekannt, dennoch
Voll Eigenschaften ist das Angesicht
Des Himmels von ihm. Die Blize nemlich
Der Zorn sind eines Gottes. Jemehr ist eins
Unsichtbar,   schiket es sich in Fremdes. Aber der Donner
Der Ruhm ist Gottes. Die Liebe zur Unsterblichkeit
Das Eigentum auch, wie das unsere,
Ist eines Gottes.

What is God? . . .

What is God? Unknown, and yet
Full of qualities is the face
Of heaven with him. For lightning flashes
And wrath are a god's. The more a thing
Is invisible   into foreignness it goes forth. But thunder
Fame are God's. And love of immortality
Possessions, too, such as ours
Are a god's.

An die Madonna

Viel hab' ich dein
Und deines Sohnes wegen
Gelitten, o Madonna,
Seit ich gehöret von ihm
In süßer Jugend;
Denn nicht der Seher allein,
Es stehen unter einem Schiksaal
Die Dienenden auch. Denn weil ich

Und manchen Gesang, den ich
Dem höchsten zu singen, dem Vater
Gesonnen war, den bat
Mir weggezehret die Schwermuth.

Doch Himmlische, doch will ich
Dich feiern und nicht soll einer
Der Rede Schönheit mir
Die heimatliche, vorwerfen,
Dieweil ich allein
Zum Felde gehe, wo wild
Die Lilie wächst, furchtlos,
Zum unzugänglichen,
Uralten Gewölbe
Des Waldes,
    das Abendland,

       und gewaltet über
Den Menschen hat, statt anderer Gottheit sie
Die allvergessende Liebe.

To the Virgin Mary

Much I have suffered
On your account
And on your son's, Our Lady,
Since first in my sweet youth
I heard of him;
For not the seer alone,
But even those who serve
A destiny rules. Because I

And many a song which to
The Highest, the Father, I once was
Disposed to sing, was lost
To me, devoured by sadness.

Yet, heavenly one, yet you
I'll celebrate and let no one
Reproach me with
The beauty of native speech,
Now that alone
I go to the field where wild
The lily grows, fearless,
To the inaccessible
Primordial vault
Of the forest,
    the Occident,

        and over mankind
In place of other deities there reigned
The all-oblivious, Love.

Denn damals sollt es beginnen
Als

Geboren dir im Schoose
Der göttliche Knabe und um ihn
Der Freundin Sohn, Johannes genannt
Vom stummen Vater, der kühne
Dem war gegeben
Der Zunge Gewalt,
Zu deuten

Und die Furcht der Völker und
Die Donner und
Die stürzenden Wasser des Herrn.

Denn gut sind Sazungen, aber
Wie Drachenzähne, schneiden sie
Und tödten das Leben, wenn im Zorne sie schärft
Ein Geringer oder ein König.
Gleichmuth ist aber gegeben
Den Liebsten Gottes. So dann starben jene.
Die Beiden,   so auch sahst
Du göttlichtrauernd in der starken Seele sie sterben.
Und wohnst deswegen

                        und wenn in heiliger Nacht
Der Zukunft einer gedenkt und Sorge für
Die sorglosschlafenden trägt
Die frischaufblühenden Kinder
Kömmst lächelnd du, und fragst, was er, wo du
Die Königin seiest, befürchte.

Denn nimmer vermagst du es

    For then it was to begin
When

Born from within you the boy
Divine and when about him
The son of your friend, named John
By his dumb father, he the bold one
To whom was given
The power of the tongue
To interpret

And the fear of the peoples and
The thunder and
The rushing waters of the Lord.

For good are statutes, but
Like dragons' teeth, they cut
And kill the living, when in anger whetted
By a lowly man or a king.
But equanimity is given
To those most loved by God. So then they died
Those two,   so you also saw
Them die, divinely mourning in your mighty soul.
And for that reason dwell

              and when in holy Night
Of coming ages someone remembers and
Is troubled for their sake who untroubled sleep
The freshly unfolding children,
Then smiling you come and ask him what,
Where you are Queen, he could fear.

For never you could be moved

Die keimenden Tage zu neiden,
Denn lieb ist dirs, von je,
Wenn größer die Söhne sind,
Denn ihre Mutter. Und nimmer gefällt es dir
Wenn rükwärtsblikend
Ein Älteres spottet des Jüngern.
Wer denkt der theuern Väter
Nicht gern und erzählet
Von ihren Thaten,

                         wenn aber Verwegnes geschah,
Und Undankbare haben
Das Ärgerniß   gegeben
Zu gerne blikt
Dann   zum
Und thatenscheu
Unendliche Reue und es haßt das Alte die Kinder.

Darum beschüze
Du Himmlische sie
Die jungen Pflanzen und wenn
Der Nord kömmt oder giftiger Thau weht oder
Zu lange dauert die Dürre
Und wenn sie üppigblühend
Versinken unter der Sense
Der allzuscharfen, gieb erneuertes Wachstum.
Und daß nur niemals nicht
Vielfältig, in schwachem Gezweige
Die Kraft mir vielversuchend
Zerstreue das frische Geschlecht, stark aber sei
Zu wählen aus Vielem das beste.

Nichts ists, das Böse. Das soll
Wie der Adler den Raub

To envy the days that are burgeoning,
But always have been pleased
When the sons are greater
Than their mother. And never you approve
When looking backwards
An older one mocks at the younger.
Who does not like to think
Of the dear fathers and tell
About their deeds,

                  but when reckless deeds were done,
And ungrateful men gave cause
For   annoyance
Too gladly then
Looks   to
And shy of action
Unending remorse and the old will hate the children.

Therefore protect them,
O heavenly one,
Those tender plants, and when
The North Wind comes or poisonous dew wafts
Or too long a drought has lasted
And when in copious flower
They sink beneath the scythe,
The all too sharp, then grant them renewal of growth.
And never, above all,
Attempting much and multifarious
In feeble branches let a power
Disperse the new generation, but strong let it be
Out of many to choose the best.

A mere nothing is Evil. This
As an eagle his prey

Mir Eines begreifen.
Die Andern dabei. Damit sie nicht
Die Amme, die
Den Tag gebieret
Verwirren, falsch anklebend
Der Heimath und der Schwere spottend
Der Mutter ewig sizen
Im Schoose. Denn groß ist
Von dem sie erben den Reichtum.
Der

Vor allem, daß man schone
Der Wildniß göttlichgebaut
Im reinen Geseze, woher
Es haben die Kinder
Des Gotts, lustwandelnd unter
Den Felsen und Haiden purpurn blühn
Und dunkle Quellen
Dir, o Madonna und
Dem Sohne, aber den anderen auch
Damit nicht, als von Knechten,
Mit Gewalt das ihre nehmen
Die Götter.

An den Gränzen aber, wo stehet
Der Knochenberg, so nennet man ihn
Heut, aber in alter Sprache heißet
Er Ossa, Teutoburg ist
Daselbst auch und voll geistigen Wassers
Umher das Land, da
Die Himmlischen all
Sich Tempel

Let someone grasp.
The others no less. So that they
Do
Not perplex the nurse
Who gives birth to day,
Wrongly sticking to home and mocking
At hardship, endlessly sit
On their mother's lap. For great
Is he whose wealth they inherit.
He

Above all, let them spare
The wilderness divinely built
In the spirit of pure law,
Whence the God's children have it,
Pleasantly strolling under
The rocks; and heaths are in purple flower
And dark the sources
For you, our Lady, and
For the son, but for the others also,
Lest as from slaves by force
The gods
Should take what is theirs.

But near the frontiers, where lies
The Knochenberg, so now it is called,
But in ancient speech its name
Was Ossa, Teutoburg also
Is there and full of spiritual waters
The country round about, where
The heavenly all
(Built) themselves temples

Ein Handwerksmann.

Uns aber die wir
Daß

Und zu sehr zu fürchten die Furcht nicht!
Denn du nicht, holde

aber es giebt
Ein finster Geschlecht, das weder einen Halbgott
Gern hört, oder wenn mit Menschen ein Himmlisches oder
In Woogen erscheint, gestaltlos, oder das Angesicht
Des reinen ehrt, des nahen
Allgegenwärtigen Gottes.

Doch wenn unheilige schon
in Menge
und frech

Was kümmern sie dich
O Gesang den Reinen, ich zwar
Ich sterbe, doch du
Gehest andere Bahn, umsonst
Mag dich ein Neidisches hindern.

Wenn dann in kommender Zeit
Du einem Guten begegnest
So grüß ihn, und er denkt,
Wie unsere Tage wohl

An artisan.

But to us who
That

Nor be too greatly afraid of fear!
For, gracious one, not you

        but there is
A gloomy race which does not like to hear
Either a demigod or when with mortals a heavenly being
Appears or in waves, amorphous, nor will honour
The face of him, the pure,
The near and omnipresent God.

But even if the unholy
        in masses
          and insolent

What do they matter to you
O Song, that are pure; indeed
I die, but you
Follow a different course, in vain
Shall the envious try to impede you.

And if in a coming age
You should meet with a good man,
Then greet him and he will think
How once our days were full

Voll Glüks, voll Leidens gewesen.
Von einem gehet zum andern

Noch Eins ist aber
Zu sagen. Denn es wäre
Mir fast zu plözlich
Das Glük gekommen,
Das Einsame, daß ich unverständig
Im Eigentum
Mich an die Schatten gewandt,
Denn weil du gabst
Den Sterblichen
Versuchend Göttergestalt,
Wofür ein Wort? so meint' ich, denn es hasset die Rede, wer
Das Lebenslicht das herzernährende sparet.
Es deuteten vor Alters
Die Himmlischen sich, von selbst, wie sie
Die Kraft der Götter hinweggenommen.

Wir aber zwingen
Dem Unglük ab und hängen die Fahnen
Dem Siegsgott, dem befreienden auf, darum auch
Hast du Räthsel gesendet. Heilig sind sie
Die Glänzenden, wenn aber alltäglich
Die Himmlischen und gemein
Das Wunder scheinen will, wenn nemlich
Wie Raub Titanenfürsten die Gaaben
Der Mutter greifen, hilft ein Höherer ihr.

Of joy, of suffering.
From one will go to another

Yet one thing remains
To be said. For almost
Too suddenly
This happiness would have been granted,
This lonely happiness: that, lacking knowledge
Of what is mine
To the shadows I would have turned,
For because you gave
To mortals
The tentative shape of gods,
Why waste a word? So then I thought, for he hates speech
Who husbands the light of life that nourishes the heart.
In ancient times
The heavenly beings themselves interpreted
How they had taken away the strength of the gods.

But we
Wrest from misfortune and hang the flags
Upon the god of victory, the liberator, and that is why
You sent enigmas. Holy are they,
The shining, but when the heavenly
Would seem quotidian and vulgar
The miracle and when, indeed,
Like stolen booty Titanic princes seize
The Mother's gifts, then One who is higher comes to her aid.

Die Titanen

Nicht ist es aber
Die Zeit. Noch sind sie
Unangebunden. Göttliches trift untheilnehmende nicht.
Dann mögen sie rechnen
Mit Delphi. Indessen, gieb in Feierstunden
Und daß ich ruhen möge, der Todten
Zu denken. Viele sind gestorben
Feldherrn in alter Zeit
Und schöne Frauen und Dichter
Und in neuer
Der Männer viel
Ich aber bin allein.

            und in den Ocean schiffend
Die duftenden Inseln fragen
Wohin sie sind.

Denn manches von ihnen ist
In treuen Schriften überblieben
Und manches in Sagen der Zeit.
Viel offenbaret der Gott.
Denn lang schon wirken
Die Wolken hinab
Und es wurzelt vielesbereitend heilige Wildniß.
Heiß ist der Reichtum. Denn es fehlet
An Gesang, der löset den Geist.
Verzehren würd' er
Und wäre gegen sich selbst

The Titans

Not yet, however,
The time has come. They still are
Untethered. What's divine does not strike the unconcerned.
Then let them reckon
With Delphi. Meanwhile in festive hours,
And so that I may rest, allow me
To think of the dead. In olden days
Died many generals
And lovely women and poets,
In modern times
A host of men.
But I am on my own.

         and sailing into the ocean
The fragrant islands ask
Where they have gone.

For something of them has been
Preserved in faithful writings
And something in lore of the age.
Much does the God reveal.
For long already the clouds
Have worked upon what's below them,
And holy wilderness, pregnant with much, has grown roots.
Hot is wealth. For we lack
Song that loosens the mind.
It would devour
And would make war on itself

Denn nimmer duldet
Die Gefangenschaft das himmlische Feuer.

Es erfreuet aber
Das Gastmahl oder wenn am Feste
Das Auge glänzet und von Perlen
Der Jungfrau Hals.
Auch Kriegesspiel

    und durch die Gänge
Der Gärten schmettert
Das Gedächtniß der Schlacht und besänftiget
An schlanker Brust
Die tönenden Wehre ruhn
Von Heldenvätern den Kindern.
Mich aber umsummet
Die Bien und wo der Akersmann
Die Furchen machet singen gegen
Dem Lichte die Vögel. Manche helfen
Dem Himmel. Diese siehet
Der Dichter. Gut ist es, an andern sich
Zu halten. Denn keiner trägt das Leben allein.

Wenn aber ist entzündet
Der geschäfftige Tag
Und an der Kette, die
Den Bliz ableitet
Von der Stunde des Aufgangs
Himmlischer Thau glänzt,
Muß unter Sterblichen auch
Das Hohe sich fühlen.
Drum bauen sie Häußer
Und die Werkstatt gehet
Und über Strömen das Schiff.

For never the heavenly fire
Will suffer captivity.

Yet men are gladdened by
The banquet, and when in celebration
Our eyes are bright, and with pearls
The virgin's neck.
Martial games no less

         and through the walks
Of gardens blares
The memory of battle and, soothed
Upon the slender breasts
Of children quiet lie
Loud weapons of their heroic ancestors.
But around me hums
The bee, and where the ploughman draws
His furrows, birds are singing
Against the light. Many give help
To Heaven. And them
The poet sees. It is good to rely
Upon others. For no one can bear this life on his own.

But when the busy day
Has been kindled
And on the chain that
Conducts the lightning
From the hour of sunrise
Glistens heavenly dew,
Among mortals also
What is high must feel at home.
That is why they build houses
And the workshop's astir
And over currents the ship.

Und es bieten tauschend die Menschen
Die Händ' einander, sinnig ist es
Auf Erden und es sind nicht umsonst
Die Augen an den Boden geheftet.

Ihr fühlet aber
Auch andere Art.
Denn unter dem Maaße
Des Rohen brauchet es auch
Damit das Reine sich kenne.
Wenn aber

Und in die Tiefe greifet
Daß es lebendig werde
Der Allerschütterer, meinen die
Es komme der Himmlische
Zu Todten herab und gewaltig dämmerts
Im ungebundenen Abgrund
Im allesmerkenden auf.
Nicht möcht ich aber sagen
Es werden die Himmlischen schwach
Wenn schon es aufgährt.
Wenn aber
            und es gehet

An die Scheitel dem Vater, daß

            und der Vogel des Himmels ihm
Es anzeigt. Wunderbar
Im Zorne kommet er drauf.

And, bartering, men hold out
Their hands to one another; pensive it is
On earth, and not for nothing
Are eyes fixed on the ground.

Yet you also sense
A different kind.
For measure demands that
Crudity, coarseness exist, so that
What is pure shall know itself.
But when

And down into the depth
To make it come to life,
Reaches he who shakes all things,
They believe the Heavenly comes
Down to the dead, and mightily
In the unfettered abyss,
The all-perceiving, light breaks.
But I do not wish to say
That the Heavenly are growing weak
Though now it erupts.
But when
                    and it rises

Up to the partings of the Father's hair, so that

            and the bird of Heaven
Makes it known to him. Then
Marvellous in anger he comes.

Einst hab ich die Muse gefragt . . .

Einst hab ich die Muse gefragt, und sie
Antwortete mir
Am Ende wirst du es finden.
Kein Sterblicher kann es fassen.
Vom Höchsten will ich schweigen.
Verbotene Frucht, wie der Lorbeer, aber ist
Am meisten das Vaterland. Die aber kost'
Ein jeder zulezt,

Viel täuschet Anfang
Und Ende.
Das lezte aber ist
Das Himmelszeichen, das reißt
       und   Menschen
Hinweg. Wohl hat Herkules das
Gefürchtet. Aber da wir träge
Geboren sind, bedarf es des Falken, dem
Befolgt' ein Reuter, wenn
Er jaget, den Flug.

Im   wenn
Und der Fürst

        und Feuer und Rauchdampf blüht
Auf dürrem Rasen
Doch ungemischet darunter
Aus guter Brust, das Labsaal

At one time I questioned the Muse . . .

At one time I questioned the Muse, and she
Replied to me,
In the end you will find it.
No mortal can grasp it.
About the Highest I will not speak.
But, like the laurel, forbidden fruit
Your country is, above all. To be tasted last
By any man,

Beginning and end
Greatly deceive us.
The last thing, however, is
The heavenly sign: it sweeps
       and   men
Away. Of this even Hercules
Was doubtless afraid. But since we are
Born lazy, the hawk is needed,
Whose flight, when he hunts,
A horseman follows.

In the   when
And the prince

        and fire and smoke are in flower
On a dry lawn
Yet unmingled on to it wells,
From a good breast, the battle's

Der Schlacht, die Stimme quillet des Fürsten.

Gefäße machet ein Künstler.
Und es kauffet

        wenn es aber
Zum Urteil kommt
Und keusch hat es die Lippe
Von einem Halbgott berührt

Und schenket das Liebste
Den Unfruchtbaren
Denn nimmer, von nun an
Taugt zum Gebrauche das Heilge.

Refreshment, the voice of the prince.

An artist makes vessels.
And they are bought

         but when
It comes to the judgement
And chastely it has been touched
By the lip of a demigod

And never now will he
Give away what's dearest to him
To those unfruitful, from now on
The holy is fit for use.

Wenn aber die Himmlischen . . .

Wenn aber die Himmlischen haben
Gebaut, still ist es
Auf Erden, und wohlgestalt stehn
Die betroffenen Berge. Gezeichnet
Sind ihre Stirnen. Denn es traf
Sie, da den Donnerer hielt
Unzärtlich die gerade Tochter
Des Gottes bebender Stral
Und wohl duftet gelöscht
Von oben der Aufruhr.
Wo inne stehet, beruhiget, da
Und dort,   das Feuer.
Denn Freude schüttet
Der Donnerer aus und hätte fast
Des Himmels vergessen
Damals im Zorne, hätt ihn nicht
Das Weise gewarnet.
Jezt aber blüht es
Am armen Ort.
Und wunderbar groß will
Es stehen.
Gebirg hänget   See,
Warme   Tiefe   es Kühlen aber die Lüfte
Inseln und Halbinseln,
Grotten zu beten,

Ein glänzender Schild
Und schnell, wie Rosen,

                    oder es schafft

But when the heavenly . . .

But when the heavenly
Have built, it is quiet
On earth, and well-fashioned stand
The mountains they struck. Their brows
Are marked. For they were hit,
When the straight daughter untenderly
Held back the Thunderer,
By the god's tremulous ray
And rebellion quenched from above
Exhales a good fragrance.
Where within, assuaged, here
And there,   is the fire.
For joy the Thunderer
Pours out and almost would have
Forgotten heaven at that time,
Enraged, if the wise had not
Warned him.
But now it blossoms
In a place of dearth.
And wonderfully great
Desires to stand.
Alpine ranges hang   sea,
Warm   deep   but the breezes cool
Islands and peninsulas,
Grottoes to pray,

A gleaming shield
And quick, like roses,

                    or else

Auch andere Art,
Es sprosset aber

          viel üppig neidiges
Unkraut, das blendet, schneller schießet
Es auf, das ungelenke, denn es scherzet
Der Schöpferische, sie aber
Verstehen es nicht. Zu zornig greifft
Es und wächst. Und dem Brande gleich,
Der Häußer verzehret, schlägt
Empor, achtlos, und schonet
Den Raum nicht, und die Pfade bedeket,
Weitgährend, ein dampfend Gewölk
          die unbeholfene Wildniß.
So will es göttlich scheinen. Aber
Furchtbar ungastlich windet
Sich durch den Garten die Irre,
Die augenlose, da den Ausgang
Mit reinen Händen kaum
Erfindet ein Mensch. Der gehet, gesandt,
Und suchet, dem Thier gleich, das
Nothwendige. Zwar mit Armen,
Der Ahnung voll, mag einer treffen
Das Ziel. Wo nemlich
Die Himmlischen eines Zaunes oder Merkmals
Das ihren Weg
Anzeige, oder eines Bades
Bedürfen, reget es wie Feuer
In der Brust der Männer sich.

Noch aber hat andre
Bei sich der Vater.
Denn über den Alpen
Weil an den Adler

A different manner creates,
But there sprouts

                very lushly an envious
Weed that dazzles, faster it shoots
Up, the awkward, for the creative
Is joking, but they
Do not understand. Too wrathfully
It grips and grows. And like a conflagration
That devours houses, it flares
Up, heedless, and does not spare
Space and a steaming cloud,
Widely in ferment, covers
                the helpless wilderness.
So it would seem divine. But
Dreadfully inhospitable through
The garden confusion winds,
The eyeless, when with clean hands
Scarcely a man can find
The way out. He goes, on a mission,
And, like an animal, searches
For what is needed. True, with his arms,
Full of foreknowledge, one may attain
The goal. For where
The heavenly need a fence or a sign
To mark their
Way, or a bath,
There is a stirring like fire
In the hearts of those men.

Yet others the Father
Keeps at his side.
For above the alps,
Because by the eagle

Sich halten müssen, damit sie nicht
Mit eigenem Sinne zornig deuten
Die Dichter, wohnen über dem Fluge
Des Vogels, um den Thron
Des Gottes der Freude
Und deken den Abgrund
Ihm zu, die gelbem Feuer gleich, in reißender Zeit
Sind über Stirnen der Männer,
Die Prophetischen, denen möchten
Es neiden, weil die Furcht
Sie lieben, Schatten der Hölle,

Sie aber trieb,
Ein rein Schiksaal
Eröffnend   von
Der Erde heiligen Tischen
Der Reiniger Herkules,
Der bleibet immer lauter, jezt noch,
Mit dem Herrscher, und othembringend steigen
Die Dioskuren ab und auf,
An unzugänglichen Treppen, wenn von himmlischer Burg
Die Berge fernhinziehen
Bei Nacht, und hin
Die Zeiten
Pythagoras

Im Gedächtniß aber lebet Philoktetes,

Die helfen dem Vater.

They must be guided, lest with their own minds
In fury they interpret,
The poets, they dwell above
The bird's flight, around the throne
Of the god of joy
And cover the abyss
For him, they who like yellow fire, when time is in spate,
Are above the brows of those men,
The prophetic, would begrudge
It them, because they love
Fear, shades of hell,

But they were driven away,
Opening up a pure
Fate, from
The holy tables of earth,
By Hercules the cleanser
Who, candid always, remains, even now,
With the ruler, and, breath-bearing, still
The Dioscuri descend and rise
On inaccessible steps, when from the heavenly fortress
The mountains draw far away
By night, and away
The times
Of Pythagoras

In remembrance, though, lives Philoctetes,

Those help the Father.

Denn ruhen mögen sie. Wenn aber
Sie reizet unnüz Treiben
Der Erd' und es nehmen
Den Himmlischen
     die Sinne, brennend kommen
Sie dann,

Die othemlosen –

Denn es hasset
Der sinnende Gott
Unzeitiges Wachstum.

For they like to rest. But when
They are roused by mischievous
Happenings on earth and the heavenly
Are robbed
            their senses, burning then
They come,

The breathless —

For the pondering god
Hates
Untimely growth.

Sonst nemlich, Vater Zevs . . .

Sonst nemlich, Vater Zevs

Denn

Jezt aber hast du
Gefunden anderen Rath

Darum geht schröklich über
Der Erde Diana
Die Jägerin und zornig erhebt
Unendlicher Deutung voll
Sein Antliz über uns
Der Herr. Indeß das Meer seufzt, wenn
Er kommt

O wär es möglich
Zu schonen mein Vaterland

Doch allzuscheu nicht,

Es würde   lieber sei
Unschiklich und gehe, mit der Erinnys, fort
Mein Leben.
Denn über der Erde wandeln

For formerly, Father Zeus . . .

For formerly, Father Zeus,

Because

But now you have
Found other counsel

That is why terribly over
The earth Diana sweeps,
The huntress, and full of anger,
Full of infinite meaning
The Lord raises his face
Upon us. While the sea sighs when
He comes

O that it were possible
To spare my fatherland

But not too timid,

It would   rather be
Unseemly and go, with the Erinnyes, away,
My life,
For above the earth move

Gewaltige Mächte,
Und es ergreiffet ihr Schiksaal
Den der es leidet und zusieht,
Und ergreifft den Völkern das Herz.

Denn alles fassen muß
Ein Halbgott oder ein Mensch, dem Leiden nach,
Indem er höret, allein, oder selber
Verwandelt wird, fernahnend die Rosse des Herrn,

Mighty powers
And their destiny grips
Him who suffers it and looks on
And grips the hearts of the peoples.

For all things he must grasp,
A demigod or a man, in the way of suffering,
By hearing it, alone, or being transformed
Himself, divining from afar the horses of the Lord,

Der Adler

Mein Vater ist gewandert, auf dem Gotthard,
Da wo die Flüsse, hinab,
Wohl nach Hetruria seitwärts,
Und des geraden Weges
Auch über den Schnee,
Zu dem Olympos und Hämos
Wo den Schatten der Athos wirft,
Nach Höhlen in Lemnos.
Anfänglich aber sind
Aus Wäldern des Indus
Starkduftenden
Die Eltern gekommen.
Der Urahn aber
Ist geflogen über der See
Scharfsinnend, und es wunderte sich
Des Königes goldnes Haupt
Ob dem Geheimniß der Wasser,
Als roth die Wolken dampften
Über dem Schiff und die Thiere stumm
Einander schauend
Der Speise gedachten, aber
Es stehen die Berge doch still,
Wo wollen wir bleiben?

Der Fels ist zu Waide gut,
Das Trokne zu Trank.

The Eagle

My father roamed, up on the Gotthard,
Where the rivers are, downward,
Perhaps to Etruria, sideways,
And by the straight way too
Over the snow,
To Olympus and Haemus
Where Athos casts its shadow,
To caves in Lemnos.
In the beginning, though,
My parents came
Out of the forests of the Indus,
The strongly fragrant.
But the first forefather
Flew across the sea,
Pondering sharply, and the golden head
Of the king was full of wonder
At the mystery of the waters,
When red the clouds were steaming
Above the ship, and the animals,
Dumbly gazing at one another,
Gave thought to food, but
Nonetheless the mountains stand still,
Where shall we settle?

The rock is good for pasture,
What is dry, for drink.

Das Nasse aber zu Speise.
Will einer wohnen,
So sei es an Treppen,
Und wo ein Häuslein hinabhängt
Am Wasser halte dich auf.
Und was du hast, ist
Athem zu hohlen.
Hat einer ihn nemlich hinauf
Am Tage gebracht,
Er findet im Schlaf ihn wieder.
Denn wo die Augen zugedekt,
Und gebunden die Füße sind,
Da wirst du es finden.
Denn wo erkennest,

But what is wet, for food.
If someone wishes to dwell,
Let it be on steps
And where a small house hangs down
Near water, there spend your days.
And what is yours
Is to draw breath.
For if someone has brought it
Up to the top by day,
In sleep he finds it again.
For where the eyes are covered
And the feet are bound,
There you will find it.
For where will you recognize,

Ihr sichergebaueten Alpen . . .

Ihr sichergebaueten Alpen!
Die

Und ihr sanftblikenden Berge,
Wo über buschigem Abhang
Der Schwarzwald saußt,
Und Wohlgerüche die Loke
Der Tannen herabgießt,
Und der Nekar

      und die Donau!
Im Sommer liebend Fieber
Umherwehet der Garten
Und Linden des Dorfs, und wo
Die Pappelweide blühet
Und der Seidenbaum
Auf heiliger Waide,

Und

Ihr guten Städte!
Nicht ungestalt, mit dem Feinde
Gemischet unmächtig

Was
Auf einmal gehet es weg
Und siehet den Tod nicht.

You firmly built Alps . . .

You firmly built Alps!
That

And you mildly glancing mountains,
Where over the bushy slope
The Black Forest rushes
And the fir tree's curl
Pours down pleasing odours
And the Neckar

        and the Danube!
In summer the garden wafts
About a loving fever,
And the village's lindens, and where
The black poplar blossoms
And the white mulberry
On a holy pasture,

And

You good cities!
Not misshapen, mingled with
The enemy, powerless

Which
All at once it goes away
And does not see death.

Wann aber

Und Stutgard, wo ich
Ein Augenbliklicher begraben
Liegen dürfte, dort,
Wo sich die Straße
Bieget, und
      um die Weinstaig,
Und der Stadt Klang wieder
Sich findet drunten auf ebenem Grün
Stilltönend unter den Apfelbäumen

Des Tübingens   wo
und Blize fallen
Am hellen Tage
Und Römisches tönend ausbeuget der Spizberg
Und Wohlgeruch

Und Tills Thal, das

But when

And Stuttgart, where
A momentary one I might be allowed
To lie buried, at the place
Where the road
Bends, and
      around the Weinstaig,
And the city's hubbub meets
Itself once more down below on the level sward
Quietly sounding among the apple trees

Of Tübingen   where
and in day's full glare
Lightning flashes fall
And the Spitzberg, resounding, yields Roman lore
And pleasing odour

And Thill's valley, which

Das nächste Beste

Dritte Fassung

      offen die Fenster des Himmels
Und freigelassen der Nachtgeist
Der himmelstürmende, der hat unser Land
Beschwäzet, mit Sprachen viel, unbändigen, und
Den Schutt gewälzet
Bis diese Stunde.
Doch kommt das, was ich will,
Wenn
Drum wie die Staaren
Mit Freudengeschrei, wenn auf Gasgogne, Orten, wo viel Gärten sind,
Wenn im Olivenland, und
In liebenswürdiger Fremde,
Springbrunnen an grasbewachsnen Wegen
Die Bäum unwissend in der Wüste
Die Sonne sticht,
Und das Herz der Erde thuet
Sich auf, wo um
Den Hügel von Eichen
Aus brennendem Lande
Die Ströme und wo
Des Sonntags unter Tänzen
Gastfreundlich die Schwellen sind,
An blüthenbekränzten Straßen, stillegehend.
Sie spüren nemlich die Heimath,
Wenn grad   aus falbem Stein,
Die Wasser silbern rieseln
Und heilig Grün sich zeigt

Whatever is Nearest

Third Version

       opened the windows of Heaven
And let loose the spirit of Night
Who takes Heaven by storm – he has talked over
Our country, with many languages, unrestrained, and
Has rolled his ball of rubble
Up to this hour.
Yet what I want shall come
When
Therefore like the starlings
With jubilant cries, when in Gascony, places with many gardens,
When in the olive country, and
In lovable foreign parts,
Fountains by pathways overgrown with grass
The trees ignorant in the desert
Are stung by the sun,
And the heart of Earth
Opens up, where round
The hill of oaks
From a burning land
The rivers and where
On Sundays amid dances
Hospitable are the thresholds
On streets all hung with garlands, quietly moving.
For it is home that they sense
When straight   from dun-coloured stone
The waters trickle silver
And holy green appears

Auf feuchter Wiese der Charente,

Die Klugen Sinne pflegend.   wenn aber
Die Luft sich bahnt,
Und ihnen machet waker
Scharfwehend die Augen der Nordost, fliegen sie auf,
Und Ek um Eke
Das Liebere gewahrend
Denn immer halten die sich genau an das Nächste,
Sehn sie die heiligen Wälder und die Flamme, blühendduftend
Des Wachstums und die Wolken des Gesanges fern und athmen Othem
Der Gesänge. Menschlich ist
Das Erkentniß. Aber die Himmlischen
Auch haben solches mit sich, und des Morgens beobachten
Die Stunden und des Abends die Vögel. Himmlischen auch
Gehöret also solches. Wolan nun. Sonst in Zeiten
Des Geheimnisses hätt ich, als von Natur, gesagt,
Sie kommen, in Deutschland. Jezt aber, weil, wie die See
Die Erd ist und die Länder, Männern gleich, die nicht
Vorüber gehen können, einander, untereinander
Sich schelten fast, so sag ich. Abendlich wohlgeschmiedet
Vom Oberlande biegt sich das Gebirg, wo auf hoher Wiese die Wälder
                                                   [sind wohl an
Der bairischen Ebne. Nemlich Gebirg
Geht weit und streket, hinter Amberg sich und
Fränkischen Hügeln. Berühmt ist dieses. Umsonst nicht hat
Seitwärts gebogen Einer von Bergen der Jugend
Das Gebirg, und gerichtet das Gebirg
Heimatlich. Wildniß nemlich sind ihm die Alpen und
Das Gebirg, das theilet die Tale und die Länge lang
Geht über die Erd. Dort aber

On a sodden meadow of the Charente,

Cultivating the prudent senses.   but when
The air becomes passable
And the north-easterly, sharply blowing,
Makes bold their eyes, they fly off
And corner by corner
Perceiving that which is dearer to them,
For always they are guided by that which is nearest,
They see the holy woods and the flame, fragrantly blossoming,
Of growth and the clouds of song far away, and breathe the breath
Of songs. Human it is
To perceive, to seek knowledge. But the Heavenly too
Have something like it about them, and in the mornings observe
The hours, and at nightfall the birds. To the Heavenly, therefore, too
This appertains. Very well, then. Before, at times when
The secret was kept, as though by nature, I should have said,
They are coming, in Germany. But now, because the earth
Is like the sea and the countries are like men
Who cannot pass one another, but almost
Are scolding one another, I speak. Nocturnally, well forged
By highlands the mountain range bends, where on the alpine pasture
                               [the woods are
Near the Bavarian plain. For mountain ranges
Extend far off and stretch beyond Amberg and
Franconian hills. Famous these are. Not for nothing
Did someone bend sideways from mountains of youth
The range and turned it to face
Towards home. For wilderness are the Alps to him and
The range that divides the valleys and sprawled full length
Runs across the earth. But there

Gehn mags nun. Fast, unrein, hatt sehn lassen und das Eingeweid
Der Erde.   Bei Ilion aber
War auch das Licht der Adler. Aber in der Mitte
Der Himmel der Gesänge. Neben aber
Am Ufer zornige Greise, der Entscheidung nemlich, die alle
Drei unser sind.

Now let it run. Almost, impurely, it showed and the entrails
Of Earth.   Near Ilion, however,
The light of the eagles was too. But in the midst
The heaven of songs. But near-by
Angry old men on the shore, of decision, that is,
Which all three are ours.

Und mitzufühlen das Leben . . .

Und mitzufühlen das Leben
Der Halbgötter oder Patriarchen, sizend
Zu Gericht. Nicht aber überall ists
Ihnen gleich um diese, sondern Leben, summendheißes auch von
                                  [Schatten Echo
Als in einen Brennpunct
Versammelt. Goldne Wüste. Oder wohlunterhalten dem Feuerstahl
                               [des lebenswarmen
Heerds gleich schlägt dann die Nacht Funken, aus geschliffnem Gestein
Des Tages, und um die Dämmerung noch
Ein Saitenspiel tönt. Gegen das Meer zischt
Der Knall der Jagd. Die Aegypterin aber, offnen Busens sizt
Immer singend wegen Mühe gichtisch das Gelenk
Im Wald, am Feuer. Recht Gewissen bedeutend
Der Wolken und der Seen des Gestirns
Rauscht in Schottland wie an dem See
Lombardas dann ein Bach vorüber. Knaben spielen
Perlfrischen Lebens gewohnt so um Gestalten
Der Meister, oder der Leichen, oder es rauscht so um der Thürme
                                 [Kronen
Sanfter Schwalben Geschrei.

Nein wahrhaftig der Tag
Bildet keine
Menschenformen. Aber erstlich
Ein alter Gedanke, Wissenschaft
Elysium.

               und verlorne Liebe
Der Turniere   Rosse, scheu und feucht

And to feel with the lives . . .

And to feel with the lives
Of demigods or the patriarchs, sitting
In judgement. Yet not everywhere are they
Impartial about these, but life, hummingly hot and the shadows' echo
As though in a focal point
Concentrated. Golden desert. Or, well maintained like the steel for
                                       [striking fire
Of the life-warm stove, then the night strikes sparks, out of polished
                                       [stones
Of day, and around nightfall still
A stringed instrument sounds. Towards the ocean hisses
The cracking shots of the hunt. But the Egyptian woman sits,
Her breast exposed, always singing because of toil her joints arthritic
In the wood, by the fire. Signifying clear conscience
Of the clouds and the lakes of the planet.
In Scotland a stream rushes on
As beside Lombardy's lake. So boys will play
Accustomed to pearl-fresh life around the figures
Of masters, or of corpses, or so round the crests of towers rushes
The crying of gentle swallows.

No indeed the day
Moulds no
Human shapes. But first
An ancient thought, erudition
Elysium.

                    and lost love
Of the tournaments   horses, shy and moist

Kolomb

Wünscht' ich der Helden einer zu seyn
Und dürfte frei, mit der Stimme des Schäfers, oder eines Hessen,
Dessen eingeborner Sprach, es bekennen
So wär' es ein Seeheld. Thätigkeit, zu gewinnen nemlich
Ist das freundlichste, das
Unter allen

Heimische Wohnung und Ordnung, durchaus bündig,
Dürre Schönheit zu lernen und Gestalten
In den Sand gebrannt
Aus Nacht und Feuer, voll von Bildern, reingeschliffenes
Fernrohr, hohe Bildung, nemlich für das Leben
Den Himmel zu fragen.

Wenn du sie aber nennest
Anson und Gama, Äneas
Und Jason, Chirons
Schüler in Megaras Felsenhöhlen, und
Im zitternden Reegen der Grotte bildete sich ein Menschenbild
Aus Eindrüken des Walds, und die Tempelherren, die gefahren
Nach Jerusalem Bouillon, Rinaldo,
Bougainville   [Entdekungsreisen
als Versuche, den hesperischen
orbis gegen den
orbis der Alten zu bestimmen]

Gewaltig ist die Zahl
Gewaltiger aber sind sie selbst

Colombo

If I desired to be one of the heroes
And freely, with the shepherd's voice or a Hessian's,
His native speech, could profess it
A seaman hero I'd be. For action, to gain is
The most amiable thing
Of all

Indigenous dwelling and order, thoroughly compact,
To learn sparse beauty and figures
Burnt into sand
Out of night and fire, full of images, telescope
Polished until it's true, high expertise, that is, for life
To question the sky.

But if you name them
Anson and Gama, Aeneas
And Jason, Chiron's
Pupil in Megara's caves in the rocks, and
In tremulous rain of the grotto a man's image is formed
From the forest's impressions, and the Templars who travelled
To Jerusalem Bouillon, Rinaldo,
Bougainville   [voyages of discovery
as attempts to distinguish
the hesperian orbis from
the orbis of the ancients]

Mighty is their number
But more mighty are they themselves

Und machen stumm

      die Männer.

Dennoch

Und hin nach Genua will ich
Zu erfragen Kolombos Haus
Wo er, als wenn
Eins der Götter eines wäre und wunderbar
Der Menschen Geschlecht,
In süßer Jugend gewohnet. Licht
Aber man kehret
Wesentlich um, wie ein
Bildermann, der stehet
Vorm Kornhaus, von Sicilien her vieleicht
Und die Bilder weiset der Länder
Der Großen auch
Und singet der Welt Pracht,

      so du
Mich aber fragest

So weit das Herz
Mir reichet, wird es gehen
Nach Brauch und Kunst.

And strike dumb

        the men.

And yet

And over to Genoa I want to go
To ask my way to Colombo's house
Where he, as though
One were one of the gods and marvellous
Were human kind,
Dwelled in sweet youth. Light
But one turns
About essentially, like a
Picture man who stands
In front of the cornhouse, from Sicily perhaps
And shows pictures of the countries
And of the great
And sings the world's glory,

        but if
You ask me

As far as my heart
Reaches, it will go
As custom and art command.

Zu Schiffe aber steigen
ils crient rapport, ils fermes maison
'tu es un saisrien'

Ein Murren war es, ungedultig, denn
Von wengen geringen Dingen
Verstimmt wie vom Schnee war
Die Gloke, womit
Man läutet
Zum Abendessen
Die Erde zornig und eilte, während daß sie schrien
Manna und Himmelsbrod
Mit Prophezeiungen und
Großem Geschrei, des Gebets mit Gunst.
Sauer wird mir dieses wenig
Geduld und Gütigkeit mein Richter und Schuzgott
Denn Menschen sind wir
Und sie glaubten, sie seien Mönche.
Und einer, als Redner
Auftrat uns als Pfarherr
Im blauen Wamms
entière personne content de son
âme difficultés connoissance
rapport tire

Doch da hinaus, damit
Vom Plaze

But they embark
ils crient rapport, ils ferment maison
'tu es un saisrien'

A murmur it was, impatient, for
By a few trifling matters
Put out of tune as by snow was
The bell with which
One rings
For supper
The earth grew angry, and hurried, while they cried
Manna and bread from Heaven
With prophecies and
Great outcry, of prayer with grace.
This irks me, little
Patience and goodness my judge and tutelary god
For we are human
And they thought they were monks.
And one as orator
As vicar appeared to us
In a blue doublet
entière personne content de son
âme difficultés connoissance
rapport tire

But out that way, so
That we'll get

Wir kommen, also rief
Gewaltig richtend
Die Gesellen die Stimme des Meergotts,
Die reine, daran
Heroen erkennen, ob sie recht
Gerathen oder nicht —

Stürzet herein, ihr Bäche
Von Leib und Gottes Gnad und Glük im seinen,
Kräfte zu begreiffen, o ihr Bilder
Der Jugend, als in Genua, damals
Der Erdkreis, griechisch, kindlich gestaltet,
Mit Gewalt unter meinen Augen,
Einschläfernd, kurzgefaßtem Mohngeist gleich mir
Erschien

Das bist du ganz in deiner Schönheit apocalyptica

moments tirées hautes sommeils der Schiffer
Kolombus aber beiseit Hypostasierung des vorigen orbis
Naiveté der Wissenschaft
Und seufzeten miteinander, um die Stunde,
Nach der Hizze des Tags.
lui a les pleures

Sie sahn nun

Es waren nemlich viele,
Der schönen Inseln.

Moving, thus
Mightily judging
The sea-god's voice called
The companions, pure voice
By which heroes recognize
Whether they've turned out right
Or not —

Rush in, you streams
Of love and God's mercy and bliss in what's his,
To understand powers, o you images
Of youth when in Genoa, then
The terrestrial orb, Greek, childlike in shape
By force under my eyes
Lulling to sleep, like the spirit of poppies compressed
Appeared to me

That is wholly you in your beauty apocalyptica.

moments tirées hautes sommeils the mariner
Colombo apart, though, hypostasis of the previous orbis
naïveté of science
And sighed among themselves, at the hour
After the day's heat.
lui a les pleures

Now they saw

For they were many,
The lovely isles.

damit
Mit Lissabon

Und Genua theilten;

Denn einsam kann
Von Himmlischen den Reichtum tragen
Nicht eins; wohl nemlich mag
Den Harnisch dehnen
            ein Halbgott, dem Höchsten aber
Ist fast zu wenig
Das Wirken   wo das Tagslicht scheinet,
Und der Mond,

      Darum auch

          so

Nemlich öfters, wenn
Den Himmlischen zu einsam
Es wird, daß sie
Allein zusammenhalten

           oder die Erde; denn allzurein ist
Entweder

      Dann aber

so that
With Lisbon

And Genoa shared;

For lonely not one
Can endure the wealth
Of the heavenly; for indeed
a demigod
Can stretch the armour, but
To the Highest
Such working is almost too little
Where daylight shines
And the moon

And therefore

so

For often, when
The heavenly grow
Too lonely, so that
Alone they hold together

or Earth; for all too pure is
Either

But then

Wenn über dem Weinberg . . .

Wenn über dem Weinberg es flammt
Und schwarz wie Kohlen
Aussiehet um die Zeit
Des Herbstes der Weinberg, weil
Die Röhren des Lebens feuriger athmen
In den Schatten des Weinstoks. Aber
Schön ists, die Seele
Zu entfalten und das kurze Leben

When there's a flaming . . .

When there's a flaming above the vineyard
And black as coal
The vineyard looks, around the
Autumn season, because
More fierily breathe the pipes of life
In the grapevine's shadows. But
Lovely it is to unfold
The soul and our brief life

Vom Abgrund nemlich . . .

Vom Abgrund nemlich haben
Wir angefangen und gegangen
Dem Leuen gleich, in Zweifel und Ärgerniß,
Denn sinnlicher sind Menschen
In dem Brand
Der Wüste
Lichttrunken und der Thiergeist ruhet
Mit ihnen. Bald aber wird, wie ein Hund, umgehn
In der Hizze meine Stimme auf den Gassen der Gärten
In denen wohnen Menschen
In Frankreich
Der Schöpfer
Frankfurt aber, nach der Gestalt, die
Abdruk ist der Natur zu reden
Des Menschen nemlich, ist der Nabel
Dieser Erde, diese Zeit auch
Ist Zeit, und deutschen Schmelzes.
Ein wilder Hügel aber stehet über dem Abhang
Meiner Gärten. Kirschenbäume. Scharfer Othem aber wehet
Um die Löcher des Felses. Allda bin ich
Alles miteinander. Wunderbar
Aber über Quellen beuget schlank
Ein Nußbaum und   sich. Beere, wie Korall
Hängen an dem Strauche über Röhren von Holz,
Aus denen
Ursprünglich aus Korn, nun aber zu gestehen, bevestigter Gesang
                                        [von Blumen als
Neue Bildung aus der Stadt, wo
Bis zu Schmerzen aber der Nase steigt

For from the abyss . . .

For from the abyss we
Began and have walked like
The lion, in doubt and annoyance,
For more sensual are men
In the blaze
Of deserts,
Drunk with light, and the spirit of animals
Joins in their rest. But soon like a dog my voice
Will walk in the heat through the alleys of gardens
In which men and women live
In France
The creator
Frankfurt, though to speak according to the shape
Of nature's imprint, human nature, I mean,
Is the navel of this earth, our time too
Is time, and of German mould.
But a wild hill looms above the slope of
My gardens. Cherry trees. A sharp breath, however,
Blows around the holes of the rock. And there I am
All things at once. But wonderfully
Over well-springs there slenderly bends
A nut tree and   Berries like coral
Hang on the shrub above wooden gutters
From which
Originally of corn, but now to be confessed, fortified song of flowers
As new education from town, where
To the point of pain in the nose

Citronengeruch auf und das Öl, aus der Provence, und es haben diese
Dankbarkeit mir die Gasgognischen Lande
Gegeben. Gezähmet aber, noch zu sehen, und genährt hat mich
Die Rappierlust und des Festtags gebraten Fleisch
Der Tisch und braune Trauben, braune
                                        und mich leset o
Ihr Blüthen von Deutschland, o mein Herz wird
Untrügbarer Krystall an dem
Das Licht sich prüfet wenn   Deutschland

A smell of lemons rises and of oil, from Provence, and it is
The Gascon regions that have given me
This thankfulness. But what tamed me, still to be seen, and fed me
Is love of rapiers and the holiday's roast meat
The table and brown grapes, brown ones
                        and read me, gather me O
You flowers of Germany, O my heart is turning
To crystal that cannot lie, in which

The light is tested when   Germany

Narcyssen . . .

Narcyssen Ranunklen und
Siringen aus Persien
Blumen Nelken, gezogen perlenfarb
Und schwarz und Hyacinthen,
Wie wenn es riechet, statt Musik
Des Eingangs, dort, wo böse Gedanken,
Liebende mein Sohn vergessen sollen einzugehen
Verhältnisse und diß Leben
Christophori   der Drache vergleicht der Natur
Gang und Geist und Gestalt.

Narcissi . . .

Narcissi, ranunculi and
Syringas from Persia
Carnations, bred
Flowers pearl-coloured
And black and hyacinths
As when there's a smell, instead of music
Of entry, there, where an evil thought,
          my son
Lovers should forget to enter into
Relationships and this life
                  Christopher's
Dragon   compares with nature's
Gait and spirit and shape

. . . der Vatikan . . .

                                der Vatikan,
Hier sind wir   in der Einsamkeit
Und drunten gehet der Bruder, ein Esel auch dem braunen
                                                [Schleier nach
Wenn aber der Tag   , allbejahend von wegen des Spotts
Schiksaale macht, denn aus Zorn der Natur-
Göttin, wie ein Ritter gesagt von Rom, in derlei
Pallästen, gehet izt viel Irrsaal, und alle Schlüssel des Geheimnisses
                                                        [wissend

Fragt bös Gewissen
Und Julius Geist um derweil, welcher Calender
Gemachet, und dort drüben, in Westphalen,
Mein ehrlich Meister.
Gott rein und mit Unterscheidung
Bewahren, das ist uns vertrauet,
Damit nicht, weil an diesem
Viel hängt, über der Büßung, über einem Fehler
Des Zeichens
Gottes Gericht entstehet.
Ach! kennet ihr den nicht mehr
Den Meister des Forsts, und den Jüngling in der Wüste, der von Honig
Und Heuschreken sich nährt. Still Geists ists. Fraun
                        Oben wohl
Auf Monte   , wohl auch seitwärts,
Irr ich herabgekommen
Über Tyrol, Lombarda, Loretto, wo des Pilgrims Heimath
            auf dem Gotthard, gezäunt, nachlässig, unter Gletschern
Karg wohnt jener, wo der Vogel
Mit Eiderdünnen, eine Perle des Meers

... the Vatican ...

the Vatican,
Here we are   in the solitude
And down below walks the brother, a donkey too according to the
                                                    [brown veil
But when the day   , all-affirming because of the mockery
Makes destinies, for out of wrath of the Nature-
Goddess, as a knight said of Rome, in suchlike
Palaces much confusion teems, and knowing all keys to the secret
Bad conscience asks
And the spirit of Julius meanwhile, who
Made calendars, and over there in Westphalia,
My honest master.
To preserve God pure and with discrimination
Is the task entrusted to us,
Lest, because much depends
On this, through a penitence, through a mistake
In the sign
God's day of judgement set in.
Oh, have you forgotten, then
The forest's master and the youth in the desert who feeds
On locusts and honey. Of the quiet spirit it is. Women
                                        Up there perhaps
On Monte,   sideways too perhaps
I stray, come down
Across Tirol, Lombardy, Loretto, where the pilgrim's home is
                on the Gotthard, fenced, carelessly, under glaciers
Poorly he lives, where the bird
With eiderdown, a pearl of the sea

Und der Adler den Accent rufet, vor Gott, wo das Feuer läuft der
[Menschen wegen
Des Wächters Horn tönt aber über den Garden
Der Kranich hält die Gestalt aufrecht
Die Majestätische, keusche, drüben
In Patmos, Morea, in der Pestluft.
Türkisch, und die Eule, wohlbekannt der Schriften
Spricht, heischern Fraun gleich in zerstörten Städten. Aber
Die erhalten den Sinn. Oft aber wie ein Brand
Entstehet Sprachverwirrung. Aber wie ein Schiff,
Das lieget im Hafen, des Abends, wenn die Gloke lautet
Des Kirchthurms, und es nachhallt unten
Im Eingewaid des Tempels und der Mönch
Und Schäfer Abschied nehmet, vom Spaziergang
Und Apollon, ebenfalls
Aus Roma, derlei Pallästen, sagt
Ade! unreinlich bitter, darum!
Dann kommt das Brautlied des Himmels.
Vollendruhe. Goldroth. Und die Rippe tönet
Des sandigen Erdballs in Gottes Werk
Ausdrüklicher Bauart, grüner Nacht
Und Geist, der Säulenordnung, wirklich
Ganzem Verhältniß, samt der Mitt,
Und glänzenden

And the eagle there calls the accent, before God, where the fire runs
                                      [because of men
But the watchman's horn rings out over the guards
The crane holds his body erect
The majestic, the chaste, over there
In Patmos, Morea, the pestilent air.
Turkish, and the owl, well-versed in writings,
Speaks like hoarse women in cities destroyed. But
They catch the meaning. Yet often like a fire
Confusion of tongues breaks out. But like a ship
That lies in the harbour, at evening, when the bell rings
Down from the church tower and reverberates in
The temple's entrails below and the monk
And shepherd take leave, from the walk
And Apollo, likewise
From Rome, suchlike palaces, say
Farewell! dirtily bitter, that's why!
Then comes the nuptial song of Heaven.
Rest of perfection. Reddish-golden. And loud sings the rib
Of the sandy globe in the work of God
A definite style of building, green night
And spirit, the pillars' order, true to
Total proportions, including the centre,
And to gleaming

Zu Sokrates Zeiten

Vormals richtete Gott.

          Könige.

     Weise.

          wer richtet denn izt?

Richtet das einige
   Volk? die heilge Gemeinde?
   Nein! o nein! wer richtet denn izt?
               ein Natterngeschlecht!   feig und falsch
                    das edlere Wort nicht mehr
               Über die Lippe
O im Nahmen
                                   ruf ich
          Alter Dämon! dich herab

Oder   sende
   Einen Helden

Oder
     die Weisheit.

In Socrates' Time

At one time God judged.

        Kings.

     Wise men.

        who, then, judges now?

Does the unanimous
  people? the holy community?
  No, oh no! who, then, judges now?
         a generation of vipers!   cowardly and lying
             the nobler word no more
       Passes the lip
O in the name
                  I call
    you down to us, ancient Daemon

Or   send
   A hero

Or

    Wisdom.

Im Walde

Du edles Wild.
Aber in Hütten wohnet der Mensch, und hüllet sich ein ins verschämte Gewand, denn inniger ist achtsamer auch und daß er bewahre den Geist, wie die Priesterin die himmlische Flamme, diß ist sein Verstand. Und darum ist die Willkür ihm und höhere Macht zu fehlen und zu vollbringen dem Götterähnlichen, der Güter Gefährlichstes, die Sprache dem Menschen gegeben, damit er schaffend, zerstörend, und untergehend, und wiederkehrend zur ewiglebenden, zur Meisterin und Mutter, damit er zeuge, was er sei geerbet zu haben, gelernt von ihr, ihr Göttlichstes, die allerhaltende Liebe.

In the Forest

You noble beast of the wilds.
But in cottages human kind dwell, and wrap themselves in the garment of shame, for more inward, more attentive too, so that they preserve the spirit as the priestess preserves the heavenly flame, such is their understanding. And for that free choice and higher power to err and to achieve have been granted to the godlike, the most dangerous of possessions, language, has been granted to human kind, so that creating, destroying and perishing, and returning to the eternally living, mistress and mother, that they may perpetuate what they are, their heritage, learnt from her, the most divine of her attributes, all-maintaining love.

Griechenland

Erste Fassung

Wege des Wanderers!

Denn   Schatten der Bäume
Und Hügel, sonnig, wo
Der Weg geht
Zur Kirche,

Reegen, wie Pfeilenregen

Und Bäume stehen, schlummernd, doch
Eintreffen Schritte der Sonne,
Denn eben so, wie sie heißer
Brennt über der Städte Dampf
So gehet über des Reegens
Behangene Mauren die Sonne

Wie Epheu nemlich hänget
Astlos der Reegen herunter. Schöner aber
Blühn Reisenden die Wege
        im Freien   wechselt wie Korn.
Avignon waldig über den Gotthardt
Tastet das Roß, Lorbeern
Rauschen um Virgilius und daß
Die Sonne nicht
Unmänlich suchet, das Grab. Moosrosen
Wachsen
Auf den Alpen. Blumen fangen
Vor Thoren der Stadt an, auf geebneten Wegen unbegünstiget
Gleich Krystallen in der Wüste wachsend des Meers.
Gärten wachsen um Windsor. Hoch
Ziehet, aus London,

Greece

First Version

                    ways of the wanderer!
For   shadows of trees
And hills, sunny where
The path runs
Up to the church,
            rain like showers of arrows,
And trees loom, drowsing, yet
Strides of the sun arrive.
For just as more hotly
It burns above the vapour of cities
So does the sun move above
The draped walls of the rain

For like ivy
Branchless the rain hangs down. But
More beautifully to travellers blossom the roads
     out in the open   changes like corn.
Avignon woody over the Gotthart
The horse gropes its way, laurels
Rustle around Vergil and, so that
Not unmanly the sun
Shall search, the grave. Moss-roses
Grow
On the Alps. Flowers begin
Before the city gates, on levelled roads, unfavoured
Like crystals growing in the desert of the sea.
Gardens grow around Windsor. High up,
From London,

Der Wagen des Königs.
Schöne Gärten sparen die Jahrzeit.
Am Canal. Tief aber liegt
Das ebene Weltmeer, glühend.

The King's coach drives on.
Fine gardens save up the season.
By the canal. But deep down lies
The level ocean, glowing.

Griechenland

Zweite Fassung

O ihr Stimmen des Geschiks, ihr Wege des Wanderers
Denn an dem Himmel
Tönt wie der Amsel Gesang
Der Wolken sichere Stimmung gut
Gestimmt vom Daseyn Gottes, dem Gewitter.
Und Rufe, wie hinausschauen, zur
Unsterblichkeit und Helden;
Viel sind Erinnerungen.
Und wo die Erde, von Verwüstungen her, Versuchungen der Heiligen
Großen Gesezen nachgeht, die Einigkeit
Und Zärtlichkeit und den ganzen Himmel nachher
Erscheinend singen
Gesangeswolken. Denn immer lebt
Die Natur. Wo aber allzusehr sich
Das Ungebundene zum Tode sehnet
Himmlisches einschläft, und die Treue Gottes,
Das Verständige fehlt.
Aber wie der Reigen
Zur Hochzeit,
Zu Geringem auch kann kommen
Großer Anfang.
Alltag aber wunderbar
Gott an hat ein Gewand.
Und Erkentnissen verberget sich sein Angesicht
Und deket die Lüfte mit Kunst.
Und Luft und Zeit dekt
Den Schröklichen, wenn zu sehr ihn
Eins liebet mit Gebeten oder
Die Seele.

Greece

Second Version

O you voices of fate, you ways of the wanderer
For on the heavens
Rings out like the blackbird's song
The clouds' even mood, well
Tempered by the existence of God, the thunder-storm.
And calls, like looking out, for
Immortality and heroes;
Memories are many.
And where the Earth, proceeding from devastations, temptations of
[the saints,

Pursues great laws, afterwards
Song-clouds, becoming visible, sing
Concord and tenderness
And the whole of heaven. For always
Nature lives. But where all too greatly
The unbound longs for death,
The Heavenly, and God's faithfulness, go to sleep,
Reason is lacking.
But like the dance
To a wedding
A great beginning can come
Even to humble things.
Everyday but marvellous
God has put on a garment.
And his face is withheld from the knowing
And covers the winds with art.
And air and time cover
The terrible one, when too much
Someone loves him with prayers, or
Else the soul.

Griechenland

Dritte Fassung

O ihr Stimmen des Geschiks, ihr Wege des Wanderers
Denn an der Schule Blau,
Fernher, am Tosen des Himmels
Tönt wie der Amsel Gesang
Der Wolken heitere Stimmung gut
Gestimmt vom Daseyn Gottes, dem Gewitter.
Und Rufe, wie hinausschauen, zur
Unsterblichkeit und Helden;
Viel sind Erinnerungen. Wo darauf
Tönend, wie des Kalbs Haut
Die Erde, von Verwüstungen her, Versuchungen der Heiligen
Denn anfangs bildet das Werk sich
Großen Gesezen nachgehet, die Wissenschaft
Und Zärtlichkeit und den Himmel breit lauter Hülle nachher
Erscheinend singen Gesangeswolken.
Denn fest ist der Erde
Nabel. Gefangen nemlich in Ufern von Gras sind
Die Flammen und die allgemeinen
Elemente. Lauter Besinnung aber oben lebt der Aether. Aber silbern
An reinen Tagen
Ist das Licht. Als Zeichen der Liebe
Veilchenblau die Erde.
Zu Geringem auch kann kommen
Großer Anfang.
Alltag aber wunderbar zu lieb den Menschen
Gott an hat ein Gewand.
Und Erkentnissen verberget sich sein Angesicht
Und deket die Lüfte mit Kunst.

Greece

Third Version

O you voices of fate, you ways of the wanderer!
For amid the blue of the school,
From afar, amid the uproar of heaven
Rings out like the blackbird's song
The clouds' happy mood, well
Tempered by the existence of God, the thunder-storm.
And calls, like looking out, for
Immortality and heroes;
Memories are many. Where ringing out
On it, as on the calf's hide,
The earth, proceeding from devastations, temptations of the saints,
For at the beginning the work is shaped,
Pursues great laws, and knowledge
And tenderness and the width of heaven, all wrapping, later becoming
Visible, sing clouds of song.
For firmly fixed is the navel
Of Earth. For captive in banks of grass are
The flames and the common
Elements. But above, all reflection, lives Aether. But silver
On pure days
Is light. As a sign of love
Violet-blue the earth.
A great beginning can come
Even to humble things.
Everyday but marvellous, for the sake of men,
God has put on a garment.
And his face is withheld from the knowing
And covers the winds with art.

Und Luft und Zeit dekt
Den Schröklichen, daß zu sehr nicht eins
Ihn liebet mit Gebeten oder
Die Seele. Denn lange schon steht offen
Wie Blätter, zu lernen, oder Linien und Winkel
Die Natur
Und gelber die Sonnen und die Monde,
Zu Zeiten aber
Wenn ausgehn will die alte Bildung
Der Erde, bei Geschichten nemlich
Gewordnen, muthig fechtenden, wie auf Höhen führet
Die Erde Gott. Ungemessene Schritte
Begränzt er aber, aber wie Blüthen golden thun
Der Seele Kräfte dann der Seele Verwandtschaften sich zusammen,
Daß lieber auf Erden
Die Schönheit wohnt und irgend ein Geist
Gemeinschaftlicher sich zu Menschen gesellet.

Süß ists, dann unter hohen Schatten von Bäumen
Und Hügeln zu wohnen, sonnig, wo der Weg ist
Gepflastert zur Kirche. Reisenden aber, wem,
Aus Lebensliebe, messend immerhin,
Die Füße gehorchen, blühn
Schöner die Wege, wo das Land

And air and time cover
The terrible one, so that not too much a man
With prayers shall love him.
Or else the soul. For long already like leaves,
To learn, or like lines and angles,
Nature lies open
And more yellow the suns and the moons,
But at times
When the ancient knowledge of earth is in danger
Of going out, amid histories, that is, grown, come to pass
And boldly fencing, as on high places God
Leads on the Earth. Unmeasured paces, though,
He limits, but like blossoms golden then
The faculties, affinities of the soul consort
So that more willingly
Beauty dwells on earth and one or the other spirit
More communally joins in human affairs.

Sweet it is then to dwell under the high shade
Of trees and hills, sunny, where the road
Is paved to church. To travellers, though,
To him whose feet, from love of life,
Measuring all along, obey him,
More beautifully blossom the roads, where the land

Pindar Fragments and Commentary
(1805)

Untreue der Weisheit

O Kind, dem an des pontischen Wilds Haut
Des felsenliebenden am meisten das Gemüth
Hängt, allen Städten geselle dich,
Das gegenwärtige lobend
Gutwillig,
Und anderes denk in anderer Zeit.

Fähigkeit der einsamen Schule für die Welt. Das Unschuldige des reinen Wissens als die Seele der Klugheit. Denn Klugheit ist die Kunst, unter verschiedenen Umständen getreu zu bleiben, das Wissen die Kunst, bei positiven Irrtümern im Verstande sicher zu seyn. Ist intensiv der Verstand geübt, so erhält er seine Kraft auch im Zerstreuten; so fern er an der eigenen geschliffenen Schärfe das Fremde leicht erkennt, deßwegen nicht leicht irre wird in ungewissen Situationen.

So tritt Jason, ein Zögling des Centauren, vor den Pelias:

ich glaube die Lehre
Chirons zu haben. Aus der Grotte nemlich komm' ich
Bei Charikli und Philyra, wo des
Centauren Mädchen mich ernähret,
Die heilgen; zwanzig Jahre aber hab'
Ich zugebracht und nicht ein Werk
Noch Wort, ein schmuziges jenen
Gesagt, und bin gekommen nach Haus,
Die Herrschaft wiederzubringen meines Vaters.

Unfaithfulness of Wisdom

O child whose love most clings
To the pontic game beast's skin,
The rock-enamoured, with all cities mix,
Praising, with good will,
That which is present,
And differently think when the times are different.

The lonely school's capacity for the world. The innocence of
pure knowledge as the soul of intelligence. For intelligence is the art
of remaining faithful in changing circumstances, knowledge the art
of being sure in one's understanding in the midst of positive errors.
If our understanding has been exercised intensely, it retains its
strength even in diffusion; inasmuch as it easily recognizes alien
things by its own honed sharpness, and so is not easily confused in
uncertain situations.

So Jason, a pupil of the centaur, confronts Pelias:

I believe I possess
Chiron's doctrine. For I come from the grotto
By Charikli and Philyra, where the
Centaur's girls fed me,
The holy; twenty years, though, I
Have spent and not one work
Or word, a dirty one, said
To them, and have returned home
To restore my father's rule.

Von der Wahrheit

Anfängerin großer Tugend, Königin Wahrheit,
Daß du nicht stoßest
Mein Denken an rauhe Lüge.

Furcht vor der Wahrheit, aus Wohlgefallen an ihr. Nemlich das erste lebendige Auffassen derselben im lebendigen Sinne ist, wie alles reine Gefühl, Verwirrungen ausgesezt; so daß man nicht irret, aus eigener Schuld, noch auch aus einer Störung, sondern des höheren Gegenstandes wegen, für den, verhältnißmäßig, der Sinn zu schwach ist.

Of Truth

Initiator of great virtue, Queen Truth,
May you not thrust
My thinking up against a coarse lie.

Fear of truth, out of liking for it. Because the first living apprehension of it in the living mind, like all pure feeling, is exposed to error; so that one does not err by one's own fault, nor by one's own disturbance, but because of the higher object for which, relatively speaking, one's mind is too weak.

Von der Ruhe

Das Öffentliche, hat das ein Bürger
In stiller Witterung gefaßt,
Soll er erforschen
Großmänlicher Ruhe heiliges Licht,
Und dem Aufruhr von der Brust,
Von Grund aus wehren seinen Winden; denn Armuth
[macht er
Und feind ist er Erziehern der Kinder.

Ehe die Geseze, der grosmännlichen Ruhe heiliges Licht, erforschet werden, muß einer, ein Gesezgeber oder ein Fürst, in reißenderem oder stetigerem Schiksaal eines Vaterlandes und je nachdem die Receptivität des Volkes beschaffen ist, den Karakter jenes Schiksaals, das königlichere oder gesammtere in den Verhältnissen der Menschen, zu ungestörter Zeit, usurpatorischer, wie bei griechischen Natursöhnen, oder erfahrener, wie bei Menschen von Erziehung auffassen. Dann sind die Geseze die Mittel, jenes Schiksaal in seiner Ungestörtheit festzuhalten. Was für den Fürsten origineller Weise, das gilt, als Nachahmung für den eigentlicheren Bürger.

Of Repose

> The public realm, if in calm weather
> A citizen has grasped that,
> Let him search out
> The holy light of lordly repose
> And from the foundations up fend it off
> From his winds, heart's turbulence; for that makes poverty
> And is inimical to educators of children.

Before laws, the holy light of lordly repose, are searched out, a legislator or prince, in the more agitated as in the constant destiny of a country, and according to the people's receptivity, must grasp the nature of that destiny, whether more kingly or more collective, in the conditions of people, more usurpatory, as with Greek sons of nature, or more experienced, as with persons of education. Then the laws are the means of maintaining this destiny undisrupted. What is valid for the prince in an original manner, is valid for the citizen as imitation.

Vom Delphin

> Den in des wellenlosen Meeres Tiefe von Flöten
> Bewegt hat liebenswürdig der Gesang.

Der Gesang der Natur, in der Witterung der Musen, wenn über Blüthen die Wolken, wie Floken, hängen, und über dem Schmelz von goldenen Blumen. Um diese Zeit giebt jedes Wesen seinen Ton an, seine Treue, die Art, wie eines in sich selbst zusammenhängt. Nur der Unterschied der Arten macht dann die Trennung in der Natur, daß also alles mehr Gesang und reine Stimme ist, als Accent des Bedürfnisses oder auf der anderen Seite Sprache.

Es ist das wellenlose Meer, wo der bewegliche Fisch die Pfeife der Tritonen, das Echo des Wachstums in den waichen Pflanzen des Wassers fühlt.

Of the Dolphin

Which in the waveless sea's deep of flutes
The song delightfully has moved.

The song of nature, in the Muses' weather, when above blossoms
the clouds hang like flakes, and above the sweetness of golden
flowers. At such a time each creature utters its tone, its faithfulness,
the way in which an organism coheres within itself. Then only the
difference in kinds makes for division in nature, so that all is more
song and pure voice than the accent of need or, on the other hand,
language.

It is the waveless sea, where the mobile fish senses the Triton's
pipe, the echo of growth in the water's soft weeds.

Das Höchste

> Das Gesez,
> Von allen der König, Sterblichen und
> Unsterblichen; das führt eben
> Darum gewaltig
> Das gerechteste Recht mit allerhöchster Hand.

Das Unmittelbare, streng genommen, ist für die Sterblichen unmöglich, wie für die Unsterblichen; der Gott muß verschiedene Welten unterscheiden, seiner Natur gemäß, weil himmlische Güte, ihret selber wegen, heilig seyn muß, unvermischt. Der Mensch, als Erkennendes, muß auch verschiedene Welten unterscheiden, weil Erkentniß nur durch Entgegensezung möglich ist. Deswegen ist das Unmittelbare, streng genommen, für die Sterblichen unmöglich, wie für die Unsterblichen.

Die strenge Mittelbarkeit ist aber das Gesez.

Deswegen aber führt es gewaltig das gerechteste Recht mit allerhöchster Hand.

Die Zucht, so fern sie die Gestalt ist, worinn der Mensch sich und der Gott begegnet, der Kirche und des Staats Gesez und anererbte Sazungen, (die Heiligkeit des Gottes, und für den Menschen die Möglichkeit einer Erkentniß, einer Erklärung) diese führen gewaltig das gerechteste Recht mit allerhöchster Hand, sie halten strenger, als die Kunst, die lebendigen Verhältnisse fest, in denen, mit der Zeit, ein Volk sich begegnet hat und begegnet. »König« bedeutet hier den Superlativ, der nur das Zeichen ist für den höchsten Erkentnißgrund, nicht für die höchste Macht.

The Supreme

> The law,
> King of all, both mortals and
> Immortals; which for that very reason
> Compellingly guides
> The justest justice with a sovereign hand.

The immediate, strictly speaking, is impossible for mortals, as for immortals; the god has to differentiate several worlds, according to his nature, because heavenly goodness, for its own sake, must be holy, unalloyed. Human beings, as cognizant ones, must also differentiate between several worlds, because cognition is possible only by contrast. That is why the immediate, strictly speaking, is impossible for mortals, as for immortals.

But the strictly mediate is the law.

And that is why, compellingly, it guides the justest justice with a sovereign hand.

Discipline, in so far as it is form in which human beings and the god meet, the laws of Church and State and inherited statutes (the god's sanctity, and for human beings the possibility of a recognition, an elucidation), these compellingly guide the justest justice with a sovereign hand, more strictly than arts they stabilize those vital conditions in which, in time, a people has encountered itself and encounters itself. 'King' here means the superlative that is only the sign for the supreme ground for cognition, not for the highest power.

Das Alter

Wer recht und heilig
Das Leben zubringt,
Süß ihm das Herz ernährend,
Lang Leben machend,
Begleitet die Hoffnung, die
Am meisten Sterblichen
Die vielgewandte Meinung regieret.

Eines der schönsten Bilder des Lebens, wie schuldlose Sitte das lebendige Herz erhält, woraus die Hoffnung kommet; die der Einfalt dann auch eine Blüthe giebt, mit ihren mannigfaltigen Versuchen und den Sinn gewandt und so lang Leben machet, mit ihrer eilenden Weile.

Old Age

Who aright and in holiness
Spends his life,
Sweetly nourishing his heart,
Making for long life,
Him hope accompanies, which
In mortals most of all governs
Opinion, their versatile minds.

One of the most beautiful images of life, how guiltless decorum preserves the living heart, from which hope comes; which then gives a bloom, too, to simplicity, with its manifold endeavours and lends skill to the mind and so makes for long life, as it speeds in its lingering.

716 · *Pindar Fragments and Commentary*

Das Unendliche

> Ob ich des Rechtes Mauer
> Die hohe oder krummer Täuschung
> Ersteig' und so mich selbst
> Umschreibend, hinaus
> Mich lebe, darüber
> Hab ich zweideutig ein
> Gemüth, genau es zu sagen.

Ein Scherz des Weisen, und das Räthsel sollte fast nicht gelöst werden. Das Schwanken und das Streiten zwischen Recht und Klugheit löst sich nemlich nur in durchgängiger Beziehung. »Ich habe zweideutig ein Gemüth genau es zu sagen.« Daß ich dann zwischen Recht und Klugheit den Zusammenhang auffinde, der nicht ihnen selber, sondern einem dritten zugeschrieben werden muß, wodurch sie unendlich (genau) zusammenhängen, darum hab' ich ein zweideutig Gemüth.

The Infinite

> Whether I climb the wall
> Of justice, the high, or crooked
> Deception's and so,
> Circumscribing myself, live
> My way out, of that
> Ambiguously I have a
> Mind to say it exactly.

A joke of the wise man, and the conundrum ought almost not to be solved. For the wavering and the conflict between justice and prudence are resolved only in open relatedness. 'Ambiguously I have a mind to say it exactly.' So that I then discover the connection between justice and prudence, a connection not to be ascribed to either of them, but to a third factor by which they are connected infinitely (exactly), for that I have an ambiguous mind.

Die Asyle

> Zuerst haben
> Die wohlrathende Themis
> Die Himmlischen, auf goldenen Rossen, neben
> Des Ozeans Salz,
> Die Zeiten zu der Leiter,
> Zur heiligen geführt des Olympos, zu
> Der glänzenden Rükkehr,
> Des Retters alte Tochter,
> Des Zevs zu seyn,
> Sie aber hat
> Die goldgehefteten, die gute,
> Die glänzendbefruchteten Ruhestätten geboren.

Wie der Mensch sich sezt, ein Sohn der Themis, wenn, aus dem Sinne für Vollkommenes, sein Geist, auf Erden und im Himmel, keine Ruhe fand, bis sich im Schiksaal begegnend, an den Spuren der alten Zucht, der Gott und der Mensch sich wiedererkennt, und in Erinnerung ursprünglicher Noth froh ist da, wo er sich halten kann.

Themis, die ordnungsliebende, hat die Asyle des Menschen, die stillen Ruhestätten geboren, denen nichts Fremdes ankann, weil an ihnen das Wirken und das Leben der Natur sich konzentrirte, und ein Ahnendes um sie, wie erinnernd, dasselbige erfähret, das sie vormals erfuhren.

The Sanctuaries

At first the
Heavenly led well-advising
Themis, on golden horses, next to
The ocean's salt,
The ages to the ladder,
The holy, of Olympos, to
The shining return,
To be the rescuer's
Ancient daughter, of Zeus,
But she, the good, gave birth to
The gold-riveted,
The shiningly fertilized places of rest.

As a man, son of Themis, settles when, out of a sense of perfection, his spirit, on earth and in heaven, found no rest, until, meeting in fate, by the traces of ancient discipline, the god and the man recognize each other, and in recollection of original need, he is glad to be where he can maintain himself.

Themis, the order-loving, gave birth to the human sanctuaries, the quiet places of rest, which nothing alien can touch, because in them the working and life of nature was concentrated, and something around them that divines, as though remembering, experiences that which they experienced formerly.

Das Belebende

Die männerbezwingende, nachdem
Gelernet die Centauren
Die Gewalt
Des honigsüßen Weines, plözlich trieben
Die weiße Milch mit Händen, den Tisch sie fort, von selbst,
Und aus den silbernen Hörnern trinkend
Bethörten sie sich.

Der Begriff von den Centauren ist wohl der vom Geiste eines Stromes, so fern der Bahn und Gränze macht, mit Gewalt, auf der ursprünglich pfadlosen aufwärtswachsenden Erde.

Sein Bild ist deswegen an Stellen der Natur, wo das Gestade reich an Felsen und Grotten ist, besonders an Orten, wo ursprünglich der Strom die Kette der Gebirge verlassen und ihre Richtung queer durchreißen mußte.

Centauren sind deswegen auch ursprünglich Lehrer der Naturwissenschaft, weil sich aus jenem Gesichtspuncte die Natur am besten einsehn läßt.

In solchen Gegenden mußt' ursprünglich der Strom umirren, eh' er sich eine Bahn riß. Dadurch bildeten sich, wie an Teichen, feuchte Wiesen, und Höhlen in der Erde für säugende Thiere, und der Centauer war indessen wilder Hirte, dem Odyssäischen Cyklops gleich; die Gewässer suchten sehnend ihre Richtung. Jemehr sich aber von seinen beiden Ufern das troknere fester bildete, und Richtung gewann durch festwurzelnde Bäume, und Gesträuche und den Weinstok, destomehr mußt' auch der Strom, der seine Bewegung von der Gestalt des Ufers annahm, Richtung gewinnen, bis er, von seinem Ursprung an gedrängt, an einer Stelle durchbrach, wo die Berge, die ihn einschlossen, am leichtesten zusammenhiengen.

The Life-Giving

> The man-subduing, after
> The Centaurs had learned
> The power
> Of honey-sweet wine, suddenly
> With hands they pushed away
> The white milk, the table, by themselves
> And drinking from the silver horns
> They besotted themselves.

The notion of centaurs must be that of the spirit of a river, inasmuch as it makes a course and limit, by force, on the originally pathless and upward growing earth.

Their image, therefore, is at those places where the bank is rich in rocks and grottoes, especially at places where originally the river left the mountain ranges and had to sweep its way diagonally across their direction.

Centaurs, therefore, in their origin are also the teachers of natural science, because from that perspective nature is best discovered.

In such regions the river originally had to meander before it could sweep a course for itself. In that way wet meadows, like those by ponds, were formed, and caverns in the earth for mammals, and at that time the centaur was a wild herdsman, like the Odyssean Cyclops; the waters, yearning, looked for their direction. But the more the dry substance of its two banks consolidated itself, and obtained direction from firmly rooted trees, and shrubs and the grapevine, the more the river, too, taking its direction from the banks, must acquire direction, until, urged on from its origin, it broke through at a place where the mountains that enclosed it were more lightly joined.

So lernten die Centauren die Gewalt des honigsüßen Weins, sie nahmen von dem festgebildeten, bäumereichen Ufer Bewegung und Richtung an, und warfen die weiße Milch und den Tisch mit Händen weg, die gestaltete Welle verdrängte die Ruhe des Teichs, auch die Lebensart am Ufer veränderte sich, der Überfall des Waldes mit den Stürmen und den sicheren Fürsten des Forsts regte das müßige Leben der Haide auf, das stagnirende Gewässer ward so lange zurükgestoßen, vom jäheren Ufer, bis es Arme gewann, und so mit eigener Richtung, von selbst aus silbernen Hörnern trinkend, sich Bahn machte, eine Bestimmung annahm.

Die Gesänge des Ossian besonders sind wahrhafftige Centauren-gesänge, mit dem Stromgeist gesungen, und wie vom griechischen Chiron, der den Achill auch das Saitenspiel gelehrt.

So the centaurs learned the power of honey-sweet wine, they took their motion and direction from the firmly shaped, richly wooded banks, and threw away the white milk and the table with their hands, the shaped ripple displaced the calm of the pond, and the way of life on the banks, too, changed, the forest's assaults with its gales and the secure princes of the woodland stirred up the leisurely life of the moors, the stagnant water was pushed back from the sheer banks to the point where it acquired tributaries and so, with a direction of its own, by itself drinking from silver horns, made a way for itself, became determinate.

The songs of Ossian especially are true centaur songs, sung with the river's spirit, and as of the Grecian Chiron, who taught Achilles to play the lyre.

Last Poems
(1807–1843)

Freundschaft, Liebe . . .

Freundschaft, Liebe, Kirch und Heilge, Kreuze, Bilder,
Altar und Kanzel und Musik. Es tönet ihm die Predigt.
Die Kinderlehre scheint nach Tisch ein schlummernd müßig
Gespräch für Mann und Kind und Jungfraun, fromme Frauen;
Hernach geht er, der Herr, der Burgersmann und Künstler
Auf Feldern froh umher und heimatlichen Auen,
Die Jugend geht betrachtend auch.

Friendship, love . . .

Friendship, love, saints and the church, images, crosses,
Altar and pulpit and music. The sermon rings out for him.
Sunday school after the meal seems drowsily leisured
Conversation for man and child and unmarried girls, pious women;
After that he, the master, the citizen and the artist
Cheerfully walks the fields and his home country's meadows,
And, reflective, young people walk too.

Wenn aus der Ferne . . .

Wenn aus der Ferne, da wir geschieden sind,
   Ich dir noch kennbar bin, die Vergangenheit
      O du Theilhaber meiner Leiden!
         Einiges Gute bezeichnen dir kann

So sage, wie erwartet die Freundin dich?
   In jenen Gärten, da nach entsezlicher
      Und dunkler Zeit wir uns gefunden?
         Hier an den Strömen der heilgen Urwelt.

Das muß ich sagen, einiges Gutes war
   In deinen Bliken, als in den Fernen du
      Dich einmal fröhlich umgesehen
         Immer verschlossener Mensch, mit finstrem

Aussehn. Wie flossen Stunden dahin, wie still
   War meine Seele über der Wahrheit daß
      Ich so getrennt gewesen wäre?
         Ja! ich gestand es, ich war die deine.

Wahrhafftig! wie du alles Bekannte mir
   In mein Gedächtniß bringen und schreiben willst,
      Mit Briefen, so ergeht es mir auch
         Daß ich Vergangenes alles sage.

Wars Frühling? war es Sommer? die Nachtigall
   Mit süßem Liede lebte mit Vögeln, die
      Nicht ferne waren im Gebüsche
         Und mit Gerüchen umgaben Bäum' uns.

If from the distance . . .

If from the distance where we went separate ways
   I'm recognizable to you still, the past,
      O you the sharer of my sufferings,
         Still can convey to you something pleasant,

Then tell me how your girl friend awaits you now?
   In those same gardens where after horrible
      And darkened years once more we're meeting,
         Here by the holy primaevum's rivers.

This much I'm bound to say, something good there was
   About your glances when in the distances
      For once you cheerfully looked round, you
         Man always shut like a clam, of gloomy

Appearance. How the hours slipped away, how calm
   My soul was at the thought of the truth that I
      Had been so long and wholly parted?
         Yes, I confessed, I was yours entirely.

Indeed! As you are trying to bring and write
   These well-known things all back to my memory,
      With letters, so it is with me, and
         All that is past I now freely speak of.

Was it in spring? In summer? The nightingale
   Lived sweetly singing with other birds that were
      Not far away within the thicket,
         And there was fragrance of trees around us.

Die klaren Gänge, niedres Gesträuch und Sand
   Auf dem wir traten, machten erfreulicher
      Und lieblicher die Hyacinthe
         Oder die Tulpe, Viole, Nelke.

Um Wänd und Mauern grünte der Epheu, grünt'
   Ein seelig Dunkel hoher Alleeen. Offt
      Des Abends, Morgens waren dort wir
         Redeten manches und sahn uns froh an.

In meinen Armen lebte der Jüngling auf,
   Der, noch verlassen, aus den Gefilden kam,
      Die er mir wies, mit einer Schwermuth,
         Aber die Nahmen der seltnen Orte

Und alles Schöne hatt' er behalten, das
   An seeligen Gestaden, auch mir sehr werth
      Im heimatlichen Lande blühet
         Oder verborgen, aus hoher Aussicht,

Allwo das Meer auch einer beschauen kann,
   Doch keiner seyn will. Nehme vorlieb, und denk
      An die, die noch vergnügt ist, darum,
         Weil der entzükende Tag uns anschien,

Der mit Geständniß oder der Hände Druk
   Anhub, der uns vereinet. Ach! wehe mir!
      Es waren schöne Tage. Aber
         Traurige Dämmerung folgte nachher.

Du seiest so allein in der schönen Welt
   Behauptest du mir immer, Geliebter! das
      Weist aber du nicht,

The clear-cut pathways, shrubs rather low and sand
    On which we walked were made more agreeable,
        More charming by the hyacinth or
            Tulip, the violet or carnation.

On walls and housefront ivy grew green, green too
    A blissful darkness made by tall avenues.
        There we spent many mornings, evenings,
            Said this and that and exchanged glad glances.

In my embrace it was that the youth revived
    Who, still forsaken, came from the very fields
        He showed to me, with such deep sadness,
            But all the names of those curious places

And all the lovely things, he remembers still
    Which, very dear to me also, are in bloom
        On blessèd shores, our native country,
            Or else concealed, from a high perspective,

Wherever men can look at the ocean too,
    But no one wants to be. Now excuse me, think
        Of her who still is glad because that
            Day so enchanting shone down upon us

Which started with confessions or holding hands
    And which united us. But ah, woe is me.
        Those days were beautiful. However,
            Sad was the twilight that followed after.

That you're so much alone in this lovely world,
    You always claim, my darling, but as for that,
        You cannot know . . .

Der Ruhm

Es knüpft an Gott der Wohllaut, der geleitet
Ein sehr berühmtes Ohr, denn wunderbar
Ist ein berühmtes Leben groß und klar,
Es geht der Mensch zu Fuße oder reitet.

Der Erde Freuden, Freundlichkeit und Güter,
Der Garten, Baum, der Weinberg mit dem Hüter,
Sie scheinen mir ein Wiederglanz des Himmels,
Gewähret von dem Geist den Söhnen des Gewimmels. –

Wenn Einer ist mit Gütern reich beglüket,
Wenn Obst den Garten ihm, und Gold ausschmüket
Die Wohnung und das Haus, was mag er haben
Noch mehr in dieser Welt, sein Herz zu laben?

Fame

With God links up the euphony that attends
A very famous ear; for great indeed
A famous life is, wonderfully clear.
On foot or else on horseback men proceed.

The pleasures of this earth, its gifts, indulgence,
The garden, tree, the vineyard with its keeper,
These seem to me a heavenly refulgence
The Spirit grants our teeming multitude's sons.

If goods in plenty blessed a man who had
Fruits to adorn his orchard, and had gold
To adorn his house and dwelling, then what more
In this world could he have to make him glad?

Auf die Geburt eines Kindes

Wie wird des Himmels Vater schauen
Mit Freude das erwachs'ne Kind,
Gehend auf blumenreichen Auen,
Mit andern, welche lieb ihm sind.

Indessen freue dich des Lebens,
Aus einer guten Seele kommt
Die Schönheit herrlichen Bestrebens,
Göttlicher Grund dir mehr noch frommt.

On the Birth of a Child

How will the heavenly Father see,
With what delight, the child more grown
Walking through wildflowers of the lea
With others dear to it, not alone.

Meanwhile be glad that you are living,
From a good soul there issues forth
The beauty of a noble striving,
Divine ends grant still greater worth.

Das Angenehme dieser Welt . . .

Das Angenehme dieser Welt hab' ich genossen,
Die Jugendstunden sind, wie lang! wie lang! verflossen,
April und Mai und Julius sind ferne,
Ich bin nichts mehr, ich lebe nicht mehr gerne!

The world's agreeable things . . .

The world's agreeable things were mine to enjoy,
The hours of youth, how long they have been gone!
Remote is April, May, remote, July;
I'm nothing now, and listless I live on.

An Zimmern

Von einem Menschen sag ich, wenn der ist gut
    Und weise, was bedarf er? Ist irgend eins
        Das einer Seele gnüget? ist ein Halm, ist
            Eine gereifteste Reb' auf Erden

Gewachsen, die ihn nähre? Der Sinn ist deß
    Also. Ein Freund ist oft die Geliebte, viel
        Die Kunst. O Theurer, dir sag ich die Wahrheit.
            Dädalus Geist und des Walds ist deiner.

To Zimmer

About a man I say, if he's virtuous
   And wise, what can he lack? Is there anything
      Could satisfy a soul? Is there a blade of corn, one
         Vine grown on earth with a fruit so mellow

That it could nourish him? What I mean is this:
   A friend quite often is the belovèd, and art
      Is much. Dear fellow, I'll tell you the truth now:
         Daedalus' spirit is yours, the forest's.

Wenn aus dem Himmel . . .

Wenn aus dem Himmel hellere Wonne sich
    Herabgießt, eine Freude den Menschen kommt,
      Daß sie sich wundern über manches
        Sichtbares, Höheres, Angenehmes:

Wie tönet lieblich heilger Gesang dazu!
    Wie lacht das Herz in Liedern die Wahrheit an,
      Daß Freudigkeit an einem Bildniß –
        Über dem Stege beginnen Schaafe

Den Zug, der fast in dämmernde Wälder geht.
    Die Wiesen aber, welche mit lautrem Grün
      Bedekt sind, sind wie jene Haide,
        Welche gewöhnlicher Weise nah ist

Dem dunkeln Walde. Da, auf den Wiesen auch
    Verweilen diese Schaafe. Die Gipfel, die
      Umher sind, nakte Höhen sind mit
        Eichen bedeket und seltnen Tannen.

Da, wo des Stromes regsame Wellen sind,
    Daß einer, der vorüber des Weges kommt,
      Froh hinschaut, da erhebt der Berge
        Sanfte Gestalt und der Weinberg hoch sich.

Zwar gehn die Treppen unter den Reben hoch
    Herunter, wo der Obstbaum blühend darüber steht
      Und Duft an wilden Heken weilet,
        Wo die verborgenen Veilchen sprossen;

When down from heaven . . .

When down from heaven there gushes a brighter bliss,
    A human joy approaches for human kind
        So that they feel amazed by much that's
            Visible, lofty and pleasing to them

How lovely, blended with it, sound holy hymns!
    How the heart laughs in canticles at the truth
        That to one image clings rejoicing!
            Over the footbridge now sheep begin their

Long track that almost takes them to glimmering woods.
    The meadows, though, all covered with flawless green,
        Are like that heath which, in a fashion
            Usual enough, is not far away from

The gloomy wood. And there, in the meadows, too
    These sheep remain. The hilltops around those parts,
        Bare, arid heights they seem, are covered
            Sparsely with oaks and uncommon spruces.

There, where the river's frolicsome ripples are,
    So that a man who passes them on his way
        Is glad to see them, there the gentle
            Shape of the hills and the vineyard rises.

Although amid the grape-vines quite steeply steps
    Descend, where high the blossoming fruit tree looms
        And on wild hedges fragrance lingers,
            Hidden the violets grow and flower,

Gewässer aber rieseln herab, und sanft
    Ist hörbar dort ein Rauschen den ganzen Tag;
        Die Orte aber in der Gegend
            Ruhen und schweigen den Nachmittag durch.

Yet waters trickle down, and though quiet, faint,
  A murmur there is audible all day long;
    The places in those parts, however,
      Rest after noon and for hours keep silence.

An Zimmern

Die Linien des Lebens sind verschieden
Wie Wege sind, und wie der Berge Gränzen.
Was hier wir sind, kan dort ein Gott ergänzen
Mit Harmonien und ewigem Lohn und Frieden.

To Zimmer

The lines of life are various; they diverge and cease
Like footpaths and the mountains' utmost ends.
What here we are, elsewhere a God amends
With harmonies, eternal recompense and peace.

Überzeugung

Als wie der Tag die Menschen hell umscheinet,
Und mit dem Lichte, das den Höh'n entspringet,
Die dämmernden Erscheinungen vereinet,
Ist Wissen, welches tief der Geistigkeit gelinget.

Conviction

Like the bright day that shines on human kind
And with a light of heavenly origin
All things obscure and various gathers in,
Is knowledge, deeply granted to the mind.

Der Frühling

Wenn auf Gefilden neues Entzüken keimt
   Und sich die Ansicht wieder verschönt und sich
      An Bergen, wo die Bäume grünen,
         Hellere Lüfte, Gewölke zeigen,

O! welche Freude haben die Menschen! froh
   Gehn an Gestaden Einsame, Ruh und Lust
      Und Wonne der Gesundheit blühet,
         Freundliches Lachen ist auch nicht ferne.

Spring

When new enchantment sprouts in the meadowlands,
   And when the view grows lovelier once again
      And over hills where trees are verdant
         Breezes more bright and small clouds are passing,

O what a joy it is for mankind! Content
   The lonely walk on river-banks, peace, delight
      And bliss of healthy vigour bloom, and
         Not far away is kind-hearted laughter.

Das fröhliche Leben

Wenn ich auf die Wiese komme,
Wenn ich auf dem Felde jezt,
Bin ich noch der Zahme, Fromme
Wie von Dornen unverlezt.
Mein Gewand in Winden wehet,
Wie der Geist mir lustig fragt,
Worinn Inneres bestehet,
Bis Auflösung diesem tagt.

O vor diesem sanften Bilde,
Wo die grünen Bäume stehn,
Wie vor einer Schenke Schilde
Kann ich kaum vorübergehn.
Denn die Ruh an stillen Tagen
Dünkt entschieden treflich mir,
Dieses mußt du gar nicht fragen,
Wenn ich soll antworten dir.

Aber zu dem schönen Bache
Such' ich einen Lustweg wohl,
Der, als wie in dem Gemache,
Schleicht durch's Ufer wild und hohl,
Wo der Steg darüber gehet,
Geht's den schönen Wald hinauf,
Wo der Wind den Steg umwehet,
Sieht das Auge fröhlich auf.

Droben auf des Hügels Gipfel
Siz' ich manchen Nachmittag,

The Merry Life

When I come to walk the meadow,
Later, reach the field below,
Still I am the tame, the pious,
As by thorns uninjured go.
In the wind my garment flutters
While I gaily think upon
What our inner life consists of
Till its dissolution's dawn.

Oh before this gentle image
Where the green trees line the sky
As before a tavern's emblem
Hardly I can just pass by.
For the peace on days all quiet
Is true excellence, in my view;
This you should not even ask me
If I am to answer you.

But towards the lovely brook now
For a pleasant path I peer
Which, as in a fine apartment,
Creeps through banks all wild and sheer,
Where the footbridge runs across it,
To the lovely woodland ways
Where the breeze blows round the footbridge
Upward happily I gaze.

Sitting on that hilltop yonder
After noon I spend my time,

Wenn der Wind umsaust die Wipfel,
Bei des Thurmes Glokenschlag,
Und Betrachtung giebt dem Herzen
Frieden, wie das Bild auch ist,
Und Beruhigung den Schmerzen,
Welche reimt Verstand und List.

Holde Landschaft! wo die Straße
Mitten durch sehr eben geht,
Wo der Mond aufsteigt, der blasse,
Wenn der Abendwind entsteht,
Wo die Natur sehr einfältig,
Wo die Berg' erhaben stehn,
Geh' ich heim zulezt, haushältig,
Dort nach goldnem Wein zu sehn.

When the wind roars round the tree crests
And I hear the clock tower chime,
Contemplation gives the heart a
Peace, whatever bodes the while,
And a soothing of the sorrows
That our reason rhymes with guile.

Dearest landscape! where the roadway
Runs right through, all level, straight,
Where the moon, the pale, is rising
When the evening wind's in spate,
Where nature's mind is very simple,
Lofty mountains loom and shine,
I go home at last, domestic,
There to see to golden wine.

Der Spaziergang

Ihr Wälder schön an der Seite,
Am grünen Abhang gemahlt,
Wo ich umher mich leite,
Durch süße Ruhe bezahlt
Für jeden Stachel im Herzen,
Wenn dunkel mir ist der Sinn,
Den Kunst und Sinnen hat Schmerzen
Gekostet von Anbeginn.
Ihr lieblichen Bilder im Thale,
Zum Beispiel Gärten und Baum,
Und dann der Steg der schmale,
Der Bach zu sehen kaum,
Wie schön aus heiterer Ferne
Glänzt Einem das herrliche Bild
Der Landschaft, die ich gerne
Besuch' in Witterung mild.
Die Gottheit freundlich geleitet
Uns erstlich mit Blau,
Hernach mit Wolken bereitet,
Gebildet wölbig und grau,
Mit sengenden Blizen und Rollen
Des Donners, mit Reiz des Gefilds,
Mit Schönheit, die gequollen
Vom Quell ursprünglichen Bilds.

The Walk

You wayside woods, well painted
On the green and sloping glade
Where I conduct my footsteps
With lovely quiet repaid
For every thorn in my bosom,
When dark are my mind and heart
Which paid from the beginning
In grief for thought and art.
You graceful views in the valley,
For instance garden and tree
And then the footbridge, the narrow,
The stream one can hardly see,
How beautiful, clear from the distance
These glorious pictures shine
Of the landscape I like to visit
When the weather is mild and fine.
The deity kindly escorts us,
At first with unblemished blue,
Later with clouds provided,
Well rounded and grey in hue,
With scorching flashes and rolling
Of thunder, and charm of the fields,
With beauty the bubbling source of
The primal image yields.

Der Kirchhof

Du stiller Ort, der grünt mit jungem Grase,
Da liegen Mann und Frau, und Kreuze stehn,
Wohin hinaus geleitet Freunde gehn,
Wo Fenster sind glänzend mit hellem Glase.

Wenn glänzt an dir des Himmels hohe Leuchte
Des Mittags, wann der Frühling dort oft weilt,
Wenn geistige Wolke dort, die graue, feuchte
Wenn sanft der Tag vorbei mit Schönheit eilt!

Wie still ist's nicht an jener grauen Mauer,
Wo drüber her ein Baum mit Früchten hängt;
Mit schwarzen thauigen, und Laub voll Trauer,
Die Früchte aber sind sehr schön gedrängt.

Dort in der Kirch' ist eine dunkle Stille
Und der Altar ist auch in dieser Nacht geringe,
Noch sind darin einige schöne Dinge,
Im Sommer aber singt auf Feldern manche Grille.

Wenn Einer dort Reden des Pfarrherrn hört,
Indeß die Schaar der Freunde steht daneben,
Die mit dem Todten sind, welch eignes Leben
Und welcher Geist, und fromm seyn ungestört.

The Churchyard

You tranquil place, all green with the new grass,
There man and woman lie, and crosses stand
Where, well escorted, friends go walking, and
Where windows are agleam with brightest glass.

When on you gleams the high celestial ray
Of noon, there spring will often linger, last,
When there the spiritual cloud, the moist, the grey
After mild nightfall in beauty hurries past.

How very still it is by that grey wall
A tree overhangs with fruit that soon may drop,
Black dewy ones, the leaves all sorrowful,
But nicely bunched, abundant is the crop.

There in the church a gloomy stillness reigns,
This night the altar, too, from pomp abstains.
Yet still there are some handsome things in it,
In summer, though, in fields chirps many a cricket.

When someone hears the vicar talking there,
While next to him there stands the crowd of friends
Who join the dead one, how his life is rare
And what a spirit, awe no disturbance rends.

Die Zufriedenheit

Wenn aus dem Leben kann ein Mensch sich finden,
Und das begreifen, wie das Leben sich empfindet,
So ist es gut; wer aus Gefahr sich windet,
Ist wie ein Mensch, der kommt aus Sturm' und Winden.

Doch besser ists, die Schönheit auch zu kennen,
Einrichtung, die Erhabenheit des ganzen Lebens,
Wenn Freude kommt aus Mühe des Bestrebens,
Und wie die Güter all' in dieser Zeit sich nennen.

Der Baum, der grünt, die Gipfel von Gezweigen,
Die Blumen, die des Stammes Rind' umgeben,
Sind aus der göttlichen Natur, sie sind ein Leben,
Weil über dieses sich des Himmels Lüfte neigen.

Wenn aber mich neugier'ge Menschen fragen,
Was dieses sei, sich für Empfindung wagen,
Was die Bestimmung sei, das Höchste, das Gewinnen,
So sag' ich, das ist es, das Leben, wie das Sinnen.

Wen die Natur gewöhnlich, ruhig machet,
Er mahnet mich, den Menschen froh zu leben,
Warum? die Klarheit ist's, vor der auch Weise beben,
Die Freudigkeit ist schön, wenn alles scherzt und lachet.

Der Männer Ernst, der Sieg und die Gefahren,
Sie kommen aus Gebildetheit, und aus Gewahren,
Es geh' ein Ziel; das Hohe von den Besten
Erkennt sich an dem Seyn, und schönen Überresten.

Contentment

When out of life a man can find his way
And comes to grasp what life is felt to be,
That's good; the man released from danger, he
Is like one saved from storm and ocean spray.

But better still if he knows beauty too,
Order, array, the worth of all that's living,
When joy comes from the labour of our striving,
Or what these days they call the ends of what they do.

The tree that sprouts, the crest of all its boughs,
The flowers that grow around the bark and bole
Are nature's, that's divine, a living whole,
Because above them heavenly breezes blow.

But when inquisitive persons now ask me
What is this thing, for feeling to risk all,
What is the aim, the gain, the destiny –
I say, that's it, it's life, like thinking, quizzical.

He whom this nature makes quite common, flat,
He minds me to live cheerfully for others' sake,
What for? For clarity wise men tremble at,
Joy is a good thing, when all folk laugh and joke.

Men's gravity, great perils, conquering zest,
These come from education and awareness
That there's a goal; the high worth of the best
Is shown by what exists, and relics in their fairness.

Sie selber aber sind, wie Auserwählte,
Von ihnen ist das Neue, das Erzählte,
Die Wirklichkeit der Thaten geht nicht unter,
Wie Sterne glänzen, giebts ein Leben groß und munter.

Das Leben ist aus Thaten und verwegen,
Ein hohes Ziel, gehaltener's Bewegen,
Der Gang und Schritt, doch Seeligkeit aus Tugend
Und großer Ernst, und dennoch lautre Jugend.

Die Reu, und die Vergangenheit in diesem Leben
Sind ein verschiednes Seyn, die Eine glüket
Zu Ruhm und Ruh', und allem, was entrüket,
Zu hohen Regionen, die gegeben;

Die Andre führt zu Quaal, und bittern Schmerzen
Wenn Menschen untergehn, die mit dem Leben scherzen,
Und das Gebild' und Antliz sich verwandelt
Von Einem, der nicht gut und schön gehandelt.

Die Sichtbarkeit lebendiger Gestalt, das Währen
In dieser Zeit, wie Menschen sich ernähren,
Ist fast ein Zwist, der lebet der Empfindung,
Der andre strebt nach Mühen und Erfindung.

But they themselves are, as are the elect,
Of them the new tells, them the old lays reflect,
The power and truth of deeds does not decay,
Like stars they shine, make life both great and gay.

Life comes from deeds and it is daring, bold,
A lofty aim, a movement more controlled,
The gait and pace, from virtue, bliss and truth,
Great gravity, and yet a candid youth.

Remorse, and all the past one's left behind
Are a quite different being, the one proves
Most fit for fame and rest and every thing that removes,
To those high regions given us, assigned;

The other leads to torment, bitter pain,
When those who trifled with their lives go down
And when the stature and the face are changed
Of one who acted badly, wrongly, self-estranged.

The living figure's visibility,
How men subsist in time, find nourishment,
Almost conflict: one lives to feel and be,
The other strives to labour and invent.

Nicht alle Tage . . .

Nicht alle Tage nennet die schönsten der,
  Der sich zurüksehnt unter die Freuden wo
    Ihn Freunde liebten wo die Menschen
      Über dem Jüngling mit Gunst verweilten.

Not any day . . .

Not any day will he call the happiest
  Who wishes he were back among pleasures where
    He had the love of friends, where others
      Dwelled on the youth with good will and favour.

Der Herbst

Die Sagen, die der Erde sich entfernen,
Vom Geiste, der gewesen ist und wiederkehret,
Sie kehren zu der Menschheit sich, und vieles lernen
Wir aus der Zeit, die eilends sich verzehret.

Die Bilder der Vergangenheit sind nicht verlassen
Von der Natur, als wie die Tag' verblassen
Im hohen Sommer, kehrt der Herbst zur Erde nieder,
Der Geist der Schauer findet sich am Himmel wieder.

In kurzer Zeit hat vieles sich geendet,
Der Landmann, der am Pfluge sich gezeiget,
Er siehet, wie das Jahr sich frohem Ende neiget,
In solchen Bildern ist des Menschen Tag vollendet.

Der Erde Rund mit Felsen ausgezieret
Ist wie die Wolke nicht, die Abends sich verlieret,
Es zeiget sich mit einem goldnen Tage,
Und die Vollkommenheit ist ohne Klage.

Autumn

The legends that depart from land and sea,
Of spirit that once was here and will return,
These turn to men, and there is much we learn
From time that, self-devoured, moves speedily.

No image of the past is quite mislaid
By Nature; summer's dogdays fade,
But back to earth at once will autumn fly;
The ghost of showers gathers in the sky.

In a short time how much has passed away!
The countryman observed behind his plough
Sees how the year meets a glad ending now;
Such images complete the human day.

The sphere of earth adorned with rocks revolves
Not like a cloud, which after dusk dissolves;
Within a golden day the earth appears,
And to perfection no complaint adheres.

Der Sommer

Das Erndtefeld erscheint, auf Höhen schimmert
Der hellen Wolke Pracht, indeß am weiten Himmel
In stiller Nacht die Zahl der Sterne flimmert,
Groß ist und weit von Wolken das Gewimmel.

Die Pfade gehn entfernter hin, der Menschen Leben
Es zeiget sich auf Meeren unverborgen,
Der Sonne Tag ist zu der Menschen Streben
Ein hohes Bild, und golden glänzt der Morgen.

Mit neuen Farben ist geschmükt der Gärten Breite,
Der Mensch verwundert sich, daß sein Bemühn gelinget,
Was er mit Tugend schafft, und was er hoch vollbringet,
Es steht mit der Vergangenheit in prächtigem Geleite.

Summer

The harvest field appears, high up there glimmers
The bright clouds' glory, while the wide sky along
In quiet night the stars' profusion shimmers.
Vast and with clouds expanded is that throng.

The paths go out still farther, human lives
Will show themselves on oceans unconcealed,
The solar day to human striving gives
A noble image, gold that mornings yield.

The garden in new colours is arrayed,
Folk marvel that their labour brings reward,
What they achieve with virtue, worthily have made,
And with the past they stand in good accord.

Der Frühling

Es kommt der neue Tag aus fernen Höhn herunter,
Der Morgen der erwacht ist aus den Dämmerungen,
Er lacht die Menschheit an, geschmükt und munter,
Von Freuden ist die Menschheit sanft durchdrungen.

Ein neues Leben will der Zukunft sich enthüllen,
Mit Blüthen scheint, dem Zeichen froher Tage,
Das große Thal, die Erde sich zu füllen,
Entfernt dagegen ist zur Frühlingszeit die Klage.

Mit Unterthänigkeit
d: 3ten März 1648.   Scardanelli.

Spring

New day descends from many a distant height,
The morning woken out of twilight shades.
It laughs to human folk adorned and bright,
Gently with joys their hearts and minds pervades.

A new life to the future shows its will,
With blossom, with the signs of happy days
The valley's width, the whole earth seems to fill,
While far away in springtime sorrow stays.

> Your humble servant

March 3rd 1648.   Scardanelli.

Der Sommer

Wenn dann vorbei des Frühlings Blüthe schwindet,
So ist der Sommer da, der um das Jahr sich windet.
Und wie der Bach das Thal hinuntergleitet,
So ist der Berge Pracht darum verbreitet.
Daß sich das Feld mit Pracht am meisten zeiget,
Ist, wie der Tag, der sich zum Abend neiget;
Wie so das Jahr verweilt, so sind des Sommers Stunden
Und Bilder der Natur dem Menschen oft verschwunden.

d. 24 Mai
   1778.   Scardanelli.

Summer

When then the blooms of springtime disappear,
Summer is here, that winds around the year.
And as the brook winds down the valley-side
So mountain splendour round it stretches wide.
The utmost splendour field and meadow bring,
Is like the day, that bends to evening;
While the year lingers on, for men a summer's day
And nature's images often will fade away.

May 24th
   1778.   Scardanelli.

Der Winter

Wenn blaicher Schnee verschönert die Gefilde,
Und hoher Glanz auf weiter Ebne blinkt,
So reizt der Sommer fern, und milde
Naht sich der Frühling oft, indeß die Stunde sinkt.

Die prächtige Erscheinung ist, die Luft ist feiner,
Der Wald ist hell, es geht der Menschen keiner
Auf Straßen, die zu sehr entlegen sind, die Stille machet
Erhabenheit, wie dennoch alles lachet.

Der Frühling scheint nicht mit der Blüthen Schimmer
Dem Menschen so gefallend, aber Sterne
Sind an dem Himmel hell, man siehet gerne
Den Himmel fern, der ändert fast sich nimmer.

Die Ströme sind, wie Ebnen, die Gebilde
Sind, auch zerstreut, erscheinender, die Milde
Des Lebens dauert fort, der Städte Breite
Erscheint besonders gut auf ungemeßner Weite.

Winter

When pale snow beautifies the meadow land
And high effulgence from the wide plain blinks,
Summer attracts us from a distance, and
Often mild spring draws near while the hour sinks.

The glorious prospect is, the air is rarer,
The wood is bright, no person, no wayfarer
Walks roads now too remote, the calm maintains
Sublimity, and yet how laughter reigns.

Spring does not shine with blossom's colour ranges,
So pleasing human kind, but stars are bright
Against the sky above, a welcome sight
Like the far sky that hardly ever changes.

The rivers are, like plains, the shapes of wildness
Are scattered also, more revealed the mildness
Of life continues, and our cities' traces
Appear most clearly on unmeasured spaces.

Der Winter

Das Feld ist kahl, auf ferner Höhe glänzet
Der blaue Himmel nur, und wie die Pfade gehen
Erscheinet die Natur, als Einerlei, das Wehen
Ist frisch, und die Natur von Helle nur umkränzet.

Der Erde Stund ist sichtbar von dem Himmel
Den ganzen Tag, in heller Nacht umgeben
Wenn hoch erscheint von Sternen das Gewimmel,
Und geistiger das weit gedehnte Leben.

Winter

The field is bare, on distant hilltop ground
The blue sky only gleams and as the footpaths go
Nature appears as all one thing, winds grow
Quite fresh, with brightness only nature wreathed around.

The hour of earth is visible from the sky
The whole day long, surrounded by bright night,
When teeming of the stars appears on high,
More spiritual this human life, stretched out.

Der Sommer

Noch ist die Zeit des Jahrs zu sehn, und die Gefilde
Des Sommers stehn in ihrem Glanz, in ihrer Milde;
Des Feldes Grün ist prächtig ausgebreitet,
Allwo der Bach hinab mit Wellen gleitet.

So zieht der Tag hinaus durch Berg und Thale,
Mit seiner Unaufhaltsamkeit und seinem Strale,
Und Wolken ziehn in Ruh', in hohen Räumen
Es scheint das Jahr mit Herrlichkeit zu säumen.

Mit Unterthänigkeit

d. 9ten Merz   Scardanelli
   1940.

Summer

Still you can see the season, and the field
Of summer shows its mildness and its pride.
The meadow's green is splendidly outspread
Where down the brook and all its wavelets glide.

So now the day moves on through hill and valley,
Not to be stopped and in its beam arrayed,
And clouds move calmly on through lofty space
As though the year in majesty delayed.

                Your humble and obedient servant
March 9th   Scardanelli
  1940.

Der Herbst

Das Glänzen der Natur ist höheres Erscheinen,
Wo sich der Tag mit vielen Freuden endet,
Es ist das Jahr, das sich mit Pracht vollendet,
Wo Früchte sich mit frohem Glanz vereinen.

Das Erdenrund ist so geschmükt, und selten lärmet
Der Schall durchs offne Feld, die Sonne wärmet
Den Tag des Herbstes mild, die Felder stehen
Als eine Aussicht weit, die Lüffte wehen

Die Zweig' und Äste durch mit frohem Rauschen
Wenn schon mit Leere sich die Felder dann vertauschen,
Der ganze Sinn des hellen Bildes lebet
Als wie ein Bild, das goldne Pracht umschwebet.

d. 15<u>ten</u> Nov.

1759.

Autumn

Nature's bright gleam is higher revelation,
Where amid many joys the day comes to its end,
It is the year in glorious consummation,
Where fruit with cheerful brightness, gleaming, blend.

Earth's globe is thus adorned, with rare alarms
Of noise through open fields, the sunshine warms
The day of autumn mildly, fields lie so
That widely they are viewed, the breezes blow

Through twigs and branches, rustling cheerfully,
Though then to emptiness the fields give way.
The total meaning of this picture lives, as might
A picture framed in glory, golden light.

Nov. 15th

1759.

Der Sommer

Im Thale rinnt der Bach, die Berg' an hoher Seite,
Sie grünen weit umher an dieses Thales Breite,
Und Bäume mit dem Laube stehn gebreitet,
Daß fast verborgen dort der Bach hinunter gleitet.

So glänzt darob des schönen Sommers Sonne
Daß fast zu eilen scheint des hellen Tages Wonne,
Der Abend mit der Frische kommt zu Ende,
Und trachtet, wie er das dem Menschen noch vollende.

mit Unterthänigkeit
Scardanelli.

d. 24 Mai
   1758.

Summer

Brooks thread the valleys, each high mountain-side
Is greening far around this vale so wide
And trees in all their leafage stand outspread
So that the brook glides down an almost hidden bed.

The lovely summer sun so shines on it
That almost the day's radiance seems to flit.
Then evening with coolness makes an end,
Seeks to perfect it and for men amend.

Your humble servant

May 24th   Scardanelli.
   1758.

Der Sommer

Die Tage gehn vorbei mit sanffter Lüffte Rauschen,
Wenn mit der Wolke sie der Felder Pracht vertauschen,
Des Thales Ende trifft der Berge Dämmerungen,
Dort, wo des Stromes Wellen sich hinabgeschlungen

Der Wälder Schatten sieht umhergebreitet,
Wo auch der Bach entfernt hinuntergleitet,
Und sicht bar ist der Ferne Bild in Stunden,
Wenn sich der Mensch zu diesem Sinn gefunden.

d. 24 Mai   Scardanelli.
  1758.

Summer

The days go by with rustling breezes, tender,
Exchanging cloud for meadows full of splendour,
The valley's end meets with the darkling hills
Yonder, where downward wound the river's rills.

The forest shadow sees expanded wide
Where downward, far away, the wavelets glide,
And in those hours far places, visible, shine
When human beings to such sense incline.

May 24th   Scardanelli.
   1758.

Der Winter

Wenn ungesehn und nun vorüber sind die Bilder
Der Jahreszeit, so kommt des Winters Dauer,
Das Feld ist leer, die Ansicht scheinet milder,
Und Stürme wehn umher und Reegenschauer.

Als wie ein Ruhetag, so ist des Jahres Ende,
Wie einer Frage Ton, daß dieser sich vollende,
Alsdann erscheint des Frühlings neues Werden,
So glänzet die Natur mit ihrer Pracht auf Erden.

Mit Unterthänigkeit

d. 24 April   Scardanelli.
  1849

Winter

When past, unseen the season's images are,
Winter's duration comes to us again;
The field is bare, the view seems milder far,
And gales blow round about and showers of rain.

A day of rest, such is the year's conclusion,
A question's tone that seeks a complement.
Then to our eyes the Spring's new growth is lent –
So Nature shines on earth in her profusion.

Your humble and obedient servant

April 24th   Scardanelli.
  1849

Der Frühling

Wenn aus der Tiefe kommt der Frühling in das Leben,
Es wundert sich der Mensch, und neue Worte streben
Aus Geistigkeit, die Freude kehret wieder
Und festlich machen sich Gesang und Lieder.

Das Leben findet sich aus Harmonie der Zeiten,
Daß immerdar den Sinn Natur und Geist geleiten,
Und die Vollkommenheit ist Eines in dem Geiste,
So findet vieles sich, und aus Natur das Meiste.

Mit Unterthänigkeit
Scardanelli.

d. 24 Mai
  1758.

Spring

When springtime from the depth returns to life,
Men are amazed, and from their minds aspire
New words, and happiness once more is rife,
And festive music rings from house and choir.

Life finds itself in seasonal harmonies,
That ever Nature, Spirit might attend our thought,
And *one* within our minds perfection is;
So, most of all from Nature, much to itself is brought.

                    Your humble and obedient servant

May 24th   Scardanelli.
  1758.

In lieblicher Bläue . . .

In lieblicher Bläue blühet mit dem metallenen Dache der Kirch-thurm. Den umschwebet Geschrei der Schwalben, den umgiebt die rührendste Bläue. Die Sonne gehet hoch darüber und färbet das Blech, im Winde aber oben stille krähet die Fahne. Wenn einer unter der Gloke dann herabgeht, jene Treppen, ein stilles Leben ist es, weil, wenn abgesondert so sehr die Gestalt ist, die Bildsamkeit her-auskommt dann des Menschen. Die Fenster, daraus die Gloken tönen, sind wie Thore an Schönheit. Nemlich, weil noch der Natur nach sind die Thore, haben diese die Ähnlichkeit von Bäumen des Walds. Reinheit aber ist auch Schönheit. Innen aus Verschiedenem entsteht ein ernster Geist. So sehr einfältig aber die Bilder, so sehr heilig sind die, daß man wirklich oft fürchtet, die zu beschreiben. Die Himmlischen aber, die immer gut sind, alles zumal, wie Reiche, haben diese, Tugend und Freude. Der Mensch darf das nachahmen. Darf, wenn lauter Mühe das Leben, ein Mensch aufschauen und sagen: so will ich auch seyn? Ja. So lange die Freundlichkeit noch am Herzen, die Reine, dauert, misset nicht unglüklich der Mensch sich mit der Gottheit. Ist unbekannt Gott? Ist er offenbar wie der Himmel? dieses glaub' ich eher. Des Menschen Maaß ist's. Voll Verdienst, doch dichterisch, wohnet der Mensch auf dieser Erde. Doch reiner ist nicht der Schatten der Nacht mit den Sternen, wenn ich so sagen könnte, als der Mensch, der heißet ein Bild der Gottheit.

———————

Giebt es auf Erden ein Maaß? Es giebt keines. Nemlich es hemmen den Donnergang nie die Welten des Schöpfers. Auch eine Blume ist schön, weil sie blühet unter der Sonne. Es findet das Aug' oft im Leben Wesen, die viel schöner noch zu nennen wären als die Blumen. O! ich weiß das wohl! Denn zu bluten an Gestalt und Herz, und ganz nicht mehr zu seyn, gefällt das Gott? Die Seele aber,

In lovely blueness . . .

In lovely blueness with its metal roof the steeple blossoms. Around it the crying of swallows hovers, most moving blueness surrounds it. The sun hangs high above it and colours the sheets of tin, but up above in the wind silently crows the weathercock. If now someone comes down beneath the bell, comes down those steps, a still life it is, because, when the figure is so detached, the man's plasticity is brought out. The windows from which the bells are ringing are like gates in beauty. That is, because gates still conform to nature, these have a likeness to trees of the wood. But purity too is beauty. Within, out of diversity a serious mind is formed. Yet these images are so simple, so very holy are these, that really often one is afraid to describe them. But the Heavenly, who are always good, all things at once, like the rich, have these, virtue and pleasure. This men may imitate. May, when life is all hardship, may a man look up and say: I too would like to resemble these? Yes. As long as kindliness, which is pure, remains in his heart not unhappily a man may compare himself with the divinity. Is God unknown? Is He manifest as the sky? This rather I believe. It is the measure of man. Full of acquirements, but poetically, man dwells on this earth. But the darkness of night with all the stars is not purer, if I could put it like that, than man, who is called the image of God.

Is there a measure on earth? There is none. For never the Creator's worlds constrict the progress of thunder. A flower too is beautiful, because it blooms under the sun. Often in life the eye discovers beings that could be called much more beautiful still than flowers. Oh, well I know it! For to bleed both in body and heart, and wholly to be no more, does that please God? Yet the soul, it is my belief,

wie ich glaube, muß rein bleiben, sonst reicht an das Mächtige auf Fittigen der Adler mit lobendem Gesange und der Stimme so vieler Vögel. Es ist die Wesenbeit, die Gestalt ist's. Du schönes Bächlein, du scheinest rührend, indem du rollest so klar, wie das Auge der Gottheit, durch die Milchstraße. Ich kenne dich wohl, aber Thränen quillen aus dem Auge. Ein heiteres Leben seh' ich in den Gestalten mich umblühen der Schöpfung, weil ich es nicht unbillig vergleiche den einsamen Tauben auf dem Kirchhof. Das Lachen aber scheint mich zu grämen der Menschen, nemlich ich hab' ein Herz. Möcht' ich ein Komet seyn? Ich glaube. Denn sie haben die Schnelligkeit der Vögel; sie blühen an Feuer, und sind wie Kinder an Reinheit. Größeres zu wünschen, kann nicht des Menschen Natur sich vermessen. Der Tugend Heiterkeit verdient auch gelobt zu werden vom ernsten Geiste, der zwischen den drei Säulen wehet des Gartens. Eine schöne Jungfrau muß das Haupt umkränzen mit Myrthenblumen, weil sie einfach ist ihrem Wesen nach und ihrem Gefühl. Myrthen aber giebt es in Griechenland.

Wenn einer in den Spiegel siehet, ein Mann, und siehet darinn sein Bild, wie abgemahlt; es gleicht dem Manne. Augen hat des Menschen Bild, hingegen Licht der Mond. Der König Oedipus hat ein Auge zuviel vieleicht. Diese Leiden dieses Mannes, sie scheinen unbeschreiblich, unaussprechlich, unausdrüklich. Wenn das Schauspiel ein solches darstellt, kommt's daher. Wie ist mir's aber, gedenk' ich deiner jezt? Wie Bäche reißt das Ende von Etwas mich dahin, welches sich wie Asien ausdehnet. Natürlich dieses Leiden, das hat Oedipus. Natürlich ist's darum. Hat auch Herkules gelitten? Wohl. Die Dioskuren in ihrer Freundschaft haben die nicht Leiden auch getragen? Nemlich wie Herkules mit Gott zu streiten, das ist Leiden. Und die Unsterblichkeit im Neide dieses Lebens, diese zu theilen, ist ein Leiden auch. Doch das ist auch ein Leiden, wenn mit Sommerfleken ist bedekt ein Mensch, mit manchen Fleken ganz überdekt zu seyn! Das thut die schöne Sonne: nemlich die

must remain pure, else on pinions the eagle reaches far as the Mighty with songs of praise and the voice of so many birds. It is the essence, the form it is. You beautiful little stream, you seem touching, as you flow so clear, clear as the eye of divinity, through the Milky Way. I know you well, but tears gush out of my eyes. A serene life I see blossom around me in the shapes of creation, because not unfittingly I compare it to the solitary doves of the churchyard. But the laughter of men seems to grieve me, for I have a heart. Would I like to be a comet? I think so. For they possess the swiftness of birds; they blossom with fire and are like children in purity. To desire more than that, human nature cannot presume. The serenity of virtue also deserves to be praised by the serious spirit which wafts between the garden's three columns. A beautiful virgin must wreathe her head with myrtle, because she is simple both in her nature and in her feelings. But myrtles are to be found in Greece.

If someone looks into the mirror, a man, and in it sees his image, as though it were a painted likeness; it resembles the man. The image of man has eyes, whereas the moon has light. King Oedipus has an eye too many perhaps. The sufferings of this man, they seem indescribable, unspeakable, inexpressible. If the drama represents something like this, that is why. But what comes over me if I think of you now? Like brooks the end of something sweeps me away, which expands like Asia. Of course, this affliction, Oedipus has it too. Of course, that is why. Did Hercules suffer too? Indeed. The Dioscuri in their friendship, did not they bear afflictions too? For to fight with God, like Hercules, that is an affliction. And immortality amidst the envy of this life, to share in that, is an affliction too. But this also is an affliction, when a man is covered with freckles, to be wholly covered with many a spot! The beautiful sun does that: for it rears

ziehet alles auf. Die Jünglinge führt die Bahn sie mit Reizen ihrer Stralen wie mit Rosen. Die Leiden scheinen so, die Oedipus getragen, als wie ein armer Mann klagt, daß ihm etwas fehle. Sohn Laios, armer Fremdling in Griechenland! Leben ist Tod, und Tod ist auch ein Leben.

up all things. It leads young men along their course with the allure-
ments of its beams as though with roses. The afflictions that
Oedipus bore seem like this, as when a poor man complains that
there is something he lacks. Son of Laios, poor stranger in Greece!
Life is death, and death is a kind of life.

Notes

Notes

THE EXCELLENT (page 61)

In November 1794 Hölderlin wrote to his friend Christian Ludwig Neuffer from Jena: '. . . a sentence which I happened to see today in the announcement of Wieland's collected works still burns in my heart. It says that Wieland's Muse began with the beginning of German poetry and will end with its decline. Wonderful! Call me a childish fool, but a thing like that can spoil a whole week for me . . .'

VANINI (page 115)

Lucilio Vanini (1585–1619) was an Italian philosopher burnt at the stake for atheism and for dabbling in magic and astrology. Hölderlin sees him as the inspired philosopher-prophet at odds with the 'nexus of rulers and clerics', and thus as a figure akin both to Empedocles and himself.

TO A PRINCESS OF DESSAU (page 147)

Alcaic ode, probably written in November 1799, after the renewed outbreak of war, to which there are several allusions in the poem. The reference to Italy suggests that the ode was addressed to the Duchess Luise of Anhalt Dessau, rather than to her daughter-in-law Amalie, a sister of Hölderlin's patron Princess Augusta of Homburg. The Duchess had travelled in Italy from 1795 to 1796. Luisium is the name of a palace near Dessau, the grounds of which Hölderlin had seen in 1795 while walking from Jena to Halle.

TO PRINCESS AUGUSTA OF HOMBURG (page 151)

Alcaic ode, written for her twenty-third birthday. The Princess was not only devoted to Hölderlin's novel *Hyperion* – the only work of his available in book form at this time – but made copies of several of his poems that might otherwise have been lost. The middle sections of the ode refer to the withdrawal of the French revolutionary troops from Homburg in March 1799. The 'hero' of the fifth stanza is most probably Napoleon, whose recent *coup d'état* was welcomed in many quarters as a promise of lasting peace in Europe. Princess Augusta's mother, Caroline, is known to have admired Napoleon.

ROUSSEAU (page 179)

This attempt to recast his Asclepiadean ode 'To the Germans' shows how much better the Alcaic form lent itself to the peculiar flow of Hölderlin's later odes. The change in subject is not so significant, since the Rousseau of this ode is a figure deeply akin to the solitary poet of the other ode.

HEIDELBERG (page 183)

Hölderlin's poem is in the Asclepiadean metre, one that he rarely chose for his longer odes. Because, for all but epigrammatic effects, this metre is far more refractory in English than in German, I was unable to make my version flow across the caesuras in the first and second lines of each strophe. My original version, therefore, did not satisfy me, being neither truly metrical nor as free as I should have made it if I had not attempted to reproduce the metre. Since later attempts proved no more satisfactory, I transposed my version into Alcaics, a form that had become congenial to me in the course of translating Hölderlin, so that I could rely on my ear for it, rather than on 'scansion' and syllable counts.

The whole vexed question of whether ancient quantitative metres can be imitated at all in English, or ought to be, must be left open here. I will mention only that the hexameters of A. H. Clough proved as flexible and natural a metre for him as the usual iambic pentameter for other English poets; and that some of Hölderlin's ode forms were successfully taken over by twentieth century poets in English, Vernon Watkins and W. H. Auden among them.

NATURE AND ART OR SATURN AND JUPITER (page 223)

The eighteenth-century preoccupation with the antinomy between Nature and Art is touched upon in the Introduction. Hölderlin identifies the triumph of Art over Nature with the triumph of Jupiter over Saturn, drawing on ancient poetic tradition, yet giving it a personal twist. Jupiter becomes closely identified with the *Zeitgeist* of his earlier ode; he is called 'Kronion' because Hölderlin identifies Kronos (Saturn) with Chronos (Time), so that Jupiter becomes both 'the son of Kronos' and a 'son of Time'. This anticipates the curious theology of the hymns, with their two parallel orders of divinity – one temporal and temporary (the gods), the other timeless and eternal (God). Compare Hölderlin's letter on the one quarrel in the world (Introduction, page 35).

SUNG BENEATH THE ALPS (page 229)

The one completed ode by Hölderlin written in a modified Sapphic metre. Hölderlin saw the Swiss Alps in 1801.

THE POET'S VOCATION (page 233)

The last line has puzzled many commentators. Hölderlin's disgust with the exploitation and debasement of religion, science and art is such that the allusion to God's absence has been construed as irony. Yet Hölderlin is quite serious in stating that the dominant trends in our civilization will never be reversed until there is a general recognition of God's absence in our lives. Only this awareness of God's absence can bring about a general *metanoia* – and so release the poet and prophet from his irreligious solitude.

VOICE OF THE PEOPLE (page 239)

Cf. S. T. Coleridge: 'I never said that the *vox populi* was of course the *vox Dei*. It may be, but it may be and with equal probability, *a priori, vox Diaboli*. That the voice of ten millions of men calling for the same thing, is a spirit, I believe; but whether that be a spirit of Heaven or Hell, I can only know by trying the thing called for by the prescript of reason and God's will' (*Table Talk*, 1888, page 160). It is such rational and moral doubts as Coleridge's that the peculiar reticence and impersonality of this ode imply from the opening lines onward; but Hölderlin's vision here is tragic rather than moral, and what the Christian moralist would see as wickedness and unreason he must affirm as a tragic sacrifice. There is no need to point out that Hölderlin's recognition of a communal 'death-wish' anticipates some of the discoveries of Freud and other psychologists.

THE BLIND SINGER (page 245)

The quotation is from the *Ajax* of Sophocles, line 706, and means 'Cruel woe has Ares lifted from our eyes'.

TIMIDNESS (page 265)

In the last strophe Hölderlin plays on various derivations from the verb *schicken* ('to send'). *Geschickt*, literally 'sent', also means 'skilful' – so that there is an etymological connection between the artist's skill and his mission or his fitness to serve, for fitness is implied in the German word *Geschicklichkeit*. Yet the nouns *Geschick* and *Schicksal* also mean fate or destiny – and again Hölderlin takes up the etymological link. These multiple meanings could be rendered only by adding alternative words in English.

GANYMEDE (page 269)

This last ode renders what Hölderlin meant by saying (in his letter to Böhlendorff) that Apollo had struck him. His 'madness', among other things, was a release from tremendous mental and spiritual exertions, and a removal from the entire sphere of human relations, human converse (*Gespräch*) and human conflict. In the last versions of these late odes Hölderlin translates personal experiences into myth, identifying himself with a centaur (Chiron) and a spirit or demigod (Ganymede).

BREAD AND WINE (page 319)

In this elegy Hölderlin develops his notion of alternating eras or cycles of Day and Night, epiphany and retraction. The conception, though new, owes something to the thought of Empedocles and his predecessors, and is pantheistic in its likening of history to natural processes. Hölderlin's purpose here is to 'justify the ways of God to Men', yet in a way consonant with his own tragic sense of life and his experience of God's absence in his own time. His notion of the 'searing beam', the unbearable brightness of God, on the other hand, is firmly rooted in Biblical, esoteric and poetic tradition. *Paradise Lost* presents parallels; and so does the poetry of William Blake, who wrote in 'The Little Black Boy':

> And we are put on earth a little space
> That we may learn to bear the beams of love.

THE NOOK AT HARDT (page 459)

Another of the fragments that Hölderlin himself salvaged as a poem complete in itself, making it one of the 'Canticles of Night' that were the last poems he sent out for publication, in December 1803. I had left it untranslated before because of its regional allusions – to Ulrich, Duke of Württemberg (1487–1550), a fighter for the Protestant cause who, when deposed and pursued in 1519, hid between sandstone rocks, the Ulrichstein, at Hardt, and was saved by a spider's web spun across the entrance. The leaning stones are above a wooded gorge between Nürtingen and Denkendorf, places in which Hölderlin spent his childhood.

FOR MOTHER EARTH (page 469)

Probably written late in 1800, and left unfinished like the Pindaric 'hymn', 'As on a holiday . . .' . An extant prose draft suggests that, as in the case of the earlier hymn, Hölderlin could not fit all he had to say into the form he had chosen – a choric form in both cases, demanding a strict balance between each group of three strophes.

The names of the three brothers have a mythical aura, but seem to be Hölderlin's own invention – a rare analogy with William Blake's names in his prophetic poems. A number of poems by Klopstock provided a precedent for the three persons of his poem.

THE RHINE (page 499)

Stanza 14, lines 12–15: The 'wise man' is Socrates in Plato's *Symposium*.

It is significant that this poem was originally dedicated and addressed not to Sinclair, but to Wilhelm Heinse, to whom 'Bread and Wine' had also been dedicated and addressed. Hölderlin changed the dedication after Heinse's death in 1803, when Sinclair and Sinclair's sovereign, the Landgrave of Homburg, were his patrons.

The original version ended as follows, with lines referring so specifically to Heinse that they had to be replaced when the dedication was changed:

> And you say to me from afar
> Out of a soul ever serene,
> What do you call good fortune,
> What misfortune? That question, my father,
> I well understand, but still in my ears
> Roars the wave that submerged me
> And I dream
> Of the ocean bed's precious pearl.

> But you, familiar with the sea
> As with firm land, look at the earth
> And at light: unlike the two seem, you think,
> But both divine, for always,
> By Aether sent to you
> A genius surrounds your brow.

These lines allude not only to Hölderlin's loss of his love, Susette – the 'precious pearl' – and so to the time when Heinse had been close to Susette and Hölderlin in Kassel and Bad Driburg, but to Heinse's exemplariness for Hölderlin as a 'father' figure and sage whose celebration of a Dionysian Greece was very different from Winckelmann's interpretation of the Hellenic ideal.

CONCILIATOR, YOU THAT NO LONGER . . . (page 513)

Stanza 4, line 7: 'The faithful cloud' is the disciples, the 'cloud of witness'.

CELEBRATION OF PEACE (page 523)

Whole books have been devoted to speculations about the identity of the 'prince of the feast-day', who has been interpreted historically (as Napoleon, because the poem was occasioned by the Treaty of Lunéville in February 1801), ideologically (as the 'genius of the German people'), allegorically (as Peace) and even, untenably, as Christ, though at one point in the poem Christ is entreated to join the prince of the feast-day. What is certain is that Hölderlin did not want to establish his identity, as we see by comparing the preliminary drafts, in which Peace is unequivocally addressed. The introduction to the prince, in the second strophe, contains a characteristic syntactical ambiguity; strictly speaking, the opening two lines should be taken to describe the 'I' of the poem, not the prince, but throughout the poem Hölderlin uses syntax for his own poetic ends, not least for the creation of suspense and mystery. The opening strophe is a striking example of Hölderlin's poetic 'architecture'. The syntactic suspension of the word 'tables', for instance, serves to give this word exactly the right place in a design at once pictorial and mythical. By the time we read the word it has been invested with all the functions and associations which Hölderlin attributes to the phenomenon.

PATMOS (*fragments of the later version*) (page 567)

More athletic in ruin (stanza 3): compare Hölderlin's letter to Böhlendorff, Introduction, pages 39–40.

THE ISTER (page 581)

'Ister' was the classical name of the Danube. 'Hertha' (stanza 3), according to Tacitus, was the *terra mater* of the ancient Germans.

MNEMOSYNE (page 587)

'Mnemosyne' means 'memory', and she was the mother of the Muses. Mourning for the past as the earlier hymns had already stated, is not permitted to the poet, who must 'collect his soul' for a different task, that of interpreting 'the signs of day', all that is present and actual. (Cf. the conclusion of 'Patmos'.) Cooking in the opening line denotes the natural process of ripening, as distinct from roasting or burning – a distinction observed in ancient sacrificial rites. Paracelsus wrote: 'The ripening of fruit is natural cookery: therefore what nature has in her, she cooks, and when it is cooked, then nature is whole.' Serpents traditionally are prophetic creatures. Since they slough their skins, they are also symbols of renewal or (in oriental and Gnostic lore) of eternity. To 'sever a lock of hair', in Greek mythology, is to mark a person out for death.

THE NYMPH (page 591)

This is D.E. Sattler's reconstruction and conflation of the three drafts previously known as 'Mnemosyne', published in his edition with a title also considered by Hölderlin for a poem of which there is no final, definitive version. I have taken the text from D.E. Sattler: *Hesperische Gesänge*, Neue Bremer Presse, Bremen 2001, and it is published here with his permission. Sattler believes that all the poems previously known as 'hymns' – and the fragments of these published by Hölderlin before he became Scardanelli – were intended to constitute a single twelve-part work which he calls 'hesperian cantos' or 'canticles'.

My Hölderlin translations, done over a period of fifty years, could not be based on Sattler's reading of the manuscripts or his construction of what might or might not have become the definitive texts. Not only did Hölderlin leave no fair copies of most of the poems and fragments in question, but there was virtually no end to his reworking even of poems that were finished once, but superseded, if only for him, by new insights, experiences and visions. I have made an exception of 'Die Nymphe' because Sattler's conflation has made a coherent poem of what were fragmentary drafts in Beissner's 'Stuttgart' edition, on which most of my texts were based.

What has become clear from D.E. Sattler's admirable and devoted work on manuscripts not so much as legible to him when he began the work is that there never will be one authentic and definitive text of poems not finalized by the poet – unless lost manuscripts reappear, as the fair copy of 'Friedensfeier' did in London as late as 1954. This is the justification for Sattler's conflation of the successive drafts of the poem formerly known as 'Mnemosyne' – and mine for adding it here, with thanks to him.

TO THE VIRGIN MARY (page 617)

By a lowly man or king: Hölderlin is thinking of Herod, who had John the Baptist decapitated, and those responsible for the death of Christ; but also of Creon whose laws (in the *Antigone*) are contrasted with the 'unwritten unalterable laws of Heaven'.

Spiritual water: This is ambiguous, since in eighteenth-century German usage *geistiges Wasser* denoted 'mineral water'. Hölderlin is referring to the mineral springs at Bad Driburg in Westphalia, where he spent part of the year 1796, not far from the Knochenberg (literally: mountain of bones), which he associates with the Thessalian mountain Ossa. This region was also the site of the battle between the Romans and the ancient Germans under Arminius; hence the allusion to Teutoburg.

To the shadows I would have turned: Once again Hölderlin alludes to the forbidden pleasure of communing with the dead and with the past. Instead, he praises the Virgin, God's representative in the present transitional age of Night or 'wilderness'. It is she who desires that the coming era, 'the germinating days', shall be greater than the era of her reign. There are allusions to traditional symbols associated with the Virgin Mary, such as lilies and the enclosed garden.

YOU FIRMLY BUILT ALPS . . . (page 655)

This poem is a fragmentary draft for one of several longer poems that Hölderlin left unfinished before a change in his personality once supposed to have set in before or just after his return from Bordeaux in 1802. Because this change, which grounded him when he had prepared for his most daring flights, was put down to his 'madness' (schizophrenia), his poems were dated accordingly. But now, almost a century and a half after his death, Hölderlin's work is not only being re-edited yet again, but radically re-interpreted in the light of new biographical research and new thinking about the whole course of his development, which – as he predicted in an early poem – was an arc that must take him back to the starting-level, though not to the starting-point.

This fragmentary draft cannot be precisely dated nor attributed with certainly to any one of the thematic complexes of drafts, fragments and reworkings contained in his loose-leaf 'Homburg Folio' – the repository of work done, or merely projected, from 1802 to 1807. The later dating has been established by D. E. Sattler, the editor of the current Hölderlin edition and of the 1986 facsimile edition of the Folio manuscripts. Sattler has shown that all the contents of the Folio are later than they had been assumed to be, and that a few of them were entered even after Hölderlin's forcible removal to the Tübingen mental clinic in 1806, if not after his discharge from it in 1807 as an 'incurable case' – given three years to live at the most, when in fact he lived on for another 36 years, as a different person and a different poet. (The Folio was taken away from Hölderlin in 1807 and handed over to his family.)

The fragment is a celebration of Hölderlin's native region, Württemberg, in line with his 'return to the source', his homecoming after the visionary 'colonization' of ancient Greece. Consonant with that, it is in his 'naïve' tone, rather than the idealistic or tragic, though it was Hölderlin's practice to make these tones alternate or modulate in completed longer poems – as in the free-verse hymns or cantos originally modelled on those of Pindar, but progressively adapted to Hölderlin's own, entirely different, needs and situation. It is the 'naïve' tone that calls for the specification of things seen, heard, smelled or recalled, down to the kinds of trees or the names of landmarks and locations.

Johann Jakob Thill was a minor Swabian poet who died in his twenties soon after Hölderlin's birth; 'his' valley was near Waiblingen in Württemberg.

. . . THE VATICAN . . . (page 685)

and over there in Westphalia, my honest master: Probably a reference to Wilhelm Heinse (cf. Introduction, page 28).

PINDAR FRAGMENTS AND COMMENTARY (page 705)

Hölderlin's translation of these Pindar fragments and his commentary on them were done in 1805 – at a time when he was regarded as incapable of intellectual effort, let alone work so concentrated, sharp and lucid. They were the last work he prepared for publication; and he wrote them in response to a comment on his 'night songs', the last poems of his own he had sent out for publication. Their reviewer had called these poems 'obscure and strange', suggesting that they needed a *commentarius perpetuus*, like the work of ancient poets – such as Pindar! Hölderlin's response explains my reason for deciding to translate his translations. They, and his commentary on them, are so intimately bound up with his own work of this period that they called for inclusion here. A few words from the commentary, in fact, appeared in Hölderlin's draft for a poem of his own in the Homburg Folio, and have been included in printed editions of his text. Again, it is Hölderlin's latest editor and interpreter, D. E. Sattler, who spotted that intrusion and recognized that Hölderlin's commentaries on Pindar shed as much light on his own work as on the fragments he chose to add to his earlier Pindar versions.

IF FROM THE DISTANCE . . . (page 729)

The only poem of this period in which Hölderlin seems to allude directly to events in his life before his removal to the clinic. Susette Gontard, if she, not a fictitious character, is meant to be the speaker, had been dead for a number of years by the time this fragmentary alcaic ode was written. The French poet Philippe Jaccottet has cited the fifth and sixth strophes of this ode as an instance of 'the moment when poetry, without seeming to do so, since it is stripped of all brilliancy, attains what for me is the highest point, [which] seems at first to be simpler than anything else. In reality, though, it is the most difficult and rarest of all.'

CONVICTION (page 747)

Inscribed in Christoph Schwab's copy of Hölderlin's first collection of poems, *Gedichte* (1826), edited by Ludwig Uhland and Gustav Schwab; the lines were written and entered there at Christoph Schwab's request, preceded by four lines of prose.

THE WALK (page 755)

Here, as elsewhere in poems written in his early years in the Tübingen tower, Hölderlin seems to interpret the 'philosophical calm' of this phase as a compensation or recompense for the stresses of his earlier life. In later years his person disappears completely from verses that have become occasional only, written not for himself but for others, at their request.

SUMMER (*'When then the blooms . . .'*) (page 771)

The fictitious date and the signature 'Scardanelli' are typical of Hölderlin's escape both from time and identity at this period. He would also call himself 'Buonarotti' or 'Scaliger Rosa'.

IN LOVELY BLUENESS . . . (page 789)

This poem is printed last because its authenticity is doubtful. It is taken from the novel *Phaeton* (1823), by Wilhelm Waiblinger, a Swabian poet who saw a great deal of Hölderlin in his later years and drew on his knowledge of him for the character of Phaeton, a sculptor. In 1822 Waiblinger mentioned in his diary that he had access to Hölderlin's unpublished work, and the prose poem in the novel is introduced as follows: 'At that time he covered with writing all the paper he could lay his hands on. Here are a few pages from his papers, which at the same time give us a deep insight into his terribly confused state of mind. In the original they are divided into lines like verses in the Pindaric manner.' The most likely hypothesis is that Waiblinger adapted the piece from one or more poems given to him by Hölderlin and now lost, possibly adding and omitting passages in the process. In 1827 Waiblinger wrote an early account of Hölderlin's 'Life, Work and Madness'.

INDEX OF GERMAN FIRST LINES

INDEX OF GERMAN TITLES

INDEX OF ENGLISH FIRST LINES

INDEX OF ENGLISH TITLES

Poetry by Michael Hamburger from Anvil

Collected Poems 1941–1994

A distinctive body of work, reflecting half a century's dedication to his art which has consistently engaged with both the natural and human world.

Late

A narrative meditation in a style akin to his 'Variations', *Late* is both an elegy for and a celebration of life towards the end of the millennium.

Intersections

A varied collection of his shorter poems written between 1994 and 1999.

A Diary of Non-Events

A year in the poet's life, blending observation of changes in the natural world with his daily life in and around his Suffolk home, as the larger concerns of the outside world intrude upon these 'non-events'.

––––––––

'Few English poets of our day can have come to their craft with the cultural and linguistic richness of Michael Hamburger . . . a thoroughly European, even cosmopolitan sensibility who is at the same time a nature poet of thoroughly English stamp. A Brechtian social and political satirist co-exists, and not always peaceably, alongside a knowledgeable naturalist who dwells among the cloudscapes and birdsong of Suffolk . . . Behind his often passionate work lies his Jewish heritage, and the catastrophe suffered by that people in this century . . . As a translator, of course, but also as a distinctive, wide-ranging poet, Hamburger has been more than usually attentive to the divisions, to the "shocks and conflicts" of his century; his work helps us share in them, and enriches our understanding.'

STEPHEN ROMER, *Agenda*

'The poems have never shouted, and in a high-volume age, they have often gone unheard, yet they are testimony of a critical imagination and very clearly "add something to the resources of their medium, language". . . . The poems will in time be recognized as his securest achievement'

MICHAEL SCHMIDT, *Agenda*

Some other German poetry from Anvil
Translated by Michael Hamburger

Paul Celan: Poems

'Celan's mysterious, spell-binding German poems have been translated into equally mysterious, equally spell-binding English verse. Through these exemplary translations the English reader can now enter the hermetic universe of a German-Jewish poet who made out of the anguish of his people, and his own representative sufferings, things of terror and beauty.'

Times Literary Supplement

Goethe: Roman Elegies
and other poems

Johann Wolfgang von Goethe (1749–1832) is mainly known in the English-speaking world as the poet of *Faust*. His other poetry, for all its richness and variety, has received comparatively little attention. This edition collects all the versions made over many years by Michael Hamburger. His selection and introduction provide a valuable account of 'a writer so many-sided as to constitute a whole literature'. Here are poems from all periods of Goethe's creative life, including a complete version of the erotic *Roman Elegies*.

Peter Huchel: The Garden of Theophrastus

Peter Huchel (1903–1981) wrote amidst the political turmoil of modern Germany. His poetry has its roots in a native place (Brandenburg) from which he was exiled in the 1970s when he was 'sent West' after long official neglect. Before that break, and through the hardship of the Second World War and its vexed aftermath, he maintained a poetry of humane commitment, formal invention and precision. His devotion to the place was also a devotion to its people, but the rural nature of the community that commanded his earliest allegiances made his radicalism unconventional.

For Michael Hamburger this book is of special importance: Huchel was a close friend and mentor of his and he has been translating his work for many years. Here he adds some new versions to his earlier translations.

Rainer Maria Rilke: Turning-Point

While Rilke has been perhaps more widely translated into English than any other modern poet, the emphasis has always been on 'major works', such as the *Duino Elegies* and *Sonnets to Orpheus*. Yet Rilke produced many more poems which got little or no airing beyond the confines of the workshop. Michael Hamburger suggests that these poems are not inferior to the poems in the collections that form the accepted corpus; rather that they did not fit in with Rilke's wish to form a definitive statement.

First published as *An Unofficial Rilke*, Hamburger's choice from the many miscellaneous poems which Rilke wrote between 1912 and his death in 1926 has been critically acclaimed for its contribution towards a more complete understanding of one of the major poets of the 20th century.

'The collusion of Hamburger the German scholar and Hamburger the poet gives the translations what is for me an unrivalled distinction.'

MICHAEL HANKE, *PN Review*

French Poetry in Bilingual Editions from Anvil

Guillaume Apollinaire: Selected Poems
Translated and introduced by Oliver Bernard

A cross-section of the dynamic French poet's work. 'Oliver Bernard's translations . . . are immediately engaging in their vividness and humour.'

CHRISTOPHER RICKS, *New Statesman*

Charles Baudelaire
Translated and introduced by Francis Scarfe
Volume I: The Complete Verse
Volume II: The Poems in Prose *with 'La Fanfarlo'*

Francis Scarfe's prose versions of the complete poetry of France's greatest nineteenth-century poet are both scrupulous and inventive. 'No one must underestimate the value of the present enterprise to even the most advanced student of French literature.'

MICHAEL GLOVER, *British Book News*

Poems of Jules Laforgue
Translated and introduced by Peter Dale

Peter Dale captures Laforgue's panache in this substantial selection from one of the quirkiest and most entertaining of French poets. 'Generally, when Dale adapts, he still manages to reproduce, conveying much of the letter of the original as well as the spirit. . . . The collection is hard to over-praise'

D.J. ENRIGHT, *The Observer*

Gérard de Nerval: The Chimeras
Translated by Peter Jay
with an essay by Richard Holmes

'The rendering of Gérard de Nerval's justly celebrated and mysteriously allusive sonnet sequence in English is a formidably difficult enterprise, and translator and publisher are to be congratulated.'

MICHAEL GLOVER, *Books and Bookmen*

Arthur Rimbaud: A Season in Hell and Other Poems
Translated by Norman Cameron
with an introduction by Michael Hamburger

In Robert Graves's opinion, Norman Cameron was unsurpassed as a translator of Rimbaud. This volume contains 33 verse poems and the whole of *Une Saison en enfer*, the extraordinary work that was Rimbaud's literary testament, his apology, and contribution to the mythology of his time.

Paul Verlaine: Women/Men
Translated by Alistair Elliot

'. . . in Verlaine's clandestine collections of erotic verse, Mr Elliot succeeds marvellously . . . astonishing, beautiful poems, astonishingly and beautifully rendered.'

D.M. THOMAS